LABOUR COSTS ADMINISTRATION IN MAJOR INDUSTRIES

LABOUR COSTS ADMINISTRATION IN MAJOR INDUSTRIES

LABOUR COSTS ADMINISTRATION IN MAJOR INDUSTRIES

By

Prashant Verma
Assistant Professor
Department of Operations Management
NIILM Centre for Management Studies
Knowledge Park - V
Greater Noida - 201 306
(India)

DISCOVERY PUBLISHING HOUSE PVT. LTD.
NEW DELHI-110 002

Published by:
Tilak Wasan
DISCOVERY PUBLISHING HOUSE PVT. LTD.
4383/4B, Ansari Road, Darya Ganj
New Delhi-110 002 (India)
Phone : +91-11-23279245; 23253475; 43596065
E-mail : discoverybooksindia@gmail.com
discoverypublishinghouse@gmail.com
namitwasan9@gmail.com
web : www.discoverypublishinggroup.com

Edition: **2019**

ISBN: 978-93-5056-726-5

Labour Costs Administration in Major Industries

Printed at:
Infinity Imaging Systems
Delhi

Acknowledgements

At the very outset I would like to express my gratitude to all those who have helped me at various stage of this research work.

During the process of research, the influence of Dr. P.C Maheshwari has been the guiding light. I am highly indebted to him for the guidance at all stages of the work, of professional and personal nature, profound knowledge of the subject and his continued interest in my work. I wish research work I plan for the future would be worthy of making him feel proud of his disciple.

I am highly indebted to Prof. K.L. Krishna, Ex Dean Delhi School of Economics for mentoring me in various meetings. Prof. K.L. Krishna, a great teacher, always knew the stages of my work and gave inputs which were of immense help. A special mention of Prof. C.P. Gupta, Ex. Professor MDI Gurgoan, for helping me in my work wherever I found myself stuck. Prof. S. Neelamegham, Ex Dean FMS Delhi and President NIILM CMS Greater Noida, for being very kind in helping me find resources and arranging the meetings with these great teachers.

With a sense of appreciation, I feel myself highly indebted to the staff and librarian of most importantly the NCEAR New Delhi; NIILM CMS; MDI Gurgoan; Ratan Tata Library, Delhi School of Economics; V.V. Giri National Labour Institute Noida and modern day technology provider Google, Wikipedia and various other online resources available on internet.

I would like to acknowledge my academic friends who liberally gave their time for various discussions on various aspects of this research work. My friend Dr. Shruti Jain, Prof. NIILM center for management studies, Greater Noida, Dr. Manoj Srivastava, Prof. MDI Gurgaon; Dr. Ashish Varma, Prof. IMT Gahaziabad; Dr. Brajesh Kumar, Managing Editor NIFM Journal of Public Financial Management and faculty member of NIFM Faridabad; and Dr. Sandhya Verma, Scientist C, DIPR lab of DRDO -New Delhi.

Last but not the least; I acknowledge the role of my family members in bringing this work to the stage of publication.

–Author

Contents

1

Introduction

INTRODUCTION

Present study is a fact finding research to understand trends and relationship between productivity, labour cost and wages administration covering four major industries of India viz. Cotton textiles, Jute, Sugar and Steel. This research would help to understand the economic performance and movements of economic factors like wage determination, productivity, technology replacements, opportunities of investment and various others during 1980-2004, the period considered for this fact finding study.

Since independence Indian economy has seen various ups and down, which were largely attributed to government policies (Ahluwalia, 1985). Various studies on Indian economy agree that the structured effort on economy, with focus on productivity and efficiency in manufacturing, started from 1980 and is continuing till date. The Industrial Policy Statement of 1980 promoted competition, technological up-gradation and modernisation in the domestic market. The policy laid the foundation for highly competitive export based high technology areas and for encouraging foreign investment in these areas, emphasising the need for productivity to be the central concern in all economic and production activities. These policies created a climate for rapid industrial growth in the country; therefore, for this fact finding study on empirical relationship between productivity, wages and labour cost administration in selected industries of India, the selection of period since 1980 is justified. Turnaround in the industrial output growth in the decade of 80's has been widely attributed to liberalisation, improvement in public investment and public sector performance. (Ahluwalia I., 1992; Nagaraj, 1990; Commission, 1981)

It is widely recognized that to assess the progress of economy and industry there shall be scientific inquiry on trends in productivity. Labour productivity is considered as an indispensible factor for rapid economic growth which is especially true for Indian economy, which is moving from agriculture dominated economy to manufacturing and services dominated economy. Given the pivotal role of labour in manufacturing sector, the understanding of prevailing relationship between productivity and labour cost; the productivity improvements and rewards labour class obtain for its contribution to output is extremely important. Usually, the economists focus on finding the links between productivity and wages and not on productivity, labour cost and wages. This kind of study would be useful from the point of view of management trying to look in the interest of producer as well as labour. The employers, in general, lay emphasis on linking wages to productivity with an aim to reduce labour cost thereby raising profitability or capital formation.

Labour cost is an important element of production cost. It is significantly connected with number of factors, such as productivity movements, technological changes and volume of production, rates of return, union activities and state intervention. Workers aspire for higher wages, while the employers resist this and try to minimise the unit labour cost. This conflict of interests often comes to fore through union activities on labours part and technological up-gradation on producer's part. In a fast growing economy technological up-gradation doesn't bring negative impact on employment, but otherwise it increases unemployment levels.

Labour cost may be studied in two ways. In the interest of producer, the study of unit labour cost is important; but, in the interest of labour it is the study of earnings. The latter may also be termed as the study of hourly labour cost, or labour cost per worker. The various studies so far made in the field of labour cost were focused on study of single variable representing the earnings of the workers (e.g. fringe benefits, survey of labour conditions etc.). Present study is an attempt to include both the interests, with emphasis on wages administration, labour cost and productivity in cotton textile, jute, sugar and steel industries of India.

Previous Research Work in this Field

The studies focusing on productivity, wages and labour cost are less in number in India. Maheshwari (1968) covered the data series from 1947 to 1962 and found that the wages increased with declining trend of labour cost, reasoning the causes as intensive use of capital in manufacturing resulting in growth of productivity and technological developments.

There are large number of studies covering productivity and wage movements in India. Verma (1973) examined the inter-regional wage variations in Indian manufacturing from 1950 to 1960. Paper attempts to explain the inter-regional wage differentials by analysing the data on trade unionism, per capita income, productivity, capital intensity, non-primary employment and consumer prices. It argued that the level of regional wage differentials can be explained by relative differentials in productivity and in trade unionism, but the change in wage differentials depends upon the changing capital intensity in respective regions.

Johri and Agarwal (1966) covering data series of 1951-61, studied inter-industry wage structures of 29 industries and found time variant weakening correlation between wages and productivity. i.e. the strength of association declined over time.

Shivamaggi, Rajgopalan, & Venkatachalam (1968) covering the data series for the period 1951-61 studied wages, labour productivity and cost of production for seven major industries including sugar. They found that the productivity has increased with increase in capital intensity and improvement in management techniques. The wages lagged behind the improvements in productivity. The age (time-period) components of total industry cost were small and wage cost ratio declined during the period.

Fonesca (1964) used the data series of 1953-63 to determine the money wages using regression, taking money wages as dependent variable and degree of unionization, cost of living and productivity as independent variables. Cost of living explained the major part of variation in money wages. The share of labour in value added by manufacturing in industrial sector showed a stagnating or falling trend.

Papola (1970), used regression analysis to study the differences in the money wages between states, taking productivity, rate of return, capital intensity and average size of units as explaining variables. He found rate of return and productivity significantly explains the variation in money wages only in few states but, the capacity has low significance in the study. Capital intensity only emerged as factor explaining difference in wages among states.

Papola (1972) used regression analysis for cotton textile industry covering the data for same period to test whether labour productivity as an independent variable affects money wages. He concluded that cost of living has highest degree of influence on money wages followed by capacity to pay. Productivity has marginal effect on money wages.

Suri & Sastry (1974) covered the data series of aggregate manufacturing sector for the period 1959-69, using regression with money wages as dependent variable and cost of living index (CPI), productivity index (value added by manufacturing per man-hour worked at current prices), employment index, capital output ratio(at current prices) and index of degree of unionization as independent variable. Correlation was found positive with all independent variables except degree of unionization. The result of regression analysis indicated the changes in money wages is largely explained by cost of living index and productivity index.

Verma (1992) in his study "Trends and Structures of Wages in Indian Industries" concluded: "wage behaviour in the industry is influenced by factors as productivity, capital intensity and inflation. Over the years, the importance of these factors has been varing. During the 50s and 60s, consumer price played a very important role in determining wages. At the same time, productivity also has impact on wages. Prices and productivity continued to have say over wages until late 70s, in more recent years capital intensity has also emerged as a factor explaining wage movements."

Kibria, Tisdell,(1985) compared the patterns of productivity progress and learning curve in jute manufacturing mills in Bangladesh, with those patterns observed for manufacturing plants in developed countries. This study is based on extensive surveys of individual mills over there life of operation, which in many cases extended up to 26 years. Authors estimated learning or productivity parameters for the start-up phase of jute manufacturing plants in Bangladesh. The author writes:

"The *[there is]* uniformity of *[productivity]* parameters in the start-up phase (Baloff, 1966a, 1967; Baloff and Kenelly, 1967; Harvey, 1976; Pegels, 1976). Typically manufacturing productivity starting from the installation of a new manufacturing process shows a period of continuous increase before it eventually levels off. It is generally believed that learning is the principal contributor to productivity increase in this phase and is likely to be confined to this phase. For this reason, the terms "start-up" and "learning" are often used interchangeably in recent literature on this subject (e.g., Pegels, 1976). It is widely believed that learning is a finite process and once it stops, the level of productivity stabilizes and remains roughly stationary thereafter (Baloff, 1966a; Hartley, 1966)."

The finding suggests both product and process innovations provide considerable opportunity for learning/adoption by the personnel responsible for manufacturing efficiency. The article suggested that the learning curve is relevant for planning the industrial output.

Jha, et.al. (1993) examined the biases of technological change, factor substitution and economies of scale in four major manufacturing industries (viz. cement, electricity and gas, cotton textiles and iron and steel) in India by estimating the translog cost functions using annual time series data covering the period 1960-61 to 1982-83. The study revealed that in cotton textiles, the technological changes enhanced use of capital and energy, but saved the labour and material. In iron cement and Steel industries, technical change has been biased towards saving of capital and use of material. These biases in technical progress have affected the factor income distributions in these industries in different ways. For example, relative to supplies of capital and energy, in iron and steel industries the workers have gained but not in cotton textiles industry.

Tulpule & Datta (1988) used data for the period 1960-83 to analyse the trends of real wages in manufacturing in India. The authors found high correlation between real wages per workers and labour productivity. The study argues that real wages rose marginally faster than national per capita real income beside that labour productivity increased faster than real wages.

Joshi and Little (1994) found that the productivity and investment increased during 1980s, especially in private manufacturing. But more systematically, Chand and Sen(2002) have recently studied the relationship between trade liberalization and productivity in manufacturing using 3-digit industry data spanning 1973-88 econometrically. They took 30 industries, which accounted for 53 per cent of gross value added and 45 per cent of employment in manufacturing over this period. These industries divide approximately equally among consumer, intermediate and capital goods. They measure protection by the proportionate wedge between the Indian and U.S. price and estimated total factor productivity growth (TFPG) in the three industry groups averaged over three non-overlapping periods: 1974-78, 1979-83 and 1984-88. They then related this productivity growth to liberalization.

Jose (1994) studied the 19 manufacturing industries for the period 1970-88 indicated that there was stagnation or even decline in productivity during 1970s whereas during 1980's there was upward acceleration in productivity among number of industries. There was 2-3% increase per annum in real earnings, by and large restricted to high wage industry where raise started in mid 70s and in other industries it started in early 80s. the study noted high degree of association between index number of real earnings and productivity in most industries.

Bhattacharya & Mitra (1994) studied the employment, labour productivity and wage rate in public and organized private sectors in the context of structural reforms for the period 1970-91 using regression analysis. They found that labour do not get full compensation for the increase in labour productivity and prices in private firms, whereas, in public enterprise wage rate is fully adjusted to price and labour productivity has partial role.

Gangopadhyay & Wadhwa (1998) studied the data for the period 1973-93 and found that rate of growth of wage earnings has been falling along with employment, the capital deepening has been accompanied by gains in labour productivity and gains in productivity is associated with falling unit labour cost. They suggested that labour productivity (output per worker) can be increased in three different ways: (a) increasing the skills in labour (b) new capacities with better technology capable of increasing output with same amount of input and (c) new techniques that substitute capital for labour and can also increase output per worker.

Kambhampati, Howell (1998) explored the impact of liberalization in India covering issues such as wages, job security and health and safety on formal sector employment in the cotton textile industry. Data was collected from Ahmedabad, Bombay, Delhi and Coimbatore between September and November 1996. The findings indicate that restructuring has led to a decline in employment levels in composite mills in the cotton textile industry in India through closure, downsizing and the shift towards more capital-intensive technologies. As wages are determined within an institutional setting, it was found that there was insignificant variation across mills as well as over time. However, the increased capital-intensity of production has resulted in an improvement in health and safety conditions within the mills, at least with respect to occupational hazards which have typified this industry in the past.

Chand and Sen (2002) did further tests by pooling their sample and employing fixed-effects estimator on 1973-88 data, to allow for intrinsic differences across industries with respect to the rate of technological progress. Their estimates show that on average one percentage point reduction in the price wedge leads to 0.1 per cent rise in the total factor productivity. For the intermediate goods sector, the effect is twice as large. The impact of the liberalization of the intermediate goods sector on productivity turns out to be statistically significant in all of their regressions (Panagariya, 2003).

Narayan (2003) in his work on selected Indian industries in organised manufacturing sector for the period 1973-96 found that labour productivity index increased at an average growth rate of 5.21%, capital intensity showed positive growth rate of 4.94% but the total factor productivity, a measure of overall productivity efficiency of the industry, had shown declining trend in paper and paperboard industry, stagnation in watches & clock and motor vehicle industry. Labour productivity and total factor productivity were found positively influenced by output. Labour enjoyed positive gains and did not participate in productivity losses.

Kambhampati, (2003), analysed the impact of 1991 reforms on manufacturing efficiency in cotton textile industry in India, through a best practice frontier for the industry and then measuring efficiency as the distance from this frontier using RBI data for the period of 1986-1994. The paper concludes that while there was considerable dispersion in efficiency levels before the reforms, this dispersion has decreased since the reforms. The location of the firm within a state and its proximity to a major urban centre has an influence on the efficiency levels of firms. This increase in manufacturing efficiency has influenced other factors such as market shares, exports and imports and capital-labour ratios.

Duque, Ramos, & Suriñach, (2006) in their study on OECD countries, on the data for the period of 1972-2004, obtained results which are in line with the predictions by wage determination theories and highlight the role of institutions in the functioning of the labour market. The study found that intensity of the relationship between wages and productivity is lower in countries with a lower union density and a higher coordination between firms in the collective bargaining process. On the contrary, other factors such as the bargaining coverage and a higher synchronization affect positively the response of wages to productivity. The bargaining level also matters and the results show that in countries with more decentralization in collective bargaining, the response of wages to productivity increases. Countries with a higher presence of small firms or higher levels of technology, productivity gains are more easily translated into wage increases.

There are recent studies on post reform data on perspectives given by Heckscher–Ohlin theory and trade-induced skill-biased technological change (SBTC) on wage inequality. Trade reforms have led to a widening of wage gap between skilled and unskilled workers, and an increase in relative skill intensity in Indian manufacturing. Sen (2008) investigated whether the trade reforms lead to wage inequality using 1973-97 data. He found that the trade-induced technological progress has led to an increase in relative skill intensity and wage inequality within industries. At the same time, the decline in protection that seems to have occurred more in unskilled labour-intensive industries has led to a relative fall in the economy-wide return to unskilled labour relative to skilled labour.

Kumar, et.al. (2008) evaluated empirically the impact of the dramatic 1991 trade liberalization in India on the industry wage structure using variation in industry wage premiums and trade policy across industries and over time. In contrast to earlier studies on developing countries, this study, using data for the period of 1980-2000, finds a strong, negative, and robust relationship between changes in trade policy and changes in industry wage premiums over time. The results were consistent with liberalization-induced productivity increases at the firm level, which get passed on to industry wages. It was found that trade liberalization has led to decreased wage inequality between skilled and unskilled workers in India.

Mitra & Ural (2008), using data for the period 1988-2000, found that Trade liberalization benefits most the export-oriented industries located in states with flexible labour-market institutions. Trade liberalization increases productivity in all industries across all states, more pronounced in states that have relatively more flexible labour markets and less protected industries. Similar effects are also found in the case of employment, capital stock and investment. Per capita state development expenditure was the strongest and the most robust predictor of productivity, employment, capital stock and investment.

OBJECTIVE, SCOPE AND LIMITATIONS OF THE STUDY

There has been a fluctuating performance of the economy since the introduction of reforms as part of a comprehensive stabilisation and structural adjustment programme in 1980 and an enormous change in the economic environment since 1991. In this process of economic reforms, international trade & industrial policies were changed, better regulatory mechanisms were evolved and privatisation was invoked. This has resulted in restructuring of public enterprises, greater internal and international competitiveness among the firms, and up-gradation of their technologies. These changes have respective influences on the composite performance of the industrial sector. In such a scenario it is important to judge the nature and pattern of efficiency and productivity at the micro or firm level and at the macro or industry level of the key industrial sector.

One of the positive fallouts of reforms of 1990's was that improving productivity became the new national priority. Productivity has its impact on costs, prices, output, profits, investment and employment trends in industry. Productivity is a measure of efficiency with which resources, both human and material are utilised, for generating goods and services. Productivity is the synonym of improved competitiveness. Enterprises are competitive when their productivity of labour and all production factors grow consistently, which allows them to reduce the unit cost of their output. Increased competitiveness of one enterprise also affects other enterprises at national and international levels, as they contribute towards the revised productivity and efficiency frontiers. Higher productivity provides funding for an organisation's expansion plans. In the short term higher productivity benefit citizens by providing better and cheaper products, and in the medium term it benefits the economy through growth in employment. Another effect of higher productivity is constant growth in wages in real terms. As a result, a country's living standard goes up when its productivity growth (in macro-terms) is sustained. Therefore, an enterprise plays the primary role in generating revenues and employment, and contributes to a lasting and balanced economic and social development. It is a well known fact that the productivity data plays a significant role in collective bargaining between labour and management (Sanga, 1964). Productivity studies about the significant variables like employment levels, production efficiencies, earnings of labour force, cost factor with respect to per worker productivity, helps the government and industry towards better economic policies and strategies.

Productivity growth depends on a number of factors, among which innovations, investments and development of human capital are the most important (Carneiro, 2007). Faster rate of economic growth can be ensured through accelerated production and higher productivity in all the branches of economic activity. Productivity of Human resources plays a significant role in determining the overall economic growth of any nation. Apart from the level of human skills, the quality of raw materials, technology employed and standard of living, which directly affects wage determination, are also responsible for productive human resources. Salter (1969) rightly remarks that "behind labour productivity lie all the dynamic forces of economic life: technical progress accumulation, enterprises, and the institutional pattern of society."

The recent economic reforms as well as some recent developments, like existence of economic and monitory union (EMU) and related social pacts in Europe and in the world economy have brought the issue of wage flexibility in organized industries to the fore (celex-text-52002DC0332, 2009). As the economy further opens up and the forces of globalisation gather strength, cost adjustments would assume increasing importance, in such scenario wage flexibility is expected to facilitate cost adjustments. The issues related to appropriate linkages among wages, productivity and profitability of enterprises would gather importance. These factors determine the competitive strength of industries or enterprises. Given this context, wages in organized industries and its relationship with productivity and labour cost need to be examined.

Objective of the Study

This is an inductive and fact finding statistical study on four major industries of India viz. Cotton Textile, Jute, Steel and Sugar for the period 1980-2004. The main objectives of the study are:

1. To estimate the trends of:
   (i) Productivity;
   (ii) Labour cost; and
   (iii) Wages.

To find the causes of trend identified.

To find the external factors affecting labour cost outside the factory (e.g. such as location, size, price movements etc.)

To find the internal factors affecting labour cost within the industry (such as productivity, capital intensity, technological movements etc.)

To measure the magnitude of the impact of factors identified.

The present study is an attempt to analyse wages as a factor of production cost and its implication on productivity and technological developments. This work will attempt to study in detail the unit labour cost from the producer's point of view as a 'cost factor' and from labour's point of view as 'earnings' with emphasis on wages and productivity.

Hypothesis

Present study is based on the following commonly held assumptions (hypothesis) to be investigated:

1. Wages and Labour Costs are directly correlated.

Productivity and total cost of production are directly correlated.

There exist a determinable relationship between unit labour cost and total cost for industries of India covered in this study

Productivity, labour costs and wages vary from industry to industry and even within the industry from region to region and from unit to unit.

There are various factors that tend to lift or lower the cost of labour, wages and productivity. But the combined as well as individual effect of these factors, vary on different conditions.

Labour is a variable factor rather than a fixed factor, therefore for industries operating under increasing return, any increase in the number of workers will improve the marginal productivity of the labour. For industries operating under diminishing return, any increase in the number of workers will decrease the marginal productivity of the labour.

Smaller industrial units have lower productivity higher labour cost and are therefore less efficient.

Limitations

The annual survey of industries is the prime source of industrial statistics in the country. However, till 1998, the survey covered only factories, bidi and cigar manufacturing units and all electricity generating, transmitting and distributing establishments which are registered under the law.

The main problem/data gaps are data on earnings need to be collected every year instead of in 4 years. There is need to collect data on wages in addition to the total labour cost of units covered under the survey.

THE SOURCE OF INFORMATION, METHODS OF APPROACH

Source of Information

Statistical data (secondary data) will be mainly collected from the "Annual Surveys of Industries" Govt. of India publications. The data are authentic, as these have been collected under the statutory obligation from the industrialist. Hard copy available in various libraries and database of ASI data on www.indiastat.com was referred.

Statistical information on various aspects of labour will be collected from Labour Bureau. The data and news articles, export import figures, capitals etc. are to be collected through Industry Analysis Service (IAS) database provided by CMIE. (Centre of Monitoring Indian Economy)

For the purpose of construction of price deflators, the data for the various price indices has been taken from monthly bulletin of *Index Numbers of Wholesale Price in India* from the office of Economic Advisor, Ministry of Industry, Government of India, Udyod Bhawan, New Delhi and from CIER's *Industrial Databook* by making suitable and necessary adjustments. The data pertaining to consumer price index are obtained from various issues of *Indian Labour Statistics* and necessary adjustments have been made for the purpose of the study. The weights for the calculation of input prices are taken from *Input-Output Transaction Tables* from CSO. Labour related other data are taken from various issues of *Indian Labour Statistics.*

Method of Approach

Theoretical discussions on productivity, wages and labour costs will be carried out so as to make logical and easily understandable interpretation. The empirical study will be divided into two parts (1) simple analytical study; and (2) econometric analysis. The problems will be identified on the basis of factual data and then inferences will be drawn on the basis of econometric models.

In order to differentiate between the real and incidental factors that influence unit labour costs, the problem will be approached in both the ways i.e. on the basis of current prices and on the basis of constant prices.

Price Movements

Since price movements do not identically affect all the factors of production, possibility of it having erroneous effect on unit labour cost looms large. Therefore, the real changes in unit labour cost due to productivity movements, intensity of capital, and technique of production cannot be captured if labour costs are computed on current prices. But, if labour costs are computed on constant prices, the hypothesis under evaluation would appear imaginary because price fluctuations brings a relative change in factors of production, which encourages or discourages the substitution of various factors and alternative methods of production. This necessitates the study of unit labour cost to be carried out on current prices of goods and services.

The fact that location factor is an important determinant of cost, further necessitates an investigation into nature and character of inter-regional trends of the industry. This will explore the possibilities and prospects of any industry for its further concentration or dispersion. Through this analysis it might be possible to identify certain broad tendencies, which are operating in the important centers of the industry, and to measure the magnitude of deviation from or degree of uniformity with general standards set by the industry as a whole.

Data Clustering on Location

Location planning is an important consideration for manufacturing units. It is an important determinant of cost hence, it is important to study the inter-regional trends in the industry. For this purpose the factual data will further be analysed on regional basis for exploring broad tendencies operating in the industry explained by location of the manufacturing units.

The size-wise approach of the problem is also necessary, as the size of the industrial unit effects labour costs and other related variables, such as productivity and intensity of capital.

Data Clustering on Size of the Industry

Size of the industry greatly influence the labour cost and other related factors because of volumes involved. It is a general perception that large units are relatively economical and have greater efficiency. The assumption shall be tested through the statistical process.

In light of the above discussion the study was required to be carried out on the basis of current prices and also on constant prices. The approach shall facilitate to differentiate between real and incidental factors influencing the unit labour cost.

Organisation of the Study

The research work focuses on the empirical testing of economic hypotheses. In the next two chapters the theoretical aspects of labour cost and methodology required for testing is discussed to facilitate better interpretation of the results. The study is divided into two parts- simple analytical study and econometric analysis. The problems are identified on the basis of factual data and then inferences are drawn on the basis of econometric models.

Part-I of Study

The study is divided in two parts the part-I will consist of statistical inquiry on factual data to prepare the background for econometric analysis.

Regional trends will be compared with the standards set by the industries. An analysis of production cost will be made on the basis of the fact that labour cost affects the total production cost.

Part-II of the Study

Part-II of the study is technical and scientific inquiry of unit labour cost. Econometric models will be formulated to identify the structures explaining the economic phenomenon. Statistical estimation will be used for estimation of impact of productivity, wage rates, technological changes and innovations on unit labour cost. The impact of rate of return, marginal productivity of factors and scale of production on unit labour cost will also be studied.

2

Research Methodology

METHODS OF ESTIMATION

Present work considered many variables and observations from published sources, which generally present the data in its basic form. This data is not always appropriate for the requirements of econometric hypothesis under investigation. Therefore certain transformations of data are carried out.

Transformation of Data

In time series data it is essential to ensure the uniformity in coverage and other details, such as the requirement of same sample size every year, measurement of variables are unit free to facilitate comparison of two different variables. To make the measurement of variables unit free certain ratios would be calculated instead of considering absolute values of the wages, capital, material and, other inputs. To facilitate further comparison the ratios were converted to index numbers.

MEASUREMENT OF IMPORTANT VARIABLES

Unit Labour Cost, Productivity, Construction of Price-Deflators

Unit Labour Cost

The unit labor costs figure is derived by comparing compensation to output. According to the Bureau of Labour Statistics(BLS), "Compensation is a measure of the cost to the employer of securing the services of labor. It includes wages and salaries (like shift differentials, all kinds of paid leave, bonus and incentive payments, and employee discounts), and employer contributions to employee-benefit plans (like medical and life insurance, workmen's compensation, and unemployment insurance)."

Output, or the value of finished goods and services, is adjusted for price change. Inter-industry transactions are excluded to avoid double-counting. The BLS stated "For example, the output of the steel industry is excluded to the extent that it is incorporated in final products such as automobiles". An index is created for the resulting output figure.

To obtain unit labor costs, the compensation index is divided by the output index. It's computed on a seasonally adjusted basis. There are two methods for measurement of unit labour cost: (1) In physical terms: expressing labour cost as per unit of product; (2) In value terms: expressing labour cost as per unit of output. The measurement of labour cost per unit of product is suitable where the output is fairly homogeneous. Since the industry under consideration produce variety of products, differing in quality and volume generated, hence it is not possible to compute the labour cost in terms of physical units, which would not be comparable. Unlike Cotton textile, Steel and Jute; sugar industry have homogeneous output but there exist a problem of allocating the 'joint cost' between the by-products generated in the process of manufacturing sugar.

Going by the above discussion for this investigation labour cost is calculated as per unit of value of output, i.e.

$$\textit{Unit Labour Cost} = \frac{\textit{Total Labour Expenditure}}{\textit{Ex Factory Value of Output}} \qquad (1)$$

Where, total labour expenditure includes salaries, wages and other benefits paid to worker. The term 'workers' exclude supervisors, technicians, clerks etc. or person employed in a confidential position. Although (Sinha & Sawhney, 1970) noted that their services are as important for the execution of work in the factory as the operators who are directly engaged in various stages of production process. The ASI gives no separate data of benefits paid to workers and persons other than workers. Therefore the labour expenditure includes total benefits paid to above discussed categories. This inclusion of other than workers shall not lead to bias because (a) the benefits constitute only two to nine percent of wages; (b) further, the proportion of 'other than workers' enjoying a part of such benefit is very small. The Labour Bureau which does not favour the inclusion of the persons other than workers in the measurement of labour input also reasons that they form very small portion of total employees in the factory. (c) Extra share of benefits so included may be compensated by the expenses on training and recruitment which is not been included in labour cost.

Industry produces diverse set of goods, expressed in different units, hence assumption of homogeneity required in measuring the output through physical output becomes meaningless. Although in case of homogeneous products, the physical output gives a better measure of productivity, since, researcher is not confronted with the problem of making adjustment for change in money value in measuring productivity over a period of time. Hence aggregation can only be done in terms of value leading to the choice between value added and gross output. If later is chosen then it becomes necessary to measure production function in terms of labour, capital and material. Majority of studies have chosen the 'value added' as a measure of output, advancing following arguments in favour: (a) It facilitates the comparison of results between different industries. (b) It facilitates aggregation of output across the industry. c) Inclusion of material as an argument in production function leads to problem of dominant variable, in such almost all the variation in output tends to get explained by the material, deviating from practical observations.

The ex-factory value of output is real total cost of production. Therefore unit labour cost is calculated as the ratio of labour expenditure to the ex-factory value of output is justified.

Productivity

Productivity can be defined as the efficiency with which inputs are transformed into meaningful outputs, through a production process. The simplistic definition is the ratio of output to input. Productivity can be measured through comparing output with single factor input (Partial Productivity Ratio), or by Total Factor Productivity which accounts for effects in total output not caused by inputs or by comparing all the inputs combined to standard form of output (Multifactor Productivity). In the case of multifactor productivity there are practical difficulties involved in taking all the factors, as they are not additive and also not in the scope of current research. Total Factor Productivity variable considers all inputs which are directly or indirectly measurable, e.g. technology growth, efficiency; quality of human resource etc. which is its major limitation also, moreover on the basis of dimensional analysis, TFP is criticized as not having meaningful units of measurement.(Cambridge capital controversy, 2009) In Indian scenario the labour input for quality differences cannot be adjusted, also lack of all the data at firm level and problem of aggregation makes this measure unreliable, more so for variety of industries under consideration in this study. Hence it would be wise to take the simple and reliable measure of partial productivity ratios. Partial productivity ratios are derived by dividing the output by relevant factor input. The most commonly used and widely reported among many possibilities of partial productivity ratios are Labour Productivity Ratio and Capital Productivity Ratio. The increase in partial productivity ratios means that over a period of time more output is possible from reduced amount of input or with same amount of input. The decline in of this ratio implies increase in unit input for per unit output concerned. The study of partial productivity ratio is helpful in measuring the savings in use of a particular factor. As long as all the partial productivity ratios move in single direction it indicates overall positive efficiency, but if the movement is in opposite direction then such inference is not easy.

This research work considers labour productivity which can be measured in two ways, either in term of physical products or in terms of value of the products. The total gross output includes all goods and services produced without deduction of intermediate products consumed in the process or for capital consumption. Some studies preferred real product estimate over gross output because the real product estimates in relation to real factor costs alone indicates change in efficiency with which basic factor in the industry are used to add value to intermediate products.

A further choice arises between Net Value Added and Gross Value Added. The former is net of capital consumption. (Denison E. , 1969) regards both Gross and Net measures as legitimate for productivity analysis. He however preferred Net Value arguing: " In so far as a large output is a proper goal of society and objective of policy, it is the net product that measures the degree of success in achieving this goal. Gross Product is larger by value of capital consumption- the quality of capital used in production- than there is to maximize the quantity of any other intermediate product...". Kendrick (1973, p. 18) shows that the trends are not affected significantly on use of Gross Value Added. Griliches and Jorgenson(1976, p. 256) argued, "Exclusion of depreciation of capital introduces and entirely arbitrary distinction between labour and capital input, since the corresponding exclusion of stock of labour service is not carried out." The present study will use Gross Value added as the measure of output. It is justified on the ground that from current data estimation of the real capital consumption is extremely difficult as ASI data records depreciation as per the rate allowed by Income Tax authorities of India, which seldom represent the real depreciation. Also, by taking Gross Value Added we are measuring both factor returns net of depreciation, thereby avoiding the bias in weighting system. Theoretically, Net Value Added (reported in ASI data) is the contribution of labour and capital in production process. The depreciation is added back to get the Gross Value Added.

This research work considers labour productivity which can be measured in two ways, either in term of physical products or in terms of value of the products. The first method relates directly to what we want to measure and is robust to price fluctuations but possess problem of summating the different outputs of variety of quality and volume manufactured. Labour productivity in terms of Gross Value of the product overcome some of these limitations but due to inadequate information on price movements the value of the output requires deflation to overcome price inflationary influence.

Labour input is considered in terms of man hour worked instead of taking number of workers employed because man hour worked in a flow is a variable as output therefore resulting in a unit free ratio for productivity.(Solow, Growth Theory: An Exposition, 1970)

$$Productivity = \frac{Output}{Man\ Hours\ Worked} \qquad (2)$$

Construction of Price-Deflators

The previous research work in productivity theory suggest the use of deflators for handling price movements of various inputs like raw material, power and fuel, capital and labour and for output consisting of variety of products in the selected industries. The most of the studies have though recognised the desirability of double deflation for arriving at real value but avoided using it in absence of suitable data or input deflator. Goldar (1987) used WPI of aggregate manufacturing for deflation to capture the movement of relative price changes in the value added, whereas Ahluwalia (1992) used WPI of concerned industry but not the double deflation. Balakrisnan and Puspangadan (1998) used material price index for the aggregate manufacturing using double deflation but this is of little use for individual industries. Pradhan and Barik (1998) derived material price index of individual industries using structural coefficient of industries from Input and Output Transactions Table. Rao (1996a) showed bias in the measurement because of fixed weights and noted double deflation method does not give error free measure. The price indices, which are used as input deflators in some of the studies been prepared by different agencies. These indices vary in their objectives, weighing systems, base year and coverage and hence cannot be readily used.

Gross value added is arrived at by adding the value of depreciation in the Net Value Added, i.e., deducting total input from total output. Now to arrive at value of Real Value Added, if we deflate the value of Gross Value Added by WPI $\left(I_{ij} = \frac{P_{ij}}{P_{oj}} \times 100 \right)$ of concerned industry, the method would be called single deflation.

$$Real\ Value\ Added_{Single\ Deflation} = (Gross\ Value\ Added) * I_{ij}$$

Here when we deflate Gross Value Added by output prices, we are ignoring the effect of material price and thereby implicitly assuming that the movement of price indices of Gross Value Added and material prices are similar. If we deflate Gross Output by Output Prices and material inputs by Input Prices, their difference would give Real Gross Value Added, Symbolically;

$$Real\ Value\ Added_{Double\ Deflation} = \frac{P_t Q_t}{P_t / P_o} - \frac{P_{mt} M_t}{P_{mt} P_{mo}}$$

Thus, in double deflation the material are weighted by base year material prices and gross output by base year output prices and their difference would give Real Gross Value Added.

For the current study the single price deflator (also, indicated by Maheshwari (1968)) will be used and is explained below:

$$I_{ij} = \frac{P_{ij}}{P_{oj}} \times 100 \tag{3}$$

Where, I_{ij} = index number of jth item in i^{th} year
P_{ij} = Price of the jth item in i^{th} year
P_{0j} = Price of the jth item in base year
Therefore, the average index of the selected variable will be:

$$I_j = \frac{1}{n} \Sigma_{i=1}^{n} I_{ij} \tag{4}$$

In order to avoid the problem of weighing, efforts are made to select those items which have more or less the same importance in the variable and constitute the major proportion of the universe.

ECONOMETRIC MODELS-NATURE OF THE MODELS, ESTIMATION OF PARAMETERS IN THE MODEL

The econometric models explain various kinds of relationships which exist among the econometric variables. The behavioural relationship have explanatory variable on one side and explained variable on the other. There can be interrelation among the explanatory variables. Econometric models in linear form, developed to study the impact of explanatory variables on labour cost wages and productivity are considered. Depending on practical feasibility number of explanatory variables are to be kept limited, also theoretical limitation of time series data analysis suggest that the number of exploratory variables are to be kept less than number of observations.

Let, $x_1 \ldots x_n$ be explanatory variables, y the dependent variable and a_0, a_t, a_n the (n+1) constant, then a linear multiple regression equation linear model can be written for the ith times series as:

$$y(t) = a_0 + a_1 x_1 (t) + \ldots + a_n x_n (t) + u(t) \tag{5}$$
$$t = 1, \ldots T$$

Where u(t) is error term and t the number of observations. The properties of the error term are as follows:

$E[u(t)] = 0$

$E[u^2(t)] = \sigma^2$ independent of t

$E[u(t)*u(t')] = 0$; $t \neq t'$

Independent variables x_i's are non stochastic

If x's are stochastic they should be distributed independently to error term u.

Independent variables x_i's are functionally independent.

The error term, therefore has mean value of zero, constant variance and are not auto-correlated.

The constant $a_0,...a_n$ are called parameters, and are unknown. These parameters are to be estimated and their significance tested. The coefficients are interpreted as the change in average value of y, when x_i changes by 1 unit, keeping $x_2,...x_n$ unchanged.

Estimation of Parameters in the Model

The principle of estimation of parameters, using statistical techniques requires following considerations:

1. How close is the estimated value to the true value of the parameters?
2. Whether all relevant variables were included in finding relationship?
3. Whether relationship identified provides good fit to the observed data?

The estimate shall be unbiased, efficient and consistent. The estimate obtained through the principle of least square ensures the above mentioned properties. The consideration of whether all relevant variables are used in the relationship is checked through significance of squared coefficient of multiple correlation (R^2) and F-statistic.

Where R^2 is obtained as:

$$R^2 = \frac{\sum_{t=1}^{T}(yo(t)-\bar{y})^2}{\sum_{t=1}^{T}(y(t)-\bar{y})^2} \tag{6}$$

$$where\ y = \frac{1}{T}\sum_{t=1}^{T} y(t) \tag{7}$$

$y_0(t)$ expected value of dependent variable y(t)

R^2 measures the proportion of variation in dependent variable explained by the explanatory variable. The value of R^2 is an indicator to significant exploratory variables If model uses appropriate explanatory variable the value of R^2 increases. To test R^2, F-statistic is used as follows:

$$F = \frac{R^2/(n-1)}{1-R^2/(T-n)} \tag{8}$$

where, T = Total number of observations,

n = Number of parameters.

Critical region with appropriate level of significance can be obtained from F-distribution with (n-1) and (T-n) degrees of freedom.

The linear as well as non linear economic models are worked out in this study. The non linear models in most of the cases are transformed in linear functions wherever necessary. For transformation of non linear model the double log transformation method is adopted for its property of constant elasticity of dependent variable w.r.t. independent variable. The double log transformation is explained below:

Let the model be: $y = a_0\ x_1^{a_1} x_2^{a_2} x_3^{a_3} \ldots x_n^{a_n}$ (9)

Taking log both sides we get

$\log y = \log a_0 + a_1 \log x_1 + a_2 \log x_2 + \ldots + a_n \log x_n$ or,

$y' = a_0 + a_1 x'_1 + a_2 x'_2 + \ldots a_n x'_n$ (10)

where, $y' = \log y$, $x'_1 = \log x_1, \ldots x'_n = \log x_n$

Specification of the Model

A regression model has a dependent variable, also called explained variable and a set of independent variables, also called explanatory variable. The variables are chosen in the light of economic theory in accordance with hypothesis under investigation. The efforts are made to obtain a model which would minimize errors in prediction and hence would be a model with greater precision.

Selection of explanatory variables: every set of possible explanatory variables are tested for their significance of R^2 value. The set of explanatory variables having significance and higher effect size i.e. value of R^2 being close to 1 is considered in the model.

ESTIMATION OF RELATIONSHIP BETWEEN OUTPUT AND INPUT, TESTING OF ECONOMIC HYPOTHESES

Estimation of Relationship Between Output and Input

A production function shows the technological relationship between the maximum output obtainable from a given set of input, viz. labour, capital, raw material, lubricants, fuel power etc. In this approach of productivity measurement the various component of productivity can be estimated through econometric functions. The production function can be used to measure the efficiency of production technology, returns to scale and the degree of substitution between factors of production. The parameter of specified function can be estimated through regression and its statistical significance tested. The direct estimation of production functions has an advantage that it is not necessary to assume competitive equilibrium for derivation of estimates. (Gujrati & Sangeetha, 2007)

The important determinants of unit labour cost are elasticity of production with respect to different inputs, marginal productivity of factors and rates of return under which industry is operating. If output is function of various inputs, mathematically it can be expressed as follows:

$P = f(L, C, R, F, U)$ (11)

Where P= output, C= Capital, L=Labour, R= Raw material, F= Lubricants, fuel, power etc. and U = The stochastic disturbance term following usual properties

The most commonly estimated Cobb-Douglas production function can be written as,

$P = AL^k C^j R^m F^n U$ (12)

Where A, k, j, m and n are the unknown parameters.

The important deductions of this well known function from theoretical economics are:

that, k, j, m and n are the elasticity of the production with respect to labour, capital, raw material and power, fuel, lubricants etc., this can be shown by taking logarithm of the function as

$$\log P = \log A + k \log L + j \log C + m \log R + n \log F + \log U \quad (13)$$

Differentiating partially w.r.t. L we have

$$\frac{1}{P}\frac{\partial P}{\partial L} = \frac{k}{L}$$

$$\text{or } k = \frac{L}{P}\frac{\partial P}{\partial L} = \textit{Elasticity of production w.r.t. labour} \quad (14)$$

Similarly,

$$j = \frac{C}{P}\frac{\partial P}{\partial C} = \textit{Elasticity of production w.r.t. capital} \quad (15)$$

$$m = \frac{R}{P}\frac{\partial P}{\partial R} = \textit{Elasticity of production w.r.t. material} \quad (16)$$

$$n = \frac{F}{P}\frac{\partial P}{\partial F} = \textit{Elasticity of production w.r.t. power, fuel etc.} \quad (17)$$

that, the sum of the exponents shows the degree of return to scale of production.

i.e.

$k + j + m + n < 1$ *means decreasing return to scale*

$k + j + m + n = 1$ *means constant return to scale*

$k + j + m + n > 1$ *means increasing return to scale*

Suppose that, each input is increased by r% then the new input will be:

$$L_1 = L\left(1 + \frac{r}{100}\right)$$

$$C_1 = C\left(1 + \frac{r}{100}\right)$$

$$R_1 = R\left(1 + \frac{r}{100}\right)$$

$$F_1 = F\left(1 + \frac{r}{100}\right)$$

Then, the output is increased by less than r%, by r%, or by more than r%; according to whether there are decreasing, constant, or increasing 'return to scale'. This is easily seen by substituting into the function:

$$= A\left\{L\left(1+\frac{r}{100}\right)\right\}^{k}\left\{C\left(1+\frac{r}{100}\right)\right\}^{j}\left\{R\left(1+\frac{r}{100}\right)\right\}^{m}\left\{F\left(1+\frac{r}{100}\right)\right\}^{n}U$$

$$P\left(1\frac{r}{100}\right)^{k+j+m+n} = A\left(1\frac{r}{100}\right)^{k+j+m+n} L^{k}C^{j}R^{m}F^{n}U \qquad (18)$$

Where, 'r' is the percentage rate of increase of P.

that, multiple of exponents with respective average productivity of the factors are the marginal productivity of the respective factors:

$$k\frac{P}{L} = \textit{Marginal productivity of labour}$$

$$j\frac{P}{C} = \textit{Marginal productivity of capital}$$

$$m\frac{P}{R} = \textit{Marginal productivity of raw material}$$

$$n\frac{P}{F} = \textit{Marginal productivity of power and fuel}$$

This can be easily seen by using the relations derived earlier (see equation 14-17), in case of the first property, marginal productivity of

labour $= \dfrac{\partial P}{\partial L}$

Then,

$$k\frac{P}{L} = \partial P / \partial L \qquad (19)$$

and so on so forth.

that, the sum of the coefficients show the degree of homogeneity of the function. If k+j+m+n is equal to unity the production function is homogeneous of first degree.

Testing the Economic Hypothesis

Empirical testing of economic hypothesis is very essential in any fact finding investigation. Attempts have been made to test hypothesis on factual data using either simple or sophisticated statistical techniques, for example, the hypothesis that wage of the worker moves faster than productivity has been tested by the analysis of indices of wages and productivity, while testing of negative association between size of the firm and labour cost has been done using Spearman's rank correlation test. Similarly ANOVA (F-test) results are reported for testing the structures of the models. The description of only important estimation is done.

The factual data is utilized as far as possible, but where complete data series are not available but is comparable, interpolations are made. For incomparable data series transformations are made. Where the results of long term trends are objectionable due to major shift in policies, the periods have been divided into parts to remove the effect of time factor. Where firm aggregation is not suitable, industry aggregation has been made. Where industry aggregation has not been found suitable, all manufacturing industries have been aggregated. Where multicollinearity among the selected variables is observed, caution has been exercised in estimation of the parameters and interpolation of the results. Where trends are affected by number of factors, graphic method has been used to make the relationship clearer.

DATA CLASSIFICATION AND TABULATION

Statistical data (secondary data) will be mainly collected from the "Annual Surveys of Industries" Govt. of India publications. The data are authentic, as these have been collected under the statutory obligation from the industrialist. It is important to describe how these data were collected by the government agencies and the related lacuna or gaps therein.

Annual Survey of Industries (ASI)

The Annual Survey of Industries (ASI) is the principal source of industrial statistics in India. It provides statistical information to assess and evaluate, objectively and realistically, the changes in the growth, composition and structure of organised manufacturing sector comprising activities related to manufacturing processes, repair services, gas and water supply and cold storage. Industrial sector occupies an important position in the Indian economy and has a pivotal role to play in the rapid and balanced economic development. The Survey is conducted annually under the statutory provisions of the Collection of Statistics Act 1953, and the Rules framed there-under in 1959, except in the State of Jammu & Kashmir where it is conducted under the State Collection of Statistics Act, 1961 and the rules framed there-under in 1964.

This survey replaced both the CMI (Census of Manufacturing Industries) and SSMI (Sample Survey of Manufacturing Industries). The ASI was launched in 1960 with 1959 as the reference year and is continuing since then except for 1972. The ASI refers to the factories defined in accordance with the Factories Act 1948, and thus has coverage wider than that of the CMI and SSMI put together.

Scope and Coverage

The ASI extends to the entire country except the States of Arunachal Pradesh, Mizoram, and Sikkim and Union Territory of Lakshadweep. It covers all factories registered under Sections 2m(i) and 2m(ii) of the Factories Act, 1948 i.e. those factories employing 10 or more workers using power; and those employing 20 or more workers without using power. The survey also covers bidi and cigar manufacturing establishments registered under the Bidi & Cigar Workers (Conditions of Employment) Act, 1966 with coverage as above. All electricity undertakings engaged in generation, transmission and distribution of electricity registered with the Central Electricity Authority (CEA) were covered under ASI irrespective of their employment size. Certain servicing units and activities like water supply, cold storage, repairing of motor vehicles and other consumer durables like watches etc. are covered under the Survey. Though servicing industries like motion picture production, personal services like laundry services, job dyeing, etc. are covered under the Survey but data are not tabulated, as these industries do not fall under the scope of industrial sector defined by the United Nations. Defense establishments, oil storage and distribution depots, restaurants, hotels, café and computer services and the technical training institutes, etc. are excluded from the purview of the Survey.

From ASI 1998-99, the electricity units registered with the CEA and the departmental units such as railway workshops, RTC workshops, Govt. Mints, sanitary, water supply, gas storage etc. are not covered, as there are alternative sources of their data compilation for the GDP estimates by the National Accounts Division of CSO.

ASI Frame and Its Updation

The ASI frame is based on the lists of registered factories/units maintained by the Chief Inspector of Factories (CIF) in each State/UT and those maintained by licensing authorities in respect of bidi and cigar establishments and electricity undertakings. Regional offices of FOD (NSSO) maintain close liaison with CIF in updating the frame every year.

Sampling Design

The primary unit of enumeration in the survey is a factory in the case of manufacturing industries, a workshop in the case of repair services, an undertaking or a licensee in the case of electricity, gas & water supply undertakings and an establishment in the case of bidi & cigar industries. The owner of two or more establishments located in the same State and pertaining to the same industry group and belonging to same scheme (census or sample) is, however, permitted to furnish a single consolidated return. Such consolidated returns are common feature in the case of bidi and cigar establishments, electricity and certain public sector undertakings.

The ASI adopted from the beginning a very simple design. All units with 50 or more workers operating with power, and units having 100 or more workers operating without power were covered under the census sector. Also 12 States/UTs, namely, Himachal Pradesh, Jammu & Kashmir, Manipur, Meghalaya, Nagaland, Tripura and Pondicherry, A&N Islands,

Chandigarh, Goa, Daman & Diu, D & N Haveli, which were industrially backward, were covered under the census sector to take complete stock of their manufacturing activities. Even the sample sector which comprised of units employing less than 50/100 workers (operating with or without power) in the major States were covered fully over a span of two years. This procedure continued till ASI 1986-87 by which time the total number of factories in the country grew enormously. Accordingly, the definition of the census sector was changed from ASI 1987-88 to the units having 100 or more workers irrespective of their operation with or without power. All the units in the frame of 12 less industrially developed States/UTs were surveyed on complete enumeration basis. The rest of the universe was covered on sampling basis through an efficient sampling design adopting State X 3 digit industry group as stratum so as to cover all the units in a span of three years. This design continued till ASI 1996-97.

Before launching of ASI 1997-98 due to constraints of resources in covering a large number of units in the survey and generating the results of the survey in time bound manner, a review of the earlier design was made and a revised design was adopted in ASI 1997-98. The census sector was defined to include units having 200 or more workers and also some Significant Units were identified from the databases of ASI 1993-94 to ASI 1995-96, which although having less than 200 workers, contributed significantly to the Value of Output in these ASI years. The complete coverage of all Units in 12 less industrially developed States/UTs, namely, Goa, Himachal Pradesh, Jammu & Kashmir, Manipur, Meghalaya, Nagaland, Tripura, A&N Islands, Chandigarh UT, D & N Haveli, Daman & Diu and Pondicherry was continued. Also, all public sector undertakings (PSUs) were included in the census sector. The rest of the universe was covered in the Sample Sector by the usual formula of determination of sample size at a given value of the precision of the estimates with at least 99 per cent chance. This approach significantly reduced the sample size in ASI 1997-98 compared to that of ASI 1996-97 while maintaining a fair level of degree of precision for the estimates up to the State level. However, in 1997-98 a consensus decision has been taken so as not to attempt for the district level estimates. This design has been more or less continued till 2003-04 with the modification that the census sector was defined to include units having 100 or more workers instead of 200 or more workers and only 5 industrially backward States/UTs, namely, Manipur, Meghalaya, Nagaland, Tripura and A&N Islands were covered in census sector. The public sector undertakings were also covered in the general scheme i.e. units having 100 or more workers in census sector and rest in sample sector. A new sampling design has been adopted from ASI 2004-05 which continued till ASI 2006-07.

The schedule is in three parts. Part I which is processed at the CSO aims to collect data on capital structure by type of assets, workforce by sex and category of workers, wage bill by type of payments, consumption by broad categories of inputs, output by type of products and by-products etc. Part II which is processed by the Labour Bureau, aims to collect data on different aspects of labour statistics, namely, working days, man- days worked, absenteeism, labour turnover, man-hours worked, earnings and social security benefits. Part III which is processed by the National Buildings Organisation, aims to collect data on housing activities, i.e. houses constructed by the employers for the benefit of their employees. Part three of the schedule has been removed from 1998-99 onwards.

Highlighting one of the limitations, up to 1996-97 while presenting data, only the reporting factories were taken into account. The aggregates based on these data, therefore, needed adjustment because of non-reporting units. The CSO, while estimating gross value added from the registered sector used to inflate the gross value added given by ASI by using the number of workers in the non-reporting units. The implicit assumption was that value added per worker in the reporting units is the same as that in the non-reporting units. This assumption was, however, not correct as one of the reasons cited in ASI reports regarding non- reporting units was that the factory remained closed for the major part of the year due to labour and management disputes.

Industrial Classification

ASI data is classified under the Standard Industrial and Occupation Classification 1962 developed on the basis of the UN International Standard Industrial Classification (ISIC) of all Economic Activities 1958 (Rev. 1). This classification was adopted from first survey of ASI in 1960. The National Industrial Classification (NIC) 1970 was developed subsequently on the basis of UNISIC 1968(Rev.2), this classification was adopted with effect from ASI 1973-74. Under this scheme the four digit classification has structured levels indicating 'Section', 'Division', 'Major Group', and 'Sub-Groups'. For the present study's data needs, data tables (1980 to 1988) with following classification were consulted: NIC code 206 for sugar, 230 to 239 for cotton textile, 250, 251, 252, 259 for Jute and 330 for steel. In this classification the first digit 2 & 3 indicates the 'Division' of Manufacturing, the second level digit code i.e. 20-21 is for manufacturing of food products, 23 for cotton textile, 25 for manufacturing of Jute, hemp and Mesta and 33 for manufacturing of Basic Metal and Alloys.

The NIC 1987 which followed UNISIC 1968 was adopted from ASI 1989-90 to ASI 1997-98. For data required in this study tables with classification number 206, 207.1 to 207.6 for Sugar, 230 to 234 and 235.1to 235.4 for cotton textile, 250, 251, 254, 257 for Jute and 330, 330.1, 330.2, 330.9 for Steel

The NIC 1998, developed on the basis of UNISIC, 1990 (Rev. 3) was used from ASI 1998-99 to ASI 2003-04. The data tables consulted were for category D, 15421 to 15427 for sugar, 01409, 17111, 17115, 17121, for cotton textile, 17119, 17125, for Jute and 27104 to 20108 for Steel.

Concepts and Definitions of Items Collected Through the Schedule of Enquiry

The concepts and definitions of items collected through ASI schedule are given below:

- *Factory* is one that is registered under sections 2m (i) and 2m (ii) of the Factories Act, 1948. The sections 2m (i) and 2m (ii) refer to any premises including the precincts thereof (a) whereon ten or more workers are working, or were working on any day of the preceding twelve months, and in any part of which a manufacturing process is being carried on with the aid of power, or is ordinarily so carried on; or (b) whereon twenty or more workers are working or were working on any day of the preceding twelve months, and in any part of which a manufacturing process is being carried on without the aid of power, or is ordinarily so carried on.
- *Fixed Capital* represents the depreciated value of fixed assets owned by the factory as on the closing day of the accounting year. Fixed assets are those that have a normal productive life of more than one year. Fixed capital includes land including lease- hold land, buildings, plant & machinery, furniture and fixtures, transport equipment, water system and roadways and other fixed assets such as hospitals, schools, etc. used for the benefit of the factory personnel.
- *Physical Working Capital* is the total inventories comprising of raw materials and components, fuels and lubricants, spares, stores and others, semi-finished goods and finished goods as on the closing day of the accounting year. However, it does not include the stock of the materials, fuels, stores, etc. supplied by others to the factory for processing and finished goods processed by the factory from raw materials supplied by others.
- *Working Capital* is the sum total of the physical working capital as already defined above and the cash deposits in hand and at bank and the net balance receivable over amounts payable at the end of the accounting year. Working capital, however, excludes unused overdraft facility, fixed deposits (irrespective of duration), advances for acquisition of fixed assets, loans and advances by proprietors and partners (irrespective of their purpose and duration), long-term loans (including interest thereon) and investments.
- *Productive Capital* is the total of fixed capital and working capital as defined above.
- *Invested Capital* is the total of fixed capital and physical working capital as defined above.
- *Gross Value of Plant and Machinery* represents the total original (un-depreciated) value of installed plant and machinery at the end of the accounting year. It includes the book value of the newly installed plants and machinery and the approximate value of rented in plants and

machinery at the time of renting-in but exclude the value of rented-out plants and machinery. Total value of all the plants and machinery acquired on hire - purchase basis is also included.

- *Workers* are defined to include all persons employed directly or through any agency whether for wages or not and engaged in any manufacturing process or in cleaning any part of the machinery or premises used for manufacturing process or in any other kind of work incidental to or connected with the manufacturing process or the subject of the manufacturing process . Labour engaged in the repair & maintenance, or production of fixed assets for factory's own use, or employed for generating electricity, or producing coal, gas etc. are included.
- *Employees* include all workers defined above and persons receiving wages and holding clerical or supervisory or managerial positions engaged in administrative office, store keeping section and welfare section, sales department as also those engaged in purchase of raw materials etc. or purchase of fixed assets for the factory as well as watch and ward staff.
- *Total Persons Engaged* include the employees as defined above and all working proprietors and their family members who are actively engaged in the work of the factory even without any pay, and the unpaid members of the co-operative societies who worked in or for the factory in any direct and productive capacity. The number of workers or employees is an average number obtained by dividing man-days worked by the number of days the factory had worked during the reference year.
- *Wages and Salaries* are defined to include all remuneration in monetary terms and also payable more or less regularly in each pay period to workers as compensation for work done during the accounting year. It includes (a) direct wages and salary (i.e., basic wages/salaries, payment of overtime, dearness, compensatory allowance, house rent and other allowances), (b) remuneration for the period not worked (i.e., basic wages, salaries and allowances payable for leave period, paid holiday, lay-off payments and compensation for unemployment, if not paid from sources other than employers), (c) bonuses and ex-gratia payment paid both at regular and less frequent intervals (i.e., incentive bonuses, good attendance bonuses, productive bonuses, profit sharing bonuses, festival or year-end bonuses, etc.). It excludes lay off payments which are made from trust or other special funds set up exclusively for this purpose i.e., payments not made by the employer. It also excludes imputed value of benefits in kind, employer's contribution to old age benefits and other social security charges, direct expenditure on maternity benefits and crèches and other group benefits. Travelling and other expenditure incurred for business purposes and reimbursed by the employer are excluded. The wages are expressed in terms of gross value i.e., before deduction for fines, damages, taxes, provident fund, employee's state insurance contribution, etc.

- *Contribution to Provident Fund and Other Funds* includes old age benefits like provident fund, pension, gratuity, etc. and employers contribution towards other social security charges such as employees state insurance, compensation for work injuries and occupational diseases, provident fund-linked insurance, retrenchment and lay- off benefits.
- *Workmen and Staff Welfare Expenses* include group benefits like direct expenditure on maternity, crèches, canteen facilities, educational, cultural and recreational facilities; and grants to trade unions, co-operative stores, etc. meant for employees.
- *Total Emoluments* is defined as the sum of wages and salaries, employers' contribution as provident fund and other funds and workmen and staff welfare expenses as defined above.
- *Total Input* comprises total value of fuels and materials consumed as well as expenditures such as cost of contract and commission work done by others on materials supplied by the factory, cost of materials consumed for repair and maintenance of factory's fixed assets including cost of repairs and maintenance work done by others to the factory's fixed assets, inward freight and transport charges, rates and taxes (excluding income tax), postage, telephone and telex expenses, insurance charges, banking charges, cost of printing and stationery and purchase value of goods sold in the same condition as purchased .
- *Total Output* comprises total ex-factory value of products and by-products manufactured as well as other receipts such as receipts from non-industrial services rendered to others, work done for others on material supplied by them, value of electricity produced and sold, sale value of goods sold in the same condition as purchased, addition in stock of semi- finished goods and own construction.
- *Depreciation* is consumption of fixed capital due to wear & tear and obsolescence during the accounting year and is taken as provided by the factory owner or is estimated on the basis of cost of installation and working life of the fixed assets.
- *Net Value Added* is arrived by deducting total input and depreciation from total output.

The data collected and analysed from ASI are presented in the appropriate chapters in the form of tables following the APA format, graphs are created wherever required for better assimilation of the result of analysis.

Consumer Price Index Numbers (For Industrial Workers)

The compilation of index numbers on uniform and scientific lines was started only after the conduct of the Family Living Surveys by the Labour Bureau during 1958-59 at 50 important industrial centres spread over length and breadth of the country on guidelines of the Technical Advisory Committee on Cost of Living Index Numbers. Since then the compilation and maintenance of Consumer Price Index Numbers are being done by the

Labour Bureau on a continuous basis. The current series (1982=100) replaced the old (1960=100) series in December, 1988 with release of October, 1988 index. (India, 2003)

Labour Bureau, is the competent authority under the Minimum Wages Act, 1948 to ascertain, from time to time, the Consumer Price Index Numbers applicable to employees employed in the Scheduled employment in respect of all undertakings in the Central Sphere and the Union Territories.

The old series of the Consumer Price Index Numbers for Industrial Workers on base 1960=100 was compiled for industrial workers relating to factories, mines and plantations. But the coverage of the Industrial Workers for 1982 series was extended to seven sectors by including four more sectors viz. (a) railways, (b) public motor transport undertakings, (c) electricity generation and distribution establishments, and (d) ports and docks. A Working Class Family is defined as one where one of the members worked as a manual worker in any of the 7 sectors listed above and which derived one half or more of its income through manual work

The Weighting Diagram for the Index was derived by conducting Working Class Family Income and Expenditure Survey, 1981-82 in all 76 selected centres. The survey was conducted over a period of 12 months in each centre during 1981-82 when an equal number of a moving sample of families was convassed every month. The data collected through this survey was thoroughly scrutinised and inconsistencies, if any, were got rectified before getting it tabulated for the purpose of derivation of Weighting Diagram.

As it was not feasible to monitor the price behaviour of all the items on which index population reported consumption expenditure (nor it is necessary) a number of representative items were retained in the index basket, which were manageable over time.

For this purpose the first step was to form group of items which meet similar or related demands of the consumers.

The total expenditure on consumption items was divided into 6 main groups viz.,

I – Food;

II – Pan, Supari, Tobacco & Intoxicants;

III – Fuel & Light ;

IV – Housing ;

V – Clothing, Bedding & Footwear ; and

VI – Miscellaneous.

In the first and the last group a few well-defined sub-groups have also been formed.

Weights, which are meant to indicate relative importance attached to different items of goods and services consumed by the index population, are determined on the basis of expenditure made by them on these goods and services. However, the expenditures on non-consumption items are excluded from the weighting diagram.

The items directly retained in the basket were those which had (a) atleast one percent expenditure in the Group/Sub-Group; (b) significant number of families reporting expenditure; and (c) could be priced satisfactorily over the life of the series. The remaining items were imputed to related items or to a group of items depending upon their similarity of want, manufacturing process or price behaviour etc. The percentage expenditure on each item in the sub-group/group represents its weight. Similarly, the percentage expenditure on sub-group/group in the Group/Total consumption expenditure represent their weight.

The retail prices used in the index calculation are those actually charged from the consumers for cash transaction and are inclusive of all indirect taxes which are payable by him. However, rebates and discounts, given to consumers in general are taken into account. The retail prices of price sensitive items such as cereals, pulses, vegetables, oils & fats etc., are collected on a weekly basis. Similarly, the prices of some other items, like cinema, furniture, utensils, clothing, house-hold appliances etc., which are known to vary less frequently are collected on monthly basis. However, the price data relating to house rent, school/college fees and books etc., are collected on six-monthly/yearly basis as these items do not show much change in their price behaviour.

The retail prices of the selected items are collected on the fixed date/ day by part-time Price Collectors, who are generally the employees of the State Governments working in the Directorate of Economics and Statistics and Labour Departments, and sent to the Headquarters for further processing. While collecting prices, various elements such as fixity of markets, shops, specifications, unit of purchase, day and time of price quotations etc. are maintained for the purpose of comparability. These price data, after cleaning it for conceptual/factual error at various levels, are utilised for the compilation of index numbers.

Compilation of Index: The index is compiled by using Laspeyres base weighted formula which is reproduced below:

$$CPIIW = \frac{\sum\left(\frac{Pn}{Po}\right)PoQo}{\sum PoQo} * 100$$

Where:

CPIIW= Consumer Price Index for Industrial Worker

P_n= Price for current year

P_0 =Price for base year

Q_0 = Quantity for base year

The index of each selected centre is compiled in several stages i.e. Sub-group, Group and General level every month.

In the first stage price quotations of an item in all outlets of all the markets in a month are averaged for a centre. On the basis of this average price, a price relative (over base period price), or item index as known in some of the countries, is worked out. However, in case of certain items which are supplied through subsidised outlets (fair price shops) first the weighted average price of open market and fair price outlets in each selected market of a centre is worked out (weight being availability ratio in the respective outlets in that month).

In the next stage a simple average of these market prices is worked out to arrive at the centre price. On the basis of this average centre price, a price relative is worked out. The sub-group or group index is worked out as a weighted average of an item/sub-group index respectively. The general index of a centre is worked out as a weighted average of group indices.

An all-India index which is weighted average of 70 centre indices is also worked out every month. The weight assigned to each centre is the proportion of the total consumption expenditure of estimated number of families allocated to a centre in the State to sum total of all such expenditure over all centres in the country.

Classification on the Basis of Location and Size

The fact that location factor is an important determinant of cost, necessitates data clustering on location for investigation into nature and character of inter-regional trends of the industry. The factual data is further analysed on regional basis for exploring broad tendencies operating in the industry explained by location of the manufacturing units.

The size-wise approach of the problem is also necessary, as the size of the industrial unit effects labour costs and other related variables, such as productivity and intensity of capital. Hence, the data shall be is also clustered on the basis of size, but data collected by ASI for the period under consideration contains fluctuating operational definitions for sampling unit and census unit, hence, it would be erroneous to club them under the assumption of similar characteristics. If we divide the data on the basis of changes observed by ASI for data collected, each period is left with very less number of data points for statistical principles to work.

3

Scope and Significance of the Study

Theoretically and empirically the study will provide scientific analysis of productivity, labour cost and wages. It will bring to light the important changes that took place during 1980 to 2004 in four major industries of India viz. Cotton textile, Jute, Steel and Sugar. This study will also identify many relationships that generally subsist and estimate the impact of factors influencing industrial productivity in India.

In every factor of production, whether it is raw material, capital equipment or a factory building, the element of labour is present. In the phase of liberalised economy wages are rising and India is facing foreign competition, this investigation may pave the way of reducing labour cost thereby more competitive trade development.

Labour being an important factor in production, abundant literature dealing with various aspects of the subject has been published. But attempts to consider wages as an element of earning for living is rare. Maheswari (1968), Brenner (2002), Kumar and Mishra (2008) and Ambedekar Institute of Labour Studies, Mumbai (2009) had done work in this area, the work needs more attention and this study is an attempt in the same direction. Wages can be viewed through two different perspectives- as a mean of livelihood (living wage) for the workers and as an element of production cost. Workers take wages as their earnings, while producers treat them as a part of their production cost. There is abundant literature available dealing wages as a part of production cost but very less detailed scientific work to analyse relationship of wage to production cost has been done. This study is an attempt to analyse wages as a factor of production cost and its impact on productivity and technological developments. Present study focuses attention on work of Maheswari (1968).

As per the theory of comparative costs, labour as an important cost element affects the international flow of goods and services. At present when wages are rising and India is facing competition from other Asian countries mainly China, for attracting MNCs to establish manufacturing units in the country, such an investigation should prove very useful in finding out the ways of reducing labour cost and searching out the possibilities of trade developments.

Study's Relevance to the Problems and Needs of the Society and the Country

Labour cost being an important element of production cost is also significantly connected with number of factors, such as, productivity movements, technological changes, volume of production, and rates of return, union activities and state intervention. In the everlasting conflict between the objectives of workers and employers, workers aspire for higher wages and employers focus on minimizing unit production cost. To attain their objectives workers form unions and engage in activities for pressurizing the employers for wage raise and employers resist these goals and try to reduce cost. One of the methods available to employers is to adopt labour saving devices available due to technological advances but, this usually increases the unemployment (keeping other variables related with economic environment constant). How much one or the other party succeeds, depends upon the conditions of the market for labour and commodity produced, on the nature of the industry and on the industrial policy of the government. But labour cost gets definitely influenced by these activities. The study attempts to study these effects.

Expected Outcome of the Study

Theoretically as well as empirically the present study will provide a scientific analysis of productivity, labour cost and wages. It will highlight the important changes that are taking place, will discover relationships their strength, trends in factors influencing industrial productivity in India. The results would provide basis for drawing many useful conclusions of the interrelationships of the share and impact of labour in total cost and its influence on productivity.

4

A Conceptual Analysis

This chapter will discuss in detail the theoretical background of concepts used in the study. The reasoning for choosing one method over other will also be explained.

CONCEPTS OF PRODUCTIVITY

Productivity can be defined as the efficiency with which inputs are transformed into meaningful outputs, through a production process. The simplistic definition is the ratio of output to input. Productivity can be measured through comparing output with single factor input (Partial Productivity Ratio), or by Total Factor Productivity which accounts for effects in total output not caused by inputs or by comparing all the inputs combined to standard form of output (Multifactor Productivity).

Brief History of Productivity Measurement

Dale W. Jorgenson's *The Economics of Productivity*, contains good description of history of productivity. The excerpts are provided in this discussion. The references made by him are also included. It is important to note here that these developments, if to be applied, require suitable data quality. In the case of Indian statistics provided by ASI or CSO it was reported by researchers in India to have found lacking uniformity and has various errors and imperfections, as is the case of most of developing nations, nevertheless the discussion is provided for conceptual clarity and hence better interpretation of results reported in successive chapters.

In early 1970's the empirically founded study of growth economics was published by Kuznet (1971) and theory of growth by Solow (1970) which summarised decade of theoretical research initiated by Roy Horrod (1939) and Evsey Domar (1946). These two works established the framework of growth models and measurements for such studies. The initial challenge to the frameworks of Kuznets and Solow was posed by Denison's magisterial study, *Why Growth Rates Differ* (1967), where Denison retained NNP as measure of national product but departed on identification of labours input he considered labour inputs in terms of hours worked and constructed constant quality measures of labour input, taking into account differences in quality of hours worked due to age, sex and education attainment of the workers. The notion of efficiency or 'total factor productivity' was introduced by Gorge Stigler(1947). Solow (1957) identified 'technical change' with shifts in production function. He attributed all of US economic growth to 'residual' growth in productivity. This residual now is known as Solow Residual. Kuznet (1978) interpreted the Solow residual as due to exogenous technological innovations. Successful attempts to provide a more convincing explanation to Solow residual ultimately led to demise of traditional framework in growth economics.

Jorgenson and Griliches (1967)challenged more seriously the traditional approach and replaced NNP with GNP as a measure of output and introduced constant quality indexes for both capital and labour inputs. They combined hours worked for each type into a constant quality index of labour input, using the index number methodology developed by Griliches (1960) for US agriculture.

Finally Griliches and Jorgenson replaced the aggregate production function employed by Danison, Kuznets and Solow with the *production possibility frontier* (Jorgenson, 1966). This allowed for joint production of consumption and investment goods from capital and labour inputs.

In the case of research on Indian economic data, the problem of estimates due to lack of sufficient data and homogeneity in it, has found traditional measurement practices more reliable, the concepts of measurement of productivity used mostly by Indian researchers is discussed below.

Partial Productivity

The partial productivity ratios, also known as 'average ratios', can be estimated using statistical procedures. These are the simplest measure of productivity and are derived by dividing the output by relevant factor input. The most commonly used and widely reported are labour productivity ratio and capital productivity ratio. The partial productivity ratio relates output to the input of a single factor and does not tells any thing about the other factors. The increase in partial productivity ratio means that over a period of time more output is possible with decreasing amount of inputs or with same amount of input, or with same outputs with lesser inputs. The inverse of these partial productivity ratios implies unit requirement of factor concerned for per unit of output. The study of partial productivity ratios is very helpful in measuring the savings in use of that particular factor over time. These ratios indicate the average productivity of that particular factor.

As long as all productivity ratios move in the same direction, a general idea can be held about the direction of overall productive efficiency. But when different ratios move in the different directions, no finite idea can be made about overall productive efficiency, such ideas, if any, can be misleading. Although, for finding the factor remuneration, factor's share etc. marginal productivity is required, which unfortunately, unlike average ratios (partial productivity ratios), cannot be estimated directly in pure statistical sense. Rosen (1959) has suggested that if data does not permit an estimation of marginal ratios, the average ratio may be used as a very rough estimation for the approximation of marginal ratio. But caution must be taken while using them.

Labour Productivity

Labour productivity is defined as the ratio of output to the ratio of labor input, while there is no ambiguity regarding the definition of labour productivity but its measurement differs due to various definitions and qualifications of numerator and denominator in the ratio, i.e., output and input. The definitions and measurement issues were discussed in Chapter 2. Labour productivity in any year may be defined as:

$$\text{Labour Productivity}_t = \frac{\text{Value of Output}_t}{\text{Value of Labour Input}_t} \qquad (1)$$

The change in labour productivity between two periods is given by ratio of productivity in two periods, symbolically:

$$\text{Index of Labour Productivity} = \frac{\text{Value of Output}_t/\text{Value of Labour Input}_t}{\text{Value of Output}_0/\text{Value of Labour Input}_0} \qquad (2)$$

Labour productivity should be interpreted with utmost caution as labour is only one of the factors of production. Changes in labour productivity should not be interpreted as change due to labour alone. The connotation attached to it of labour efficiency can be misleading as the labour productivity here is purely in statistical sense, any factor affecting output and labour input may cast influence on labour productivity.

The concept of output per person is representative of the efficiency of enterprise in utilisation labour force, rather than efficiency of labour in the unit time. The output per person is related to the abilities and the will of the labour to work. Beri (1962) remarked that labour productivity as measure of efficiency is quite misleading, especially in underdeveloped countries, where labour is cheaper and abundantly available and there has been greater amount of capital increase. Salter (1969) pointed that measurement of productivity as given above does not measure anything peculiar to labour and that increased capital or material may raise labour productivity while labour itself remain passive. Subrahmanyam(1984) argued that when an appreciable increase in productivity is witnessed, our first line of inquiry shall be directed towards verifying whether large, perhaps uneconomic, increase in capital is at the bottom of it? Sinha and Sawhney(1970) argued that an increase in labour productivity measures the savings in the cost of labour used in producing a given output but whether it amounts to reduction in real cost of other factors of production, depends upon direction of changes in the cost of other factors of production. Thus labour productivity so obtained should not be purely relied in linking wages with productivity

Despite the limitations discussed above the Labour Productivity is computed. It is easy to compute and is relatively more reliable. Labour is the only active factor which is directly productive. Other factors such as production means are passive in nature and contribute to productivity of labour during the course of production.

Capital Productivity

The capital productivity index reflects the efficiency in utilisation of capital. It may be defined as:

$$Capital\ Productivity_t = \frac{Value\ of\ Output_t}{Value\ of\ Input_t} \qquad (3)$$

and a change in productivity between two periods can be measured by the ratio of capital productivity in two periods. Symbolically:

$$Index\ of\ Capital\ Productivity = \frac{Value\ of\ Output_t\ /Value\ of\ Input_t}{Value\ of\ Input_0/\ Value\ of\ Input_0} \qquad (4)$$

Like labour productivity this measure also has its limitations as those of partial productivity ratios discussed above.

Total Factor Productivity

In the literature Total Factor Productivity and Technological Progress is seen as synonymous, although the distinction lies. The meaning or various aspects of technology or technological progress was explored in details by Marjit and Singh(1995) one of the dimension is taken as technology referring to collection of techniques used to convert various inputs in given quantity of outputs. Technological progress indicates advancement in this knowledge. Total factor productivity, which extends the concept of single factor or partial productivity is defined as ratio of gross output to the weighted combination of inputs. The changes in TFP can take place due to various reasons such as technological progress, experiential learning curve, improved labour skills, better maintenance procedures, better management labour relationships etc. hence TFP is a regarded as a better measure of growth in productivity. TFP is measured under two different approaches (i) A non-parametric index number approach (b) a parametric production function approach.

Index Number Approach

For measurement of TFP separate input and output indexes from prices and quantity data are computed. This approach makes TFP free from bias of explicit functional form. If we take the difference between the growth in output and growth in aggregate inputs we get TFP growth for the period under consideration. Solow residual which indicate technological progress can be obtained if weights of inputs for aggregation is known. Solow (1957) derived analytically the unique weights for such aggregation and has shown that residual growth indicates technological progress. There are various index numbers developed which are consistent and differ from each other on the basis of aggregation scheme or underlying production function. Following are most commonly indexes used:

Kendrick Index: this index measures the average productivity of an arithmetic combination of labour and capital with base period factor prices. Kendrick describes it as "the fact that our total factor input index is the weighted arithmetic mean of labour and capital input indices (rather than geometric mean) implies logarithmic linear relationship with in successive sub periods". This TFP measure is based on linear production function of the form:

$$Output = \alpha.\ Labour + \beta.Capital \tag{5}$$

A weighted input index is prepared by combining labour and capital inputs using appropriate weights. The scheme of weighing can be either price of the labour and capital or percentage of labour and capital in total value added. To obtain total input index the aggregation of weighted inputs of labour and capital is done, similarly the index of the output is also prepared. The ratio of output to total input index yields the arithmetic Kendrick's TFP index. Symbolically for time t:

$$TFPK_t = \frac{Index\ of\ Output_t}{\alpha.Labour_t + \beta.Capital_t} \tag{6}$$

Mehta (1980) has pointed some technical lacuna in this form of index. By rewriting the function as Index of Output$_t$ = TFPKt = (α.Labour$_t$ + β.Capital$_t$) Mehta indicated the lacuna that regardless of upward movement in Capital in relation to labour, this ratio remains same. Thus marginal rate of substitution is assumed implying the assumption of linear production function, perfect competition, perfect substitutability between labour and capital. In Kendrik's TFP Index Weights are not derived using statistical estimation, they are factor's share in income. For the base year the value of index is 1. The index can be genralised to allow for more than two factors.

Solow Index: Solow's geometric measure is based on neo-classical multiplicative production function. It assumes constant return to scale, Hicks-neutral technical change, competitive equilibrium and weights of factors determined by marginal products. The multiplicative production function is given by:

Output = *A* (*t*) *Labour*$^{\alpha}$ *Capital*$^{\beta}$

$P = A\,(t){:}L^{\alpha}\,K^{\beta}$ (7)

Where, α β and A(t) are unknown parameters. A(t) measures the cumulated effect of technological shifts over time.

Taking log and total differentiating the function with respect to time we have,

$$\frac{\dot{P}}{P} = \frac{\dot{A}}{A} + \alpha\frac{\dot{L}}{L} + \beta\frac{\dot{K}}{K} \qquad (8)$$

Where, dot (·) represents derivations with respect to time. For discrete changes the above equation can be written as:

$$\frac{\Delta A}{A} = \frac{\Delta P}{P} - \left(\alpha\frac{\Delta L}{L} + \beta\frac{\Delta K}{K}\right) \qquad (9)$$

Where $\frac{\Delta A}{A}$ is the rate of change of TFP; $\frac{\Delta P}{P}$ is rate of change of output, $\frac{\Delta L}{L}$ is rate of change of labour and $\frac{\Delta K}{K}$ is rate of change of capital; a and b are the share of labour and capital in total income. Thus, rate of change of TFP is the difference between the rate of change of the output and the weighted sum of rate of change of inputs.

Under the constant rate of return, when α+β=1, from eq.(7) we have;

$$\frac{P}{L} = A(t)(K/L)^{\beta} \qquad (10)$$

and TFP is given by:

$$\frac{\Delta A}{A} = \left(\frac{\Delta P}{P}\Big/\frac{P}{L}\right) - \beta\left(\frac{\Delta K}{L}\Big/\frac{K}{L}\right) \qquad (11)$$

Thus under the assumption of constant return to scale the rate of TFP is the difference between rate of change of output per unit of labour and rate of change of capital per unit of labour multiplied by capital share in output.

Once computation of $\frac{\Delta A}{A}$ is done for different year with the help of equation 11 above, an index of TFP A(t) for each year can be derived from the identity

$A(t+1) = A\,(t)\,(t + {}^{\Delta A}/_{A})$ (12)

measuring cumulative effect of shift over time. A(0) is one by assumption representing base year technology.

Solow model can also be used to separate the effect of technical progress and capital accumulation in TFPG. The basic procedure is to estimate the contribution made to growth in output by increase in inputs of labour and capital by multiplying the observed increase in factor price. and deducting the result from the overall growth in output. To decompose labour productivity change due to technological progress and due to capital intensity, the equation is:

$$\left(\frac{\Delta P}{P}\Big/\frac{P}{L}\right) = \frac{\Delta A}{A} + \beta\left(\frac{\Delta K}{L}\Big/\frac{K}{L}\right) \tag{13}$$

Equation above indicates that labour productivity is compounded of changes in capital intensity and changes in technical progress.

To identify the change in labour productivity due to technological progress we need to identify the total rise in productivity (equation 14), the increase in labour productivity solely due to capital intensity (equation 15), the difference between these two gives rise in labour productivity due to technological progress (equation 16)

$$\frac{\Delta P}{L} = \left(\frac{P}{L}\right)_t - \left(\frac{P}{L}\right)_0 \tag{14}$$

The labour productivity in year t is deflated by A(t) of the same year. This is net of technical change and attributable to capital intensity

$$\left(\frac{\Delta P}{L}\right)_{K/L} = \left[\left[\left(\frac{P}{L}\right)_t / A(t)\right] - \left(\frac{P}{L}\right)_0\right] \tag{15}$$

$$\left(\frac{\Delta P}{L}\right)_{tp} = \frac{\Delta P}{L} - \left(\frac{\Delta P}{L}\right)_{K/L} \tag{16}$$

Translog Index: Translog index is an improvement over Solow's Index. Solow's index works on discrete set of price and quantity data. The Transcendental Logarithmic (Translog) uses 'flexible' functional form of production function. This index is derived from translog production function under the assumption of constant return to scale and competitive equilibrium. It also assumes that factor price is paid according to marginal productivity. This index is discrete version of continuous Divisia Index. The Continuous Divisia Index of rate of technological progress is given by

$$S_T = \left(\frac{\delta LnY}{\delta t}\right) - \left[\left(S_k \frac{LnK}{\delta t}\right) + \left(S_L \frac{LnL}{\delta t}\right)\right] \quad (17)$$

Where S_k and S_L are marginal shares of factor input, the terms in [ ] can be rewritten as Divisia index of input i.e. $\left(\frac{\delta LnI}{\delta t}\right)$, the discrete time frame conversion of the equation 36 is written as:

$$\Delta S_T = \Delta LnY - (\check{S}_K \Delta LnK + \check{S}_L \Delta LnL) \quad (18)$$

Where,

$$\check{S}_K = \frac{1}{2}\left[S_K(t) + S_K(t-1)\right] \quad (19)$$

$$\check{S}_L = \frac{1}{2}\left[S_L(t) + S_L(t-1)\right] \quad (20)$$

$$\Delta LnY = \Delta LnY(t) - \Delta LnY\,(t-1) \quad (21)$$

$$\Delta LnK = \Delta LnK(t) - \Delta LnK\,(t-1) \quad (22)$$

$$\Delta LnL = \Delta LnL(t) - \Delta LnL\,(t-1) \quad (23)$$

ΔS_T is called the Translog index of the rate of technological change.

Subrahmanyam (1984) has highlighted certain bias which affects the accuracy of the non parametric approach. It fails to distinguish scales effect from the effect of neutral technical progress. Under economies of scale, TFP overestimates effect of technological progress. The production function approaches, a parametric approach, overcomes these deficiencies. This research work has used the parametric methods, these are discussed below.

Production Function Approach

A production function shows the technological relationship between the maximum output obtainable from a given set of input, viz. labour, capital, raw material, lubricants, fuel power etc. In this approach of productivity measurement the various component of productivity can be estimated through econometric functions. The production function can be used to measure the efficiency of production technology, returns to scale and the degree of substitution between factors of production. The parameter of specified function can be estimated through regression and its statistical significance tested. The direct estimation of production functions has an advantage that it is not necessary to assume competitive equilibrium for derivation of estimates. (Gujrati & Sangeetha, 2007)

The important determinants of unit labour cost are elasticity of production with respect to different inputs, marginal productivity of factors and rates of return under which industry is operating. If output is function of various inputs, mathematically it can be expressed as follows:

$$P = f(L, C, R, F, U) \tag{24}$$

Where P= output, C= Capital, L=Labour, R= Raw material, F= Lubricants, fuel, power etc. and U = the stochastic disturbance term following usual properties

The most commonly estimated Cobb-Douglas production function can be written as,

$$P = AL^kC^jR^mF^nU \tag{25}$$

Where A, k, j, m and n are the unknown parameters.

The important deductions of this well known function from theoretical economics are:

that, k, j, m and n are the elasticity of the production with respect to labour, capital, raw material and power, fuel, lubricants etc., this can be shown by taking logarithm of the function as

$$\log P = \log A + k \log L + j \log C + m \log R + n \log F + \log U \tag{26}$$

Differentiating partially w.r.t. L we have,

$$\frac{1}{P}\frac{\partial P}{\partial L} = \frac{k}{L}$$

$$\text{or, } k = \frac{L}{P}\frac{\partial P}{\partial L} \textit{ Elasticity of production w.r.t. labour} \tag{27}$$

Similarly,

$$j = \frac{C}{P}\frac{\partial P}{\partial C} = \textit{Elasticity of production w.r.t.capital} \tag{28}$$

$$m = \frac{R}{P}\frac{\partial P}{\partial R} = \textit{Elasticity of production w.r.t.material} \tag{29}$$

$$n = \frac{F}{P}\frac{\partial P}{\partial F} = \textit{Elasticity of production w.r.t. power, fuel etc.} \tag{30}$$

that, the sum of the exponents shows the degree of return to scale of production.

i.e.

$k + j + m + n < 1$ *means decreasing return to scale*

$k + j + m + n = 1$ *means constant return to scale*

$k + j + m + n > 1$ *means increasing return to scale*

Suppose that, each input is increased by r% then the new input will be:

$$L_1 = L\left(1 + \frac{r}{100}\right)$$

$$C_1 = C\left(1+\frac{r}{100}\right)$$

$$R_1 = R\left(1+\frac{r}{100}\right)$$

$$F_1 = F\left(1+\frac{r}{100}\right)$$

Then, the output is increased by less than r%, by r%, or by more than r%; according to whether there are decreasing, constant, or increasing 'return to scale'. This is easily seen by substituting into the function:

$$P\left(1+\frac{r}{100}\right)^{k+j+m+n} = A\left(1+\frac{r}{100}\right)^{k+j+m+n} L^k C^j R^m F^n U \tag{31}$$

Where, 'r' is the percentage rate of increase of P.

that, multiple of exponents with respective average productivity of the factors are the marginal productivity of the respective factors:

$$k\frac{P}{L} = \textit{Marginal productivity of labour}$$

$$j\frac{P}{C} = \textit{Marginal productivity of capital}$$

$$m\frac{P}{R} = \textit{Marginal productivity of raw material}$$

$$n\frac{P}{F} = \textit{Marginal productivity of power and Fuel}$$

This can be easily seen by using the relations derived earlier, in case of the first property, marginal productivity of labour = $\frac{\partial P}{\partial L}$

Then,

$$k\frac{P}{L} = \partial P / \partial L$$

and so on so forth.

that, the sum of the coefficients show the degree of homogeneity of the function. If k+j+m+n is equal to unity the production function is homogeneous of first degree.

UNIT LABOUR COST, LABOUR EXPENDITURE

Theory of Wages

The study of wages as reward to labour led to many theories. Wage was thought of as minimal means of survival, in 1776 Adam Smith proposed 'Labour theory of value' stating that although the wages administered will vary depending on skill and job, but it cannot go below a specific level. Adam smith believed that reward to labour is determined by contribution he makes to the creation of wealth. The labor theories of value (LTV) are economic theories of value according to which the values of commodities are related to the labor needed to produce them. Marx among first writers of political economy propagated distribution of the relative share of the total output between capital and labour. According to marginal productivity theory, the rate of increase in real wages and the rate of increase in real productivity should be similar in long run. Hicks and Marshall's advancement in law of marginal productivity affirmed the most fundamental principle of theory of wages that, any increase in real wages can take place only through improvements in productivity. As per the theory of effective wage, the wage rate acts as motivation for the workers productivity, the rise in productivity leads to adoption of new technology as a result the improvement in workers skill leads to further improvement in productivity.

In the developing country like India the studies done so far are less in number to capture and represent the dynamism of wage determination practices. In India the wage determination is faced with the conflict of the higher need of workers and the desire of manufacturer to keep production cost to minimum. The production cost is significantly related to number of factors such as productivity movements, technological changes, volume of production, and rate of return, union activities and state intervention.

The government's influence on wage movements in the economy, as state's intervention or wage settings in PSU, is very substantial. In the organized segment of the economy, this influence is quite pervasive. Given the dominance of the public sector in the organized segment of the economy wage movements in the private sector gets influenced by those in the public sector. In the organized sector, wage movements seem to have discouraged employment growth by encouraging growth of capital intensity (Kambhampati & Howell, 1998). What are the effects of these wage movements on productivity need to be investigated.

Despite of rising wages, it is interesting to note that there was a declining trend of unit labour cost in the major industries of India (Maheshwari, 1968). This decline has mainly been caused by the growth of productivity and technological developments involving intensive use of capital in manufacturing process. For the period 1947-1962 the proportion of labour cost to the total cost was highest in the cotton textile industry, low in Iron and Steel and Jute industry, lowest in Sugar industry. As such, the comparative capacity of an industry to absorb labour was highest in cotton textile, iron and steel and jute industries than in sugar industry.

The theory of comparative costs suggests that labour as an important cost element affects the international flow of goods and services. At present when wages are rising and India is facing foreign competition, the investigation looking into ways of reducing labour cost and searching the possibilities of trade developments would be very useful.

Labour Cost is a part of production cost spent on labour. In the case of individual industries the labour cost is not as important as is the cost of other factors, but in case of economy as a whole, labour cost is very important as a share of labour in GNP. Thus from the point of view of economy as a whole labour cost in any individual industry, does not wholly depend on the wage bill paid in this particular industry but also upon the salaries and wages paid in other industries which supply materials and other constituents that enter into the total costs of commodities produced by an industry. From this point of view of an individual industry, the proportion of salaries and wages paid in other industries is merged into the cost of plants and materials.

The present study is concerned with labour cost in industries, therefore, the cost of labour within the sector is considered.

Labour cost in terms of input is called cost per man hour or per worker. Labour cost in terms of output is termed as cost per unit of product or in other words unit labour cost. Generally, labour cost is considered in terms of input which does not convey a meaningful idea of the cost of production or efficiency in use of labour. Labour cost per worker can also be taken as the earnings per worker which again is inadequate to an idea of production cost until we know the required number of worker hours involved in production of a unit.

Both ways of measurement are ill equipped to indicate efficiency in use of labour, because wage determination is affected by factors beyond the control of industry such as union activities, state intervention, cost of living and the agricultural prices. On the other hand, unit labour cost is a fraction of total cost, therefore it offers assessment of proportion which labour cost bears to total cost. It does also indicate for efficiency in use of labour because the unit labour cost is not just a function of any single wage rate but is a resultant of five factors: (i) complex interactional behavior of entire galaxy of quoted wages (ii) the quantitative importance of various labour grades (iii) productivity of labour (iv) volume of production and (v) capacity to pay. That is, there can be significant change in unit labour cost of a firm with absolutely no change in any quoted wage, if there is an intra firm shift in number of man hour contributed by different grades/class of workers to produce a unit of product. Similarly there can be significant change in unit labour cost with no change in wage rate if there is a change in the productivity of labour. There can also be a change in unit labour cost without any change in wage rates, if there is a change in the volume of production. In today's technological dependent, mechanised modern industries labour becomes a fixed cost irrespective of machine produces 10 or 100 units.

The factors mentioned above are not entirely independent. Volume of production has an important bearing on productivity of labour, labour productivity bears a positive relation with changes in wage levels. Therefore, the interaction of these factors ultimately determines the trends of labour costs over long period of time.

The existence of so many intervening variables as indicated above clearly shows that labour cost per worker or per man hour is only a single variable that affects unit labour cost. Thus, changes in labour cost per worker have very minor effect on cost of production, while changes in unit labour cost have a significant role in production function. Rising unit labour costs encourages the substitution of capital for labour; hence the employer's interest in unit labour cost is more than the wage bill.

Unit Labour Cost

The labour cost like cost of other factors of production can be measured in terms of a unit of output or in terms of unit of input. In case of unit of output, labour cost is the ratio of total labour expenditure in terms of money to total output produced in physical terms. In case of unit of input, it is defined as the multiple of the hours worked to produce a unit of output and hourly labour cost. Unit labour cost will be same if calculated in either way. Algebraically,

If,

QT= Quantity produced

LC = Total labour expenditure

HW= Total man-hours worked

Then, *Unit Labour Cost* $= \frac{\text{LC}}{\text{QT}}$ (in terms of output)

$$\textit{Hourly Labour Cost} = \frac{LC}{HW}$$

$$\textit{Hours worked to produce a unit of product} = \frac{HW}{QT}$$

Therefore, in terms of input:

$$\textit{Unit Labour cost} = \frac{\text{HW}}{\text{QT}} \times \frac{\text{LC}}{\text{HW}} \times \frac{\text{LC}}{\text{QT}}$$

The ASI data reports the total man-days-worker and not total man hours worked. For conversion the guidelines laid by Factory Act 1948, is used where 'Week' is defined as the 7 day period starting from Saturday.

Labour is required to work for 48 hours in a week. First day of the week is off for workers with certain conditions. And Labour is required to work for 9 hours in a day whereas there shall be a break after continuous work of not more than 5 hours. The ASI figures were multiplied by 9 to obtain Total man-hours worked.

In addition to the unit labour cost, there are some very important questions which revolve around the appropriate meaning of the numerator and the denominator of unit labour cost ; namely 'labour expenditure' and 'quantity produced' i.e. output.

Labour Expenditure

Labour expenditure or labour cost covers all the expenses that are incurred on labour as a factor of production but there are certain conceptual difficulties concerning the following constituents:

1. the treatment of the salaries paid to the persons other than the workers
2. the treatment of fringe benefits
3. the treatment of expenditure which cannot be easily allocated to a single factor of production.

Treatment of Salaries

The salaries paid to people holding positions of supervisors or management or confidential positions or are employed in distributive activities such as sales and advertising shall be considered as labour cost or not is a debated question. In some of the studies related to labour cost, "salaries" have been included, while in others they have been excluded. Sinha & Sawhney, (1970) noted that their services are as important for the execution of work in the factory as the operators who are directly engaged in various stages of production process. The ASI gives no separate data of benefits paid to workers and persons other than workers. Therefore the labour expenditure includes total benefits paid to above discussed categories. This inclusion of other than workers shall not lead to bias because a) the benefits constitute only two to nine percent of wages b) further, the proportion of 'other than workers' enjoying a part of such benefit is very small. The Labour Bureau which does not favour the inclusion of the persons other than workers in the measurement of labour input also reasons that they form very small portion of total employees in the factory. 3) Extra share of benefits so included may be compensated by the expenses on training and recruitment which is not been included in labour cost. According to the principles of cost accounting, "salaries" should not be included in the labour cost. They should be considered as the cost of organization, which is another factor of production. Further, it may also be helpful to separate wages and salaries from the standpoint of cost-price relationships. This is because cost accountants tend to make this distinction and to treat wages as a more variable cost than salaries, which are customarily regarded as semi-variable manufacturing expenses.

Treatment of Fringe Benefits, Treatment of Non-Benefit Payments

The second factor is the treatment of fringe benefits. Fringe benefits may be taken to include all supplements legally required or voluntarily paid or provided in kind for the welfare of the workers. These payments and benefits constitute an important portion of the income and welfare of the employees. At the same time they add to the labour cost of the industry and impose an extra burden on the employers.

Generally, these extra costs of labour are ignored by economists as well as in popular discussion since daily or hourly rates of earnings are taken as the unit in study of labour cost. This type of treatment obscures the importance of fringe benefits because many of the items of benefits such as housing, recreational, cultural amenities and paid holidays are difficult to express in terms of daily remuneration. To get a true estimate of labour costs, the economists must take fringe benefits into account especially when studies suggest such cost can be considerable proportion of the total labour cost (ILO, 1959).

Treatment of Non-Benefit Payments

There is certain expenditure which is incurred on labour but they do not necessarily benefit labour, such as, recruitment and training expenses. Such expenditure are defined by the ILO as "other payments related to labour cost" and are treated separately from principal labour cost items. These benefit payments do not constitute the income of the workers but from the point of view of the employers, these are the items of labour cost and must be included in total labour cost.

Treatment of Cost Not Allocated to a Single Factor of Production

Sometimes factory overhead charges are confused with labour costs, as these can be allocated either to factory costs or to labour costs. Such items include among others, the furnishing of in-plant employee needs; for example expenditure incurred on safety clothing, devices provided to workers. As these expenditure are related to workers, it is essential to caution against the tendency of treating this as labour cost. In fact it is closely associated with work environment and, therefore, should be excluded from the labour cost.

Quantity Produced (Output)

The measurement of unit labour cost is difficult due to the fact that labour expenditure data are available by industry or by unit and output is reported by products. Moreover, since nearly all industries produce a variety of products, substantial difficulties exist in the allocation of labour expenditure to the different types of products, again mathematically it is not appropriate to add up heterogeneous output of different qualities, type and sizes, produced by an industry into a meaningful aggregate. But, to solve the problem of finding out the denominator of unit labour cost, technical methods of cost accounting can be used. Hence, attempts would be made

(a) to break down labour cost by products to arrive at unit labour costs of individual products (b) to combine products data into industry aggregate so as to arrive at unit labour cost for an industry. The methods used in the present study have been discussed in Chapter II, "Methods of Estimation". We must understand an important limitation of the study of unit cost of a single product. A Product manufactured by different producers cannot be of standard specification, quality and pattern from year to year; therefore, any change in the cost of production from time to time cannot easily be taken as the effect of technical changes and shifts in the relative price of the factors.

Unit Labour Cost and Total Costs

The discussion below highlights the significance of the ratio of unit labour cost to total cost. A systematic analysis of this relationship would include the study of the causes that bring changes in unit labour cost and their impact on total cost. Change in unit labour cost may be caused by the personal efficiency of labour, factor's substitution and technical change. Each of such factors may be expected to involve a distinctive pattern of production cost such as:

1. if increased labour efficiency were the dominating influence, then, it is expected that only labour cost would be affected;
2. if factor substitution were the main cause, one should expect some cost to rise and others to fall; and
3. if improved technology were the major influence a completely difference pattern of cost behavior would appear.

To obtain a satisfactory explanation one can proceed by setting up a number of alternative hypotheses as the reasons for these changes in costs and test them in an empirical study.

Efficiency of Labour

Unit labour cost may be affected by variations in the degree of efficiency with which labour works. Increase efficiency affects the labour cost but not necessarily affects the production cost, because there is no reason to expect that it also affects the material and other factor costs. Anyhow, it could be argued that efficient labour would lead to economies in the use of material and better utilization of capital equipment. However, such saving would be unlikely to be of sufficient magnitude to account for the savings in material and in capital costs.

FACTOR SUBSTITUTION

Factors substitution affects the unit cost to both factors; the substitute and the substituted. If capital is substituted for labour, naturally the cost of labour will decrease and the cost of capital will rise, thus, the net reduction in total cost is always less than the change in either labour cost or capital cost, and the substitution might be expected to lead to relative shares of different costs in an industry's total cost. The extent of changes in shares caused by factor substitution depends upon: (i) the magnitude of the shift in relative factor prices, and (ii) the elasticity of substitution.

Relative Factor Prices

The impact of substitution on the cost of production is the resultant of three factors; the wage rate, the interest rate and the price of capital goods. Since changes in relative prices of labour and capital play an important part in the substitution process, relative changes in wage rate, interest rate and prices of capital goods induce the substitution of labour or of capital in place of each other. It is often argued that because capital goods are also produced with help of labour, rises in wage rates result in an increase in the prices of capital goods and thus discourage substitution of capital equipments for labour. Therefore, the relative change in the prices of capital goods is more important.

This argument, first advanced by Shove, is valid if at all, only in short-team equilibrium: but it is not a valid argument for a developing economy experiencing technical progress that an increase in wage rates is always accompanied by an equal rise in the prices of capital goods (Flatau, 2002). The essence of technical progress is that it enables the producer to manufacture the commodities more economically and thus reduce the prices of the same in the market. It is one of the main justifications for introducing the price of capital goods as an explicit variable in the analysis of substitution.

Elasticity of Substitution

Production process is a technical relationship of factors of production. What proportion of each factor would be required is dependent on techniques of production, and how much a factor can substitute another is called the elasticity of substitution. The question of elasticity of substitution is important for total cost of production because the change in shares of factors is the function of two opposing influence. As labour becomes costly relative to capital, labour costs tend to rise relative to cost of capital goods but, when as a result capital is substituted for dearer labour, initial change in share in total cost may either be under or over compensated. Interpretation of elasticity of substitution is as follows:

1. when elasticity of substitution is unity, the opposing influences exactly counter balance themselves and are unchanged;
2. when the elasticity is less than unity, labour cost rises relative to capital costs; and
3. when the elasticity is greater than unity, labour costs fall relative to capital costs.

Therefore, the magnitude of changes in relative factors' prices and elasticity of substitution decides the impact of labour cost on total cost.

TECHNICAL CHANGE

Efficiency of labour and substitution of capital directly affect labour cost and indirectly the cost of other factors. But, technologies change simultaneously affects all factors of production. Improvisation developed on existing techniques involve, the use of faster and better machines, economies in utilization and generation of power, improved designs and layouts to minimize idle time, the use of automatic controls, the reduction in waste of material and other resources, and continuity of operation. These advances tend to effect a saving in all factors and lead to a general reduction in costs. Technical innovations brings savings on all factors of production through minimizing human touch or inputs, Thus saves labour in greater degree and affects unit labour cost in a larger proportion than the total unit cost. An intensive use of new technique implies an increase in capital intensity and changes in production methods. It almost always leads to an increase in labour productivity, where it is applied; and reduces the labour input required per unit of production. Technical change makes it possible to reduce labour force in the processes or it increases the volume of production. In some cases it makes it possible to achieve both these effects simultaneously.

MEASUREMENT OF CAPITAL INPUT

The measurement of Capital intensity posses various problems in econometric Studies. Laxminarayan (2003, pp. 25-32) in his work has discussed in details the various views on measurement. In the current study we have considered Fixed Capital to measure capital intensity, leaving the aggregation of working capital. In this context, Sinha and Sawney remarked: "while the importance of working capital to industrial productivity cannot be denied, the inventory and cash holdings are more often determined by supply and market expectations than technological pipeline requirements and have, therefore, far less bearing on productivity than fixed investment. Also the available data on inventories and cash are as on the last day of the year and not average holding of working capital through the year which alone may be appropriately related to annual flow of output". op.cit. (op.cit. Narayan, 2003).

UNIT LABOUR COST AS AN "INDEX OF TOTAL COST"

The discussion as given above makes it clear that the relation-ship that exists between unit labour costs and total costs is indefinite and not exact. The next logical question would seem to be to what extend the looseness and flexibility of relationship impairs our ability to predict changes in the unit total cost on the basis of unit labour cost data alone.

Statistically, it is not reliable attempt to predict the change in the total cost solely on the basis of labour cost data. There are so many intervening variables between the initial change in unit labour cost and the final changes in unit total cost certainly, which makes the use of unit labour cost as an index of total cost little unreliable.

Changes in unit labour cost do not in any way suggest the proportional changes in the total costs, as labour cost is not the sole element of production cost. Since labour cost is a part of total cost, even where wage increases result in higher unit labour cost, the effect on the total cost would be lesser than the change in unit labour cost. In short, percentage change in total costs would be less than the percentage change in the unit labour cost , for example (hypothetical), if labour cost is 20% of total costs, and if there is a 50% increases in this cost the total cost may increases only by 10% approximately.

Wage increases or decreases may also raise or reduce the prices of non-labour factors. There are cases in which wage increases exerted such strong pressure on a firm than it enters in fierce negotiation and was able to secure a reduction in its material prices. Moreover, the possibility that there may be an autonomous change in non-labour costs completely unrelated to the increase in unit labour costs, e.g. sudden world-wide reduction in the supply of raw materials might raise costs apart from any change in wage rates. Consequently unit labour cost data is unable to predict the changes in total costs.

The only conclusion that seems to emerge from this theoretical discussion is that changes in unit labour costs do bring changes in unit total costs but that the magnitude of change is very difficult to measure on the basis of the unit labour cost data alone or on the basis of the changes in wage rates.

VIEWS OF WAGE FIXING AUTHORITIES ON WAGE-PRODUCTIVITY RELATIONSHIP

Keynes after 1930's financial depression denounced the doctrine that government should not interfere in commercial affairs, and advocated state intervention for guiding the economic development. He suggested state intervention to remove very low and oppressive wages. Since then, the nations have experimented with wage fixing authorities to protect the labour community from oppression and include them in benefits of economic growth. Occasionally the purpose behind the state intervention has been the maintenance of industrial peace in the sphere of wages- the main bone of contention between employees and workers. Sometimes especially during the periods of economic depression, state regulation of wages has been designed to speed up the pace of economic recovery. Similarly, preventing an inflammatory spiral and maintaining economic stability during war times has been another objective of regulation of wages by the state (Narayan, 2003, pp58). Therfore, it can be said that wage administration or regulation is an instrument of planned economimc development.

Laxmi Narayan (2003, pp 58-61) in his study on Productivity and Wages in Indian Industries, sites various wages boards views on its administration and fixing policies, the author writes:

[1]In the determination of wages in Indian industries, the productivity wage relationship has been most vexed and indecisive problem. It has been

1 op. cit, 58; Report of committee on Fair Wages, para 15; Report of National Commission on Labour, para 15.10, pp 222; Report of the Committee on Sharing Gains of Productivity, March 1967, pp 8-9; Report of Study Group on Productivity and Incentives, pp 79-81.

theoretically agreed by parties that wages should move so as to bear a positive relationship with productivity. The Royal Commission on Wages, the Fair Wages Committee, The Committee on Sharing the Gains of Productivity, the Study Group on Productivity and Incentives, and the Five Year Plans have therefore emphasized the significance of the factor in the domain of wages. The workers, employers and economist too regarded 'productivity' as one of the criteria in wage determination. But when the question of practical application of this principle comes before wage fixing authorities, the whole issue boils down to the state of indifference in views of the conflicting argument put forward by the employers and employees. While the importance of productivity-wage relationship cannot be denied, we don't find any accepted approach to wage-productivity relationship in India (for that matter anywhere accept annual improvement factor at some places). The wage fixing authorities don't appear to have given importance to productivity. Productivity is referred as one of the factors determining actual wages.

The central wage boards considered the productivity factor, that is, whether wages should be linked to performance. For example Sugar Wage Board observed: "In a progressive economy, wage should be the function of productivity. In the major organized industries gradually the stage is being reached when further wage increase can come only out of increased productivity. It is imperative that the worker realizes that no real wage increase can flow out of government decree. Higher productivity alone can bring down the cost of production, afford higher wages and arrest inflationary trends"[2]. The wage boards, however, observed that term 'productivity of the industry' is a complex issue as productivity is end product of a combination of factors and it is not an easy task to distinguish the contributing factors and still more difficult to distinguish the degree of importance of these factors.

In view of complex nature of productivity, the wage boards, while admitting that here was an overall increase in the productivity, found it very difficult to apportion the increase in productivity between the various factors of production including labour.

---

2 op.cit., 59, Sugar Wage Board, para 183, 193.

5

Factual Setting of the Problem and Preparation of Data Tables

Present study is a fact finding research to understand trends and relationship between productivity, labour cost and wages administration covering four major industries of India viz. Cotton textiles, Jute, Sugar and Steel. At the very outset it would be appropriate to discuss the industrial policy, which guides the economic progress and movement of national economy, which would help to understand various trends expected in outcome of research.

Indian Industrial Policies

The industrial policies define the economic performance and movements of economic factors like wage determination, productivity, technology replacements, opportunities of investment and various others. In 1948, immediately after independence, Government introduced the Industrial Policy Resolution. This outlined the approach to industrial growth and development and emphasised the importance of securing a continuous increase in production and ensuring its equitable distribution in terms of wages and earning in general. The first five year plan spanning from 1951-1956 gave importance to agriculture, irrigation and energy, transport, land rehabilitation. The focus was to maximize the output from agriculture, which would then provide the impetus for industrial growth. The first plan succeeded in fulfilling the targets. The target growth rate was 2.1 per cent annual gross domestic product (GDP) growth; the achieved growth rate was 3.6 per cent. After the adoption of the Constitution and the socio-economic goals, the Industrial Policy was comprehensively revised and adopted in 1956. The second five year plan (1956-1960) was socialistic in nature and followed the Mahalanobis Model. It gave prominence to industry and agricultural programmes, the programmes were formulated to meet the raw material requirement of the industry besides food need of growing population. This period witnessed heavy inflation due to unfavourable monsoon in 1957-58 and 1959-60 and also the Suez crisis. The second five year plan achieved 4% growth rate against 4.5% targeted. Third plan (1960-1966) put emphasis on becoming self reliant in agriculture and industry. The plan aimed to increase national income by 30% and agriculture production by 30%. The country faced wars with China in 1962 and with Pakistan in 1965 and bad monsoon in almost all the years, leading to sluggish economic performance. During these years the objective of import substitution was seen as sacrosanct. In order to prevent monopolies and to promote economic developments in backward areas, unfeasible manufacturing units were augmented with subsidies. Ahluwalia(1985) identified that the industrial policy framework was the main reason for productivity slow down in mid sixties. Under this period 5 steel plants, a hydro-electric power project were created, production of coal increased and the large enterprises in seventeen industries were nationalized. This is when India got its License Raj, the bureaucratic control over the economy. Licenses were required for starting new companies, the Government prevented businesses from shutting down even when they were losing money. This policy contributed towards increasing number of sick industries. The third five year plan achieved 2.2% growth rate against 5.6% targeted.

From 1966 to 1968 annual plans were introduced. Economy, during this period was under recession. Fourth five year plan 1969-1974 had sluggish growth of 3.3% against the targeted 5.7% growth. To meet new challenges, from time to time, the industrial policies were modified through statements in 1973, 1977 and 1980. The Industrial Policy statement of 1973, among other things, identified high-priority industries where investment from large industrial houses and foreign companies was permitted. The fifth five year plan (1975-1979) for the first time had targets based on GDP rather than net national income. The plan targeted 4.4% the growth rate and achieved 5.2% growth. The Industrial Policy Statement of 1977 laid emphasis on de-centralisation and on the role of small-scale, tiny and cottage industries.

Sixth five year plan (1979-1983 and 1981 to 1985) saw political turbulence in the country, economy had growth target of 5.2% and achieved 6% growth. The Industrial Policy Statement of 1980 focused attention on the need for promoting competition, technological up-gradation and modernisation in the domestic market. The policy laid the foundation for an increasingly competitive export based high technology areas and for encouraging foreign investment in these areas, emphasising the need for productivity to be the central concern in all economic and production activities. These policies created a climate for rapid industrial growth in the country. Turnaround in the industrial output growth in the decade of 80's has been widely attributed to liberalisation, improvement in public investment and public sector performance. (Commission, 1981)

The Seventh Plan of 1985 recognised the need to consolidate on these strengths and to take initiatives to prepare Indian industry to respond effectively to emerging challenges. A number of policy and procedural changes were introduced in 1985 and 1986 aimed at increasing productivity, reducing costs and improving quality. The accent was on opening the domestic market to increased competition and readying our industry to stand on its own in the face of international competition. The public sector was freed from a number of constraints and given a larger measure of autonomy. 1989-91 was a period of political instability in India and hence no five year plan was implemented. Between 1990 and 1992, there were only Annual Plans. Industrial policy 1991 focused on the technological and managerial modernisation of industry as the key instrument for increasing productivity and improving our competitiveness in the world (Industrial Policy, 1991).

The eighth plan of 1992-97 focused on human development, higher participation of private companies in creating infrastructure and bringing economic efficiency. In this period the growth rate achieved was 6.8%. In the ninth plan of 1998-2002 targeted accelerated growth rate of economy with stable prices, priority was on infrastructure development through greater private participation, increase in agricultural and rural income, technology up-gradation and system improvements.

Industrial Growth Rate during the Period of Study

The initial break in India's growth rate can be detected in the year 1977-78 when the economy grew at 7.7 per cent followed by 5.6 per cent in 1978-79. But growth remained fragile and achieved an average of only 4.1 per cent over the ten-year period of 1977-to 1988. The average of growth rates during the seven-year period from 1981 to 1988 was 4.8 per cent which was below the 5.2% rate achieved in the Fifth Five Year Plan (1974-1979). The average growth rate over the three-year period from 1987-88 to 1990-91 was 7.6 per cent. Growth picked up in a major way only in 1988-89 when it registered 10.6 per cent rate. It is the average annual growth of 7.6 per cent achieved during the three-year period of 1988-91 that largely accounts for the 5.6 per cent growth during 1981-91. As a major outcome of the fragility of growth, the economy crash-landed in 1991-92 hitting the low growth rate of 0.5 per cent. After the July 1991 reform, growth exhibited greater stability, with the growth rate shifting upward by approximately half per cent on the average during the 1990s. These turbulent periods of growth makes the period of 1980-2004 more suitable for empirical fact finding study of this nature.

Table 5.1 suggest that compounded growth rates for industries under consideration was on an average more in 1980s than in 1990s. the variation in growth was although more in 1990s except for jute, hemp and mesta sector.

Table 5.1: Growth Trends of Two-digit Industrial Categories of Industrial Production

Category (NIC- 1970)	1980s IIP with base 1980-81=100			1990s IIP with base 1993-94=100			
	Weight	Growth	CV	Weight	Growth*	Growth$	CV
20-21 Food products	5.33	3.9	12.8	9.08	3.6	3.2	13.3
23 Cotton textiles	12.31	2.7	9.4	5.52	2.1	3.6	14.3
25 Jute, hemp and mesta	2.00	1.2	7.4	0.59	0.8	0.7	6.5
33 Basic metal and alloys	9.80	5.8	17.7	7.45	3.9	5.9	21.7

* Compound growth rate for the period 1994-95 to 2002-03 with base 1993-94 = 100.

$ Compound growth rate for the period 1990-91 to 2002-03 and the data for the period 1990-91 to 1993-94 were obtained by the method of slicing.

Summing up, circa 1980, the economic policies held India's growth dubbed as the Hindu rate of growth. This did not mean that India produced less manufacturing goods as a whole, but the composition of its manufacturing activity was unusual: India produced more than its share of capital- and skill-intensive goods, while underutilising its abundant labour. India was highly diversified in its manufacturing even in 80's, and a portion of its labour force was highly skilled, due to government's emphasis on science, higher education and leading-edge technologies for the public sector (Rajan, 2005).

In the period 1992 to 2001, industrial production grew at an average rate of 6.46% per annum (MoF, 2002). This growth was mainly on account of the manufacturing and electricity sectors, while the mining and quarrying sector witnessed much lower growth rates in production. The overall industrial growth path in the decade of 1990s has been marked by cyclical fluctuations with the industrial growth rate increasing to a high of 11.6% in 1995/96 before falling to 3.4% in 1998/99. There was a significant improvement in overall growth in industrial value added (6.4%) in 1999/2000 due to acceleration in growth rate of the manufacturing and construction sectors. The growth rate declined to 5% in 2000-01 (MoF, 2002). The targeted growth rate for the industrial sector in the Tenth Plan period was over 10%, in line with a targeted GDP growth rate of 8% (Approach to the Tenth Five Year Plan (2002-07), 2001a).

PREPARATION OF DATA TABLES

The concepts and definitions of items collected through ASI schedule are discussed in Chapter 2, under 'Concepts and Definitions of Items Collected Through the Schedule of Enquiry' the demo table from ASI is presented below:

Table 5.2: Demo Table Structure of ASI Data

Selected Characteristics by Industry Group (3-Digit) for Factory Sector under Annual Survey of Industries in India (NIC : 200 to 207) (1980-1981)

(Values are in Rs. Lakhs, Man-Days in Thousand and Others in Number)

Industry Group	200	201	202	203	204	205	206	207
(1)	(2)	(3)	(4)	(5)	(6)	(7)	(8)	(9)
1. No. of Factories	22	258	157	237	6923	499	304	2084
2. Fixed Capital	1201	11805	1289	1893	11939	1464	56283	4694
3. Working Capital	358	5347	1256	322	13197	584	10711	1697
4. Invested Capital	1685	18344	3064	3171	30792	2501	103254	6857
5. Outstanding Loan	330	9611	2241	2906	16704	1530	76034	3521
6. No. of Workers	2618	23324	9137	8401	122020	11734	315655	130826
7. Mandays-Workers	829	8660	2071	2285	26671	3427	34863	13219
8. No. of Employees	3449	36850	11651	10939	153113	15604	463454	145360
9. Mandays-Employees	1089	13491	2610	2965	33762	4469	52415	14836
10. Total Persons Engaged	3451	36947	11745	11063	162453	16300	470298	148428
11. Wages to Workers	195	1636	231	262	3516	469	7783	1431
12. Total Emoluments	297	3110	432	425	6095	747	13019	1678
13. Old Age Benefits	6	180	30	18	112	40	1057	12
14. Social Security Benefits	3	47	11	7	90	25	146	2
15. Other Benefits	9	66	9	13	46	25	163	20006
16. Fuels Consumed	141	2422	162	345	2373	506	3833	1091
17. Material Consumed	2240	55850	3873	12138	136934	8780	79405	15198
18. Total Inputs	2689	62619	4656	13806	157377	9908	98854	18076
19. Products	2821	65218	4888	14339	151968	11286	117013	20447
20. Value of Output	3275	67349	5288	15187	168620	11526	120648	21071
21. Depreciation	113	1184	182	221	1146	190	6052	474
22. Net Value Added	473	3545	451	1159	10097	1438	15732	2520
23. Rent Paid	20	81	33	76	450	71	67	28
24. Interest Paid	88	813	201	313	5242	160	12181	443
25. Net Income	365	2652	218	770	4405	1207	3485	2049
26. Net Fixed Capital Formation	5	798	59	-35	1233	150	299	135
27. Gross Fixed Capital Formation	119	1982	241	186	2379	330	6361	609

(Table Contd...)

(1)	(2)	(3)	(4)	(5)	(6)	(7)	(8)	(9)
28. Addition in Stock of								
(i) Material, Fuel Etc.	65	443	-2	-131	915	259	2267	74
(ii) Semi-Finished Goods	-1	-103	25	-61	-16	2	153	27
(iii) Finished Goods	43	-470	153	96	-487	-2	-33575	-273
(iv) Total	107	-130	175	-96	412	258	-31156	-171
29. Gross Capital Formation	226	1852	416	90	2791	588	-24795	438
30. Profits	50	-751	-263	307	-1938	369	-10901	-19649

The 30 items are labeled and would be referred as row 1 to row 30. The value figures in ASI data are given in Rs. lakhs for all India, for states, 1984, 1996 onwards are given in Rs lakhs, in 1983 values are given in Rs. lakh for Delhi, Karnataka, Rajasthan, Tamilnadu, Uttar Pradesh and West Bengal, all other years had values in Rs. thousands. In some cases the only 2 digit data for 1983-84 was found, instead of using 2 digit summary data, the previous year figures were duplicated as dirty estimate. It is to be noted that since 1998-99 the published tables had different serial number of the row titles mentioned in above demo table. Efforts are made to rearrange 1998 data tables to maintain the row serial numbers as stated above. NIC 97 was applicable since 1998 onwards the 3 digit data tables represented category aggregates which might not be complete representative of the industry considered in this research work. Moreover even though the index number approach is considered, it was not possible to obtain the linking factor for various variables required especially the labour data. Hence for development of the models data from 1980 to 1997-98 is considered and separate models were created for data ranging 1998-2005. Wherever possible, comparisons are drawn.

Unit Labour Cost

The unit labour cost as discussed in previous chapter is calculated as:

$$\text{Unit labour cost} = \frac{\text{Total Labour Expenditure}}{\text{Real Total Cost of Production}}$$

$$= \frac{\text{Total Labour Expenditure}}{\text{Ex Factory value of output}}$$

$$= \frac{\text{Wage to workers + Total emoulments + Old age benefits + Social security benefits}}{\text{Value of output}}$$

Referring the demo table,

$$\text{Unit labour cost} = \frac{\text{Sum of figures in row 11, 12, 13, 14}}{\text{Figure in row 20}}$$

The tables on unit labour cost were utilized in analysis under Chapter 5. Unit labour cost of tables are labeled as Table 5.4 to Table 5.7.

Wage Cost per worker

$$\text{Wage cost per worker} = \frac{\text{Wage of workers}}{\text{No. of workers}}$$

Referring the demo table,

$$\text{Wage cost per worker} = \frac{\text{Figure in Row 11}}{\text{Figure in Row 6}}$$

The tables on wage cost per worker are utilized in analysis under chapter 5, the tables are labeled as Table 5.9 to Table 5.12.

Capital Labour Ratio

In the current study we have considered Fixed Capital to measure capital intensity. In socialist economics, an indicator that characterizes the quantity of fixed production assets in branches of material production on a per-worker basis. The ratio is obtained by dividing the book value of these assets for a given year by the number of workers employed during that year.

$$\text{Capital Labour Ratio} = \frac{\text{Fixed Capital}}{\text{No. of Workers}}$$

Referring the demo table,

$$\text{Capital Labour Ratio} = \frac{\text{Figure in Row 2}}{\text{Figure in Row 6}}$$

The tables on capital labour ratio are utilized in analysis under chapter 5, the tables are labeled as Table 5.13 to Table 5.16.

Production, Volume of Employment and Output per worker

$$\text{Output Per Worker} = \frac{\text{Value of Output (Rs. Lakhs)}}{\text{No. of Workers (Thousands)}}$$

Referring the demo table,

$$\text{Output Per Worker (Rs. lakh per thousand workers} = \frac{\text{Figure in Row 20}}{\text{Figure in Row 6}}$$

The tables on output per worker are utilized in analysis trends of production under chapter 5, the tables are labeled as Table 5.17 to Table 5.20.

For productivity employee payments relationships, Index on Output per man hour and compensation per man hour are calculated.

$$Output\ Per\ Manhour = \frac{Value\ of\ Output\ (Rs.\ Lakhs)}{Mandays\ Workers * 9\ (hours)}$$

Referring the demo table,

$$Output\ Per\ Manhour = \frac{Figure\ in\ row\ 20}{9 * Row\ number\ 7}$$

In accordance with factory act 1948, 9 is multiplied in the denominator to convert figures in man-hours.

$$Compensation\ per\ manhour = \frac{Wages\ to\ workers\ (Rs.\ Lakhs)}{Mandays\ Workers * 9\ (hours)}$$

Referring the demo table,

$$Compensation\ per\ manhour = \frac{Figures\ in\ Row\ 11}{9 * Row\ number\ 7}$$

Output per man-hour and Compensation per man-hour values are used to understand the productivity-employee payment relationship in Chapter 5 through Table 5.21

Unit Labour Cost on Current Price and Constant Price

The unit labour cost as discussed in previous chapter is calculated as

$$Unit\ labour\ cost = \frac{Total\ Labour\ Expenditure}{Real\ Total\ Cost\ of\ Production}$$

$$= \frac{Sum\ of\ figures\ in\ row\ 11, 12, 13, 14}{Figure\ in\ row\ 20}$$

$$Unit\ Labour\ cost\ (single\ deflation) = \frac{Nominal\ Wage\ rate\ (Rs.\ per\ worker)}{Real\ Value\ Added\ (deflated)/No.\ of\ Workers}$$

$$= \frac{Nominal\ Wage\ rate\ (Rs.\ per\ worker)}{Real\ Value\ Added/CPIIW/No.\ of\ Workers}$$

Where, CPIIW (Consumer Price index for Industrial worker) is used as deflator.

Referring the demo table,

$$Unit\ Labour\ Cost\ at\ Constant\ Price = \frac{Sum\ of\ figures\ in\ row\ 11, 12, 13, 14}{Figure\ in\ row\ 20 * CPIIW} * 100$$

The Labour Bureau, Ministry of Labour and Employment, Government of India publishes the CPIIW, method of splicing the index numbers is used with linking factor of 4.75 to change the base to 1960=100. The base is then shifted to 1980=100

Table 5.3: Consumer Price Index for Industrial Workers (1980-2005)

Year	1980	1981	1982	1983	1984	1985	1986	1987	1988
CPIIW	100	113	122	136	148	156	169	184	201
Year	1989	1990	1991	1992	1993	1994	1995	1996	1997
CPIIW	208	227	258	289	307	339	373	407	436
Year	1998	1999	2000	2001	2002	2003	2004		
CPIIW	493	516	537	558	581	604	626		

(Base 1980=100)

The comparative analysis of unit labour cost at current price and constant price of 1980 is presented in Chapter 5 through Table 5.22.

Non Labour Cost

The Ex Factory value of output is broken into different percentage components of Material Consumed, Fuel Consumed, Labour expenditure and Margins.

Referring the demo table

$$\%\ Material\ Cost = \frac{Figure\ in\ row\ 17}{Figure\ in\ row\ 20}$$

$$\%\ Fuel\ Consumed = \frac{Figure\ in\ row\ 16}{Figure\ in\ row\ 20}$$

$$\%\ Labour\ Cost = \frac{Sum\ of\ Figure\ in\ row\ 11, 12, 13, 14}{Figure\ in\ row\ 20}$$

% Margin = 100 – (% material cost + % fuel cost + % Labour cost)

The analysis is presented in the table 6.19 to table 6.22.

THE LONG TERM TREND OF UNIT LABOUR COST, WAGES AND PRODUCTIVITY IN COTTON TEXTILE, JUTE, STEEL AND SUGAR FOR THE PERIOD 1980-2004

Long Term Trend of Unit Labour Cost

Trends of unit labour cost in steel industry in India and regions of India are tabulated below.

Table 5.4: Trends of Unit Labour Cost in Steel Industry in India and Regions of India

	All India	Andhra Pradesh	Bihar	Delhi	Karnataka	Maharastra	Punjab	Uttar Pradesh	West Bengal
1980-81	100	100	100	100	100	100	100	100	100
1981-82	120	69.72	69.17	122.2	93.64	91.96	104.5	99.69	92.3
1982-83	146.1	53.76	60.91	96.58	101.6	103.2	106	98.26	94.75
1983-84	162.6	61.2	79.93	4202	101.6	124.3	119.5	98.26	94.75
1984-85	167.8	56.6	66.87	81.81	114.4	113.4	111.3	102.1	138.6
1985-86	186.7	60.01	72.29	77.64	118.3	108.1	101.6	66.22	99.1
1986-87	182	59.23	82.2	96.67	106.9	91.95	93.45	95.85	118.5
1987-88	187.1	67.89	84	97.13	95.15	100.8	103.4	97.33	113.7
1988-89	211.1	67.23	87.38	113.6	100.2	84.52	102.6	72.44	99.56
1989-90	259	46.12	81.83	107.9	89.96	78.6	78.65	67.76	114.7
1990-91	465.4	78.59	63.85	95.57	82.86	76.85	74.89	60.45	110.2
1991-92	599.4	102.7	26.41	84.14	76.95	76.15	77.83	60.45	103.4
1992-93	605.6	92.83	60	80.95	88.33	61.28	89.15	49.7	98.98
1993-94	772.1	104	84.85	84.26	76.62	66.87	81.4	47.18	115.4
1994-95	946.4	89.4	86.37	151.2	57.01	77.62	83.94	47.18	103.1
1995-96	1043	87.82	86.9	106.9	57.01	57.94	80.27	46.41	115.5
1996-97	1050	83.18	91.57	104.1	83.29	63.47	79.82	44.97	111.8
1997-98	1033	68.72	60.74	54.96	80.66	68.68	69.44	35.04	98.33
1998-99**	100	100	100	100	100	100	100	100	100
1999-2000	92.69	93.57	0.43	324.6	106.9	25.77	126.2	141.5	70.96
2000-01	103	119.2	0.6	117.3	79.04	29.45	96.57	92.94	46.92
2001-02	106.1	99.1	0.61	147.1	61.61	26.37	84.29	48.79	31.03
2002-03	118.8	86.94	0.54	214.1	54.25	20.53	88.12	62.31	35.59
2003-04	131.9	70.34	0.85	124.9	48.95	14.66	73.43	54.14	30.64
2004-05	127.9	63.97	0.65	228.5	35.12	10.99	60.66	40.59	19.97

** Index numbers with base 1998-99.

The critical analysis of the table 5.4 above suggest the downward tendency of unit labour cost in all India during the period 1980-81 to 1997-98 witnessing around 33% decline. The unit labour cost in all India basis witnessed increase during 1983-85 and then in 1995-96

Comparing the regional figures Karnataka, Maharastra, Punjab, Uttar Pradesh and West Bengal indicated varying decline in unit labour cost with 1983-85 data bringing an upward movement. Bihar the most important region of production of iron and steel indicates marginal decline in the figures, sharper decline was seen during 1991-93. Delhi also indicated trends similar to Bihar whereas Andhra Pradesh after a sharp decline in 1982-83 has witnessed upward movement in the unit labour cost.

Trends of unit labour cost in sugar industry in India and regions of India are tabulated below.

Table 5.5: Trends of Unit Labour Cost in Sugar Industry in India and Regions of India

	All India	Bihar	Maharastra	Tamilnadu	UP
1980-81	100	100	100	100	100
1981-82	66.45	87.97	69.79	86.79	84.49
1982-83	54.5	82.89	68.66	67.08	91.44
1983-84	77.39	64.42	81.05	67.08	91.44
1984-85	73.8	124.4	131.3	111.6	101.9
1985-86	66.42	128.6	89.24	95.88	104.5
1986-87	62.13	90.35	85.68	79.89	97.1
1987-88	59.67	91.4	99.94	84.58	91.81
1988-89	55.76	90.13	75.23	81.2	87.54
1989-90	77.39	75.76	92.21	78.68	87.78
1990-91	66.77	86.11	87.62	83.83	90.33
1991-92	62.31	69.61	95.47	86.33	90.33
1992-93	59.44	89.42	98.14	81.26	88.56
1993-94	41.79	84.37	85.73	81.62	76.92
1994-95	49.72	75.78	74	69.77	69.28
1995-96	62.75	58.33	90.46	67.3	74.47
1996-97	59.49	65.17	95.68	75.67	84.32
1997-98	54.9	57.75	100.6	83.98	71.47
1998-99**	100	100	100	100	100
1999-2000	106.9	94.85	102.3	70.37	91.82
2000-01	95.72	95.42	93.5	76.91	82.58
2001-02	96.95	111.3	101	86.28	82.8
2002-03	88.53	124.2	105.6	88.95	85.09
2003-04	84.67	129.1	115	82.6	77.31
2004-05	89.68	132.5	93	92.13	70.13

** Index numbers with base 1998-99.

All India figures of labour cost trends in Sugar industry shows similar trends of decline with an up-word fluctuations in 1983-85 and then in 1989-90.

Wherein the decline of various size is seen in regional figures Sharpest in Bihar then in UP, Tamilnadu and almost no decline in Maharastra.

Trends of unit labour cost in Jute industry in India and regions of India are tabulated below:

Table 5.6: Trends of Unit Labour Cost in Jute Industry in India and Regions of India

	All India	Andhra Pradesh	Uttar Pradesh	West Bengal
1980-81	100	100	100	100
1981-82	111	111.3	117.6	111.7
1982-83	117.4	130.6	107.6	116.3
1983-84	109.4	126.5	107.6	116.3
1984-85	92.66	122.1	90.76	91.94
1985-86	89.04	89.35	49.42	93.4
1986-87	134.8	148.8	19.58	133.9
1987-88	138	174.6	118.7	139.2
1988-89	126.8	154.4	90.08	125.9
1989-90	117.1	115.6	127.1	112.7
1990-91	111.5	121.5	91.09	109.3
1991-92	120.2	132.8	91.09	59.85
1992-93	142.1	135.1	137.7	138.8
1993-94	122	126.8	107.1	119.4
1994-95	119.9	133.1	58.84	114.3
1995-96	120.9	119.6	105	117
1996-97	101.5	138.2	105.3	105.3
1997-98	127.2	152.3	142.1	122.3

* Category merged with cotton textile from 1998 onwards.

Labour cost trends in all India depict on the lines similar to West Bengal- the important regional centre of production. There is an upward movement in unit labour cost with decline in 1984-86. In Andhra Pradesh and Uttar Pradesh although there is an upward movement but Uttar Pradesh has witnessed decline in unit labour cost during 1984-87, and Andhra Pradesh during 1985-86.

Trends of unit labour cost in cotton textile industry in India and regions of India are tabulated below:

Table 5.7: Trends of Unit Labour Cost in Cotton Textile Industry in India and Regions of India

	All India	Andhra Pradesh	Delhi	Maharastra	Madhya Pradesh	Punjab	Rajasthan	Tamilnadu	UP	West Bengal
1980-81	100	100	100	100	100	100	100	100	100	100
1981-82	96.16	99.68	93	95.53	107.9	106.1	82.73	102.4	112.3	99.59
1982-83	97.93	93.26	100.3	105.1	98.34	93.45	102.4	98.32	105.2	96.37
1983-84	104.4	101.8	96.01	110.9	105.2	109.2	91.74	98.62	112.6	114.6
1984-85	101.5	100.8	96.01	108.9	111.9	92.78	100.2	94.09	109.5	102.3
1985-86	94.65	90.98	93.01	101.9	106.3	104.2	108.4	84.56	111.8	107.9
1986-87	104.3	109.1	93.89	114.7	113.9	99.68	100.7	100	132.9	112.5
1987-88	98.73	99.16	92.59	116.2	109.3	101.8	112.2	95.06	112.8	111
1988-89	88.09	72.29	61.2	105.6	97.7	106.1	79.06	86.23	108.5	112.4
1989-90	84.01	68.11	90.59	101.8	82.71	99.07	68.83	74.13	96.41	95.38
1990-91	81.72	69.38	70.99	95.65	83.96	91.99	75.03	73.07	114	105.2
1991-92	75.19	61.99	66.54	89.23	89.07	77.39	68.97	66.88	96.41	106.7
1992-93	73.05	64.39	61.73	95.94	67.96	93.01	68.8	64.01	112.2	84.72
1993-94	69.42	46.34	52.18	114.5	56.17	84.2	58.35	60.32	101.3	69.27
1994-95	53.6	50.84	43.29	79.96	31.56	61.49	56.38	52.21	74.31	67.52
1995-96	55.86	55.34	48.75	79.65	28.52	81.5	58.62	54.17	77.87	77.92
1996-97	50.12	97.44	54.13	79.54	19.78	85.88	51.66	54.8	79.7	83.42
1997-98	45.83	32.41	36.92	74.49	16.24	95.45	55.23	47.98	59.79	45.78
1998-99**	100	100	100	100	100	100	100	100	100	100
1999-2000	93.61	110.1	87.57	94.58	31.77	70.43	87.75	110.6	83.61	84.51
2000-01	92.42	106.2	177.7	85.18	27.74	107.5	92.29	105.3	65.75	93.25
2001-02	92.82	126.3	163.4	96.1	27.3	123.7	95.33	101.1	66.08	91.78
2002-03	91.35	100.2	60.34	89.22	25.03	97.3	87.38	96.11	66.88	92.89
2003-04	81.83	93.13	25.02	77.92	25.55	91.86	85.15	80.99	54.15	86.73
2004-05	77.12	127.6	207.6	66.43	22.09	85.31	81.71	70.67	45.15	85.85

** Index numbers with base 1998-99.

Except Maharastra and Punjab there is a sharp decline of almost 50% in unit labour cost in cotton textile industry. The period of 1983-87 indicates a period of typical rise in unit labour cost, thereafter there is a decline, in general, in all the centers of production.

Long Term Trend of wage Rate

Analysis of index number of wage rates in India at current price and constant price was carried out for the industries considered.

The chart of index numbers of wages at current price presents an upward movement in wages led by sugar and jute industries. But the current price figures can be misleading therefore the index numbers of wages at constant price was calculated.

Fig. 5.1: Index number of wage rates in India at current price (base 1981)

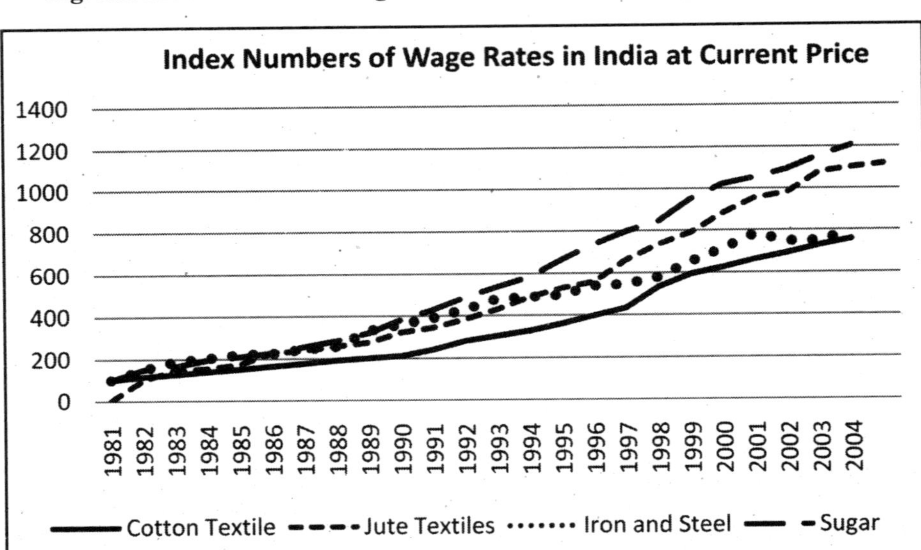

Compiled from the statistics released by: Previous Year Issues of Indian Labour Year Book, Ministry of Labour, Govt. of India

It is clear from the chart that the movement of wage rate remained relatively flat in cotton textile, iron and steel had upward movement during 1980s and declining movement in 1990s, in year 2001 and 2002 it again witnessed the upward movement. Jute and sugar industries maintained the upward movement in wage rate during the period 1980-2004. The table presented below from the statistics published by Ministry of Labour, Govt. of India also confirms the above interpretation.

Fig. 5.2: Index number of wage rates in India at constant price (base 1981)

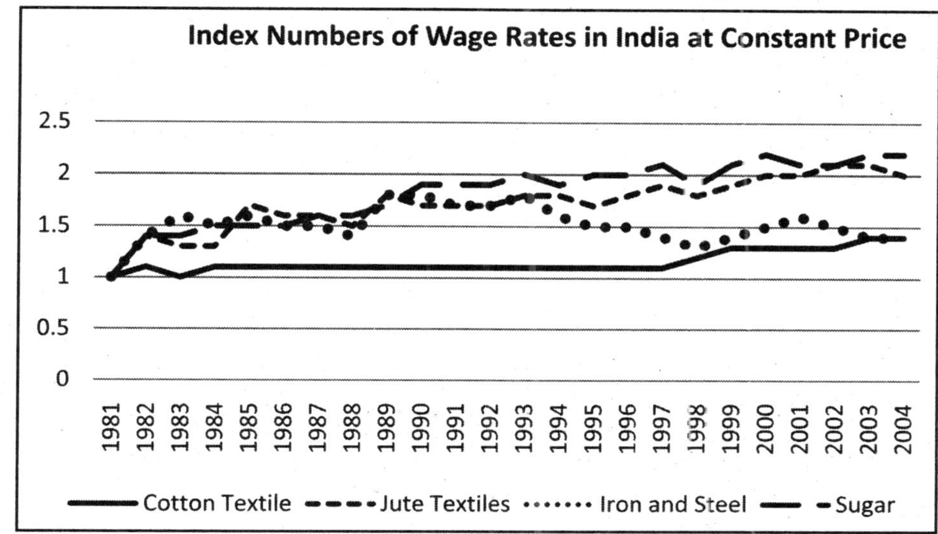

Compiled from the statistics released by: Previous Year Issues of Indian Labour Year Book, Ministry of Labour, Govt. of India

Table 5.8: Trend in Average Daily Wage Rates and Real Wage Rates of Workers in Textile Garment Industries at First Round Reference Year Price in India

	Percentage Change in Cotton		Percentage Change in Jute	
	Wage Rate at Current Price	Wage Rate at Constant Price	Wage Rate at Current Price	Wage Rate at Constant Price
First Round (1958)	–	–	–	–
Second Round (1963)	52.78	13.32	15.26	-14.5
Third Round (1975)	180.27	9.32	282.44	40.78
Fourth Round (1987)	129.67	3.1	174.85	42.3
Fifth Round (1994)	90.54	0	111.47	3.32
Sixth Round (2006)	64.64	-24.58	136.04	26.29

Source: Ministry of Labour & Employment, Govt. of India.

Long Term Trend of Wage Cost per Worker

The declining trends in general for the industries concerned are in line with the finding of for the data 1947-62 (Maheshwari, 1968). The tables below present the trends in the wage cost per worker for the selected industries. There is a general upward trend in wage cost per worker in all these industries.

Table 5.9: Trends of Wage Cost per Worker in Cotton Textile Industry in India and Regions of India

	All India	Andhra Pradesh	Delhi	Maharastra	Madhya Pradesh	Punjab	Rajasthan	Tamilnadu	UP	West Bengal
1980-81	100	100	100	100	100	100	100	100	100	100
1981-82	106.2	108.7	107.9	104.3	104.9	114.4	104.9	105	115.6	105.2
1982-83	113.7	127.1	144.8	101.6	124	111.8	129.6	114.3	119.8	121.7
1983-84	138.2	161.8	162.7	137.7	143.7	133.9	137.2	125.4	144.1	131.1
1984-85	154	184.6	162.7	158.7	159.8	118.6	149.3	136.9	147	142.7
1985-86	162.2	169.4	174.9	176.5	161	161.7	158.9	136.9	163.8	164.8
1986-87	182.6	207.1	187.7	205.6	179.1	172	180.4	160.5	173.9	186
1987-88	197.6	229.9	244.7	205	176.7	202.9	193.8	187.1	183.3	202.6
1988-89	219.2	221.7	278	229.1	210.8	206.4	186.8	220.3	193.8	209.9
1989-90	240.1	260.2	271.2	251.9	231.1	304.2	205.5	230.1	221.3	231.2
1990-91	272.5	280.2	300.5	295.8	242.4	317.9	291.1	255.7	249.5	259.6
1991-92	302.1	300.3	288.4	350.3	241.7	380.6	321.2	275.6	221.3	286.6
1992-93	336.8	359.3	337.2	369.9	254.3	420.4	347.2	335.3	282.5	349.7
1993-94	344.5	358.5	385.7	373	270.3	432.4	380.4	333.5	317.4	353.7
1994-95	386.8	433.7	393.5	462.8	273.4	466.1	415.6	377.8	318.3	397.9
1995-96	435.8	483	453.9	468.5	268.3	552.8	456.4	450.5	381.1	455
1996-97	443.2	508.2	325.8	479	284.1	650.2	466.1	462.4	408.5	476.7
1997-98	467.7	482.9	340.6	525	310.5	623.7	519.1	443.6	433.97	478.8
1998-99**	100	100	100	100	100	100	100	100	100	100
1999-2000	108.25	114.58	116.86	1042.76	192.2	107.65	100.99	96.74	102.85	105.05
2000-01	116.93	115.82	130.69	110.43	207.12	118.29	118.79	108.13	118.83	111.15
2001-02	117.35	89.92	113.05	107.53	212.49	124.54	117.89	101.86	131.3	122.98
2002-03	122.76	105.5	145.09	113.29	216.89	118.62	118.74	104.19	137.06	125.66
2003-04	122.26	115.71	147	112.96	241.45	128.36	121.66	102.08	114.75	121.2
2004-05	126.34	121.28	155.99	116.91	242.48	143.64	129.82	103.54	124.12	122.15

** Index numbers with base 1998-99.

Table 5.10: Trends of Wage Cost per Worker in Steel Industry in India and Regions of India

	All India	Andhra Pradesh	Bihar	Delhi	Karnatka	Maharastra	Punjab	UP	West Bengal
1980-81	100	100	100	100	100	100	100	100	100
1981-82	111.9	228.7	113.1	152.8	94.53	110.2	121.6	115.3	115.2
1982-83	131	300.7	139.7	147.3	104.5	144.5	125.6	127.1	125.3
1983-84	145.6	303.6	142.6	144.5	73.97	166.8	164.1	127.1	63.2
1984-85	172.1	333.8	148.5	155.4	148.2	185.3	170.4	164.8	169.9
1985-86	170.7	393.9	176.8	165.2	163.9	205.4	181.2	166.7	152.5
1986-87	178.9	421.1	156.5	188.5	183.4	236.2	213.4	219.5	180.2
1987-88	200.3	402.1	185.7	206.1	177.1	246.7	226.6	226.4	198
1988-89	242.8	395.5	234.3	269.4	233.1	300.6	243.1	271.6	225.6
1989-90	267.2	413.3	287.2	329.7	268.8	310.9	288.9	305.4	230
1990-91	274.6	483.9	315.9	305.4	308.6	347.6	328.6	338.8	252
1991-92	204.4	589.6	106.2	436.3	316.6	393.5	385.1	338.8	278.9
1992-93	241	1226	95.58	424.1	373.8	394.4	400.4	365.6	294.3
1993-94	340.7	1531	632.9	485.6	405.2	421.1	436.1	363.5	343.1
1994-95	488.2	1740	684.1	588.5	407.6	526.2	488.6	363.5	354.1
1995-96	570.9	1824	710.9	616.5	407.6	551.1	575.8	367.7	472
1996-97	659.2	4822	824.9	587.2	492.8	528.2	578.4	436.4	472
1997-98	671.8	4464	859	603.9	524.3	624	614.7	446.2	479
1998-99**	100	100	100	100	100	100	100	100	100
1999-2000	109.2	107.2	15.35	102.7	75.79	98.06	101	85.46	160.2
2000-01	132	173.3	21.61	117.4	82.01	114	102.8	108.3	128
2001-02	131.9	149.7	19.73	111.3	69.5	120.7	104.9	98.4	126.6
2002-03	149.3	179.3	22.21	122.8	88.11	143.7	115.6	131.5	146.8
2003-04	158.5	196.5	24.59	138.4	114.8	148.1	132.2	134.8	148.4
2004-05	143.3	180.9	20.86	131.4	108.8	161.3	135.3	131.3	169

** Index numbers with base 1998-99

Table 5.11: Trends of Wage Cost per Worker in Jute Industry in India and Regions of India

	All India	Andhra Pradesh	UP	West Bengal
1980-81	100	100	100	100
1981-82	111	108	125.3	104.8
1982-83	117.4	113.7	121.4	108
1983-84	109.4	126	121.4	108
1984-85	92.66	135.6	205	140.1
1985-86	89.04	173.8	208.3	175
1986-87	134.8	190	139.9	197.3
1987-88	138	236.6	292.7	189.1
1988-89	126.8	240.7	284.2	226.2
1989-90	117.1	189.7	325.1	252.7
1990-91	111.5	286	384.1	294.1
1991-92	120.2	286.8	384.1	302.1
1992-93	142.1	284.9	479.8	360.3
1993-94	122	381	450	402.5
1994-95	119.9	469.2	532.3	423.5
1995-96	120.9	541.4	460	468.4
1996-97	101.5	451.8	623.2	519.7
1997-98	127.2	618.8	739.5	632.2

* Category merged with cotton textile from 1998 onwards.

Table 5.12: Trends of Wage Cost per Worker in Sugar Industry in India and Regions of India

	All India	Bihar	Maharastra	Tamilnadu	UP
1980-81	100	100	100	100	100
1981-82	124.1	104.6	136.1	128.2	118.9
1982-83	192.1	230	218.9	222.2	183.5
1983-84	103.4	476.7	337.3	222.2	183.5
1984-85	107.3	627.8	386	455	289.1
1985-86	108.1	693	421.3	497	304.8
1986-87	108.1	751.9	446.9	567.5	347.1
1987-88	161.2	919.7	528.7	580.6	432
1988-89	193.1	1027	631.5	699.6	495.7
1989-90	191.8	1084	784.5	837.4	508
1990-91	251.6	1071	895.6	896.8	675.2
1991-92	266.5	1501	936.2	1046	675.2
1992-93	300.3	1587	1050	1166	857.8
1993-94	307.1	1623	1188	1287	888.7
1994-95	372.5	1842	1406	1556	1071
1995-96	377.7	2500	1650	1736	1148
1996-97	412	2244	2281	1808	1326
1997-98	489.8	3988	1701	1801	1428
1998-99**	100	100	100	100	100
1999-2000	109.7	95.19	101.9	117.6	90.37
2000-01	118.2	105.5	100.6	127.1	108.5
2001-02	122.5	117.9	109	127.9	117.1
2002-03	128.8	113.1	103.1	129.3	121.1
2003-04	121.5	126	101.5	128.2	119.6
2004-05	125.1	127.6	106.2	134.2	123.6

** Index numbers with base 1998-99.

The analysis of the tables above indicates that wage cost per worker in all the selected industries has a general increasing trend. In most of the cases the wage cost in cotton industry has been more than four times, in iron and steel industry more than six times lead by Andhra Pradesh and Bihar. In jute and Sugar the all India figures are drastically lower than the most important regional figures which indicate the new center of production and related manufacturing is having very less wage cost thereby bringing down the national average. Trend similar to jute is seen in the sugar industry where national average of increase in wage rate over the time period being close to five times, the traditional centers have witnessed the increase more than thrice the national average.

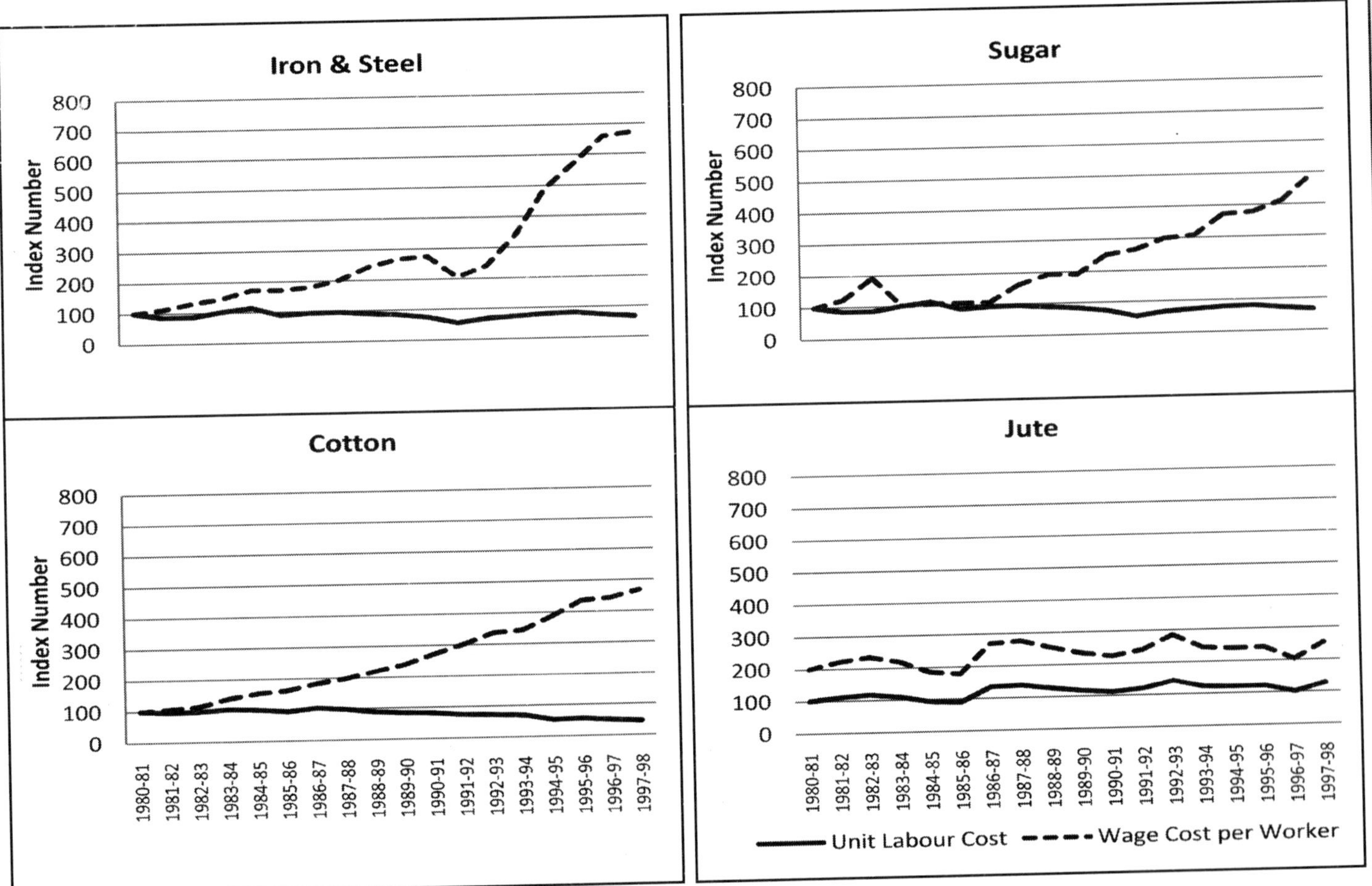

Fig. 5.3: Index number of unit labour cost and wage cost per worker in India at current price (base 1980)

The chart (figure 5.3) compares the unit labour cost and wage cost per worker on all India figures. Except Jute industry, in all other industries the wage rate has a general increasing trend and unit labour cost has a general declining trend. The past researchers, has attributed this behaviour of inverse relation to the technological changes.

Long Term Trend of Capital Labour Ratio per Worker

Rising wages induce intensive use of capital. If capital is substituted for labour due to higher wage bills, the decline in unit labour cost is implicit. Thus the intensive use of capital may be an important factor that has reduced the unit labour cost.

Intensity of capital can be measured in terms of capital-labour ratios. Capital labour ratios when show rising trends indicate increasing role of capital in manufacturing. Trends of these ratios in selected major industries of India are given in the following tables. While calculating the capital-labour ratios, only fixed capital is taken, as working capital stocks, raw material and cash balances/outstanding loan does not in any way convey the idea of substitution of capital in place of labour.

Table 5.13: Indices of Capital Labour Ratio in Sugar Industry in India and Regions of India

	All India	Bihar	Maharastra	Tamilnadu	UP
1980-81	100	100	100	100	100
1981-82	103.6	104.5	107.3	106.9	104
1982-83	126	250.4	146.3	145	130.4
1983-84	35.9	487.2	243.3	145	130.4
1984-85	39.09	801.3	389.5	254.1	204
1985-86	52.05	1536	337.9	313.6	249.7
1986-87	52.05	988.4	415.6	318.3	282.2
1987-88	46.33	1067	456.4	311.9	316.5
1988-89	36.91	1217	412.4	387	378.7
1989-90	50.2	2244	660.4	660.3	473.4
1990-91	48.31	2044	599.7	2005	672.5
1991-92	52.55	3314	632.3	1073	672.5
1992-93	37.1	3383	770.1	1328	796.5
1993-94	35.21	5264	1146	1786	1158
1994-95	50.27	6583	1194	1581	1807
1995-96	73.92	9436	1130	1851	1887
1996-97	61.95	8176	1229	2062	2419
1997-98	527.5	15002	1409	2375	2766
1998-99**	100	100	100	100	100
1999-2000	97.99	114.4	89.35	135.37	98.6
2000-01	114.69	136.83	95.99	134.74	151.79
2001-02	124.92	127.61	120.06	147	132.29
2002-03	140.09	104.46	131.44	138.66	149.03
2003-04	141.21	109.71	158.34	140.66	130.27
2004-05	14.97	118.36	194.04	152.47	147.88

** Index numbers with base 1998-99.

Table 5.14: Indices of Capital Labour Ratio in CottonTextile Industry in India and Regions of India

	All India	Andhra Pradesh	Delhi	Maharastra	Madhya Pradesh	Punjab	Rajasthan	Tamilnadu	UP	West Bengal
1980-81	100	100	100	100	100	100	100	100	100	100
1981-82	117.3	124.5	111.2	103.2	99.17	132.9	112.2	125.2	116	115
1982-83	141.8	127.4	184.3	155	130.6	119.7	153.5	152.1	119.6	148.5
1983-84	171.9	221.6	249.3	176.7	184.4	173.1	209.4	170.6	130.3	153.1
1984-85	205.2	238.1	249.3	189.5	200.1	193.9	248.8	192.8	158.8	161.7
1985-86	244.4	279	211.4	190.1	223	243.6	278	210.8	263.6	176.6
1986-87	252.3	287.8	235.6	212.6	293.3	211.9	274.4	226.2	189.9	199.8
1987-88	267.4	311.6	245	229.2	244.3	290.7	261.5	232.2	215.6	242.8
1988-89	322.4	303.9	232.8	297.2	270.8	285.2	234.5	298.8	197	277
1989-90	332	408.1	365.1	319	318.2	295.3	194.7	291.1	230.7	388.2
1990-91	403.8	410.5	234.2	387.6	266.4	418.5	256.9	434.1	279.7	246.9
1991-92	477.4	454.5	271.3	533.1	419.9	561.2	380.5	484.4	230.7	290.3
1992-93	628	634.7	542.2	633.3	793.1	562.3	460.5	618.3	304.3	441.7
1993-94	791.3	739	798.8	692.4	1574	880.9	375.5	730.8	414.6	517.3
1994-95	1153	865.7	1093	1289	3102	1172	698	945.6	610.8	888.1
1995-96	1459	1342	1211	1351	2550	1207	1089	1254	1063	1019
1996-97	1749	1275	1338	1352	2994	1384	1594	1631	1525	963.7
1997-98	2246	1681	2477	1393	4277	1471	961.6	1363	5E+05	4240
1998-99**	100	100	100	100	100	100	100	100	100	100
1999-2000	123.8	90.49	52.55	958.1	118.7	112.6	86.66	112.2	142.5	0.17
2000-01	123.3	85.41	79.51	105.2	163.9	68.05	87.71	100.5	181.1	122.4
2001-02	119.7	54.77	55.64	109.9	176.3	68.16	106.4	102.9	210.6	125.8
2002-03	123.1	83.69	193.3	154	163.2	83.55	94.74	120.1	180.5	128
2003-04	130.1	86.9	175.6	118.7	176.8	82.74	96.53	120.4	211.2	148
2004-05	137.4	61.99	59	139.2	176.1	99.26	102.1	143.6	239.6	137.5

** Index numbers with base 1998-99

Table 5.15: Indices of Capital Labour Ratio in Jute Industry in India and Regions of India

	All India	Andhra Pradesh	Uttar Pradesh	West Bengal
1980-81	100	100	100	100
1981-82	117.6	106.3	132.8	118.5
1982-83	131.9	108.9	173.7	133.6
1983-84	154.6	134.3	173.7	133.6
1984-85	174.9	130.9	250.4	193.1
1985-86	226.3	147.2	804.6	234.6
1986-87	198.9	235	2056	190.5
1987-88	283	261.6	1080	302.6
1988-89	492.4	278.9	909.9	613.2
1989-90	488.1	317.7	841.5	583
1990-91	626.8	311.8	942.8	767.5
1991-92	687.9	354.7	942.8	842.5
1992-93	565.5	485.6	745	670.7
1993-94	718.6	379.1	2184	804.2
1994-95	775.1	459.4	7214	853.7
1995-96	948	548.9	2212	1092
1996-97	1108	489.7	1543	1277
1997-98	954.3	657.5	1845	1080

The observations strongly point towards the inverse association between unit labour cost and the capital labour ratio. Rising capital labour ratio do not always mean substitution of the capital, if these are caused by inflation. Also new tecnological changes usually demand more skilled labour which is costlier than semi skilled or non skilled labour. The relationship modeling would point towards imbeded relationship between these variables.

Long Term trends in Productivity

Trend of production, volume of employment and output per worker are given in tables ahead in order to assess the comparative role of labour in production. If output is increasing but a certain input factor is not increasing in the same proportion, there are two possible explanations for the phenomenon; either the requirements of that particular factor have decreased and alternative combinations of factors are being used, or the productivity of that factor has increased. But in both these cases , the effect on unit cost will be the same, i.e. reduction in cost of that particular factor in question.

The output perworkers figures in the tables suggest that either unit requirement of labour is decreasing or technological changes have made labour more productive.

Table 5.16: Indices of Capital Labour Ratio in Steel Industry in India and Regions of India

	All India	Andhra Pradesh	Bihar	Delhi	Karnataka	Maharastra	Punjab	Uttar Pradesh	West Bengal
1980-81	100	100	100	100	100	100	100	100	100
1981-82	120	357.3	107.6	230.4	89.35	61.76	115.8	102.4	142.4
1982-83	146.1	781	130.1	306.7	93.35	111.4	141.5	99	170.2
1983-84	162.6	474.5	132.2	5.79	66.08	134.2	184.2	99	85.88
1984-85	167.8	986.3	142.7	341	141.4	153.3	204.4	133	197.6
1985-86	186.7	756.7	134.9	319.7	149.4	163	207.1	159.2	240.4
1986-87	182	589.7	115	334.9	174.6	191.6	264.7	213.2	198.7
1987-88	187.1	591.4	114.4	436.7	190.1	186.1	245.2	340.2	216.1
1988-89	211.1	543.4	120.2	635.7	186.1	476	319.3	312.6	311
1989-90	259	649.4	155	510.1	172.1	749.7	351.8	337.4	451.2
1990-91	465.4	11694	171.1	590.5	200.8	898.6	431.4	430.4	605.2
1991-92	599.4	12527	246.6	908.5	297.2	1214	567.5	430.4	1251
1992-93	605.6	16031	210.1	1065	424	1207	803.4	522.6	1489
1993-94	772.1	15198	356.9	2003	825.6	1870	1320	1186	1652
1994-95	946.4	14581	380.5	7855	1191	2122	1352	1186	1705
1995-96	1043	11430	419.5	2089	1191	3473	1406	1462	2044
1996-97	1050	4139	496.9	1202	1108	4228	1467	1596	2028
1997-98	1033	11657	504.2	8310	2231	4220	1896	2200	1928
1998-99**	100	100	100	100	100	100	100	100	100
1999-2000	92.69	75.68	7164	87.67	31.77	150.6	80.49	280.9	757.3
2000-01	103	85.92	3574	146.7	36.82	178	166	672.3	703.2
2001-02	106.1	79.62	3873	120.6	32.13	217.3	149.3	219.4	829.3
2002-03	118.8	108.1	2513	91.46	36.04	301.8	152.6	305	797.2
2003-04	131.9	98.12	1885	118.6	48.01	450.1	153.8	205.1	751
2004-05	127.9	83.05	2354	105.3	33.29	378.6	216	248.4	861.8

** Index numbers with base 1998-99

Table 5.17: Productivity, Workers Employed and Output per Worker in Iron and Steel Industry in India and Regions of India

	All India			Andhra Pradesh			Bihar			Delhi		
	Workers Employed	Production (Rs. Lakhs)	Output per Worker (Rs. Lakhs per Worker)	Workers Employed	Production (Rs. Lakhs)	Output per Worker (Rs. Lakhs per Worker)	Workers Employed	Production (Rs. Lakhs)	Output per Worker (Rs. Lakhs per worker)	Workers Employed	Production (Rs. Lakhs)	Output per Worker (Rs. Lakhs per Worker)
1980-81	233658	441057	1.89	11893	7041.6	0.59	60017	87306.71	1.45	1302	3490.9	2.68
1981-82	238729	590840	2.47	3287	7417.4	2.26	63577	152548.9	2.4	1450	4636.96	3.2
1982-83	235799	683802	2.9	2526	10316.81	4.08	62532	207725	3.32	1597	6396.97	4.01
1983-84	245142	664372	2.71	4100	13676.97	3.34	66652	170500.6	2.56	4908	175.71	0.04
1984-85	282368	836999	2.96	3910	16069.9	4.11	61929	221238.9	3.57	1796	9449.85	5.26
1985-86	256458	915564	3.57	4410	20032.14	4.54	65825	228231.7	3.47	2591	15096.96	5.83
1986-87	276799	990519	3.58	5894	27463.91	4.66	86970	243607.2	2.8	2270	12050.11	5.31
1987-88	282213	1103459	3.91	5777	22423.47	3.88	90081	279593.1	3.1	2423	13876.04	5.73
1988-89	270567	1417514	5.24	6476	24677.12	3.81	89777	346716	3.86	2361	15875.46	6.72
1989-90	243054	1570041	6.46	5651	29477.59	5.22	75741	406523.9	5.37	1495	12409.11	8.3
1990-91	276579	2137059	7.73	26444	110300.7	4.17	78591	601105.9	7.65	2836	26078.71	9.2
1991-92	234663	2001197	8.53	25723	102105.1	3.97	62935	540437.3	8.59	2807	39919.27	14.22
1992-93	288758	2773092	9.6	20736	183857.7	8.87	76058	634197.2	8.34	2170	33975.07	15.66
1993-94	273710	2919590	10.67	20998	204338.5	9.73	62265	697720.3	11.21	2354	39131.12	16.62
1994-95	268083	3324219	12.4	20576	268105	13.03	65739	783750.5	11.92	1386	15558.17	11.23
1995-96	285687	4070078	14.25	25569	346790.9	13.56	69555	871038.4	12.52	1712	27645.15	16.15
1996-97	248219	4427523	17.84	7321	148492.5	20.28	63466	830411.3	13.08	775	12334.56	15.92
1997-98	262130	5355614	20.43	22542	979388.5	43.45	56732	1238333	21.83	727	22827.01	31.4
1998-99	319744	6245180	19.53	22915	441781	19.28	38283	21611	0.56	2435	66237	27.2

(Table Contd...)

	All India			Andhra Pradesh			Bihar			Delhi		
	Workers Employed	Production (Rs. Lakhs)	Output per Worker (Rs. Lakhs per Worker)	Workers Employed	Production (Rs. Lakhs)	Output per Worker (Rs. Lakhs per Worker)	Workers Employed	Production (Rs. Lakhs)	Output per Worker (Rs. Lakhs per worker)	Workers Employed	Production (Rs. Lakhs)	Output per Worker (Rs. Lakhs per Worker)
1999-00	331011	7073520	21.37	27159	599789	22.08	2501	50707	20.27	2007	17281	8.61
2000-01	282909	6855475	24.23	20095	563184	28.03	1627	33015	20.29	1586	43164	27.22
2001-02	267637	7152450	26.72	19841	577689	29.12	1410	25924	18.39	906	18653	20.59
2002-03	264535	9542243	36.07	18353	729612	39.75	1398	32494	23.24	1195	18653	15.61
2003-04	268459	11927154	44.43	18237	982097	53.85	2068	33695	16.29	1046	31522	30.14
2004-05	294973	18627630	63.15	24098	1313833	54.52	1574	28622	18.18	1070	16735	15.64

(Table Contd...)

	Karnatka			Maharastra			Punjab			UP			West Bengal		
	Workers Employed	Production (Rs. Lakhs)	Output per Worker (Rs. Lakhs per Worker)	Wor-kers Emp-loyed	Production (Rs. Lakhs)	Output per Worker (Rs. Lakhs per Worker)	Workers Emp-loyed	Production (Rs. Lakhs)	Worker (Rs. Lakhs per Worker)	Workers Emp-loyed	Production (Rs. Lakhs)	Worker (Rs. Lakhs per Worker)	Wor-kers Emp-loyed	Produc-tion (Rs. Lakh)	Worker (Rs. Lakhs per Worker)
1980-81	10063	18214.03	1.81	16934	49516.26	2.92	14639	35281.56	2.41	7928	14945.33	1.89	48585	66959.26	1.38
1981-82	13001	23666.08	1.82	15724	53917.7	3.43	14307	40600.44	2.84	8301	18077.29	2.18	50625	86405.97	1.71
1982-83	13617	25578.93	1.88	17368	68568.28	3.95	14912	43186.56	2.9	8777	21273.99	2.42	47863	88325.19	1.85
1983-84	19236	25578.93	1.33	16781	62915.79	3.75	12648	42629.91	3.37	8777	21273.99	2.42	94861	88325.19	0.93
1984-85	11593	27441.75	2.37	15216	72028.52	4.73	11950	45779.37	3.83	8219	24447.13	2.97	69995	119054.5	1.7
1985-86	10151	26763.25	2.64	15034	79709.67	5.3	14402	63698.84	4.42	7722	34221.3	4.43	67241	130375.9	1.94
1986-87	10068	32490.94	3.23	15855	111143	7.01	12834	70905.2	5.52	8296	35953.23	4.33	59391	115038.8	1.94
1987-88	9574	35736.77	3.73	16889	111584	6.61	17562	93613.58	5.33	10671	43945.98	4.12	55502	124714.3	2.25
1988-89	8625	40322.12	4.68	17017	173801	10.21	14118	83256.64	5.9	7408	48634.64	6.57	49431	153354.2	3.1
1989-90	7781	49465.82	6.36	16146	180595.7	11.19	13643	126440.9	9.27	8544	70663.71	8.27	42298	120036.1	2.84
1990-91	7239	56573.07	7.82	16548	224547.6	13.57	11127	126660.1	11.38	7075	78239.01	11.06	54865	190603.6	3.47
1991-92	8520	66507.91	7.81	13518	212100	15.69	12941	166391.6	12.86	7075	78239.01	11.06	47137	201324	4.27
1992-93	7782	64173.38	8.25	16253	320039.8	19.69	13320	159949.9	12.01	6973	93490.05	13.41	52629	239139.5	4.54
1993-94	6554	66143.95	10.09	16557	317584.7	19.18	14355	201871.5	14.06	5989	91084.78	15.21	53699	226243.9	4.21
1994-95	8166	113136	13.85	15459	322688.6	20.87	12086	193958.9	16.05	5989	91084.78	15.21	56664	287249.5	5.07
1995-96	8166	113136	13.85	18233	545625.5	29.93	14448	283863.6	19.65	6009	91674.83	15.26	50652	317260.5	6.26
1996-97	9418	126956.7	13.48	14990	429121	28.63	12033	240070.8	19.95	5858	107606.1	18.37	50619	326593.1	6.45
1997-98	7253	104010.8	14.45	13344	440671.6	33.02	11066	273225.1	24.69	4209	108584.8	25.8	54831	367128.5	6.7
1998-99	5765	210218	36.46	27517	776216	28.21	9385	252614	26.92	5629	201496	35.8	59227	258826	4.37
1999-00	9622	248713	25.85	25099	799271	30.74	15697	338146	21.54	9634	208232	21.61	43629	430388	9.86
2000-01	7361	278484	37.83	24938	779947	31.28	13224	378796	28.64	4864	202882	41.71	48766	581477	11.92
2001-02	9470	389550	41.14	23214	858555	36.98	13822	463109	33.51	5794	418270	72.19	45054	803025	17.82
2002-03	8544	506002	59.22	25393	1436121	56.56	12099	427125	35.3	5300	400433	75.55	44354	799397	18.02
2003-04	7088	606225	85.53	25548	2085204	81.62	11458	555389	48.47	5817	518275	89.1	40324	853402	21.16
2004-05	8901	1005663	112.98	31422	3727096	118.61	13395	803907	60.02	6683	773903	115.8	41578	1537708	36.98

Table 5.18: Productivity, Workers Employed and Output per Worker in Cotton Textile Industry in India and Regions of India

	All India			Andhra Pradesh			Delhi			Maharastra			Madhya Pradesh	
	Workers Employed	Production (Rs. Lakhs)	Worker (Rs. Lakhs per Worker)	Workers Employed	Production (Rs. Lakhs)	Worker (Rs. Lakhs per Worker)	Workers Employed	Production (Rs. Lakhs)	Output per Worker (Rs. Lakhs per Worker)	Workers Employed	Production (Rs. Lakhs)	Worker (Rs. Lakhs per Worker)	Workers Employed	Production (Rs. Lakhs)
1980-81	946679	523818	0.55	39348	18194.77	0.46	15510	5538.58	0.36	209023	112352.04	0.54	56774	20555.93
1981-82	887880	539931	0.61	42363	21490.61	0.51	6006	2388.3	0.4	181695	105172.45	0.58	59995	21167.02
1982-83	926193	595592	0.64	44535	27710.16	0.62	15482	7883.95	0.51	165464	87910.51	0.53	56357	25740.87
1983-84	915265	668627	0.73	41475	30180.7	0.73	11934	7414.76	0.62	163508	108977.24	0.67	52225	26010.33
1984-85	838079	704746	0.84	55734	46457.12	0.83	11934	7414.76	0.62	153378	119870.19	0.78	45646	23985.25
1985-86	781235	747457	0.96	49376	41464.22	0.84	11408	8324.53	0.73	153469	142903.41	0.93	48253	26743.8
1986-87	788740	768777	0.97	41034	36059.4	0.88	10927	8113.41	0.74	166008	159260.55	0.96	48369	28975.25
1987-88	734898	819056	1.11	36742	39318.34	1.07	10282	10186.23	0.99	137307	130429.55	0.95	42048	25759.95
1988-89	706499	989800	1.4	42039	60191.58	1.43	8477	11555.36	1.36	135865	160577.24	1.18	38854	33063.09
1989-90	712046	1154790	1.62	44292	79668.84	1.8	5446	8307.68	1.53	146254	198232.05	1.36	41284	42580.46
1990-91	688276	1283248	1.86	48407	89560.43	1.85	6272	9410.81	1.5	139273	232226.65	1.67	43792	47295.88
1991-92	650580	1465110	2.25	44555	99963.48	2.24	6221	10330.63	1.66	125242	265858.65	2.12	36950	37659.55
1992-93	660182	1707794	2.59	48935	126382.83	2.58	4918	9610.7	1.95	137245	293381.86	2.14	27599	42447.85
1993-94	667722	1893284	2.84	54564	203308.74	3.73	4150	10967.92	2.64	137516	245676.36	1.79	28229	53262.02
1994-95	638815	2679372	4.19	51829	210633.3	4.06	4217	14254.53	3.38	115550	389963.7	3.37	31410	106876.16

(Table Contd...)

	All India			Andhra Pradesh			Delhi			Maharastra			Madhya Pradesh	
	Workers Employed	Production (Rs. Lakhs)	Worker (Rs. Lakhs per Worker)	Workers Employed	Production (Rs. Lakhs)	Worker (Rs. Lakhs per Worker)	Workers Employed	Production (Rs. Lakhs)	Output per Worker (Rs. Lakhs per Worker)	Workers Employed	Production (Rs. Lakhs)	Worker (Rs. Lakhs per Worker)	Workers Employed	Production (Rs. Lakhs)
1995-96	699564	3052347	4.36	61804	254346.22	4.12	2314	8040.73	3.47	136659	434650.64	3.18	39715	143249.46
1996-97	667443	3394500	5.09	56397	142630.51	2.53	4233	10171.73	2.4	133474	441280.07	3.31	37915	214973.44
1997-98	676893	4088106	6.04	55728	420098.61	7.54	4300	68013	15.82	131218	533077.43	4.06	42196	323659.34
1998-99	1016800	6497035	6.39	29692	199226	6.71	350	2610	7.46	128930	989595	7.68	71341	316928
1999-00	967929	7152196	7.39	29569	206539	6.98	489	4866	9.95	12739	1078022	84.62	38955	358795
2000-01	952940	7703542	8.08	29262	214149	7.32	552	3027	5.48	118242	1176547	9.95	34168	388355
2001-02	873906	7060113	8.08	53710	256552	4.78	556	2869	5.16	102396	876727	8.56	30240	358284
2002-03	857235	7361070	8.59	36633	258896	7.07	160	2869	17.93	96728	942749	9.75	30527	402603
2003-04	827579	7900393	9.55	40225	335320	8.34	379	16608	43.82	89049	990918	11.13	27130	390331
2004-05	849414	8891203	10.47	49827	317903	6.38	348	1950	5.6	82790	1118356	13.51	26116	436366

(Table Contd...)

MP	Punjab			Rajasthan			Tamilnadu			UP			West Bengal		
Output per Worker (Rs. Lakhs per Worker)	Workers Employed	Production (Rs. Lakhs)	Output per Worker (Rs. Lakhs per Worker)	Workers Employed	Production (Rs. Lakhs)	Output per Worker (Rs. Lakhs per Worker)	Workers Employed	Production (Rs. Lakhs)	Output per Worker (Rs. Lakhs per Worker)	Workers Employed	Production (Rs. Lakhs)	Output per Worker (Rs. Lakhs per Worker)	Workers Employed	Production (Rs. Lakhs)	Output per Worker (Rs. Lakhs per Worker)
0.36	19063	18006.1	0.94	26828	22407.77	0.84	132684	93072.99	0.7	62919	31658.16	0.5	53422	20972.86	0.39
0.35	27193	27596.29	1.01	21632	21483.12	0.99	135614	98249.92	0.72	64199	32529.22	0.51	55019	22775.24	0.41
0.46	16877	19020.49	1.13	27214	26512.25	0.97	138213	112174.37	0.81	66809	38542.8	0.58	51112	25238.27	0.49
0.5	19846	23423.59	1.18	27283	31103	1.14	138478	123407	0.89	71206	45377	0.64	55290	25036	0.45
0.53	14953	21802.21	1.46	24847	28782.85	1.16	144424	146931.35	1.02	65362	43544.9	0.67	59972	33215.54	0.55
0.55	16596	25665.88	1.55	24110	34183.21	1.42	147482	167032.75	1.13	65484	47823.88	0.73	41699	25550.56	0.61
0.6	17068	28638.07	1.68	25723	36188.85	1.41	145582	162853.55	1.12	65667	42404.29	0.65	36445	25336.05	0.7
0.61	22006	42068.82	1.91	25690	36736.85	1.43	153783	211503.94	1.38	66623	55209.01	0.83	33650	24343.43	0.72
0.85	25389	48909.53	1.93	23158	47336.94	2.04	156850	284766.24	1.82	53003	48416.57	0.91	25817	19948.23	0.77
1.03	25028	73918.87	2.95	22686	58020.98	2.56	156363	346312.89	2.21	64334	75399.68	1.17	31821	31496.05	0.99
1.08	27868	94444.92	3.39	26151	78988.74	3.02	156812	387371.12	2.47	52926	59445.07	1.12	27258	27390.31	1
1.02	17251	84201.28	4.88	26457	97545.49	3.69	164393	477885.19	2.91	64334	75399.68	1.17	25828	28311.13	1.1
1.54	27270	119541.45	4.38	24623	99613.15	4.05	170074	598872.93	3.52	47081	62793.54	1.33	25214	44410.1	1.76
1.89	26544	137320.76	5.17	24517	125751.39	5.13	176311	699723.86	3.97	43538	77172.51	1.77	25820	53630.93	2.08
3.4	25636	199242.94	7.77	25286	147350.84	5.83	188286	982677.58	5.22	39173	93861.77	2.4	23785	58281.77	2.45
3.61	25036	170939.86	6.83	23035	143848.03	6.24	191741	1084304.45	5.66	40053	102003.48	2.55	24039	59538.97	2.48
5.67	27221	206574.97	7.59	23696	170342.26	7.19	204839	1219761.3	5.95	38683	107662.94	2.78	29021	69429.7	2.39
7.67	26958	179665.06	6.66	22833	171354.15	7.5	221866	1512381.74	6.82	44809	191315.88	4.27	23152	109118.95	4.71
4.44	45087	423574	9.39	55513	436124	7.86	185242	1325591	7.16	50134	244489	4.88	194434	400137	2.06
9.21	44440	638112	14.36	61365	554815	9.04	202778	1269784	6.26	32616	195667	6	170498	436158	2.56
11.37	44921	464354	10.34	54290	548987	10.11	200632	1474572	7.35	26746	235744	8.81	192037	471075	2.45
11.85	41599	393559	9.46	56799	551807	9.72	193063	1392179	7.21	22263	215713	9.69	167123	460854	2.76
13.19	39817	456067	11.45	56193	599893	10.68	197309	1530699	7.76	22366	223526	9.99	173201	482186	2.78
14.39	37201	488335	13.13	56596	635274	11.22	192274	1734114	9.02	24143	249504	10.33	164185	472167	2.88
16.71	39069	617973	15.82	59243	739497	12.48	192290	2016085	10.48	18693	250626	13.41	171303	501610	2.93

Table 5.19: Productivity, Workers Employed and Output per Worker in Jute Industry in India and Regions of India

	All India			Andhra Pradesh			UP			West Bengal		
	Workers Employed	Production (Rs. Lakhs)	Output per Worker (Rs. Lakhs per Worker)	Workers Employed	Production (Rs. Lakhs)	Output per Worker (Rs. Lakhs per Worker)	Workers Employed	Production (Rs. Lakhs)	Output per Worker (Rs. Lakhs per Worker)	Workers Employed	Production (Rs. Lakhs)	Output per Worker (Rs. Lakhs per Worker)
1980-81	248546	86568	0.348298	14389	6846.63	0.475824	6385	2274.71	0.356258	214100	72419.36	0.33825
1981-82	218807	72830	0.33285	15787	7189.96	0.455435	6547	2486.67	0.379818	183735	58644.71	0.319181
1982-83	234961	76466	0.325441	13228	5392.17	0.407633	6434	2595.22	0.40336	202377	64129.1	0.316879
1983-84	200885	76279	0.379715	14627	6940.39	0.474492	6434	2595.22	0.40336	202377	64129.1	0.316879
1984-85	264944	142051	0.536155	27692	14503.35	0.523738	10133	8213.61	0.81058	210758	110090.4	0.522354
1985-86	193686	132158	0.682331	14875	13622.03	0.915767	5029	8034.2	1.597574	162408	102660.3	0.632114
1986-87	191373	96947	0.506587	16296	9699.94	0.595234	415	1345.36	3.241831	159697	79253.85	0.496276
1987-88	179249	87895	0.490351	12902	8173.27	0.633489	4216	3739.98	0.887092	149015	68973.78	0.462865
1988-89	190584	120354	0.631501	13830	10073.99	0.728416	4653	5273.7	1.133398	160697	98778.37	0.614687
1989-90	187000	141269	0.755449	12381	9991.47	0.807	4442	4013.37	0.903505	161155	123810.1	0.768267
1990-91	179982	166790	0.926704	13860	15375.87	1.10937	3941	5852.99	1.485154	153725	140869.6	0.916374
1991-92	180604	156961	0.869089	14034	14327.18	1.020891	3941	5852.99	1.485154	151309	129463.3	0.855622
1992-93	179400	159956	0.891616	9501	9583.8	1.008715	4532	5626.58	1.241523	154866	137966.6	0.890877
1993-94	156956	178790	1.139109	9025	12960.57	1.436074	3982	6219.66	1.561944	132266	150192.8	1.135536
1994-95	164911	207005	1.255253	6219	10055.62	1.616919	1160	3897.41	3.359836	149510	189392.7	1.266756
1995-96	234345	324437	1.384442	5821	12495.12	2.146559	4004	6214.79	1.552145	214592	294392.6	1.371871
1996-97	178100	313368	1.759506	6850	10998.41	1.605607	5706	12034.28	2.109057	164629	272025.1	1.652352
1997-98	191564	330877	1.72724	6751	13020.09	1.928617	4510	8524.74	1.890186	171034	297620.9	1.740127

* category merged with cotton textile from 1998 onwards

Table 5.20: Productivity, Workers Employed and Output per Worker in Sugar Industry in India and Regions of India

	All India			Bihar			Maharastra			Tamilnadu			UP		
	Workers Emp-loyed	Production (Rs. Lakhs)	Worker (Rs. Lakhs) per Worker	Workers Emp-loyed	Production (Rs. Lakhs)	Worker (Rs. Lakhs) per Worker	Workers Emp-loyed	Production (Rs. Lakhs)	Worker (Rs. Lakhs) per Worker	Workers Emp-loyed	Production (Rs. Lakhs)	Worker (Rs. Lakhs) per Worker	Workers Emp-loyed	Production (Rs. Lakhs)	Worker (Rs. Lakhs) per Worker
1980-81	446481	141719	0.32	32917	5728.28	0.17	59063	40386.74	0.68	20201	11922.93	0.59	196530	48471.65	0.25
1981-82	455397	229594	0.5	30477	6409.28	0.21	61744	80782.48	1.31	19836	17185.31	0.87	207891	72210.77	0.35
1982-83	419671	325447	0.78	25907	12188.71	0.47	50698	105635.7	2.08	12871	24943.06	1.94	187646	95623.11	0.51
1983-84	137422	30812	0.22	15200	18409.56	1.21	36803	100992	2.74	12871	24943.06	1.94	187646	95623.11	0.51
1984-85	116612	28000	0.24	9584	8347.59	0.87	32321	81848.85	2.53	8552	20537.13	2.4	133892	92869.57	0.69
1985-86	107824	31661	0.29	6592	6038.45	0.92	31584	100545.6	3.18	8021	25856.91	3.22	117619	86662.05	0.74
1986-87	107824	31661	0.29	8139	11312.21	1.39	30918	110218.1	3.56	8961	37844.68	4.22	119854	107682.01	0.9
1987-88	106335	47138	0.44	8409	14243.96	1.69	31011	112855.4	3.64	10027	40863.18	4.08	133803	155117.29	1.16
1988-89	93515	50907	0.54	9460	18361.05	1.94	36708	202480.1	5.52	9924	50090.74	5.05	129468	184903.78	1.43
1989-90	106661	49127	0.46	9033	22093.06	2.45	37093	208087.2	5.61	10173	65787.91	6.47	140231	211469.35	1.51
1990-91	89279	56535	0.63	11257	23619.13	2.1	38883	257570.8	6.62	11407	71663.81	6.28	128884	246970.12	1.92
1991-92	83577	55073	0.66	8525	31369.78	3.68	44827	287155	6.41	11458	81849.14	7.14	128884	246970.12	1.92
1992-93	87470	61760	0.71	10925	32570.14	2.98	41732	311001.1	7.45	11494	102275.36	8.9	134392	338695.03	2.52
1993-94	82674	86475	1.05	8374	27982.8	3.34	37129	350868.9	9.45	10877	111012.13	10.21	125223	379351.03	3.03
1994-95	79936	95864	1.2	7981	34425.87	4.31	39244	501514.4	12.78	10754	156548.27	14.56	118240	484211.81	4.1
1995-96	75468	88882	1.18	5554	42163.44	7.59	45551	551173.2	12.1	11275	184171.47	16.33	114699	469559.39	4.09
1996-97	75685	91930	1.21	8333	48173.62	5.78	43187	581817.4	13.47	13400	201947.81	15.07	123777	585707.03	4.73
1997-98	71843	106272	1.48	4436	45068.56	10.16	34220	390897.6	11.42	11757	165899.08	14.11	103612	562511.76	5.43
1998-99	551108	3988430	7.24	4180	40527	9.7	53263	825199	15.49	88293	416364	4.72	96271	732456	7.61
1999-00	569730	4321322	7.58	4839	47087	9.73	65078	1004677	15.44	66716	525609	7.88	92482	692490	7.49
2000-01	562026	4820613	8.58	4648	49807	10.72	75581	1259330	16.66	64563	503267	7.79	77757	777129	9.99
2001-02	547950	4623798	8.44	5360	55019	10.26	70131	1171688	16.71	61911	432701	6.99	73492	790837	10.76
2002-03	536574	4758598	8.87	4614	40730	8.83	70041	1059328	15.12	64057	439232	6.86	80976	876728	10.83
2003-04	538184	4547558	8.45	5019	47514	9.47	59967	820280	13.68	62015	454006	7.32	78857	928188	11.77
2004-05	533508	5051133	9.47	4683	43719	9.34	50475	892744	17.69	65272	448483	6.87	75485	1012474	13.41

CAUSATIVE FACTORS – INTENSITY OF CAPITAL, PRODUCTION, NATURE OF EMPLOYMENT AND OUTPUT PER WORKER, PRODUCTIVITY-EMPLOYEE PAYMENTS

If growth rate of productivity outstrips the rate of wage increase, decline in unit labour cost is genuine and vice-versa. Table5.21 below provides the necessary data to compare the growth rates of productivity and wages of all India figures in the selected industries.

Table 5.21: Growth of Productivity and Wages in Selected Industries (all India)

	Iron & Steel		Sugar		CottonTextile		Jute	
	Output per man hour	Compen-sation per man hour	Output per man hour	Compen-sation per man hour	Output per man hour	Compen-sation per man hour	Output per man hour	Compen-sation per man hour
1980-81	100	100	100	100	100	100	100	100
1981-82	129.7722	110.7833	137.4505	107.4018	112.6545	108.8577	96.06802	106.1421
1982-83	150.035	127.9757	160.6738	126.3291	116.3649	113.8305	97.59926	113.7324
1983-84	137.4817	139.3802	51.05895	74.73229	120.205	125.7902	113.7788	122.9938
1984-85	147.1235	161.2084	56.31828	79.84689	139.5342	141.3555	161.1037	147.603
1985-86	179.7114	162.2095	72.14117	84.32275	159.5519	149.6692	191.358	170.7007
1986-87	177.9526	167.952	72.14117	84.32275	160.537	166.3922	145.2499	196.3719
1987-88	194.3063	187.8911	85.49561	98.67086	184.6439	181.1305	143.3617	196.6393
1988-89	261.7209	228.9265	89.30026	100.5307	232.6873	201.4628	131.0676	227.4722
1989-90	322.9247	252.1154	96.2836	127.2732	266.6352	218.4211	216.068	249.8905
1990-91	318.4649	257.9636	116.4885	146.8955	302.4742	244.6339	256.4795	284.5928
1991-92	423.9859	191.8075	126.1648	161.981	373.8492	277.4588	258.3765	313.2088
1992-93	477.3437	226.1168	136.1958	183.8766	431.2261	310.6439	264.1951	370.5448
1993-94	535.4879	322.8947	205.9885	191.9876	472.4291	317.5794	316.1923	386.6204
1994-95	612.5652	455.2747	222.1766	219.0165	689.8277	351.981	353.486	419.8819
1995-96	710.8448	537.6622	236.0886	240.3109	704.7587	389.4627	395.2755	472.2901
1996-97	886.0471	618.0803	233.666	251.5781	836.7935	403.5063	501.4029	514.7573
1997-98	1071.779	665.1927	270.1201	283.9094	1007.777	431.7834	529.4185	675.7993
1998-99	746.2934	431.0444	725.8896	406.1385	879.6007	396.8428	#	#
1999-00	861.1657	496.3553	748.0265	438.0143	999.222	421.9862	#	#
2000-01	906.6104	556.9273	830.2647	463.3524	1104.888	460.6954	#	#
2001-02	988.9024	550.4905	834.3157	490.3297	1099.816	460.552	#	#
2002-03	1337.633	624.3988	856.3119	503.6446	1171.274	482.7073	#	#
2003-04	1659.08	667.713	864.3688	503.4426	1311.701	484.284	#	#
2004-05	2394.446	612.7654	950.5368	508.7451	1433.93	498.9452	#	#

category merged with cotton textile from 1998 onwards.

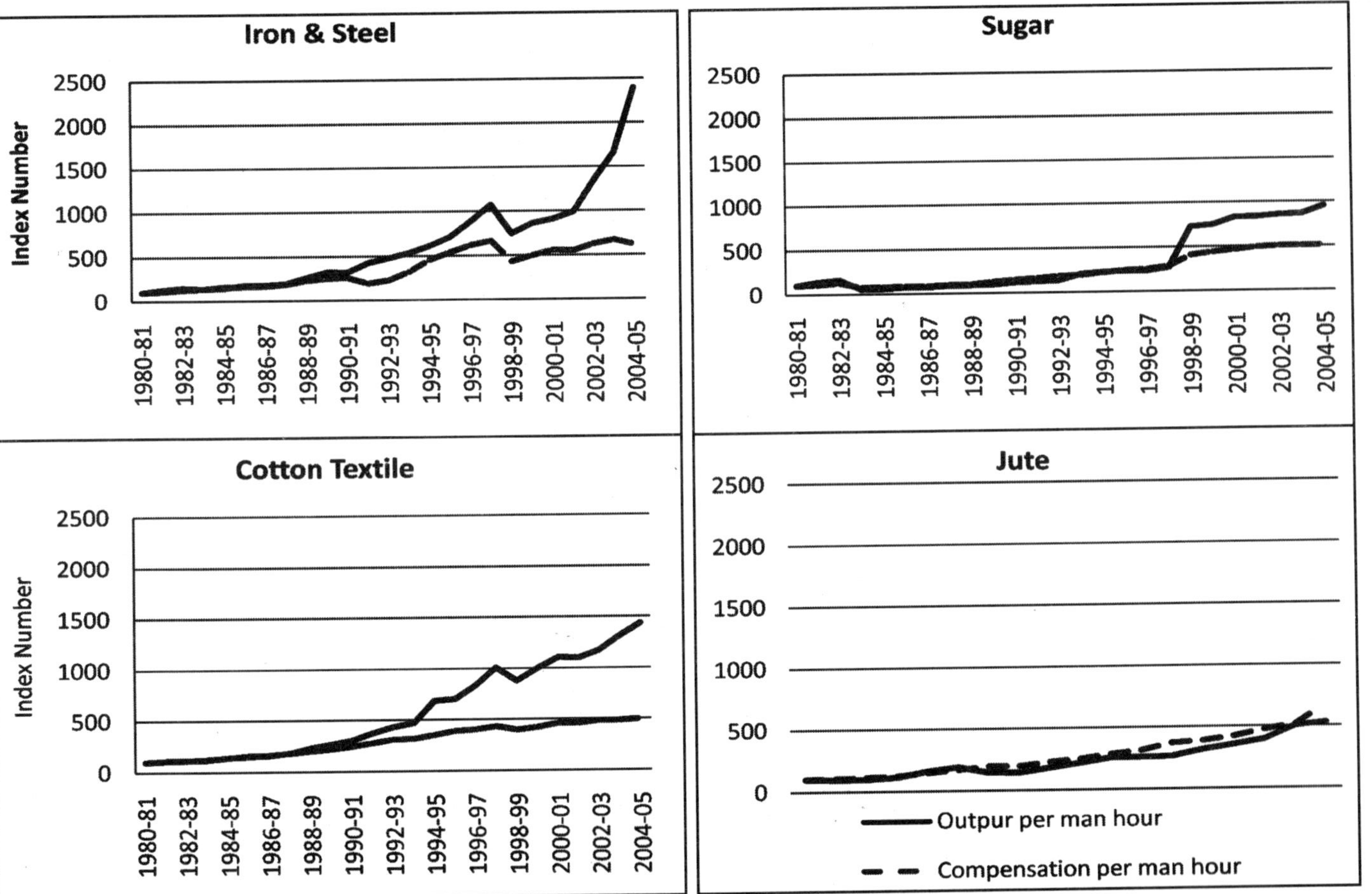

Fig. 5.4: Index number of growth of productivity and wages in selected industries of India at current price (base 1980)

The visual representation of the data indicates that output per hour increased at a faster rate in the selected industries except Jute. The respective indices of output per man hour has raised from 100 in 1980 to 2394, 951, 1433 in iron & steel, sugar and cotton textile respectively. Whereas, the indices of compensation per man-hour has risen to 613, 509, 499 respectively. In iron and steel, the productivity started picking from 1985 onwards; in sugar from 1998 onwards and in cotton textiles from 1987 onwards.

The results stated above need to checked against incidental fluctuation in prices. Since while estimating the unit labour cost, both output and labour expenditure has been taken on current price, the impact of price fluctuation may mislead the trends.. to remove these impacts, the unit labour cost is revised converting the figures to constant price through single deflation.

RELATIONSHIPS AND REVISED TRENDS, TRENDS OF NON-LABOUR COSTS.

The table given below consists of unit labour cost at current price and also at constant price with base 1980.

Table 5.22: Comparative Trends of Unit Labour Cost in the Selected Industries of India on Current Price and Constant Price of 1980.

All India	Iron & Steel		Sugar		Cotton		Jute	
	Current Price Estimates	Constant Price Estimates	Current Price Estimates	Constant Price Estimates	Current Price Estimates	Constant Price Estimates	Current Price Estimates	Constant Price Estimates
1980-81	100	100	100	100	100	100	100	100
1981-82	86.1	89.87	86.1	66.45	96.16	91.14	110.96	105.24
1982-83	86.74	80.38	86.74	54.5	97.93	83.96	117.4	107.41
1983-84	102.58	93.64	102.58	77.39	104.36	83.41	109.43	114.92
1984-85	113.57	109.28	113.57	73.8	101.5	77.49	92.66	132.01
1985-86	88.95	96.15	88.95	66.42	94.65	70.63	89.04	105.23
1986-87	94.51	94.49	94.51	62.13	104.32	71.54	134.76	120.7
1987-88	96.08	91.74	96.08	59.67	98.73	68.31	138.02	125.34
1988-89	89.59	91.41	89.59	55.76	88.09	61.67	126.79	127.92
1989-90	84.17	93.74	84.17	77.39	84.01	64.66	117.12	137.11
1990-91	74.33	81.05	74.33	66.77	81.72	62.21	1[illegible]1.5	132.73
1991-92	54.37	55.29	54.37	62.31	75.19	57.61	120.24	129.02
1992-93	67.48	61.29	67.48	59.44	73.05	49.97	142.12	136.07
1993-94	73.84	69.69	73.84	41.79	69.42	48.71	122.03	106.39
1994-95	79.44	72.34	79.44	49.72	53.6	37.09	119.87	108.75
1995-96	81.52	72.76	81.52	62.75	55.86	42.22	120.88	112.41
1996-97	73.27	68.93	73.27	59.49	50.12	39.79	101.53	114.65
1997-98	66.55	62.94	66.55	54.9	45.83	34.9	127.21	143.61
1998-99**	100	100	100	100	100	100	#	#
1999-00	99.79	95.08	99.79	106.85	93.61	92.99	#	#
2000-01	106.36	100.21	106.36	95.72	92.42	92.38	#	#
2001-02	96.38	87.24	96.38	96.95	92.82	88.81	#	#
2002-03	80.82	75.01	80.82	88.53	91.35	82.94	#	#
2003-04	69.68	76.15	69.68	84.67	81.83	80.13	#	#
2004-05	44.31	56.92	44.31	89.68	77.12	73.67	#	#

category merged with cotton textile from 1998 onwards.

** Index numbers with base 1998-99.

The revised trends calculated at constant price of 1980 reiterate that unit labour cost has declining trend except for the early 1980s for selected industries. The Jute industry has increasing unit labour cost trends. It points out that in Iron & Steel, sugar and Cotton textile industry the technical changes seem most deemed explanation for the decline in unit labour cost and growth in productivity.

Trends of non Labour Cost

Since the labour cost is a substantial proportion of total cost, changes in labour cost affects the cost of production. The larger the proportion of labour cost to total cost –the greater will be the percentage change in the total cost as a consequence of a given change in labour cost. Despite the declining unit labour cost increase in total cost indicates towards the role of non-labour cost components. If the unit labour cost see a decline due to substitution of capital then consequently capital cost will certainly increase.

The trends of non-labour cost can be analysed if gross value of output is broken up into different components. Data tables below present the per cent breakup of the gross value of output of the selected industries.

Table 5.23: Percentage Components of Gross Value of output for Iron and Steel Industry at Current Price.

Year	% Material Cost at Current Price	% Fuel Consumed	% Labour Cost	% Margin
1980-81	54.08	13.35	16.1	16.47
1981-82	50.9	11.27	13.86	23.97
1982-83	44.0	11.16	13.97	30.87
1983-84	53.15	14.44	16.52	15.89
1984-85	57.2	13.45	18.28	11.07
1985-86	56.64	13.04	14.32	16
1986-87	60.95	12.95	15.22	10.88
1987-88	60.36	12.94	15.47	11.23
1988-89	57.22	11.2	14.42	17.16
1989-90	61.53	11.21	13.55	13.71
1990-91	53.05	10.19	11.97	24.79
1991-92	63.96	11.55	8.75	15.74
1992-93	60.67	11.24	10.87	17.22
1993-94	57.81	11.49	11.89	18.81
1994-95	57.45	12.08	12.79	17.68
1995-96	55.79	12.67	13.12	18.42
1996-97	48.89	13.59	11.8	25.72
1997-98	46.99	12.18	10.72	30.11
1998-99	52.03	12.22	3.55	32.2
1999-00	54.06	11.93	3.54	30.47
2000-01	56.24	13	3.78	26.98
2001-02	59.76	13.19	3.42	23.63
2002-03	57.28	12.81	2.87	27.04
2003-04	52.3	15.65	2.47	29.58
2004-05	57.42	9.34	1.57	31.67

Table 5.24: Percentage Components of Gross Value of output for Sugar Industry at Current Price

Year	% Material Cost at Current Price	% Fuel Consumed	% Labour Cost	% Margin
1980-81	66.75	3.47	17.73	12.05
1981-82	69.38	2.66	13.75	14.21
1982-83	69.36	2.52	13.74	14.38
1983-84	62.99	8	20.64	8.37
1984-85	68.71	7.25	20.03	4.01
1985-86	72.71	6.31	16.52	4.46
1986-87	72.71	6.31	16.52	4.46
1987-88	73.76	6.62	16.7	2.92
1988-89	71.5	6.38	15.52	6.6
1989-90	72.13	6.6	19.17	2.1
1990-91	75.63	6.64	17.94	-0.21
1991-92	75.07	7.26	18.06	-0.39
1992-93	76.56	7.1	19.3	-2.96
1993-94	73.39	5.19	13.1	8.32
1994-95	82.77	6.04	13.96	-2.77
1995-96	73.6	6.66	14.59	5.15
1996-97	76.8	7.93	15.44	-0.17
1997-98	76.63	7.02	15.6	0.75
1998-99	67.43	3.09	3.64	25.84
1999-00	68.6	3.08	3.81	24.51
2000-01	70.16	3.12	3.63	23.09
2001-02	67.22	3.29	3.82	25.67
2002-03	67.96	3.45	3.82	24.77
2003-04	67.41	4.49	3.79	24.31
2004-05	66.49	4.02	3.48	26.01

Table 5.25: Percentage Components of Gross Value of output for Cotton Industry at Current Price.

Year	% Material Cost at Current Price	% Fuel Consumed	% Labour Cost	% Margin
1980-81	56.17	7.08	30.65	6.1
1981-82	72.38	7.21	29.47	-9.06
1982-83	60.93	8.04	30.01	1.02
1983-84	58.32	9.14	31.99	0.55
1984-85	62.39	8.75	31.11	-2.25
1985-86	61.88	10.29	29.01	-1.18
1986-87	57.37	10.61	31.97	0.05
1987-88	60.64	9.95	30.26	-0.85
1988-89	63.64	8.66	27	0.7
1989-90	60.38	8.33	25.75	5.54
1990-91	59.41	8.63	25.05	6.91
1991-92	65.08	8.1	23.04	3.78
1992-93	65.2	8.85	22.39	3.56
1993-94	64.85	9.24	21.28	4.63
1994-95	67.19	7.65	16.43	8.73
1995-96	69.44	8.2	17.12	5.24
1996-97	61.13	8.07	15.36	15.44
1997-98	62.45	8.01	14.05	15.49
1998-99	60.33	8.97	5.79	24.91
1999-00	58.94	10.39	5.42	25.25
2000-01	60.9	10.56	5.35	23.19
2001-02	61.63	10.37	5.38	22.62
2002-03	58.79	11.01	5.29	24.91
2003-04	58.39	12.37	4.74	24.5
2004-05	61.64	10.35	4.47	23.54

Table 5.26: Percentage Components of Gross Value of output for Jute Industry at Current Price.

Year	% Material Cost at Current Price	% Fuel Consumed	% Labour Cost	% Margin
1980-81	48.51	5.03	49.36	-2.9
1981-82	51.41	6.38	54.77	-12.56
1982-83	52.53	7.27	57.95	-17.75
1983-84	57.41	6.75	54.01	-18.17
1984-85	63.22	5.33	45.73	-14.28
1985-86	71.71	5.56	43.95	-21.22
1986-87	51.71	8	66.51	-26.22
1987-88	51.24	7.92	68.12	-27.28
1988-89	53.41	7.62	62.58	-23.61
1989-90	56.99	7.33	57.81	-22.13
1990-91	59.71	6.89	55.03	-21.63
1991-92	52.66	7.75	59.35	-19.76
1992-93	51.95	8.93	70.14	-31.02
1993-94	54.32	8.01	60.23	-22.56
1994-95	53.53	8.27	59.16	-20.96
1995-96	59.13	8.06	59.66	-26.85
1996-97	53.45	8.12	50.11	-11.68
1997-98	45.72	9.14	62.79	-17.65

The tables above indicate that material cost make biggest share in iron and steel industry, followed by labour and fuel in close proximity. In the cotton textile industry material cost is biggest component and then next big component is of labour cost followed by fuel and lubricants (in the range of 7 to 12%). In sugar industry the composition is majorly consist of material cost and labour cost, the fuel cost is marginal in the range of 2 to 8 per cent. In jute industry the fuel and lubricants proportion lie between 5 to 9 per cent and remaining is shared approximately equally by the labour and material cost. In iron & steel industry and cotton industry the labour cost has decreased and material cost has increased. Whereas in sugar industry the decrease in labour cost is much higher than the decrease in material cost, in jute industry the labour cost increased but the material cost decreased in a fluctuating manner.

6

Data Analysis

INTER-INDUSTRY COMPARISON OF PRODUCTIVITY LABOUR COST IN COTTON TEXTILE, JUTE, STEEL AND SUGAR FOR THE PERIOD 1980-2004

General trends of productivity and wages identified in the previous chapter indicate the general trends and do not cover the details of the problem under study. Labour cost may vary from industry to industry and even within industry across regions and from unit to unit. Therefore in this comparative study the share of labour as a factor of production would be measured. This chapter would attempt to study the following:

1. Inter-industry comparison of labour cost: this would help in measuring the comparative potential of labour in different industry.
2. Inter-regional comparison of labour cost and
3. Size-wise comparison of labour cost, types of ownership

Inter-Industry Comparison of Labour Cost in Cotton Textile

There is a difference between the volume of employment provided by the industry and its potentiality as provider of employment. The volume of employment is determined by the growth of an industry, while the potentiality is determined by the proportion of the labour's share in the total cost. An industry has a greater capacity of employment in its manufacturing process if the proportion of the labour cost is high. The table below provides an inter-industry comparison of labour cost in the selected industries.

The table 6.1 indicate the labour cost has a decreasing trend in Iron & steel, Sugar; has fluctuating decreasing trend and increasing trend in jute industry. The proportion of the labour cost to the total cost is highest in jute, then similar proportion in sugar and cotton textile and least in iron & steel industry. These figures indicate comparative intensity of the industry to absorb labour, and labour intensity required in the process of manufacturing. These trends are very much different than the trends during 1942-62 period, where proportion of labour cost was highest in cotton textile, low in iron & steel and jute and lowest in sugar industry (Maheshwari, 1968). These contrast indicate that over the decades the use of capital has changes the complete scenario in the industries.

Table 6.1: Inter Industry Comparison of Labour Cost in Iron & Steel Industry

	Iron & Steel	Sugar	Cotton	Jute
1980-81	16.1	17.73	30.65	49.36
1981-82	13.86	13.75	29.47	54.77
1982-83	13.97	13.74	30.01	57.95
1983-84	16.52	20.64	31.99	54.01
1984-85	18.28	20.03	31.11	45.73
1985-86	14.32	16.52	29.01	43.95
1986-87	15.22	16.52	31.97	66.51
1987-88	15.47	16.7	30.26	68.12
1988-89	14.42	15.52	27	62.58
1989-90	13.55	19.17	25.75	57.81
1990-91	11.97	17.94	25.05	55.03
1991-92	8.75	18.06	23.04	59.35
1992-93	10.87	19.3	22.39	70.14
1993-94	11.89	13.1	21.28	60.23
1994-95	12.79	13.96	16.43	59.16
1995-96	13.12	14.59	17.12	59.66
1996-97	11.8	15.44	15.36	50.11
1997-98	10.72	15.6	14.05	62.79
1998-99	3.55	3.64	5.79	#
1999-00	3.54	3.81	5.42	#
2000-01	3.78	3.63	5.35	#
2001-02	3.42	3.82	5.38	#
2002-03	2.87	3.82	5.29	#
2003-04	2.47	3.79	4.74	#
2004-05	1.57	3.48	4.47	#

category merged with cotton textile from 1998 onwards

(Labour output as percentage of ex-factory value of output in selected industries)

INTER-REGIONAL COMPARISON OF PRODUCTIVITY, LABOUR COST AND WAGES IN COTTON TEXTILE, JUTE, STEEL AND SUGAR FOR THE PERIOD 1980-2004

Inter-Regional Comparison in Cotton Textile

Labour cost as expressed in percentage of value of output has been calculated region wise and is presented for the selected industries below. The table 6.2 presents the comparative figures across regions of manufacturing of cotton textile industry.

Table 6.2: Inter Regional Comparison of Labour Cost in Cotton Textile Industry

	Delhi	Maharashtra	Madhya Pradesh	West Bengal	Uttar Pradesh	Tamilnadu	Andhra Pradesh	Rajasthan	Punjab
1980-81	52.94	36.06	43.62	43.34	35.09	25.94	19.96	17.24	10.7
1981-82	49.23	34.45	47.07	43.16	39.42	26.56	19.9	14.26	11.36
1982-83	53.11	37.89	42.89	41.77	36.92	25.51	18.62	17.65	10
1983-84	50.83	39.98	45.89	49.68	39.5	25.59	20.31	15.81	11.68
1984-85	50.83	39.28	48.78	44.34	38.42	24.41	20.13	17.27	9.93
1985-86	49.24	36.75	46.35	46.77	39.21	21.94	18.16	18.68	11.15
1986-87	49.7	41.37	49.69	48.77	46.64	25.95	21.77	17.36	10.67
1987-88	49.02	41.9	47.69	48.12	39.58	24.66	19.8	19.34	10.89
1988-89	32.4	38.08	42.61	48.7	38.06	22.37	14.43	13.63	11.36
1989-90	47.95	36.7	36.07	41.34	33.83	19.23	13.6	11.86	10.6
1990-91	37.58	34.49	36.62	45.57	39.99	18.96	13.85	12.93	9.84
1991-92	35.23	32.18	38.85	46.26	33.83	17.35	12.37	11:89	8.28
1992-93	32.68	34.6	29.64	36.72	39.39	16.61	12.86	11.86	9.95
1993-94	27.62	41.29	24.5	30.02	35.54	15.65	9.25	10.06	9.01
1994-95	22.92	28.84	13.76	29.26	26.08	13.55	10.15	9.72	6.58
1995-96	25.8	28.72	12.44	33.77	27.33	14.05	11.05	10.1	8.72
1996-97	28.65	28.68	8.63	36.15	27.97	14.22	19.45	8.9	9.19
1997-98	19.54	26.86	7.08	19.84	20.98	12.45	6.47	9.52	10.22
1998-99	3.75	6.53	13.99	23.26	7.38	4.68	4.75	4.09	3.19
1999-00	3.29	6.18	4.44	19.66	6.17	5.17	5.23	3.59	2.25
2000-01	6.67	5.56	3.88	21.69	4.85	4.92	5.04	3.78	3.43
2001-02	6.13	6.3	3.82	21.35	4.87	4.73	6	3.9	3.94
2002-03	2.27	5.83	3.5	21.6	4.93	4.5	4.76	3.57	3.1
2003-04	0.94	5.09	3.57	20.17	3.99	3.79	4.42	3.48	2.93
2004-05	7.79	4.34	3.09	19.97	3.33	3.31	6.06	3.34	2.72

(Labour output as percentage of ex-factory value of output in selected industries)

In the time period of 1980-81 to 1997-98, there are two different sets of regional groups on the basis of labour cost. Set one consists of Delhi, Maharashtra, Madhya Pradesh, West Bengal and Uttar Pradesh. In this set the proportion of labour cost is higher than the other set. In 1980s the highest cost was in Delhi (53%) and lowest in this set was of Uttar Pradesh (35%). The proportion of labour cost moderated to similar structures after 1989 onwards averaging to 30%. Historically 1942-1962 period also has the same set of regions in high proportional labour cost (Maheshwari, 1968). Madhya Pradesh is the only region which belong first to the high cost region set and after 1989 onwards moved to the lower proportion of labour cost regions in set two. Set two consist of Tamilnadu, Andhra Pradesh, Rajasthan and Punjab. This set in 1980s has highest cost proportion in Tamilnadu (26%) and lest in Punjab (10%). The proportion of labour cost moderated to similar structures after 1989 onwards averaging to 12%.

Generally, keeping other factors constant, it seems that there exists a direct relationship between the wages and labour cost. The table 6.3, present the wage cost figures. The association between these figures in table 6.2 and table 6.3 is negative.

Table 6.3: Inter Regional Comparison of Wage Cost per Worker in Cotton Textile Industry

	Delhi	Maharashtra	Madhya Pradesh	West Bengal	Uttar Pradesh	Tamilnadu	Andhra Pradesh	Rajasthan	Punjab
1980-81	78.17	78.71	67.15	72.91	73.99	78.28	39.5	55.66	42.83
1981-82	84.33	82.13	70.46	76.72	85.53	82.17	42.93	58.4	49
1982-83	113.22	79.98	83.25	88.73	88.65	89.46	50.19	72.16	47.87
1983-84	127.15	108.41	96.52	95.57	106.65	98.17	63.91	76.35	57.36
1984-85	127.15	124.94	107.31	104.04	108.73	107.17	72.92	83.11	50.8
1985-86	136.71	138.94	108.13	120.18	121.19	107.16	66.9	88.43	69.27
1986-87	146.71	161.85	120.29	135.6	128.65	125.62	81.79	100.41	73.65
1987-88	191.26	161.39	118.64	147.7	135.63	146.48	90.78	107.85	86.91
1988-89	217.31	180.34	141.53	153.05	143.41	172.44	87.57	104	88.39
1989-90	211.99	198.3	155.17	168.59	163.74	180.16	102.76	114.36	130.28
1990-91	234.9	232.85	162.81	189.27	184.59	200.16	110.67	162.02	136.14
1991-92	225.41	275.77	162.32	208.93	163.74	215.72	118.62	178.76	162.98
1992-93	263.56	291.2	170.77	254.97	209.07	262.49	141.89	193.24	180.05
1993-94	301.51	293.57	181.5	257.9	234.84	261.06	141.59	211.76	185.18
1994-95	307.62	364.28	183.62	290.12	235.5	295.74	171.31	231.33	199.62
1995-96	354.8	368.81	180.17	331.72	282.02	352.64	190.75	254.03	236.76
1996-97	254.64	377.06	190.79	347.55	302.23	361.94	200.72	259.44	278.45
1997-98	266.28	413.26	208.54	349.07	321.12	347.22	190.71	288.96	267.13
1998-99	280	501.33	212.98	478.64	359.76	334.71	318.6	321.38	299.64
1999-00	327.2	5227.73	409.34	502.83	370	323.8	365.04	324.55	322.57
2000-01	365.94	553.63	441.11	532.02	427.5	361.91	369.01	381.78	354.44
2001-02	316.55	539.09	452.55	588.63	472.35	340.92	286.5	378.88	373.18
2002-03	406.25	567.95	461.92	601.47	493.07	348.73	336.12	381.6	355.45
2003-04	411.61	566.33	514.23	580.1	412.83	341.67	368.65	390.98	384.61
2004-05	436.78	586.11	516.43	584.65	446.53	346.57	386.42	417.23	430.39

(Values in Rs. 000 per worker)

Table 6.4 below presents the output per man hour, generally based on collective bargaining of labour for share in productivity indicate that there is a direct relationship between productivity and wage. This general principle is evident in the table 6.3 and table 6.4 where the association between Delhi and Maharashtra is weaker than other region.

Table 6.4: Inter Regional Comparison of Output per Man-hour in Cotton Textile Industry

	Delhi	Maharastra	Madhya Pradesh	West Bengal	Uttar Pradesh	Tamilnadu	Andhra Pradesh	Rajasthan	Punjab
1980-81	0.14	0.2	0.14	0.15	0.17	0.25	0.2	0.32	0.35
1981-82	0.15	0.23	0.14	0.15	0.18	0.26	0.23	0.38	0.35
1982-83	0.16	0.22	0.17	0.18	0.2	0.28	0.27	0.36	0.46
1983-84	0.21	0.23	0.18	0.16	0.21	0.3	0.27	0.42	0.41
1984-85	0.21	0.27	0.18	0.2	0.23	0.35	0.31	0.44	0.52
1985-86	0.24	0.32	0.2	0.21	0.25	0.4	0.33	0.53	0.54
1986-87	0.26	0.32	0.22	0.25	0.22	0.38	0.33	0.51	0.62
1987-88	0.3	0.33	0.23	0.26	0.29	0.46	0.4	0.53	0.67
1988-89	0.43	0.4	0.3	0.29	0.31	0.6	0.58	0.76	0.71
1989-90	0.49	0.47	0.36	0.36	0.4	0.73	0.69	0.92	1.02
1990-91	0.47	0.56	0.4	0.35	0.39	0.79	0.72	1.07	1.23
1991-92	0.53	0.7	0.39	0.39	0.4	1.01	0.9	1.3	1.73
1992-93	0.63	0.76	0.61	0.58	0.47	1.18	0.96	1.41	1.67
1993-94	0.85	0.64	0.75	0.72	0.61	1.31	1.42	1.93	1.85
1994-95	1.1	1.16	1.3	0.84	0.86	1.68	1.52	2.07	2.77
1995-96	1.16	1.11	1.4	0.84	0.86	1.75	1.57	2.25	2.34
1996-97	1.04	1.16	2.31	0.84	0.91	1.91	0.92	2.66	2.51
1997-98	6.95	1.41	3.48	1.33	1.62	2.36	2.71	2.68	2.19
1998-99	1.9	2.07	1.02	0.72	1.55	2.05	1.9	2.07	2.47
1999-00	2.66	2.21	2.4	0.83	1.75	1.83	2	2.41	3.83
2000-01	1.56	2.67	3	0.81	2.49	2.14	2.13	2.65	2.76
2001-02	1.71	2.35	3.2	0.85	2.69	2.12	1.45	2.62	2.58
2002-03	5.23	2.66	3.63	0.88	2.78	2.25	2.16	2.89	3.21
2003-04	10.67	3.11	3.91	0.91	3.07	2.65	2.39	3.03	3.71
2004-05	1.9	3.7	4.55	0.93	3.76	3.04	1.93	3.33	4.32

(Values in Rs. 000 per hour)

Productivity figures in different region show that improvement in productivity is highest for Punjab, then Rajasthan and lowest in West Bengal. Madhya Pradesh has moved rapidly up since 1989 clocking highest in productivity in year 1997-98. The faster improvement in productivity of labour has been one of the causative factors that reduce labour cost in certain regions in spite of higher wages.

Regional differential of labour cost are also caused by variation in the techniques of production. Techniques of production determine the proportion of each factor. In some regions the industry is highly mechanized and therefore has greater proportion of capital and lower proportion of labour than the regions where industry is not so mechanized. Naturally the labour cost will be lower in regions where the capital labour ratios are high and will be higher where capital labour ratios are low. Table 6.5 presents the interregional capital labour ratio figures. The table below indicates that the negative association labour cost is strong in all regions and relatively weaker in Maharashtra and West Bengal.

Table 6.5: Inter Regional Comparison of Capital Labour Ratio Cotton Textile Industry

	Delhi	Maharastra	Madhya Pradesh	West Bengal	Uttar Pradesh	Tamilnadu	Andhra Pradesh	Rajasthan	Punjab
1980-81	0.07	0.12	0.07	0.1	0.13	0.16	0.1	0.12	0.13
1981-82	0.07	0.12	0.07	0.11	0.15	0.2	0.13	0.13	0.17
1982-83	0.12	0.18	0.09	0.15	0.15	0.24	0.13	0.18	0.16
1983-84	0.17	0.21	0.12	0.15	0.17	0.27	0.23	0.24	0.23
1984-85	0.17	0.22	0.13	0.16	0.2	0.31	0.25	0.29	0.25
1985-86	0.14	0.22	0.15	0.17	0.34	0.34	0.29	0.32	0.32
1986-87	0.16	0.25	0.19	0.2	0.24	0.36	0.3	0.32	0.28
1987-88	0.16	0.27	0.16	0.24	0.28	0.37	0.33	0.3	0.38
1988-89	0.16	0.35	0.18	0.27	0.25	0.48	0.32	0.27	0.37
1989-90	0.24	0.38	0.21	0.38	0.3	0.47	0.43	0.23	0.39
1990-91	0.16	0.46	0.18	0.24	0.36	0.7	0.43	0.3	0.55
1991-92	0.18	0.63	0.28	0.28	0.3	0.78	0.48	0.44	0.74
1992-93	0.36	0.75	0.52	0.43	0.39	0.99	0.67	0.54	0.74
1993-94	0.53	0.82	1.04	0.51	0.53	1.17	0.77	0.44	1.16
1994-95	0.73	1.52	2.04	0.87	0.79	1.52	0.91	0.81	1.54
1995-96	0.81	1.59	1.68	1	1.37	2.01	1.41	1.27	1.58
1996-97	0.89	1.59	1.97	0.94	1.96	2.62	1.34	1.85	1.82
1997-98	1.65	1.64	2.82	4.14	6.8	2.19	1.76	1.12	1.93
1998-99	1.45	5.01	4.41	0.68	3.44	2.97	6.22	4.02	6.81
1999-00	0.76	47.99	5.24	0	4.9	3.33	5.63	3.49	7.68
2000-01	1.15	5.27	7.23	0.83	6.23	2.98	5.31	3.53	4.64
2001-02	0.81	5.51	7.78	0.85	7.25	3.06	3.41	4.23	4.64
2002-03	2.81	7.72	7.2	0.87	6.21	3.57	5.21	3.81	5.69
2003-04	2.55	5.95	7.8	1.01	7.27	3.58	5.41	3.88	5.64
2004-05	0.86	6.97	7.77	0.93	8.25	4.27	3.86	4.11	6.76

(Values in Rs. lakh per thousand workers)

Inter-Regional Comparison in Jute

Labour cost as expressed in percentage of value of output has been calculated region wise and is presented for the Jute industry below. The table 6.6 presents the comparative figures across regions of manufacturing of jute industry. The table 6.7, present the wage cost figures. Table 6.8 presents the output per man hour and Table 6.9 presents the interregional capital labour ratio figures.

Table 6.6: Inter Regional Comparison of Labour Cost in Jute Industry

	Andhra Pradesh	Uttar Pradesh	West Bengal
1980-81	31.35	39.04	52.42
1981-82	34.89	45.89	58.54
1982-83	40.95	41.99	60.98
1983-84	39.66	41.99	60.98
1984-85	38.29	35.43	48.19
1985-86	28.01	19.29	48.96
1986-87	46.65	7.64	70.19
1987-88	54.72	46.35	72.95
1988-89	48.39	35.17	65.99
1989-90	36.23	49.61	59.09
1990-91	38.1	35.56	57.28
1991-92	41.63	35.56	31.37
1992-93	42.36	53.76	72.75
1993-94	39.74	41.82	62.57
1994-95	41.72	22.97	59.93
1995-96	37.51	41	61.31
1996-97	43.32	41.12	55.19
1997-98	47.76	55.46	64.08

Category merged with cotton textile from 1998 onwards, (Labour output as percentage of ex-factory value of output in selected industries)

Table 6.7: Inter Regional Comparison of Wage Cost per Worker in Jute Industry

	Andhra Pradesh	Uttar Pradesh	West Bengal
1980-81	64.79	61.8	77.59
1981-82	70	77.42	81.3
1982-83	73.69	75.02	83.8
1983-84	81.61	75.02	83.8
1984-85	87.84	126.66	108.69
1985-86	112.6	128.74	135.77
1986-87	123.07	86.43	153.12
1987-88	153.31	180.89	146.72
1988-89	155.93	175.62	175.52
1989-90	122.93	200.9	196.08
1990-91	185.3	237.36	228.21
1991-92	185.84	237.36	234.4
1992-93	184.61	296.49	279.59
1993-94	246.85	278.07	312.3
1994-95	303.97	328.92	328.61
1995-96	350.78	284.26	363.46
1996-97	292.74	385.12	403.23
1997-98	400.92	456.98	490.57

(Values in Rs. 000 per worker)

Table 6.8: Inter Regional Comparison of Output per Man-hour in Jute Industry

	Andhra Pradesh	Uttar Pradesh	West Bengal
1980-81	0.16	0.15	0.12
1981-82	0.15	0.14	0.12
1982-83	0.14	0.17	0.12
1983-84	0.16	0.17	0.12
1984-85	0.18	0.26	0.2
1985-86	0.31	0.54	0.22
1986-87	0.2	1.28	0.18
1987-88	0.19	0.3	0.17
1988-89	0.24	0.42	0.22
1989-90	0.36	0.33	0.27
1990-91	0.35	0.54	0.32
1991-92	0.36	0.54	0.32
1992-93	0.38	0.45	0.33
1993-94	0.46	0.58	0.39
1994-95	0.52	1.22	0.44
1995-96	0.74	0.88	0.48
1996-97	0.68	0.68	0.58
1997-98	0.81	0.48	0.64

(Values in Rs. 000 per hour)

Table 6.9: Inter Regional Comparison of Capital Labour Ratio Jute Industry

	Andhra Pradesh	Uttar Pradesh	West Bengal
1980-81	0.05	0.04	0.04
1981-82	0.05	0.06	0.04
1982-83	0.05	0.07	0.05
1983-84	0.07	0.07	0.05
1984-85	0.06	0.11	0.07
1985-86	0.07	0.35	0.08
1986-87	0.11	0.89	0.07
1987-88	0.13	0.47	0.11
1988-89	0.14	0.39	0.22
1989-90	0.15	0.36	0.21
1990-91	0.15	0.41	0.28
1991-92	0.17	0.41	0.3
1992-93	0.24	0.32	0.24
1993-94	0.18	0.94	0.29
1994-95	0.22	3.11	0.31
1995-96	0.27	0.95	0.39
1996-97	0.24	0.67	0.46
1997-98	0.32	0.8	0.39

(Values in Rs. lakh per thousand workers)

Table 6.6 indicates that the proportion of labour cost is highest in West Bengal and lowest in Uttar Pradesh. The association between the wages and labour cost indicated by figures in table 6.6 and table 6.7 is positive in Uttar Pradesh and Andhra Pradesh (r= .329, .327 respectively) and weak positive in West Bengal (r=.109). Association between wage cost and productivity is very high in Andhra Pradesh and West Bengal (r=.958 and .987) and weak in Uttar Pradesh (r=.395). Association between labour cost and capital labour ratio is positive in Andhra Pradesh (r=.386) and negative in Uttar Pradesh(r=-.35) and West Bengal (r=-04).

Inter-Regional Comparison in Steel

Labour cost as expressed in percentage of value of output has been calculated region wise and is presented for the Steel industry below. The table 6.10 presents the comparative figures across regions of manufacturing of steel industry. The table 6.11, present the wage cost figures. Table 6.12 below presents the output per man hour and Table 6.13 presents the interregional capital labour ratio figures.

Table 6.10: Inter Regional Comparison of Labour Cost in Steel Industry

	Andhra Pradesh	Bihar	Delhi	Karnataka	Maharashtra	Punjab	Uttar Pradesh	West Bengal
1980-81	9.85	23.57	4.17	15.24	8.36	4.43	7	25.67
1981-82	6.87	16.3	5.1	14.27	7.69	4.63	6.98	23.69
1982-83	5.29	14.36	4.03	15.48	8.63	4.7	6.88	24.32
1983-84	6.03	18.84	175.44*	15.48	10.4	5.3	6.88	24.32
1984-85	5.57	15.76	3.42	17.44	9.49	4.93	7.14	35.57
1985-86	5.91	17.04	3.24	18.02	9.04	4.51	4.63	25.43
1986-87	5.83	19.37	4.04	16.29	7.69	4.14	6.71	30.42
1987-88	6.68	19.8	4.05	14.5	8.43	4.58	6.81	29.18
1988-89	6.62	20.59	4.74	15.28	7.07	4.55	5.07	25.55
1989-90	4.54	19.29	4.51	13.71	6.57	3.49	4.74	29.45
1990-91	7.74	15.05	3.99	12.63	6.43	3.32	4.23	28.27
1991-92	10.11	6.22	3.51	11.73	6.37	3.45	4.23	26.54
1992-93	9.14	14.14	3.38	13.46	5.13	3.95	3.48	25.4
1993-94	10.24	20	3.52	11.68	5.59	3.61	3.3	29.63
1994-95	8.8	20.36	6.31	8.69	6.49	3.72	3.3	26.47
1995-96	8.65	20.48	4.46	8.69	4.85	3.56	3.25	29.63
1996-97	8.19	21.58	4.34	12.69	5.31	3.54	3.15	28.71
1997-98	6.77	14.32	2.29	12.29	5.74	3.08	2.45	25.24
1998-99	3.82	159.19*	1.06	2.43	6.86	1.05	0.85	15.66
1999-00	3.57	0.68	3.45	2.6	1.77	1.32	1.2	11.11
2000-01	4.55	0.96	1.25	1.92	2.02	1.01	0.79	7.35
2001-02	3.79	0.96	1.57	1.5	1.81	0.88	0.41	4.86
2002-03	3.32	0.86	2.28	1.32	1.41	0.92	0.53	5.57
2003-04	2.69	1.36	1.33	1.19	1.01	0.77	0.46	4.8
2004-05	2.44	1.03	2.43	0.85	0.75	0.64	0.34	3.13

(Labour output as percentage of ex-factory value of output in selected industries), *unusual low value of output reported.

Table 6.11: Inter Regional Comparison of Wage Cost per Worker in Steel Industry

	Andhra Pradesh	Bihar	Delhi	Karnataka	Maharashtra	Punjab	Uttar Pradesh	West Bengal
1980-81	23.89	134.91	42.72	104.31	85.52	44.13	47.58	132.59
1981-82	54.62	152.57	65.28	98.6	94.25	53.67	54.85	152.73
1982-83	71.83	188.5	62.94	109	123.56	55.42	60.49	166.07
1983-84	72.51	192.39	61.74	77.16	142.63	72.41	60.49	83.79
1984-85	79.74	200.33	66.38	154.53	158.48	75.18	78.4	225.24
1985-86	94.07	238.55	70.55	170.97	175.67	79.95	79.33	202.18
1986-87	100.57	211.17	80.54	191.31	202.05	94.18	104.42	238.89
1987-88	96.03	250.51	88.05	184.74	210.95	100.02	107.73	262.55
1988-89	94.46	316.01	115.1	243.17	257.06	107.27	129.22	299.16
1989-90	98.73	387.42	140.86	280.41	265.88	127.51	145.32	304.9
1990-91	115.58	426.22	130.47	321.83	297.27	144.99	161.19	334.1
1991-92	140.83	143.26	186.38	330.21	336.52	169.93	161.19	369.82
1992-93	292.75	128.94	181.15	389.89	337.27	176.7	173.95	390.18
1993-94	365.66	853.85	207.42	422.6	360.11	192.45	172.96	454.94
1994-95	415.6	922.83	251.38	425.18	450.01	215.61	172.96	469.44
1995-96	435.77	959.05	263.35	425.18	471.3	254.09	174.94	625.85
1996-97	1151.79	1112.86	250.84	514.02	451.74	255.24	207.61	625.84
1997-98	1066.13	1158.87	257.98	546.83	533.68	271.27	212.3	635.07
1998-99	736.37	898.62	289.53	887.6	554.46	281.83	304.14	684.25
1999-00	789.24	137.94	297.46	672.73	543.71	284.58	259.91	1095.97
2000-01	1275.84	194.22	339.85	727.89	632.09	289.62	329.36	876.02
2001-02	1102.06	177.3	322.3	616.9	669.42	295.69	299.28	865.98
2002-03	1320.17	199.57	355.65	782.07	796.99	325.73	400	1004.33
2003-04	1446.89	220.99	400.57	1019.05	821.36	372.67	409.83	1015.45
2004-05	1332.23	187.42	380.37	965.96	894.25	381.19	399.37	1156.53

(Values in Rs. 000 per worker)

Table 6.12: Inter Regional Comparison of Output per Man-hour in Steel Industry

	Andhra Pradesh	Bihar	Delhi	Karnataka	Maharashtra	Punjab	Uttar Pradesh	West Bengal
1980-81	0.36	0.45	1	0.59	1.07	1.07	0.76	0.45
1981-82	0.89	0.75	1.03	0.6	1.26	1.2	0.87	0.56
1982-83	1.47	1.02	1.52	0.62	1.46	1.25	0.91	0.6
1983-84	1.26	0.79	0.01	0.46	1.29	1.26	0.91	0.32
1984-85	1.46	1.1	2	0.77	1.61	1.46	0.96	0.54
1985-86	1.59	1.07	2.25	0.86	1.85	1.64	1.65	0.61
1986-87	1.69	0.86	1.99	1.03	2.36	2.04	1.45	0.62
1987-88	1.39	0.95	2.14	1.17	2.26	1.86	1.5	0.71
1988-89	1.38	1.18	2.34	1.54	3.45	2.15	2.36	1
1989-90	1.96	1.64	3.24	2.09	3.91	3.37	3.07	0.91
1990-91	1.34	2.34	3.46	2.56	4.62	4.36	3.93	1.1
1991-92	1.25	2.63	5.19	2.58	5.16	4.62	3.93	1.35
1992-93	2.95	2.55	5.42	2.74	6.79	3.93	4.97	1.44
1993-94	3.16	3.44	6.06	3.5	6.55	5.1	5.6	1.34
1994-95	4.15	3.65	4.1	4.54	6.75	5.8	5.6	1.6
1995-96	4.37	3.88	5.86	4.54	9.6	6.93	7.19	1.96
1996-97	6.55	4.01	6.32	4.73	8.97	7.08	6.98	2.04
1997-98	43.18	5.99	11.69	3.9	9.21	8.05	7.05	2.29
1998-99	4.66	0.13	7.73	8.69	7.03	7.26	9.07	1.32
1999-00	5.93	8	2.64	6.84	0.03	6.36	6.37	2.52
2000-01	6.98	6	8.09	9.59	7.95	8.14	10.96	3.02
2001-02	7.37	5.61	5.97	10.7	8.95	9.39	19.36	4.34
2002-03	10.03	7.14	4.97	15.38	13.61	9.98	17.96	4.44
2003-04	13.26	5.05	8.38	20	19.38	13.52	23.09	5.21
2004-05	13.78	5.62	4.78	27.78	28.66	16.59	27.98	9.24

(Values in Rs. 000 per hour)

Table 6.13: Inter Regional Comparison of Capital Labour Ratio Steel Industry

	Andhra Pradesh	Bihar	Delhi	Karnataka	Maharashtra	Punjab	Uttar Pradesh	West Bengal
1980-81	0.23	2.91	0.11	0.59	0.59	0.15	0.31	0.64
1981-82	0.83	3.13	0.26	0.52	0.36	0.17	0.32	0.91
1982-83	1.81	3.79	0.34	0.55	0.66	0.21	0.31	1.09
1983-84	1.1	3.85	0.01	0.39	0.79	0.27	0.31	0.55
1984-85	2.29	4.16	0.38	0.83	0.91	0.3	0.41	1.27
1985-86	1.76	3.93	0.36	0.88	0.96	0.3	0.49	1.54
1986-87	1.37	3.35	0.37	1.03	1.13	0.39	0.66	1.28
1987-88	1.37	3.33	0.49	1.12	1.1	0.36	1.06	1.39
1988-89	1.26	3.5	0.71	1.09	2.81	0.47	0.97	2
1989-90	1.51	4.51	0.57	1.01	4.43	0.52	1.05	2.9
1990-91	27.14	4.98	0.66	1.18	5.31	0.64	1.34	3.89
1991-92	29.07	7.18	1.01	1.75	7.18	0.84	1.34	8.03
1992-93	37.2	6.12	1.19	2.49	7.13	1.18	1.62	9.56
1993-94	35.27	10.39	2.23	4.85	11.05	1.94	3.68	10.61
1994-95	33.84	11.08	8.74	7	12.54	1.99	3.68	10.95
1995-96	26.52	12.22	2.33	7	20.52	2.07	4.54	13.13
1996-97	9.6	14.47	1.34	6.51	24.99	2.16	4.95	13.03
1997-98	27.05	14.68	9.25	13.11	24.93	2.79	6.82	12.38
1998-99	31.1	0.11	1.26	233.7	14.97	2.36	8.76	1.59
1999-00	23.54	8.08	1.11	74.24	22.55	1.9	24.6	12.01
2000-01	26.72	4.03	1.85	86.05	26.65	3.92	58.87	11.15
2001-02	24.76	4.37	1.53	75.09	32.52	3.53	19.21	13.15
2002-03	33.62	2.83	1.16	84.22	45.18	3.61	26.71	12.64
2003-04	30.52	2.13	1.5	112.19	67.38	3.63	17.96	11.91
2004-05	25.83	2.66	1.33	77.8	56.67	5.1	21.76	13.67

(Values in Rs. lakh per thousand workers)

Table 6.10 indicates that the proportion of labour cost is highest in West Bengal and lowest in Punjab and Delhi. The association between the wages and labour cost indicated by figures in table 6.10 and table 6.11 is positive in Bihar (r= .39) and positive in all other regions whereas it is weakest in Delhi (r= -.264). Association between wage cost and productivity is very high in Punjab and Uttar Pradesh (r=.954 and .917) and weak in Bihar (r=.113). Association between labour cost and capital labour ratio is meagerly positive in Andhra Pradesh (r=.0183) and negative in other states highest in Punjab (r= -.886) and Maharashtra (r= -.878) and lowest in Bihar(r= -.215).

Inter-Regional Comparison in Sugar

Labour cost as expressed in percentage of value of output has been calculated region wise and is presented for the Steel industry below. The table 6.14 presents the comparative figures across regions of manufacturing of sugar industry. The table 6.15, present the wage cost figures. Table 6.16 below presents the output per man hour and Table 6.17 presents the interregional capital labour ratio figures.

Table 6.14: Inter Regional Comparison of Labour Cost in Sugar Industry

	Bihar	Maharashtra	Tamilnadu	Uttar Pradesh
1980-81	28.17	13.92	16.36	20.13
1981-82	24.78	9.71	14.2	17.01
1982-83	23.35	9.56	10.98	18.41
1983-84	18.15	11.28	10.98	18.41
1984-85	35.03	18.27	18.27	20.52
1985-86	36.23	12.42	15.69	21.04
1986-87	25.45	11.93	13.07	19.55
1987-88	25.75	13.91	13.84	18.49
1988-89	25.39	10.47	13.29	17.63
1989-90	21.34	12.83	12.88	17.67
1990-91	24.25	12.2	13.72	18.19
1991-92	19.61	13.29	14.13	18.19
1992-93	25.19	13.66	13.3	17.83
1993-94	23.77	11.93	13.36	15.49
1994-95	21.34	10.3	11.42	13.95
1995-96	16.43	12.59	11.01	14.99
1996-97	18.36	13.32	12.38	16.98
1997-98	16.27	14	13.74	14.39
1998-99	4.81	3.58	4.45	4.6
1999-00	4.57	3.66	3.13	4.22
2000-01	4.59	3.35	3.42	3.79
2001-02	5.36	3.62	3.84	3.8
2002-03	5.98	3.78	3.96	3.91
2003-04	6.21	4.12	3.67	3.55
2004-05	6.38	3.33	4.1	3.22

(Labour output as percentage of ex-factory value of output in selected industries)

Table 6.15: Inter Regional Comparison of Wage Cost per Worker in Sugar Industry

	Bihar	Maharashtra	Tamilnadu	Uttar Pradesh
1980-81	17.24	29.63	32.39	20.34
1981-82	18.03	40.31	41.51	24.17 .
1982-83	39.65	64.86	71.97	37.31
1983-84	82.19	99.93	71.97	37.31
1984-85	108.25	114.36	147.39	58.79
1985-86	119.49	124.84	160.99	61.98
1986-87	129.64	132.42	183.82	70.6
1987-88	158.57	156.65	188.05	87.86
1988-89	177.07	187.11	226.62	100.82
1989-90	186.82	232.44	271.25	103.31
1990-91	184.72	265.35	290.47	137.32
1991-92	258.85	277.38	338.7	137.32
1992-93	273.63	311.22	377.57	174.46
1993-94	279.79	352.12	416.71	180.74
1994-95	317.58	416.58	503.96	217.83
1995-96	431.11	488.98	562.4	233.48
1996-97	386.91	675.82	585.73	269.64
1997-98	687.56	503.88	583.44	290.34
1998-99	466.75	554.96	209.78	349.64
1999-00	444.31	565.57	246.61	315.96
2000-01	492.25	558.06	266.7	379.28
2001-02	550.19	604.64	268.26	409.45
2002-03	527.96	572.01	271.32	423.37
2003-04	588.16	563.41	269	418.19
2004-05	595.56	589.2	281.61	432.3

(Values in Rs. 000 per worker)

Table 6.16: Inter Regional Comparison of Output per Man-hour in Sugar Industry

	Bihar	Maharashtra	Tamilnadu	Uttar Pradesh
1980-81	0.25	0.58	0.49	0.24
1981-82	0.36	0.88	0.64	0.31
1982-83	0.37	1.09	0.95	0.34
1983-84	0.51	0.98	0.95	0.34
1984-85	0.33	0.91	0.76	0.36
1985-86	0.34	1.16	1.07	0.39
1986-87	0.55	1.26	1.38	0.46
1987-88	0.58	1.28	1.29	0.54
1988-89	0.66	1.76	1.56	0.61
1989-90	0.85	1.92	2.09	0.76
1990-91	0.8	2.2	2.03	0.87
1991-92	1.3	2.2	2.31	0.87
1992-93	1.05	2.6	2.94	1.14
1993-94	1.24	3.28	3.33	1.44
1994-95	1.58	4.39	4.57	1.89
1995-96	2.74	4.04	5.21	1.95
1996-97	2.11	4.39	4.61	2.1
1997-98	2.21	3.34	3.79	2.02
1998-99	1.99	3.1	1.57	2.63
1999-00	2.5	3.41	2.4	2.50
2000-01	2.68	3.61	2.42	3.19
2001-02	2.89	3.59	2.23	3.41
2002 03	2.64	3.4	2.24	3.29
2003-04	2.55	3.05	2.4	3.7
2004-05	2.67	3.67	2.23	4.19

(Values in Rs. 000 per hour)

Table 6.17: Inter Regional Comparison of Capital Labour Ratio Sugar Industry

	Bihar	Maharashtra	Tamilnadu	Uttar Pradesh
1980-81	0.03	0.33	0.26	0.07
1981-82	0.03	0.35	0.28	0.08
1982-83	0.07	0.48	0.37	0.1
1983-84	0.14	0.8	0.37	0.1
1984-85	0.23	1.29	0.68	0.15
1985-86	0.44	1.12	0.81	0.19
1986-87	0.28	1.37	0.82	0.21
1987-88	0.31	1.51	0.8	0.24
1988-89	0.35	1.36	1	0.28
1989-90	0.65	2.18	1.7	0.35
1990-91	0.59	1.98	5.17	0.5
1991-92	0.95	2.09	2.77	0.5
1992-93	0.97	2.54	3.42	0.59
1993-94	1.52	3.78	4.61	0.86
1994-95	1.9	3.94	4.08	1.35
1995-96	2.72	3.73	4.77	1.41
1996-97	2.35	4.06	5.32	1.8
1997-98	4.32	4.65	6.12	2.06
1998-99	5.31	4.75	1.8	3.22
1999-00	6.08	4.25	2.43	3.18
2000-01	7.27	4.56	2.42	4.89
2001-02	6.78	5.7	2.64	4.27
2002-03	5.55	6.24	2.49	4.81
2003-04	5.83	7.52	2.53	4.2
2004-05	6.29	9.22	2.74	4.77

(Values in Rs. lakh per thousand workers)

Table 6.14 indicates that the proportion of labour cost is highest in Bihar and lowest in Maharashtra. The association between the wages and labour cost indicated by figures in table 6.14 and table 6.15 is negative, highest in Uttar Pradesh (r= -.923) and lowest, very weak, in Tamilnadu (r= -.06). Association between wage cost and productivity is very high in Andhra Pradesh and West Bengal (r=.958 and .987) and weak in Uttar Pradesh (r=.395). Association between labour cost and capital labour ratio is positive in Andhra Pradesh (r=.386) and negative in Uttar Pradesh(r=-.35) and West Bengal (r=-04).

SIZE-WISE COMPARISON OF LABOUR COST, TYPES OF OWNERSHIP

The table below present growth in the number of sugar factories registered in the country during 1982-95.

Table 6.18: Sugar Factories Active During 1982–95

	Pre-1947		1947-1990		1991-1995		Total	
	Private	Coop	Private	Coop	Private	Coop	Private	Coop
East UP	21	0	0	7	4	0	25	7
West UP	16	0	6	24	9	1	31	25
UP total	37	0	6	31	13	1	56	32
West Maharashtra	7	2	3	62	0	9	10	73
East Maharashtra	0	0	0	29	0	6	0	35
Maharashtra total	7	2	3	91	0	15	10	108

There were about 113 sugar factories in the UP state in March 2003 of which 45 were in the private sector, 37 in the public sector and 31 in the cooperative sector. During 2000-01, 47 sugar factories in eastern UP, 41 in central UP and 25 in western UP were in operation in the state.

Table 6.19: Sector-wise and zone-wise Establishment of Sugar Factories in U.P.

	Western			Central			Eastern		
Year	Private	Public	Coop.	Private	Public	Coop.	Private	Public	Coop.
Before 1960	9	7	1	10	5	1	17	17	Nil
1961-70	0	0	1	0	0	1	0	0	0
1971-80	1	0	3	1	3	7	0	3	3
1981-90	0	0	1	0	1	9	1	0	4
1991-02	1	1	0	3	0	0	2	0	0
Total	11	8	6	14	9	18	20	20	7

Table 6.20: Number of Factories, their Crushing Capacity and Crushing duration Across Various Sectors and zones of UP: 2001-02

Zone/Sector	Crushing Capacity (%) (TCD)	Crushing Duration (Days)	No. of Mills (%)
Eastern			
Public	23	129	43
Private	58	137	43
Co-operative	19	132	15
Total (numbers)	**86808**		**47**
Central			
Public	19	135	18
Private	47	142	47
Co-operative	34	139	35
Total (numbers)	**107636**		**41**

(Table Contd...)

Western			
Public	18	154	32
Private	67	162	44
Co-operative	16	161	24
Total (numbers)	**86829**		**25**

The private sector with 41 sugar factories had the crushing capacity of 159400 TCD, commanding nearly 55 per cent share in the total cane crushed, while the public and cooperative sectors had 20 and 25 per cent shares, respectively. This clearly reflects the lower capacity of plants in these two sectors. Most of the plants had the capacity of 2500 TCD or even less in these sectors, which eventually affected the performance of factories.

The crushing duration of factories across different zones of UP varied between 129 days and 162 days in 2000-01, with maximum in western zone, followed by central and eastern zones. The private sector generally crushed the cane for a longer period, than by co-operative and public sectors, contrary to the popular belief that the private sector is whimsical about their opening and closing dates of the cane crushing, coupled with lesser duration of operation.

The efficiency of sugar processing industry across various regions and sectors in UP was estimated by pooling the factory/firm-specific efficiencies. It is seen from Table below that the private sector factories in the western region belonged to the most efficient category (84.29%), while the cooperative sector mills in the eastern region were the least efficient, with efficiency level of around 60 per cent.

The average efficiency of cooperative sector was low due to the presence of few factories, operating at less than 50 per cent of the efficiency level. However, the public sector sugar factories had almost a similar efficiency range in all the three regions, highest (75.28%) being in the western region. Thus, public sector was found about 10 per cent more. (Singh, Singh, & Singh, 2007)

Table 6.21: Efficiency of Sugar Processing Industry Across Regions and Sectors in UP

Zone/Sector	Private	Public	Co-operative	Total
Central	79.37	73.87	66.31	73.18
	(70.42-88.25)	(63.79-80.72)	(58.72-79.39)	
Western	84.29	75.28	70.63	76.73
	(78.89-92.06)	(64.50-82.94)	(62.65-80.63)	
Eastern	80.30	70.83	60.82	70.65
	(75.75-86.97)	(61.87-77.57)	(45.24-72.99)	
Total	81.32	73.33	65.92	73.52

Note: Figures within the parentheses indicate efficiency ranges.

Region wise analysis in the table shows that the (real) sugar price dropped in UP and rose in Maharashtra during this period. The (real) cane price reported is the actual factory average for the Maharashtra coops, while for UP is the state advised price. The UP factories are supposed to pay this price, but often delay payments and accumulate substantial arrears. In Maharashtra the coops paid a higher average cane price than did the private factories. However we know that the cooperatives achieved higher cane quality and recovery rates, so it is not clear if coops paid a better price to their growers than the private factories once quality differences are adjusted for. Over time the statutory cane price in UP did not change in real terms, while the coops in Maharashtra paid better prices. Finally the price of the leading competing crop dropped in all regions, a factor which presumably stimulated growth of cane supplies.

Table 6.22: Cane Supply, Quality and Recovery Rates 1982-1995

	Annual Cane Crushed Factory Average ('000 quintals/year)		Pol Rate Factory Average (%)		Recovery Rate Factory Average (%)	
	Private	Coop	Private	Coop	Private	Coop
East UP 1982	2260	1018	12	11.74	82.48	83.25
East UP 1995	3992	1861	11.69	11.63	84.79	85.75
West UP 1982	4552	2369	12.22	11.65	82.76	84.24
West UP 1995	5968	3260	11.91	11.75	85.93	86.62
West Mah 1982	2824	4173	12.9	13.19	84.25	84.26
West Mah 1995	3153	5035	12.84	12.99	86.15	86.34
East Mah 1982	N.A.	2543	N.A.	12.25	N.A.	83.05
East Mah 1995	N.A.	2777	N.A.	12.16	N.A.	85.04

Table above presents average per-factory cane supply, quality and recovery rates for the different region-factory types in 1982 and 1995. In UP the private factories operated ona substantially larger scale than the coops, with the converse true in West Maharashtra. The UP private factories and the West Maharashtra coops had the biggest scales, with the former slightly bigger. The East Maharashtra coops were almost half the size of the West Maharashtra coops. Cane quality measured by the pol per cent — the single most important determinant of quality, as our production function estimates will show — were generally higher in Maharashtra than UP. In Maharashtra the coops had a higher pol rate than the privates, with the opposite true in UP. A similar cross-sectional comparison emerges for the factory recovery rate. Over time, however, the pol rate tended to decline, while the factory recovery rate improved.

In steel industry Capacity underutilization presents a major drawback, as in other industrial sectors. Capacity utilisation, as measured by total output divided by installed capacity multiplied by 100, has historically been fluctuating. From a low start in 1970-71 of 67 per cent average capacity utilisation, it increased to 75 per cent in 1980-81 and declined again thereafter to around 65 per cent in 1990-91. In 2000-01, however, it improved again to 79 per cent. It needs to be mentioned that the range of capacity utilisations amongst the plants is considerable. In 1970-71 it ranged between 40 per cent and 86 per cent, and in 1977-78 two plants even registered capacity utilisation of over 94 per cent. However, the capacity utilisation in mini steel plants is usually low largely due to inadequate supply of scrap and power.(Burange & Yamini, 2010)

Table 6.23: Capacity Utilisation of Crude Steel (%)

Year	Capacity Utilisation of Crude Steel (%)
1970-71	67
1980-81	75
1990-91	65
2000-01	79
2001-02	82
2002-03	86
2003-04	88
2004-05	91
2005-06	91
2006-07	89
2007-08	91

Source: JPC (2007) and Other Sources.

Industrial terminology defines 'size' as 'scale', meaning thereby the scale of production, output or of production. The size of an industrial unit is measured by any of the following criteria:

1. the size of the plant
2. the amount of capital invested
3. the volume of employment
4. the physical volume of production
5. the annual economic value of output
6. the quantity of raw material consumed.

Each of these has its own advantage and limitations. The accuracy, adequacy and utility of measurement depends upon the nature of the study and data available. In this study no of workers employed is been considered as the criteria of size.

Size wise labour cost has been analysed and is presented in the following table.

Table 6.24: Labour Cost in Iron and Steel Industry according to the Size of the Factory

Size	No. of Factories included in Sample	% of Labour Cost
Group-I: Small sized units (having less than 250 workers)	112	7.67
Group-II: Medium sized units (having 250 to 2000 workers)	16	10.99
Group-III: Large sized units (having 2000 to 5000 workers)	3	19.21
Group-IV: Largest size (having more than 5000 workers)	4	20.06

Table 6.25: Labour Cost in Cotton Textile Industry according to the Size of the Factory

Size	No. of Factories included in Sample	% of Labour Cost
Group-I: Small sized units (having less than 250 workers)	163	13.14
Group-II: Medium sized units (having 250 to 2000 workers)	220	21.96
Group-III: Large sized units (having 2000 to 5000 workers)	104	26.59
Group-IV: Largest size (having more than 5000 workers)	22	26.92

Table 6.26: Labour Cost in Sugar Industry according to the Size of the Factory

Size	No. of Factories included in Sample	% of Labour Cost
Group-I: Small sized units (having less than 250 workers)	37	12.65
Group-II: Medium sized units (having 250 to 2000 workers)	97	9.18
Group-III: Large sized units (having 2000 to 5000 workers)	43	10.43
Group-IV: Largest size (having more than 5000 workers)	3	12.20

Table 6.27: Labour Cost in Jute Industry according to the Size of the Factory

Size	No. of Factories included in Sample	% of Labour Cost
Group-I: Small sized units (having less than 250 workers)	1	20.22
Group-II: Medium sized units (having 250 to 2000 workers)	30	23.71
Group-III: Large sized units (having 2000 to 5000 workers)	58	21.05
Group-IV: Largest size (having more than 5000 workers)	7	21.37

A critical analysis of these tables suggest that large and largest size units have higher labour cost with exception being are Sugar industries where small units and Jute where medium sized units have highest labour cost.

TYPE OF OWNERSHIP AND LABOUR COST

The industrial units are operated in the form of sole trader ship, partnership, companies and cooperatives. In the table below the labour cost is calculated for different types of ownership.

Table 6.28: Labour Cost in Iron and Steel Industry according to the Type of Ownership

Ownership	No. of Factories included in Sample	% of Labour Cost
Sole Traders	16	8.78
Partnerships	76	7.11
Ltd. Companies		
Private	20	12.67
Public	21	19.34
Others	1	13.53

Table 6.29: Labour Cost in Cotton Textile Industry according to the Size of the Factory

Ownership	No. of Factories included in Sample	% of Labour Cost
Sole Traders	36	11.7
Partnerships	62	16.39
Ltd. Companies		
Private	68	19.42
Public	25	25.36
Others	18	25.27

Table 6.30: Labour Cost in Sugar Industry according to the Size of the Factory

Ownership	No. of Factories included in Sample	% of Labour Cost
Sole Traders	11	9.17
Partnerships	26	11.34
Ltd. Companies		
Private	26	10.53
Public	99	10.06
Others	18	6.57

Table 6.31: Labour Cost in Jute Industry according to the Size of the Factory

Ownership	No. of Factories included in Sample	% of Labour Cost
Sole Traders	1	22.89
Partnerships	1	26.69
Ltd. Companies		
Private	11	23.12
Public	83	21.28

The analysis of above tables lends support to the assumption that private firms are more efficient in using labour than other type of ownership. In iron and Steel and cotton textile industries the labour cost is lower in units run as sole trader ship or partnership than those run under cooperatives or public limited companies. The possible theoretical reason could be that the incentive of profit in private firms is more or less same as in partnership firms because the public is not invited to subscribe the shares.

In sugar industry, the labour cost is lowest in co-operatives, and lower in sole trader-ship firms than in partnership or private companies. In jute industry the labour cost is lowest in public ltd. Companies and highest in partnership firms. This exception result in jute industry may have statistical errors in its genesis because of sampling proportions.

The present investigation thus measures the proportion of labour cost to the total costs and identifies the factors which causes differences in labour cost industry to industry and within industry, from region to region and from one scale of production to another scale of production. It also suggests the factors which affect labour cost in different types of ownership, differences in wage rates, diversified rates of productivity growth, varying degrees of capital intensity and different profit initiatives are main factors that affect the labour cost.

The inter industry comparison of labour cost suggest that the potential of industry as a provider of employment is highest in cotton textile, lowest in sugar industry. The inter regional comparison of labour cost suggest, from the point of view of labour, that there are possibilities that industry can disperse to new locations in search of reduced labour costs.

7

Study of Variables Involved

Econometric model is considered for scientific study of the problem in hand. The cost of producing a commodity is dependent on quality of the product, volume of production, prices of the factors used in the production and rate of return under which the industry operates. The econometric model is supposed to estimate these relationships statistically. In order to know the combined as well as individual affects of all these factors, it is essential to establish certain models. The estimation of these models will explain the effect of individual factors on unit labour cost.

THE MODEL

It is postulated that unit labour cost (y), the dependent variable is function of various explanatory variables, x_1, x_2... x_n. In the linear regression form it can be expressed as:

$$y = a_0 + a_1x_1 + a_2x_2 + \dots + a_nx_n$$

Where 'y' is the dependent variable and 'x_i' is independent or explanatory variable, 'a_i' are known as the multiple regression coefficient which measures the impact of respective variable on unit labour cost.

EXPLANATORY VARIABLE

As explained in the conceptual analysis unit labour cost is not a simple function of wage rate but the resultant of many variables or factors. The direction of change in unit labour cost is mainly determined by conflicting or allied influence of Wages, Productivity, Volume of production, Technology Cost of other Input Factors, Rate of return, Trade Cycles, Labour Turnover. The influences of all these factors are studied independently.

1. **Wages:** The impact of wage change constitutes the primary factor that brings changes in labour cost. Wages have their direct and positive effect. If wages rise, unit labor cost must also rise and vice- versa. But in practice this is not always the case. First the wage adjustment may have direct effect on productivity. It is well known that increase in real wages improves the efficiency of the workers. If output per man hour is increased faster than wage rate, the fall in unit labour cost is implicit in spite of rising wages. Secondly, a wage adjustment may alter output per man hour by making it profitable for the industry to make minor or major changes in the manufacturing process, resulting in better combination of the input factors. Thirdly, rising wages may inspire the management to use labour more efficiently and economically by employing total quality management principles, identifying efficient workers and retrenching ill efficiency, thereby, bringing relatively profitable situation than the previous to wage increase.
2. **Productivity:** Labour productivity has inverse relationship with labour cost. Industries which have achieved greater increase in output per man-hour have been able to set off the effect of increased wages by getting a reduction in unit labour cost. What all other factors affect productivity would be dealt separately, it makes no difference whether higher productivity is achieved by increase in wages or by bringing technological changes, but unit labour cost is definitely affected by the variations in the productivity. The magnitude of the impact however depends upon the factors that bring productivity movements. Some factors cause productivity improvements without any extra remuneration to the labour. Certain examples to this are greater efficiency in labour management, improved methods of production. Some factors affect both productivity and labour compensation for example increase in efficiency of labour due to higher compensation as cause of higher motivation. Naturally, the impact on unit labour cost would greater in the former case than latter.
3. **Volume of Production:** In the industries every worker through its utilization has an annual-capacity-output, within the capacity boundaries the cost remain fixed, whether or not the labour is utilized or not. Therefore, so long as the volume of production remains smaller than the capacity of the worker engaged, the unit labour cost will also remain higher. So long as these being equal, the unit labour cost remains lower. Volume of labour also affects the unit labour cost in another way.

   In every industry there are two types of labour engagements-time related and job piece related. The cost of piece related work varies with volume of production but the cost of time related labour is fixed over wide range of output. the greater the output, the smaller would become the proportion of fixed labour cost. Hence, increase in the volume of production decreases the cost of labour per unit of the product.

According to the micro-economic point of view, the Government has guaranteed the working population with some minimum standards of living and formulates the policies to maintain reasonable level of employment. This has imposed a fixed cost of labour for the economy as a whole. Industries have to pay certain minimum wage and other facilities to their workers and cannot retrench them at will. These imposed burden of cost can be minimized per unit of product by increasing the volume of production. If volume of production remains below the capacity of workers, the unit labor cost witness increase.

4. **Technology:** Salter defined the rate of technological advance with reference to rate at which unit cost falls when factor price are constant. In general this corresponds to the improved methods of production which new technology makes possible. In absolute terms it is both labour saving in short term and capital saving in long term. It leads to a whole new range of alternate techniques within which it is possible to increase production. The saving on factor of production depends upon the rate or elasticity of substitution and nature of the invention.

   Some economists suggest that wage pressure may provide stimulus to reduce costs (Hicks). They believe that rise in wages relative to the rate of interest will induce the discovery of methods which saves labour. According to this theory the frequency of labour saving inventions depends upon the rate of increase in wages relative to the interest rates. On the other hand, Bloom and Northrup said "other economists, however, contend that because of the unpredictable nature of process of invention, wage increase do not necessarily call forth any increase in number of labour saving discoveries." According to this view most technological advances would be labour saving because of the continuing high cost of labour as an element of cost of production and because most inventions are designed to lighten the arduousness of work (Bloom & Northrup, 1958).

   Whatever the cause may be that bring technological changes- high wages, interest rate or any other economic or social motivations, it is true that most of the development aims to save labour, which in turn reduces the unit labour cost.

5. **Cost of input factors:** Unit labour cost is also affected by unit cost of other input factors. Unit labour cost is ratio of labour expenditure to the output. Where, output is constituent of all inputs, therefore, any disproportional change in the price of the input will affect he unit labour cost.

   In actual life, the price of some factors move slowly than some other factors of input. When there is non-proportional change in price of all input factors, unit labour cost is definitely affected cost of other input factors.

6. **Rate of return:** Unit cost of any factor depends on the rate of return, under which an industry is operating. It is a law of economics that increasing return implies decreasing cost whereas diminishing return implies increasing cost. If an industry is operating under increasing return, any increase in the scale of its production may reduce the unit cost of production, in spite of no change in the prices of the factors. On the other hand, if an industry is operating under diminishing return, any increase in its scale of production may increase the unit cost.

   Rate of return measure the extent to which fixed factor have been utilized. If fixed factors are not fully utilized another doses of variable factors are required to exploit the installed capacity of the industrial unit, which results in a more than proportional increase in production. Similarly, when certain factors are fully utilized and additional doses of variable factors are employed, the result will be smaller increase in production than the proportional increase in input. Thus, increasing return means under-use of the installed capacity and diminishing return means fuller use of the capacity.

   Labour is a variable factor rather than a fixed factor. In industries that are operating under increasing return, any increase in the number of the workers will improve the marginal productivity of labour and thereby reduce the cost of labour per unit of product. On the other hand, in industries which are operating under diminishing return any increase in the number of workers will decrease the marginal productivity of labour and thereby increase the average cost of labour per unit of output.

7. **Trade cycles:** cost of production is also influenced by what is going in the economy at large. Expanding business activity means rising demand for most commodities. It is very difficult for an industry to accommodate rising demand for its product without an increase in the cost of production. The management may find it necessary to employ inexperienced or otherwise less efficient workers in a booming labour market. Competition or fear of losing business during a strike may force up wages. All these developments tend to increase cost. On the other hand in a period of contracting business, management may be able to retrench its less efficient workers and will get workers at lower wages due to surplus labour in the market, which will reduce the cost of labour.

   While interpreting the impact of trade-cycles on labour cost, one should be cautious about the technical conditions of an industry. At the beginning of an expansion, many of the facilities in use must be working at less than their optimum capacity and an increase in production up to the most efficient level tend to lower labour cost in spite of paying higher wages. Similarly, the utilization of capacity below the efficient level during the contracting period may enhance the labour cost, in spite of low wages in the market.

8. **Labour Turnover:** It is evident that there will always have to be some 'mobility' in the working community, otherwise, it will stagnate; and to that extent there will also have to be some labour turn-over. It is the first approximation of the instability of the labour force. The constant flow of workers in and out of employment affects productivity and labour cost. On one hand, it reduces the output, on the other it increases the expenditure which is incurred on labour. Labour turnover therefore, has a severe effect on unit labour cost.

   It is very difficult to estimate the incidence of labour turn over on unit labour cost because its effects are manifold. They can be analysed under following heads:

   (*i*) Loss caused by outgoing worker:

   (*a*) Output lost due to Lower effort of the intending leavers;

   (*b*) Wastage and spoilage of work due to the apathy of the outgoing workers;

   (*c*) Level of output lowered because production workers are partly effective until the vacancies are filled;

   (*d*) Machinery stands idle due to the unfilled vacancies not offset by the reserves of the workers and surplus labour in other department;

   (*e*) Money lost, invested on the training of the outgoing workers; and

   (*f*) Financial loss incurred, as the ongoing workers generally give-out trade secrets to competitors.

   (*ii*) Replacement cost of labour turnover:

   (*a*) Recruitment expenses: these expenses involve charges of advertisement, test, selection and travelling allowances given to the prospective candidates for interview;

   (*b*) Training Expenses of the replaced workers;

   (*c*) Inefficiency of the new workers: Incoming replacements do not attain the experienced workers' level of production for some time (the degree of wasted effort being dependent on the requirements of the Job) and causes excessive scrap and waste;

   (*d*) Defective work: Inexperienced and new workers perform defective work. Where the material used is of high value, the cost of defective work may have serious repercussions on the cost of production.

   (*iii*) Preventive cost of labour turnover:

   (*a*) Personnel-administration: Extra staff is needed to maintain a good relationship between management and workers.

   (*b*) Prospects of extra-increment, promotion, welfare activities: the provision of these facilities is given in order to retain the services of the employees. The Psychological effect of having these prospects available is a reduction, however small, in labour turnover.

(*c*) Pension and Provident fund Schemes: The inherent desire for the security Of the future in the employment of industrial undertaking reduces labour turnover in establishments which provide pension and provident funds to their employees.

(*d*) Reserve of Labour force: To offset the disruptive effects of labonr turnover, a reserve is held in labour force.

The analysis of the cost of labour turnover depicts a phase of industrial phenomenon which has immense repercussions on the efficiency of the productive efforts and results in the incurrence of heavy expenditure with little or no return. Whatever difficulty may be in the segregation of these labour costs on a scientific basis as they are interwoven with the normal costs of production, it is necessary to consider labour turnover as one of the factors that affect unit-labour cost.

SELECTION OF VARIABLES

For the purpose of theoretical discussion, factors that affect unit labour cost may be extended to any number, but In the regression based models all of these cannot be included as explanatory variables, as it is difficult to measure all of them. Such variables may be trade cycles, efficiency or inefficiency of management, industrial Policy of the government and various labour laws. In practice it is very difficult to get data on these factors. Therefore, the only possible way is to select the most important variables and to introduce in the model a random variable whose behaviour is known. The random variable or disturbance term will represent the influence of all omitted factors.

The most important factors, such as wages, productivity, technological developments and costs of other inputs have been included as the explanatory variables of unit labour cost. Owing to the difficulty of measurement, rates of return and size of the industrial units (Volume of production) have been left in the present model.

Thus the model will be:

Unit Labour Cost (*ULC*) = *f* (*WA*, *UC*, *LP*, *CL*, *U*)

Where,

WA = Average wage Rate

UC = Unit material cost

LP = Labour productivity

CL = Intensity of capital (as pseudo measurement of technological changes)

U = Random Error or disturbance term

Let,

ULC = y

WA = x_1, UC = x_2, LP = x_3, CL = x_4

x_{ki} represents the value of x_k in the ith year

k = 1, 2, 3 and 4

The function in linear form can be written as:

$y_i = a_0 + a_1x_1 + a_2x_2 + a_3x_3 + a_4x_4 + u_i$

Where u_i follows normal distribution $N(0,\sigma^2)$

MEASUREMENT OF VARIABLES

The data published by ASI is considered in the study rather than the absolute values ratios are obtained to convert them to indices to achieve uniformity in units of measurement. This also facilitates better interpretation of the results. The calculation and theoretical explanation of the variables is discussed in chapter 2, 4 and 5.

Following variables are considered:

Average Wage Rate

Only productive workers have been taken into account. Persons other than workers holding position of supervision or management or employed in a confidential position have been left out. Average wage rate is obtained through Total Labour expenditure divided by number of productive workers.

Unit Material Cost

Instead of taking costs of all inputs, only material cost has been taken into account, because it constitutes a significant proportion of the production cost. Being a variable cost, it has a closer relation with labour cost than any other inputs. The cost of materials consumed has been divided by the output to arrive at the unit material cost.

Technological Change

Technological change implies improved techniques of production. New techniques generally involve greater use of capital. Intensity of capital is a suitable quantitative measurement of technological change.

Intensity of capital is a different version of capital-labour ratio. Capital per worker can easily be estimated. For capital-labour ratios, only fixed capital is considered. The working capital-stock of raw material, stores, spares, finished products, work in progress and cash balances does not in any way convey the idea of capital intensity for the purpose of technological change.

MEASUREMENT OF UNIT LABOUR COST AT CONSTANT PRICE

To distinguish between the real and incidental impact of one factor on the other the variables needed to be deflated. Price behaviour is one thing which influences all the input factors. Therefore it is necessary to remove the influence of price behaviour and measure the real impact of the factors on unit labour cost. Once the influence of price movement is removed, data is based on constant price line over the period under study, the inclusion of wage rates and unit material cost as an explanatory variable in model does not seem to be realistic as the fixed wage rates and stable cost of material can not explain the variance in unit labour cost. This consideration requires revision in the model.

THE REVISED MODEL

The most relevant variable that seem to explain the change in unit labour cost of an industry under stable prices are productivity and techniques of production, the latter differing when varying amount of capital are used. In mathematical term the model is expressed as follows:

Deflated labour cost = f (productivity, capital intensity)

If,

dlc = deflated unit labour cost

lp = labour productivity

cl = cpital intensity

U = random error

The linear functional form of the relationship will be

$d_{lc} = a_0 + a_1 lp + a_2 cl + U$

The non linear relationship function will be

$dlc = a_0 lp^{a1} cl^{a2} U$

The function is linear on double log transformation

$\log (dlc) = a_0 + a_1 \log (lp) + a_2 \log (cl) + U$

Let,

log (dlc) = y′

log (lp) = x_1'

log (cl) = x_2'

Then,

$y' = a_0 + a_1 x'_1 + a_2 x'_2 + U$

This model differs only in the number of explanatory variables included and in the procedure of measurement of variables

MEASUREMENT OF VARIABLES

The data is taken from ASI publication of industrial statistics, the variables are deflated using price index numbers. Methods are explained in chapter 4 and 5.

ESTIMATION

Time-series data have been fitted with least square estimates and coefficient of multiple correlations has been estimated to measure the proportion of the variability in unit labour cost explained by the model.

The estimation of the parameters involved in the model has been made with the choice of the functional form of the relationship. Both linear and non-linear relationships between the variable is included.

Separate models have been constructed for each selected industry and within an industry for different regions. The statistical results of these models are reported industry-wise.

The price-movements also influence unit labour cost, therefore, models have been reconstructed so as to remove the influence of price-movements as correctly as possible.

8

The Measurement of Productivity, Labour Cost and Wage Function in Cotton Textile, Jute, Steel and Sugar Industries of India for the Period 1980-2004

The econometric models discussed in the previous chapter make it possible for us to estimate the impact of the various factors on unit labour cost. In the present chapter the estimation of function on the basis of pan India data is done. Interpretation of the results on consolidated tables is done industry wise. The formal introduction and precision of theory is abandoned in favour of the empirical results. Theory is used for interpretation of the results.

So as to find the differences in impact of different factors on unit labour cost on the basis of geographical location, the estimation of model on the basis of data restricted to geographical location-regions was considered in next chapter. To avoid repetition, the interpretation of each analysis table is not given immediately after it the collected interpretation is built on industry wise results. The same theme is followed in the next chapter having models based on regional comparisons, where interpretation is reconstructed on the similar basis as that of estimated national model.

Since the unit labour cost is taken as function of average wage-rate, unit material cost, productivity and intensity of capital; necessary data is needed to measure these variables in quantitative terms. The relevant variables are transformed into indices. Test of significance is carried out for analysis.

The data from 1980-1997 (18 time series observations) would be considered for model building and data from 1998-2004 would be considered as 'hold-out' period for validation of the models. This selection of the period is also attributed to ASI merging the jute data with cotton-textile from 1998 onwards. Keeping the time-series similar would ensure proper inter-industry comparisons.

In times series samples we ought to find the fairly high degree of correlation between labour and capital. Traditionally, all inputs move in same direction. When inputs – labour, capital, raw material and fuel are transformed into output, there is an unidirectional behavior amongst the various inputs. It is very rare that some input factors are reduced while others enhanced when output is to be increased. Thus the inter-directional movement of the input factor causes high inter-correlations between the independent variables. The presence of inter-correlation among the independent variables is termed as multicollinearity in econometrics. The presence of multicollinearity leads to uncertainty in the results. Multicollinearity increases the standard errors of the coefficients. Increased standard errors in turn means that coefficients for some independent variables may be found not to be significantly different from 0, whereas without multicollinearity and with lower standard errors, these same coefficients might have been found to be significant and the researcher may not have come to null findings in the first place. In other words, multicollinearity misleadingly inflates the standard errors. Thus, it makes some variables statistically insignificant while they should be otherwise significant. Multicollinearity is judged through correlation matrix of independent variables or variance inflation factor in estimated equation. Other signs to detect multicollinearity are: (a) getting non-significant β coefficient where theoretically it should be significant, (b) sign of β coefficient is not logical.

Econometric theory of linear regression based models suggests that the highly correlated independent variables shall be avoided in model building. Situations in which the correlation between independent variables is greater than the correlation of these variables with dependent variable shall be avoided. According to Klien, "intercorrelation or multicollinearity is not necessary a problem unless it is highly relative to the overall degree of multiple correlation among all variables simultaneously. Production function with overall correlations much in excess of 0.95, as often occurs in practice can be well estimated with intercorrelation between labour and capital as high as 0.8 to 0.9". The models estimated below conform to the checks suggested on multicollinearity. While building the models the capital intensity and technological changes are used interchangeably in search of better model with respect to indicators like: residual sum of square and Akaike Information Criteria. The results given in the form of tables in this chapter and chapter 9, also have reported p-value of F-test (Prob(F-statistic)) which is used for hypothesis testing on multiple regression model.

ESTIMATION OF UNIT LABOUR COST FUNCTION IN IRON AND STEEL INDUSTRY:

The necessary data to estimate the model of unit labour cost in iron and steel industry of India are given in table 8.1: the variable (X4) Capital intensity = fixed capital is redefined as X4 = Technological changes= fixed capital/worker as the models resulted in lower Akaike Information Criteria (AIC) score and Schwarz criterion (SC) score.

Table 8.1: Estimated Linear Models Iron and Steel Industry at Current Price-all India

Variable	Coefficient	Std. Error	t-Statistic	Prob.
C	106.1701	21.79224	4.871923	0.0003
X1	0.218406	0.048915	4.464991	0.0006
X2	-0.186023	0.200163	-0.929359	0.3696
X3	-0.137574	0.033582	-4.096708	0.0013
X4	-0.040112	0.018990	-2.112331	0.0546
R-squared	0.797975	Mean dependent var		84.06188
Adjusted R-squared	0.735813	S.D. dependent var		14.53907
S.E. of regression	7.472951	Akaike info criterion		7.090590
Sum squared resid	725.9850	Schwarz criterion		7.337916

Prob(F-statistic) 0.000189

Estimation Equation:

Y = C(1) + C(2)*X1 + C(3)*X2 + C(4)*X3 + C(5)*X4

Substituted Coefficients:

Y = 106.1701405 + 0.2184064712*X1 - 0.1860231783*X2 - 0.1375738914*X3 - 0.04011230439*X4

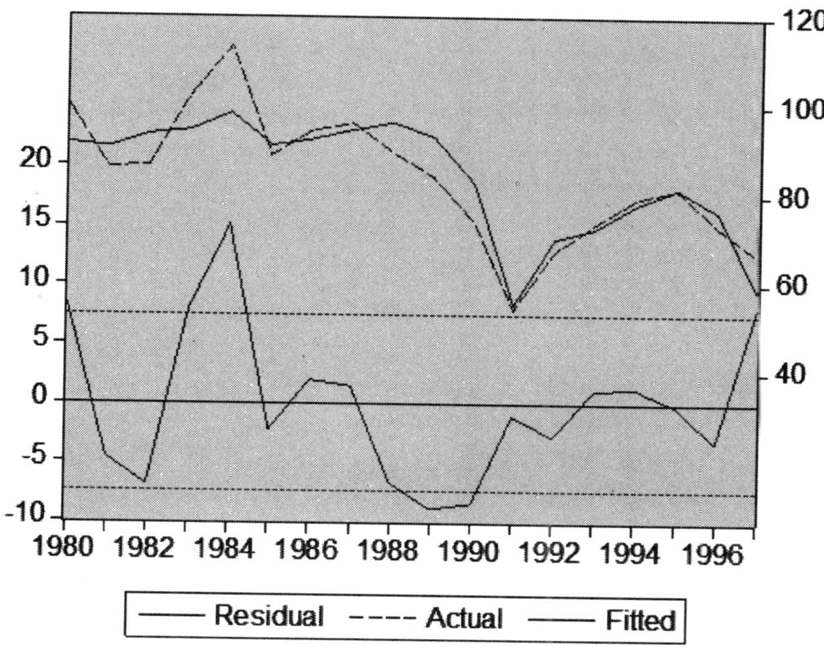

Fig. 8.1: Line Chart Estimated Linear Models Iron and Steel Industry at Current Price-all India

Table 8.2: Estimated Non Linear Models Iron and Steel Industry at Current Price- All India

Variable	Coefficient	Std. Error	t-Statistic	Prob.
C	5.258335	0.186159	28.24653	0.0000
LOG(X1)	0.942889	0.029540	31.91878	0.0000
LOG(X2)	-0.131354	0.038524	-3.409695	0.0047
LOG(X3)	-0.939157	0.035957	-26.11899	0.0000
LOG(X4)	-0.021304	0.021856	-0.974755	0.3475
R-squared	0.994324	Mean dependent var		4.416834
Adjusted R-squared	0.992577	S.D. dependent var		0.178959
S.E. of regression	0.015418	Akaike info criterion		-5.276421
Sum squared resid	0.003090	Schwarz criterion		-5.029095

Prob(F-statistic) 0.000000

Estimation Equation:

LOG(Y) = LOG(C(1)) + C(2)*LOG(X1) + C(3)*LOG(X2) + C(4)*LOG(X3) + C(5)*LOG(X4)

Substituted Coefficients:

LOG(Y) = LOG(192.161354092557) + 0.9428893237*LOG(X1) - 0.1313541245*LOG(X2) - 0.9391573795*LOG(X3) - 0.02130410025*LOG(X4)

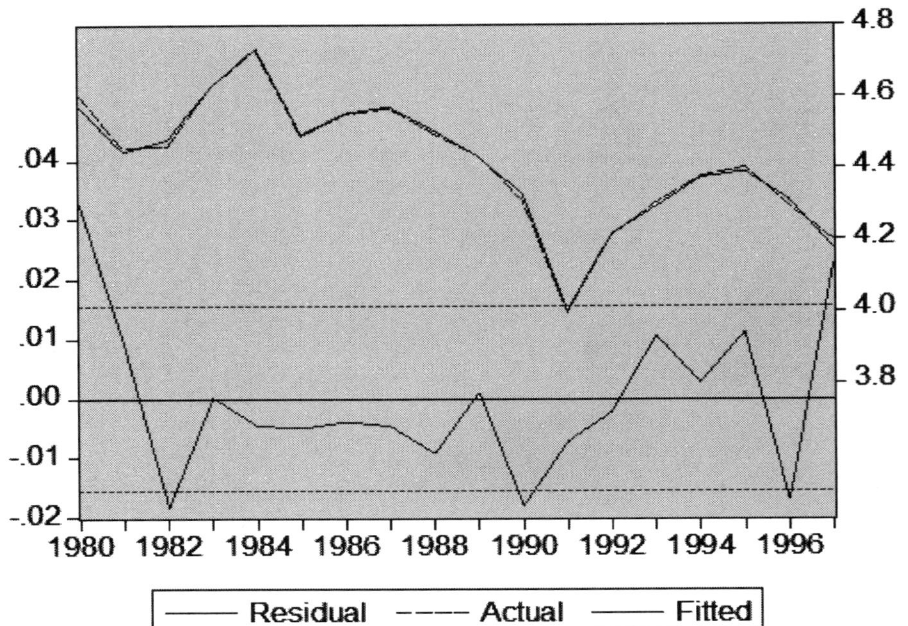

Fig. 8.2: Line Chart Estimated Non Linear Models Iron and Steel Industry at Current Price-All India

The significant values of both the models reveals the validity of the hypothesis that changes in productivity and intensity of capital are most powerful factors that affect unit labour cost in current price data. The linear model explains 73.58 % of variance in unit labour cost and the nonlinear model explains 99.25 % of variance in unit labour cost.

The coefficient of the variables (say x1=average wage rate) indicate that if other variables remain constant for every one per cent increase in the (say x1) the unit labour cost increases by 0.218 in liner model and 0.924 in non linear model. Similarly the coefficients of other variables in the linear and non linear model can be explained.

The non linear functional form of the relationship provides better fit to the data as R2 value for non linear model is higher. The coefficient of x4 = technological change in both form of equation is non-significant and coefficient of x2 (unit material cost is not significant in linear form. The non significance of unit material cost is understandable, the index numbers suggest that it remained flat in the period of study and declined in the late 90s. Both the models suggest the key determinants of unit labour cost are average wage rate and productivity.

Table 8.3: Estimated Linear Models Iron and Steel Industry at Constant Price- All India

Variable	Coefficient	Std. Error	t-Statistic	Prob.
C	93.50384	16.02393	5.835262	0.0001
X1	0.582475	0.082363	7.072032	0.0000
X2	-0.102619	0.067528	-1.519662	0.1525
X3	-0.456039	0.083273	-5.476415	0.0001
X4	-0.005608	0.011743	-0.477560	0.6409
R-squared	0.944477	Mean dependent var		82.49844
Adjusted R-squared	0.927393	S.D. dependent var		15.24211
S.E. of regression	4.107079	Akaike info criterion		5.893434
Sum squared resid	219.2853	Schwarz criterion		6.140760

Prob(F-statistic) 0.000000

Estimation Equation:

Y = C(1) + C(2)*X1 + C(3)*X2 + C(4)*X3 + C(5)*X4

Substituted Coefficients:

Y = 93.50384059 + 0.5824750033*X1 - 0.1026194521*X2 - 0.4560385179*X3 - 0.005608185319*X4

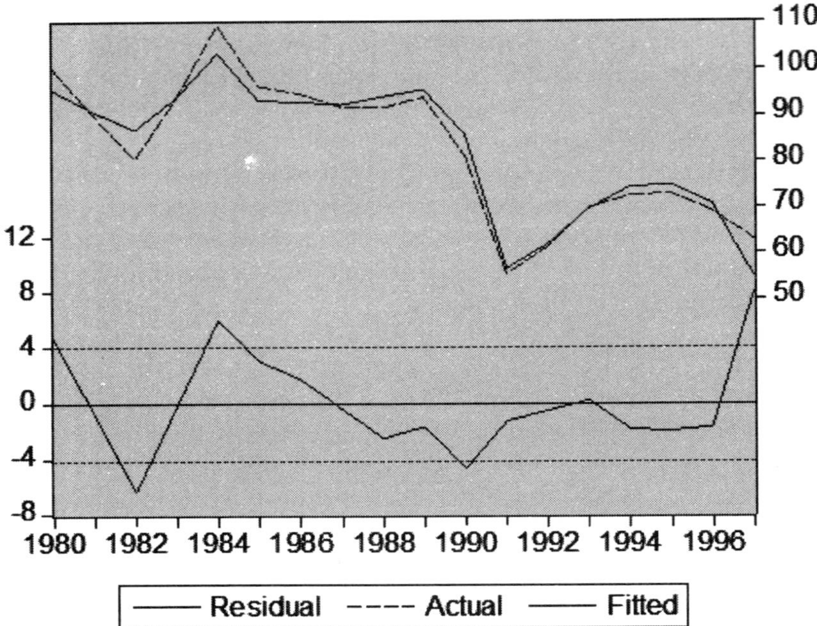

Fig. 8.3: Line Chart Estimated Linear Models Iron and Steel Industry at Constant Price- All India

Table 8.4: Estimated Non Linear Models Iron and Steel Industry at Constant Price- All India

Variable	Coefficient	Std. Error	t-Statistic	Prob.
C	4.740178	0.385557	12.29436	0.0000
LOG(X1)	0.946515	0.033377	28.35825	0.0000
LOG(X2)	-0.059832	0.041930	-1.426959	0.1772
LOG(X3)	-0.881795	0.059309	-14.86792	0.0000
LOG(X4)	-0.039438	0.023832	-1.654833	0.1219
R-squared	0.995924	Mean dependent var		4.395765
Adjusted R-squared	0.994670	S.D. dependent var		0.192632
S.E. of regression	0.014063	Akaike info criterion		-5.460342
Sum squared resid	0.002571	Schwarz criterion		-5.213017

Prob(F-statistic) 0.000000

Estimation Equation:

LOG(Y) = LOG(C(1)) + C(2)*LOG(X1) + C(3)*LOG(X2) + C(4)*LOG(X3) + C(5)*LOG(X4)

Substituted Coefficients:

LOG(Y) = LOG(114.454543137301) + 0.9465153165*LOG(X1) - 0.05983225452*LOG(X2) - 0.881794655*LOG(X3) - 0.03943842199*LOG(X4)

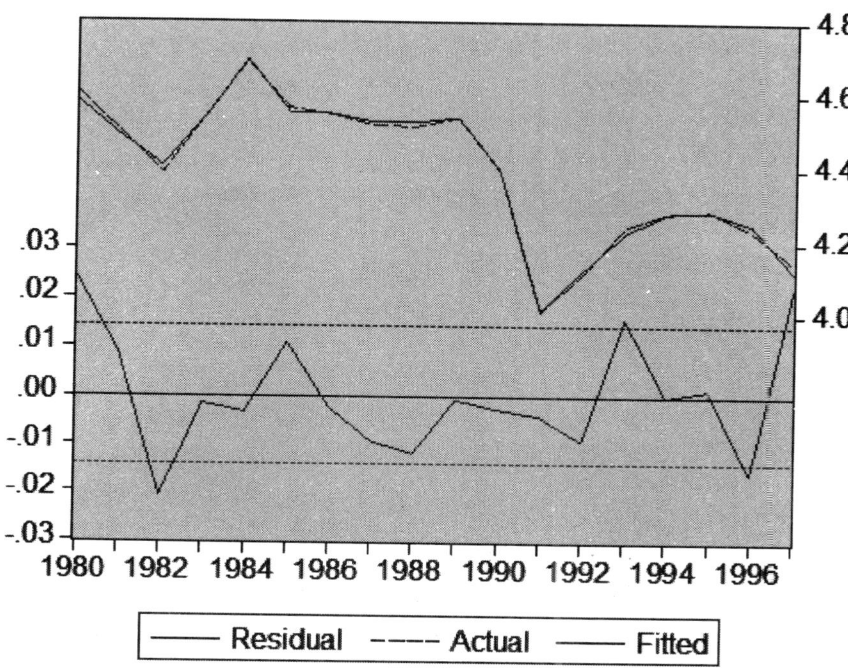

Fig. 8.4: Line Chart Estimated Non Linear Models Iron and Steel Industry at Constant Price- All India

Significant value of R^2 in both models establishes the hypothesis that changes in changes in average wage rate and productivity are the most powerful factors that affect the unit labour cost iron and steel industry at national level in an economy which has no price-movements.

ESTIMATION OF UNIT LABOUR COST FUNCTION IN COTTON TEXTILE INDUSTRY

Table 8.5: Estimated Linear Models Cotton Textile Industry at Current Price- All India

Variable	Coefficient	Std. Error	t-Statistic	Prob.
C	134.4487	11.60194	11.58847	0.0000
X1	0.009418	0.029582	0.318363	0.7553
X2	-0.211682	0.105031	-2.015427	0.0650
X3	-0.145385	0.031705	-4.585558	0.0005
X4	0.033234	0.009376	3.544672	0.0036
R-squared	0.983692	Mean dependent var		81.91797
Adjusted R-squared	0.978674	S.D. dependent var		19.90690
S.E. of regression	2.907064	Akaike info criterion		5.202297
Sum squared resid	109.8632	Schwarz criterion		5.449623

Prob (F-statistic) 0.000000

Estimation Equation:

Y = C(1) + C(2)*X1 + C(3)*X2 + C(4)*X3 + C(5)*T

Substituted Coefficients:

Y = 134.4486685 + 0.009417898161*X1 - 0.2116822436*X2 - 0.1453845754*X3 + 0.0332340468*T

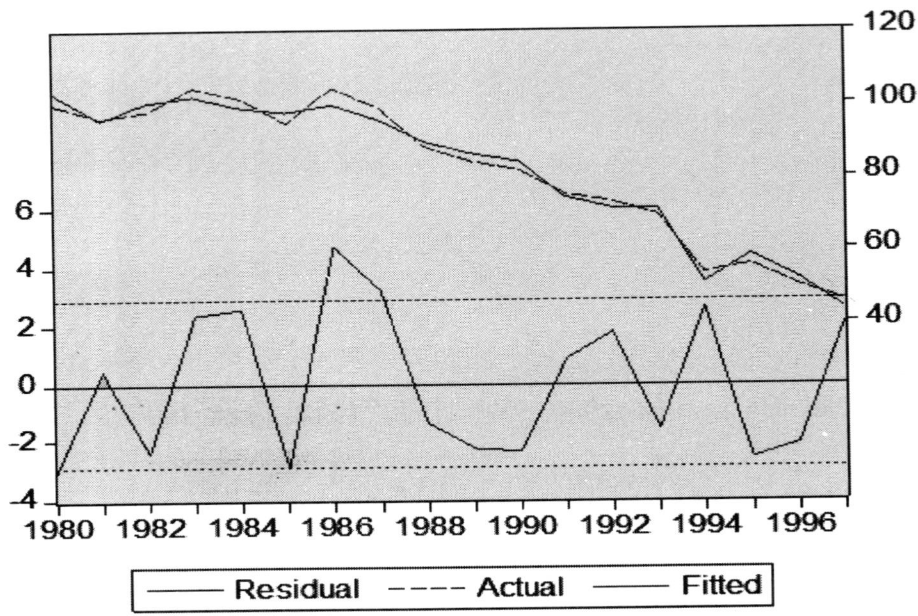

Fig. 8.5: Line Chart Estimated Linear Models Cotton Textile Industry at Current Price- All India

Table 8.6: Estimated Non Linear Models Cotton Textile Industry at Current Price- All India

Variable	Coefficient	Std. Error	t-Statistic	Prob.
C	4.780542	0.298025	16.04072	0.0000
LOG(X1)	0.737019	0.037090	19.87131	0.0000
LOG(X2)	0.062150	0.061751	1.006454	0.3326
LOG(X3)	-0.774148	0.040994	-18.88436	0.0000
LOG(X4)	-0.062728	0.027285	-2.299014	0.0387
R-squared	0.997797	Mean dependent var		4.373381
Adjusted R-squared	0.997120	S.D. dependent var		0.271844
S.E. of regression	0.014590	Akaike info criterion		-5.386852
Sum squared resid	0.002767	Schwarz criterion		-5.139526

Prob(F-statistic) 0.000000

Estimation Equation:

LOG(Y) = LOG(C(1)) + C(2)*LOG(X1) + C(3)*LOG(X2) + C(4)*LOG(X3) + C(5)*LOG(X4)

Substituted Coefficients:

LOG(Y) = LOG(119.168896955344) + 0.7370192095*LOG(X1) + 0.06214987235*LOG(X2) - 0.7741481388*LOG(X3) - 0.06272754644*LOG(X4)

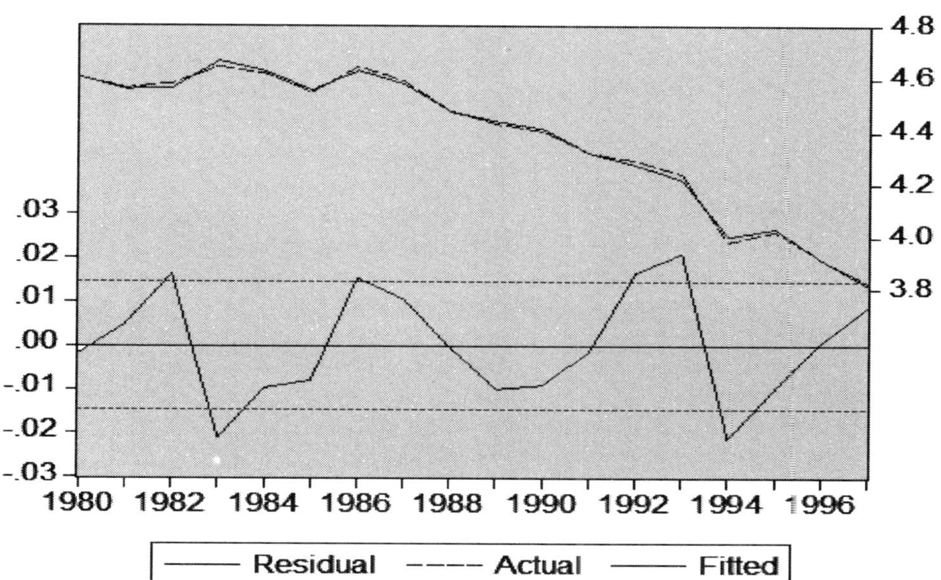

Fig. 8.6: Line Chart Estimated Non Linear Models Cotton Textile Industry at Current Price- All India

Table 8.7: Estimated Linear Models Cotton Textile Industry at Constant Price - All India

Variable	Coefficient	Std. Error	t-Statistic	Prob.
C	144.8106	36.08196	4.013379	0.0015
X1	-0.393019	0.306365	-1.282846	0.2219
X2	0.056582	0.146927	0.385100	0.7064
X3	-0.248212	0.078936	-3.144471	0.0078
X4	0.000767	0.006115	0.125412	0.9021
R-squared	0.947040	Mean dependent var		63.62755
Adjusted R-squared	0.930744	S.D. dependent var		19.12619
S.E. of regression	5.033347	Akaike info criterion		6.300181
Sum squared resid	329.3496	Schwarz criterion		6.547506

Prob(F-statistic) 0.000000

Estimation Equation:

Y = C(1) + C(2)*X1 + C(3)*X2 + C(4)*X3 + C(5)*X4

Substituted Coefficients:

Y = 144.81059 - 0.3930189443*X1 + 0.05658166908*X2 - 0.2482120742*X3 + 0.0007669138472*X4

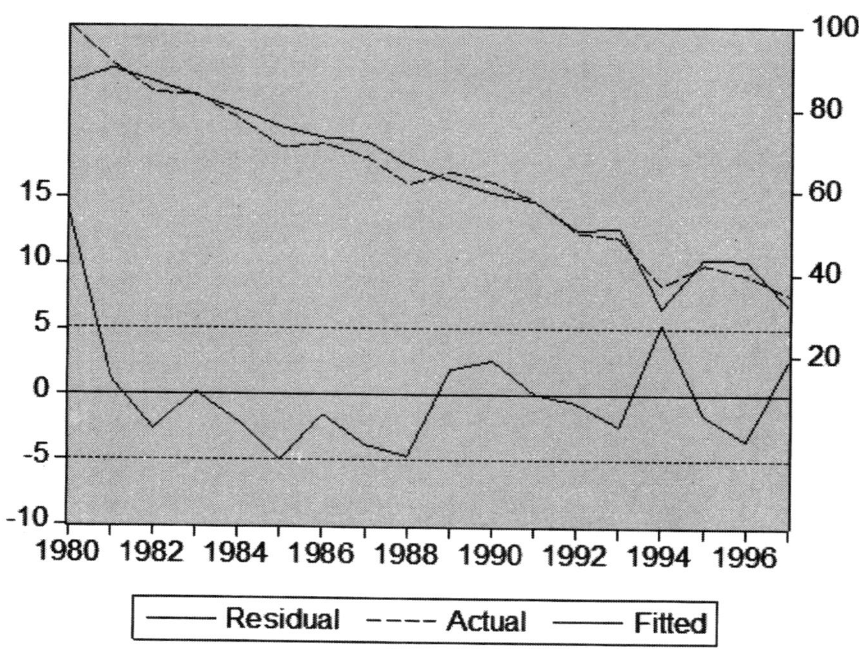

Fig. 8.7: Line Chart Estimated Linear Models Cotton Textile Industry at Constant Price - All India

Table 8.8: Estimated Non Linear Models Cotton Textile Industry at Constant Price - All India

Variable	Coefficient	Std. Error	t-Statistic	Prob.
C	5.649101	0.722396	7.819952	0.0000
LOG(X1)	0.539333	0.142098	3.795510	0.0022
LOG(X2)	0.091937	0.071708	1.282104	0.2222
LOG(X3)	-0.797922	0.092942	-8.585194	0.0000
LOG(X4)	-0.069394	0.029910	-2.320067	0.0372
R-squared	0.996761	Mean dependent var		4.107673
Adjusted R-squared	0.995765	S.D. dependent var		0.315973
S.E. of regression	0.020563	Akaike info criterion		-4.700532
Sum squared resid	0.005497	Schwarz criterion		-4.453206

Prob(F-statistic) 0.000000

Estimation Equation:

LOG(Y) = LOG(C(1)) + C(2)*LOG(X1) + C(3)*LOG(X2) + C(4)*LOG(X3) + C(5)*LOG(X4)

Substituted Coefficients:

LOG(Y) = LOG(284.035995259114) + 0.5393329232*LOG(X1) + 0.09193684486*LOG(X2) - 0.7979221673*LOG(X3) - 0.06939371837*LOG(X4)

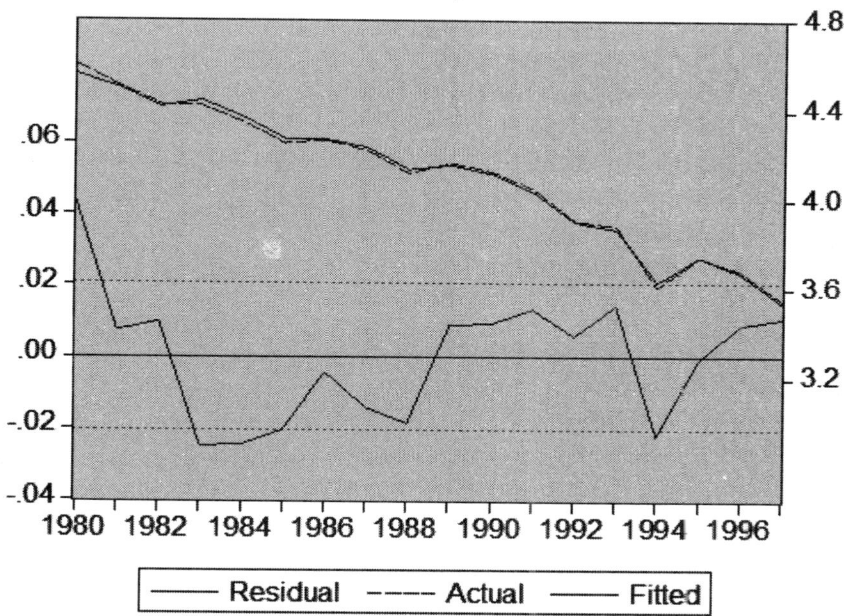

Fig. 8.8: Line Chart Estimated Non Linear Models Cotton Textile Industry at Constant Price- All India

The Cotton Textile Industry of India is widely scattered over the country. At the national level, the non linear models provide a better fit. Coefficient of unit material cost is non-significant in both the models the hypothesis fails to reject that the coefficient is zero. The coefficient of Technological changes is having positive association with unit labour cost. The cost rises with the rise of capital-labour ratios. In order to support the validity of empirical results, the necessary implications are:

1. The capital is invested in cotton textile industry to rationalize the cost. But such rationalization is opposed by labour union as it causes retrenchment. As result of negotiations the technically unskilled labour are also not retrenched and new workforce is hired to run the machinery. The total labour expansion increases the account on labour but due to more efficient machinery the per unit output cost reduces. But reduction in the unit labour cost on the account of improvement of output per worker will be represented by the parameter of x3 (productivity) which is -0.1453 and not by coefficient of x4 (technological changes).

2. The impact of x3 and x4 on y may be affected by the presence of multicollinearity. Generally, output per worker increases when capital per worker also increases.
3. The rise in capital-labour ratios may be owing to the high price of capital goods and imposition of heavy import duty on foreign machinery. This becomes clear when the constant price model provides non-significant coefficient for x4.
4. Insignificant coefficient of x2 in all the models confirms the possibilities of underutilization of installed capacities in the industry, use of old plants, and recruitment of workers of higher grades in manufacturing process.

ESTIMATION OF UNIT LABOUR COST FUNCTION IN SUGAR INDUSTRY:

For estimation of linear models for sugar industry at constant price, the linear relationship between the dependent(y) and independent variables x1, x2 x3 and x4 did not result in significant relationship. The assumptions of least square method were tested. The independent variables x1 and x3 show high correlation and all independent variables do not have high correlation with dependent variable. No heteroskedasticity was found in the series of error terms but, serial correlation was present. The serial correlation was addressed by introducing the dependent variable with lag1 as independent variable. For comparisons the model was redeveloped by using forward pass method to identify appropriate independent variables. The variable x4 (technological change) is replaced by xd4 (capital intensity). The models so obtained were compared on Akaike Information Criteria and sum of squares residuals. The model developed by addressing serial correlation problem of the error terms was found appropriate.

Table 8.9: Estimated Linear Models Sugar Industry at Current Price- All India

Variable	Coefficient	Std. Error	t-Statistic	Prob.
C	186.9591	40.39117	4.628712	0.0005
X1	0.278157	0.063848	4.356520	0.0008
X2	-0.781680	0.403000	-1.939654	0.0744
X3	-0.442731	0.075955	-5.828822	0.0001
X4	-0.007521	0.019474	-0.386220	0.7056
R-squared	0.775517	Mean dependent var		93.47212
Adjusted R-squared	0.706446	S.D. dependent var		12.99599
S.E. of regression	7.041311	Akaike info criterion		6.971599
Sum squared resid	644.5407	Schwarz criterion		7.218924

Prob (F-statistic) 0.000000

Estimation Equation:

Y = C(1) + C(2)*X1 + C(3)*X2 + C(4)*X3 + C(5)*X4

Substituted Coefficients:

Y=186.9590847+0.2781568794*X1-0.7816797635*X2-0.4427310002*X3-0.007521208997*X4

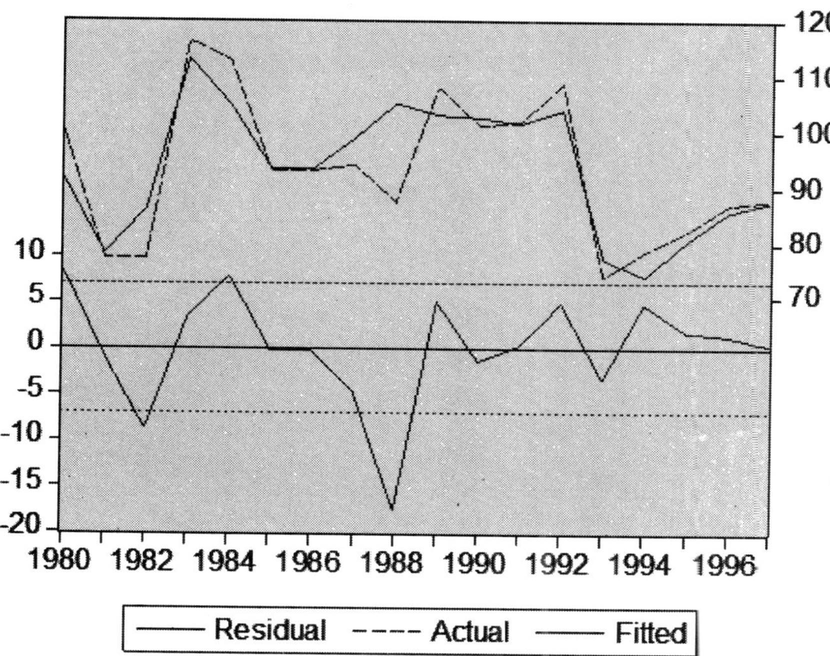

Fig. 8.9: Line Chart Estimated Linear Models Sugar Industry at Current Price - All India

Table 8.10: Estimated Non Linear Models Sugar Industry at Current Price-All India

Variable	Coefficient	Std. Error	t-Statistic	Prob.
C	6.240981	2.146956	2.906898	0.0122
LOG(X1)	0.400881	0.116776	3.432889	0.0045
LOG(X2)	-0.253738	0.498403	-0.509102	0.6192
LOG(X3)	-0.566917	0.116130	-4.881724	0.0003
LOG(X4)	0.034861	0.038093	0.915137	0.3768
R-squared	0.730647	Mean dependent var		4.528532
Adjusted R-squared	0.647769	S.D. dependent var		0.139145
S.E. of regression	0.082581	Akaike info criterion		-1.919930
Sum squared resid	0.088656	Schwarz criterion		-1.672604

Prob (F-statistic) 0.000000

Estimation Equation:

LOG(Y) = LOG(C(1)) + C(2)*LOG(X1) + C(3)*LOG(X2) + C(4)*LOG(X3) + C(5)*LOG(X4)

Substituted Coefficients:

LOG(Y) = LOG(513.361986993367) + 0.4008806199*LOG(X1) - 0.2537382143*LOG(X2) - 0.566916799*LOG(X3) + 0.03486059945*LOG(X4)

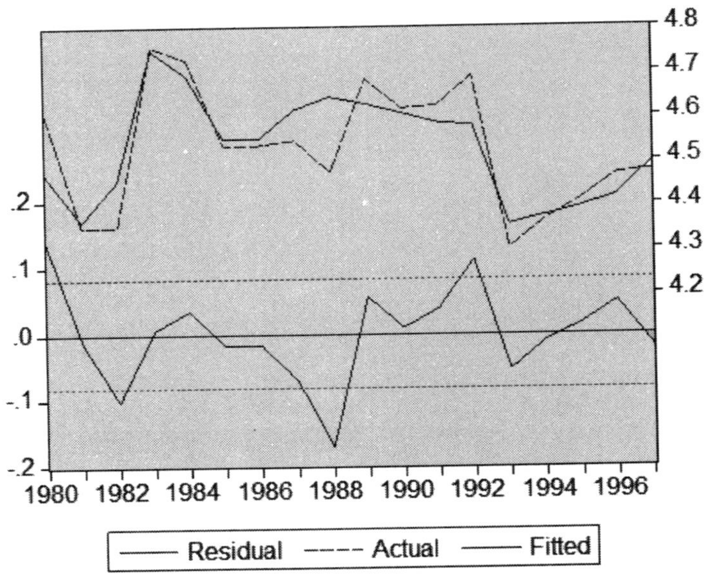

Fig. 8.10: Line Chart Estimated Non Linear Models Sugar Industry at Current Price- All India

Table 8.11: Estimated Linear Models Sugar Industry at Constant Price- All India

Variable	Coefficient	Std. Error	t-Statistic	Prob.
C	56.98428	28.69473	1.985880	0.0725
X1	0.381979	0.203439	1.877605	0.0872
X2	-0.108917	0.283421	-0.384294	0.7081
X3	-0.408095	0.143730	-2.839307	0.0161
X4	-0.010535	0.016825	-0.626146	0.5440
Y(-1)	0.327183	0.147512	2.218008	0.0485
R-squared	0.567918	Mean dependent var		61.80444
Adjusted R-squared	0.371517	S.D. dependent var		9.347898
S.E. of regression	7.410723	Akaike info criterion		7.114297
Sum squared resid	604.1069	Schwarz criterion		7.408373

Prob (F-statistic) 0.042594

Estimation Equation:

Y = C(1) + C(2)*X1 + C(3)*X2 + C(4)*X3 + C(5)*X4 + C(6)*Y(-1)

Substituted Coefficients:

Y = 56.98428099 + 0.3819785764*X1 - 0.108916846*X2 - 0.4080946919*X3 - 0.01053510003*X4 + 0.3271831067*Y(-1)

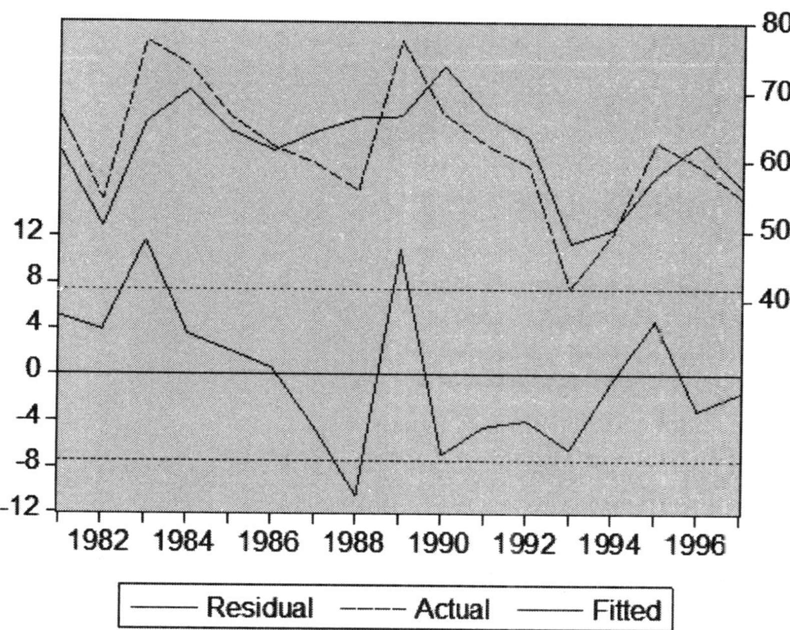

Fig. 8.11: Line Chart Estimated Linear Models Sugar Industry at Constant Price- All India

Table 8.12: Estimated Non Linear Models Sugar Industry at Constant Price - All India

Variable	Coefficient	Std. Error	t-Statistic	Prob.
C	2.932723	1.932209	1.517808	0.1573
LOG(X1)	0.481983	0.233472	2.064417	0.0634
LOG(X2)	0.128386	0.395227	0.324840	0.7514
LOG(X3)	-0.683107	0.188449	-3.624891	0.0040
LOG(X4)	0.016328	0.048209	0.338685	0.7412
LOG(Y(-1))	0.350344	0.143855	2.435400	0.0331
R-squared	0.661447	Mean dependent var		4.112744
Adjusted R-squared	0.507559	S.D. dependent var		0.156591
S.E. of regression	0.109886	Akaike info criterion		-1.308178
Sum squared resid	0.132825	Schwarz criterion		-1.014102
Prob(F-statistic)	0.020572			

Estimation Equation:

LOG(Y) = LOG(C(1)) + C(2)*LOG(X1) + C(3)*LOG(X2) + C(4)*LOG(X3) + C(5)*LOG(X4) + C(6)*LOG(Y(-1))

Substituted Coefficients:

LOG(Y) = LOG (18.7787026889802) + 0.4819827382*LOG(X1) + 0.128385663*LOG(X2) - 0.6831071533*LOG(X3) + 0.016327812*LOG(X4) + 0.3503437374*LOG(Y(-1))

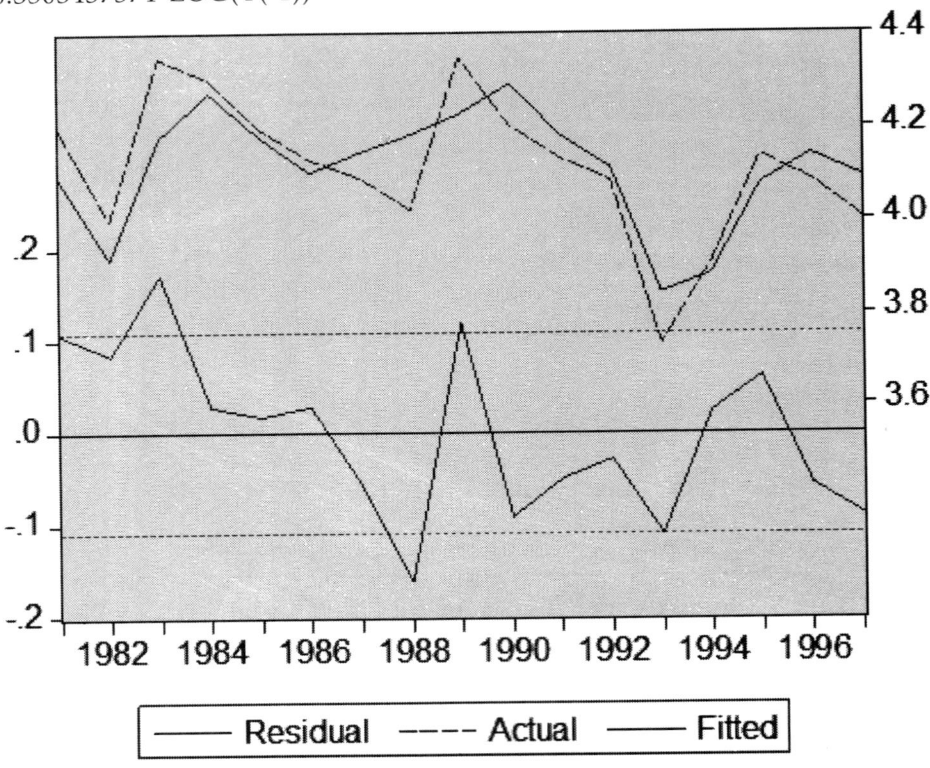

Fig. 8.12: Line Chart Estimated Non Linear Models Sugar Industry at Constant Price- All India

In the models with current price and constant price the productivity is the key variable which explains the variation in the unit labour cost. Which indicates that productivity has not been affected by price variation and is been identifies as very effective in reducing (negative sign of the coefficient) the unit labour cost. The lower R2 value indicates there are other factors which lurks and are capable of explaining the variation in the unit labour cost.

ESTIMATION OF UNIT LABOUR COST FUNCTION IN JUTE INDUSTRY

Table 8.13: Estimated Linear Models Jute Industry at Current Price - All India

Variable	Coefficient	Std. Error	t-Statistic	Prob.
C	145.4536	17.40589	8.356572	0.0000
X1	0.360666	0.058627	6.151879	0.0000
X2	-0.269872	0.145326	-1.857018	0.0861
X3	-0.432324	0.066213	-6.529287	0.0000
X4	0.009448	0.016575	0.570043	0.5784
R-squared	0.858241	Mean dependent var		116.7529
Adjusted R-squared	0.814623	S.D. dependent var		14.69873
S.E. of regression	6.328600	Akaike info criterion		6.758168
Sum squared resid	520.6654	Schwarz criterion		7.005494

Prob (F-statistic) 0.000020

Estimation Equation:

Y = C(1) + C(2)*X1 + C(3)*X2 + C(4)*X3 + C(5)*X4

Substituted Coefficients:

Y = 145.4535667 + 0.3606661162*X1 - 0.2698723996*X2 - 0.4323240354*X3 + 0.009448266486*X4

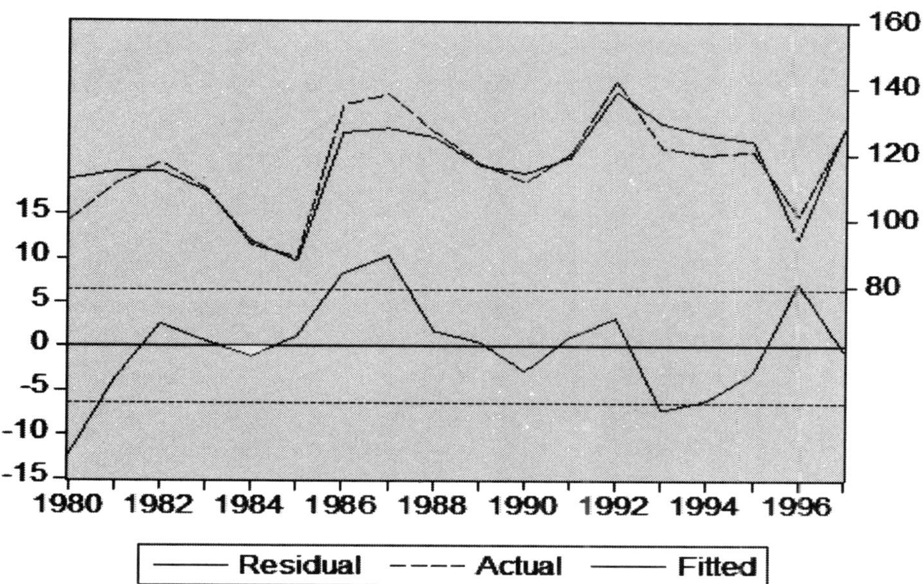

Fig. 8.13: Line Chart Estimated Linear Models Jute Industry at Current Price - All India

Table 8.14: Estimated Non Linear Models Jute Industry at Current Price- All India

Variable	Coefficient	Std. Error	t-Statistic	Prob.
C	5.307275	0.433851	12.23293	0.0000
LOG(X1)	0.951055	0.091241	10.42353	0.0000
LOG(X2)	-0.142795	0.086675	-1.647482	0.1234
LOG(X3)	-0.934660	0.071987	-12.98366	0.0000
LOG(X4)	-0.016855	0.039225	-0.429692	0.6745
R-squared	0.960508	Mean dependent var		4.752314
Adjusted R-squared	0.948357	S.D. dependent var		0.129325
S.E. of regression	0.029389	Akaike info criterion		-3.986242
Sum squared resid	0.011228	Schwarz criterion		-3.738916

Prob (F-statistic) 0.000000

Estimation Equation:

LOG(Y) = LOG(C(1)) + C(2)*LOG(X1) + C(3)*LOG(X2) + C(4)*LOG(X3) + C(5)*LOG(X4)

Substituted Coefficients:

LOG(Y) = LOG(201.79955686393) + 0.9510551444*LOG(X1) - 0.1427950238*LOG(X2) - 0.9346604704*LOG(X3) - 0.01685462907*LOG(X4)

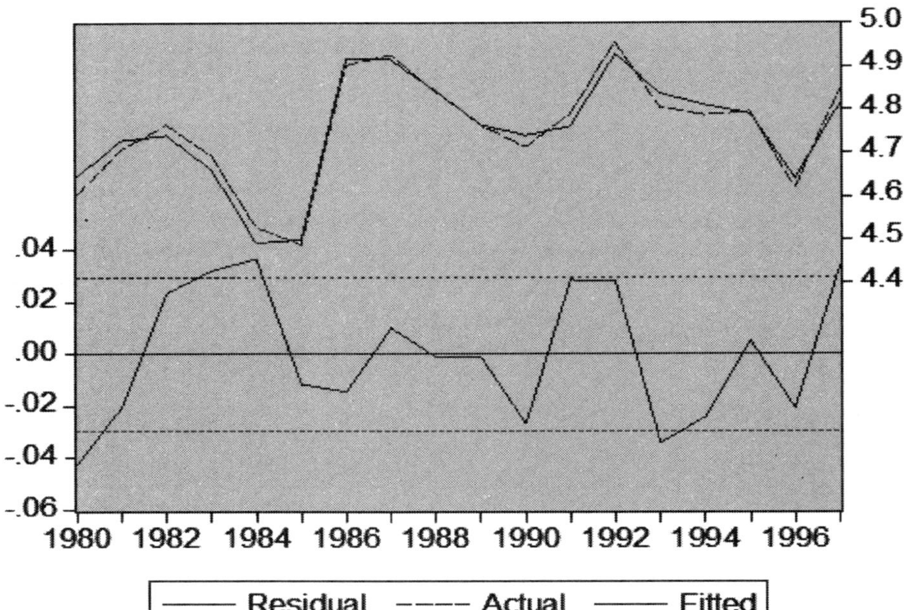

Fig. 8.14: Line Chart Estimated Non Linear Models Jute Industry at Current Price- All India

Table 8.15: Estimated Linear Models Jute Industry at Constant Price - All India

Variable	Coefficient	Std. Error	t-Statistic	Prob.
C	144.1453	9.994995	14.42174	0.0000
X1	1.032995	0.087429	11.81526	0.0000
X2	-0.070704	0.045418	-1.556730	0.1435
X3	-1.407806	0.083713	-16.81705	0.0000
X4	0.005334	0.004177	1.277148	0.2239
R-squared	0.964802	Mean dependent var		119.9728
Adjusted R-squared	0.953972	S.D. dependent var		13.29837
S.E. of regression	2.853059	Akaike info criterion		5.164793
Sum squared resid	105.8193	Schwarz criterion		5.412119

Prob (F-statistic) 0.000000

Estimation Equation:

Y = C(1) + C(2)*X1 + C(3)*X2 + C(4)*X3 + C(5)*X4

Substituted Coefficients:

Y = 144.1452656 + 1.032994511*X1 - 0.07070390626*X2 - 1.407806258*X3 + 0.005334226765*X4

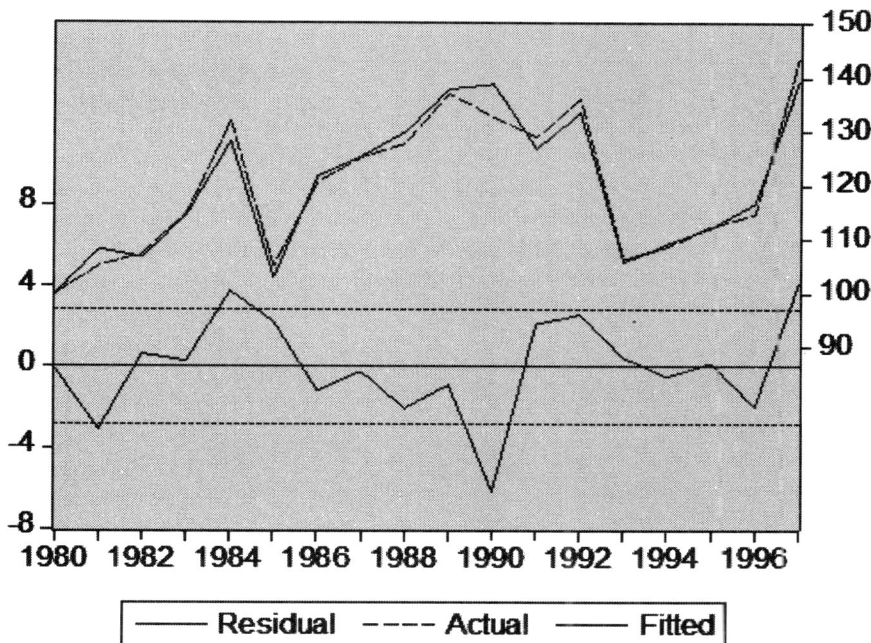

Fig. 8.15: Line Chart Estimated Linear Models Jute Industry at Constant Price - All India

Table 8.16: Estimated Non Linear Models Jute Industry at Constant Price - All India

Variable	Coefficient	Std. Error	t-Statistic	Prob.
C	6.009241	0.438535	13.70298	0.0000
LOG(X1)	0.933796	0.100483	9.293058	0.0000
LOG(X2)	-0.126028	0.052540	-2.398683	0.0322
LOG(X3)	-1.137924	0.066999	-16.98425	0.0000
LOG(X4)	0.026642	0.016964	1.570469	0.1403
R-squared	0.964789	Mean dependent var		4.781478
Adjusted R-squared	0.953955	S.D. dependent var		0.110646
S.E. of regression	0.023742	Akaike info criterion		-4.412971
Sum squared resid	0.007328	Schwarz criterion		-4.165646

Prob (F-statistic) 0.000000

Estimation Equation:

LOG(Y) = LOG(C(1)) + C(2)*LOG(X1) + C(3)*LOG(X2) + C(4)*LOG(X3) + C(5)*LOG(X4)

Substituted Coefficients:

LOG(Y) = LOG(407.174351590769) + 0.9337956116*LOG(X1) - 0.1260276158*LOG(X2) - 1.137923789*LOG(X3) + 0.02664170043*LOG(X4)

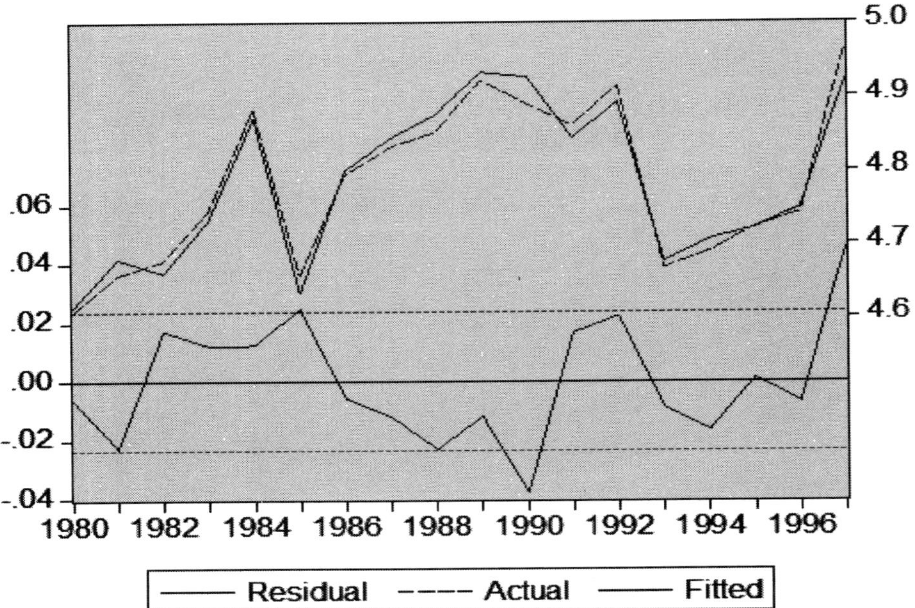

Fig. 8.16: Line Chart Estimated Non Linear Models Jute Industry at Constant Price- All India

The models with current price and constant price have high R2 values and finds average wage rate (x1) and productivity as the explanatory variables for variance in unit labour cost in jute industry at India level.

CONCLUSION

The important inference dawn from the models, designed to estimate the potential influence of factors that have affected the unit labour cost. The non linear functions provide better fit to the data in all the industries considered in the research work. Productivity has been the key variable which explains significantly the variation in the unit labour cost in industries. There is a decline in unit labour cost in all the industries under consideration at the national level. In next chapter regional models are studied and analysed.

9

The Measurement of Regional Wage Function in Cotton Textile, Jute, Steel and Sugar Industries of India

After estimating the models at national levels, the estimate of models for different important regions were developed for all industries under consideration. The results on the basis of R2 and coefficients of independent variables can be interpreted in the similar way as done in models for national level. The results given also have reported p-value of F-test (Prob(F-statistic)) which is used for hypothesis testing on multiple regression model.

For Iron and Steel industry eight regions were considered viz. Andhra Pradesh, Bihar, Delhi, Karnataka, Maharashtra, Punjab, Uttar Pradesh and West Bengal. The analysis tables are presented below.

ESTIMATION OF UNIT COST LABOUR FUNCTION IN REGIONAL IRON AND STEEL INDUSTRY:

Table 9.1: Estimated Linear Models for Regional Iron and Steel Industry at Current Price-Andhra Pradesh

Variable	Coefficient	Std. Error	t-Statistic	Prob.
C	39.44083	20.31366	1.941591	0.0782
X1	0.010107	0.004482	2.254927	0.0455
X2	0.163020	0.171059	0.953005	0.3611
X3	-0.004192	0.001615	-2.595089	0.0249
X4	0.001798	0.000448	4.016550	0.0020
D(Y)	0.227179	0.151005	1.504446	0.1606
R-squared	0.851327	Mean dependent var		73.46938
Adjusted R-squared	0.783748	S.D. dependent var		17.32340
S.E. of regression	8.055877	Akaike info criterion		7.281245
Sum squared resid	713.8687	Schwarz criterion		7.575320

Prob(F-statistic) 0.000302

Estimation Equation:

Y = C(1) + C(2)*X1 + C(3)*X2 + C(4)*X3 + C(5)*X4 + C(6)*D(Y)

Substituted Coefficients:

Y = 39.44082512 + 0.01010676456*X1 + 0.163020477*X2 - 0.004192059041*X3 + 0.001797739537*X4 + 0.2271790324*D(Y)

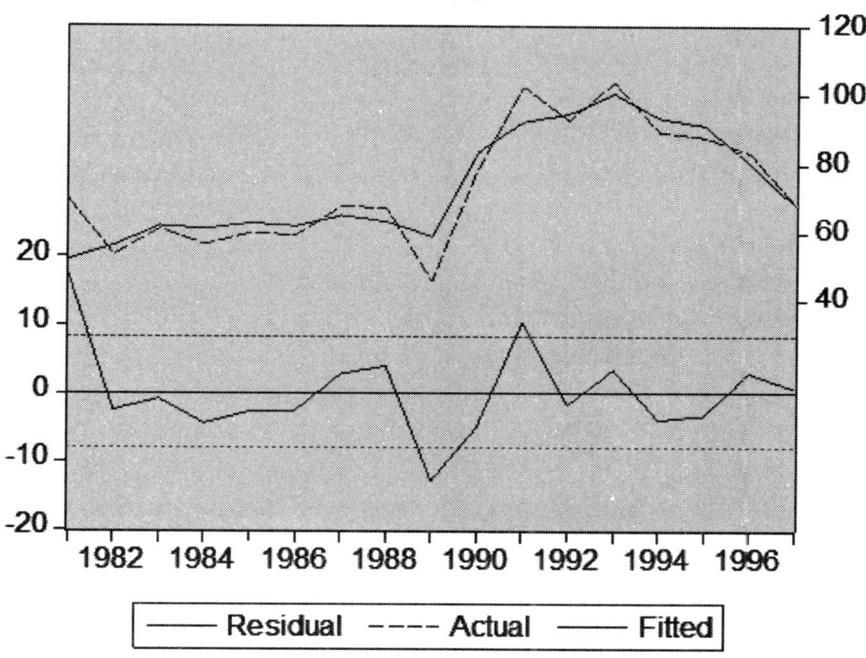

Fig. 9.1: Line Chart Estimated Linear Models for Regional Iron and Steel Industry at Current Price-Andhra Pradesh

Table 9.2: Estimated Non Linear Models for Regional Iron and Steel Industry at Current Price- Andhra Pradesh

Variable	Coefficient	Std. Error	t-Statistic	Prob.
C	6.122868	1.463951	4.182427	0.0011
LOG(X1)	0.297645	0.175538	1.695614	0.1138
LOG(X2)	-0.389114	0.281497	-1.382303	0.1902
LOG(X3)	-0.359321	0.139994	-2.566686	0.0234
LOG(REPX4)	0.044052	0.034667	1.270728	0.2261
R-squared	0.665119	Mean dependent var		4.289338
Adjusted R-squared	0.562079	S.D. dependent var		0.242073
S.E. of regression	0.160193	Akaike info criterion		-0.594740
Sum squared resid	0.333604	Schwarz criterion		-0.347415
Prob(F-statistic)	0.004345			

Estimation Equation:

LOG(Y) = C(1) + C(2)*LOG(X1) + C(3)*LOG(X2) + C(4)*LOG(X3) + C(5)*LOG(REPX4)

Substituted Coefficients:

LOG(Y) = 6.122868074 + 0.297645474*LOG(X1) - 0.3891141063*LOG(X2) - 0.3593208368*LOG(X3) + 0.04405236638*LOG(REPX4)

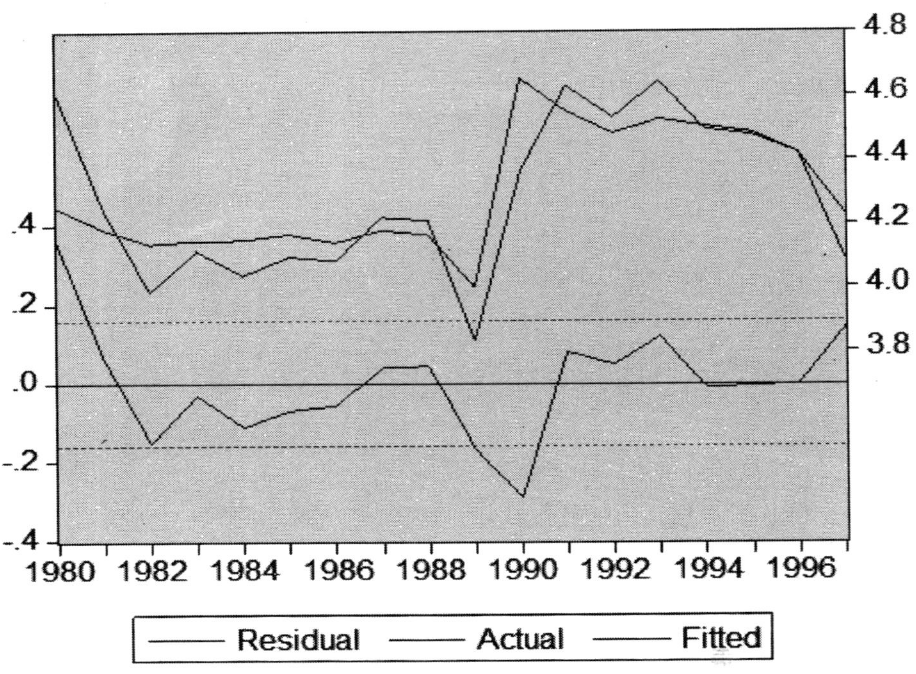

Fig. 9.2: Line Chart Estimated Non Linear Models for Regional Iron and Steel Industry at Current Price- Andhra Pradesh

Table 9.3: Estimated Non Linear Models for Regional Iron and Steel Industry at Constant Price- Andhra Pradesh

Variable	Coefficient	Std. Error	t-Statistic	Prob.
C	6.716755	1.336449	5.025822	0.0002
LOG(X1)	0.315343	0.205241	1.536453	0.1484
LOG(X2)	-0.459043	0.236757	-1.938879	0.0745
LOG(X3)	-0.418357	0.136962	-3.054545	0.0092
LOG(REPX4)	0.038886	0.029009	1.340505	0.2030
R-squared	0.670345	Mean dependent var		4.252373
Adjusted R-squared	0.568913	S.D. dependent var		0.253013
S.E. of regression	0.166121	Akaike info criterion		-0.522062
Sum squared resid	0.358752	Schwarz criterion		-0.274737

Prob (F-statistic) 0.000000

Estimation Equation:

LOG(Y) = C(1) + C(2)*LOG(X1) + C(3)*LOG(X2) + C(4)*LOG(X3) + C(5)*LOG(REPX4)

Substituted Coefficients:

LOG(Y) = 6.716755137 + 0.3153430383*LOG(X1) - 0.4590430932*LOG(X2) - 0.4183567225*LOG(X3) + 0.03888629238*LOG(REPX4)

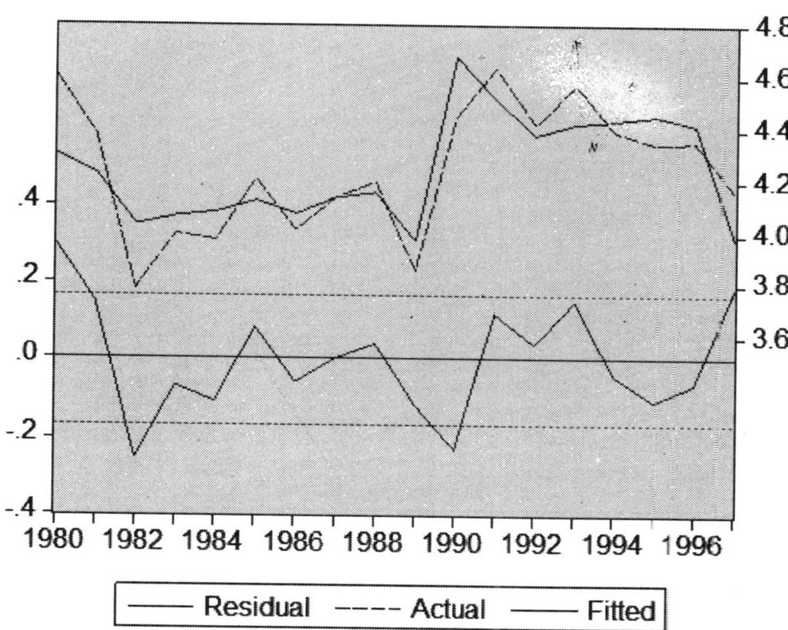

Fig. 9.3: Line Chart Estimated Non Linear Models for Regional Iron and Steel Industry at Constant Price- Andhra Pradesh

Table 9.4: Estimated Linear Models for Regional Iron and Steel Industry at Constant Price-Andhra Pradesh

Variable	Coefficient	Std. Error	t-Statistic	Prob.
C	52.42138	22.82171	2.296996	0.0423
X1	0.026581	0.026951	0.986254	0.3452
X2	0.035102	0.152292	0.230491	0.8219
X3	-0.012724	0.008303	-1.532316	0.1537
X4	0.001589	0.000577	2.751300	0.0188
D(Y)	0.301135	0.153974	1.955758	0.0764
R-squared	0.741257	Mean dependent var		70.75516
Adjusted R-squared	0.623647	S.D. dependent var		16.91213
S.E. of regression	10.37519	Akaike info criterion		7.787276
Sum squared resid	1184.090	Schwarz criterion		8.081351

Prob(F-statistic) 0.000000

Estimation Equation:

Y = C(1) + C(2)*X1 + C(3)*X2 + C(4)*X3 + C(5)*X4 + C(6)*D(Y)

Substituted Coefficients:

Y = 52.42137907 + 0.02658062392*X1 + 0.03510185409*X2 - 0.01272355105*X3 + 0.001588760436*X4 + 0.3011350091*D(Y)

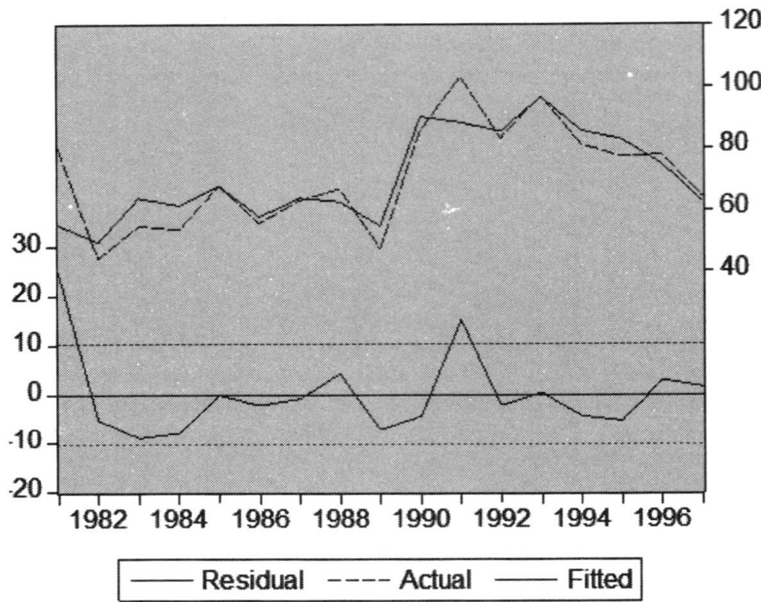

Fig. 9.4: Line Chart Estimated Non Linear Models Jute for Regional Iron and Steel Industry at Constant Price-Andhra Pradesh

The linear models are more efficient than the non linear model. The amount of variance explained in unit labour cost by the model is low and hence indicate towards other important factor which influence the movement of unit labour cost in Andhra Pradesh.

Table 9.5: Estimated Linear Models for Regional Iron and Steel Industry at Current Price- Bihar

Variable	Coefficient	Std. Error	t-Statistic	Prob.
C	65.67547	9.096173	7.220120	0.0000
X1	0.188034	0.022161	8.484802	0.0000
X2	0.182435	0.103319	1.765743	0.1009
X3	-0.121895	0.016128	-7.557933	0.0000
X4	-0.073140	0.051553	-1.418722	0.1795
R-squared	0.892595	Mean dependent var		74.73645
Adjusted R-squared	0.859547	S.D. dependent var		16.87930
S.E. of regression	6.325855	Akaike info criterion		6.757301
Sum squared resid	520.2137	Schwarz criterion		7.004626

Prob(F-statistic) 0.000003

Estimation Equation:

Y = C(1) + C(2)*X1 + C(3)*X2 + C(4)*X3 + C(5)*X4

Substituted Coefficients:

Y = 65.67546522 + 0.1880341827*X1 + 0.1824350456*X2 - 0.1218945681*X3 - 0.07314004039*X4

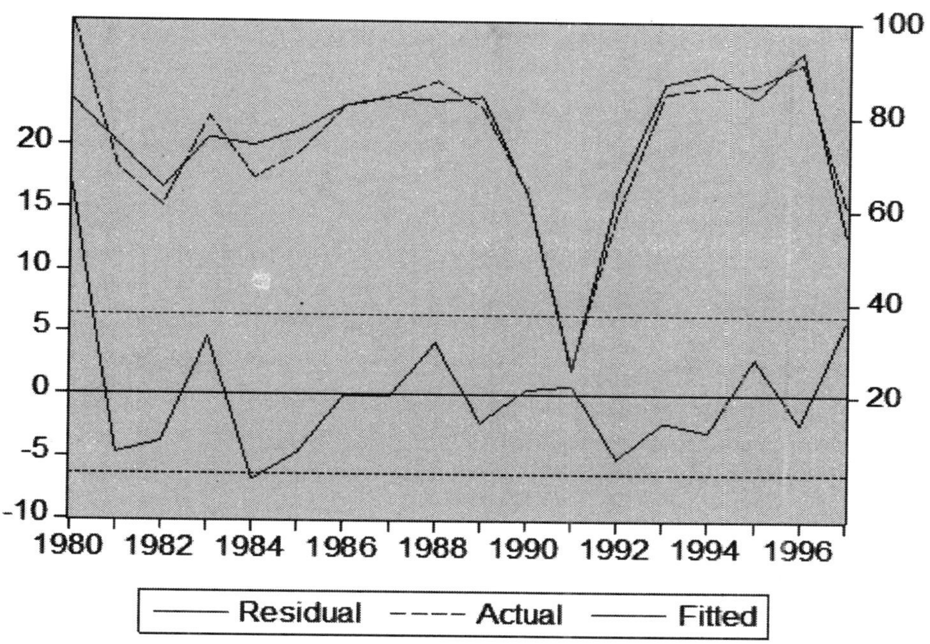

Fig. 9.5: Line Chart Estimated Linear Models for Regional Iron and Steel Industry at Current Price- Bihar

Table 9.6: Estimated Linear Models for Regional Iron and Steel Industry at Constant Price- Bihar

Variable	Coefficient	Std. Error	t-Statistic	Prob.
C	83.41909	6.695124	12.45968	0.0000
X1	0.465397	0.034327	13.55789	0.0000
X2	0.007600	0.042850	0.177368	0.8620
X3	-0.409353	0.028224	-14.50356	0.0000
X4	0.010562	0.016379	0.644869	0.5302
R-squared	0.968626	Mean dependent var		73.09635
Adjusted R-squared	0.958972	S.D. dependent var		16.86026
S.E. of regression	3.415105	Akaike info criterion		5.524427
Sum squared resid	151.6183	Schwarz criterion		5.771752

Prob(F-statistic) 0.000000

Estimation Equation:

Y = C(1) + C(2)*X1 + C(3)*X2 + C(4)*X3 + C(5)*X4

Substituted Coefficients:

Y = 83.41908723 + 0.4653966321*X1 + 0.007600283292*X2 - 0.4093531895*X3 + 0.0105620471*X4

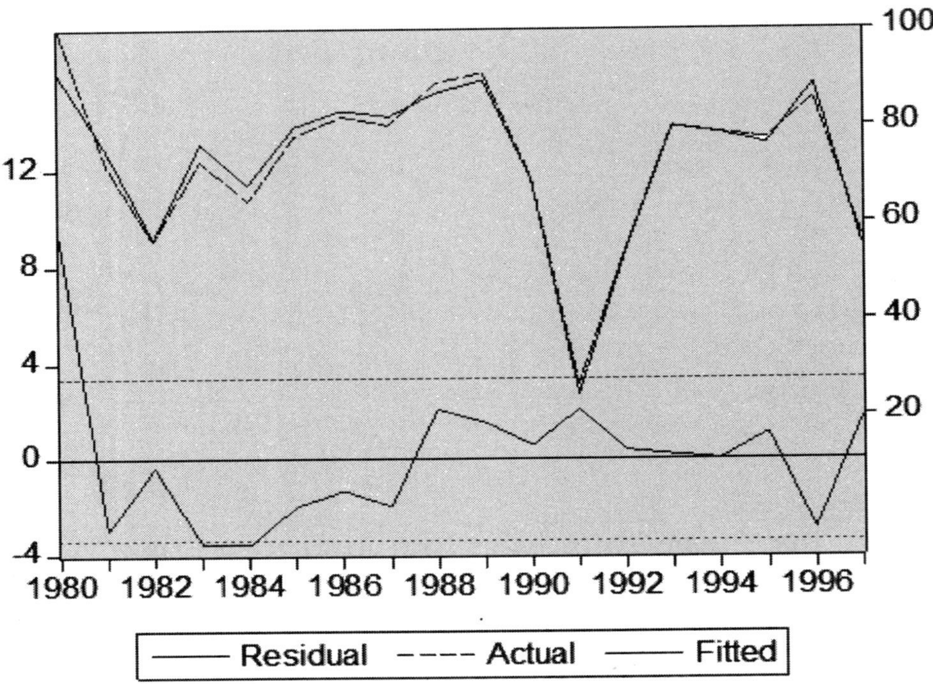

Fig. 9.6: Line Chart Estimated Linear Models for Regional Iron and Steel Industry at Constant Price- Bihar

Table 9.7: Estimated Non Linear Models for Regional Iron and Steel Industry at Current Price- Bihar

Variable	Coefficient	Std. Error	t-Statistic	Prob.
C	4.712395	0.158318	29.76530	0.0000
LOG(X1)	0.999994	0.025057	39.90843	0.0000
LOG(X2)	-0.007305	0.034205	-0.213558	0.8342
LOG(X3)	-1.026343	0.031309	-32.78128	0.0000
LOG(X4)	0.011408	0.040797	0.279629	0.7842
R-squared	0.993438	Mean dependent var		4.280163
Adjusted R-squared	0.991419	S.D. dependent var		0.295539
S.E. of regression	0.027377	Akaike info criterion		-4.128100
Sum squared resid	0.009743	Schwarz criterion		-3.880774

Prob(F-statistic) 0.000000

Estimation Equation:

LOG(Y) = C(1) + C(2)*LOG(X1) + C(3)*LOG(X2) + C(4)*LOG(X3) + C(5)*LOG(X4)

Substituted Coefficients:

LOG(Y) = 4.71239458 + 0.999994085*LOG(X1) - 0.007304694445*LOG(X2) - 1.026342722*LOG(X3) + 0.01140800591*LOG(X4)

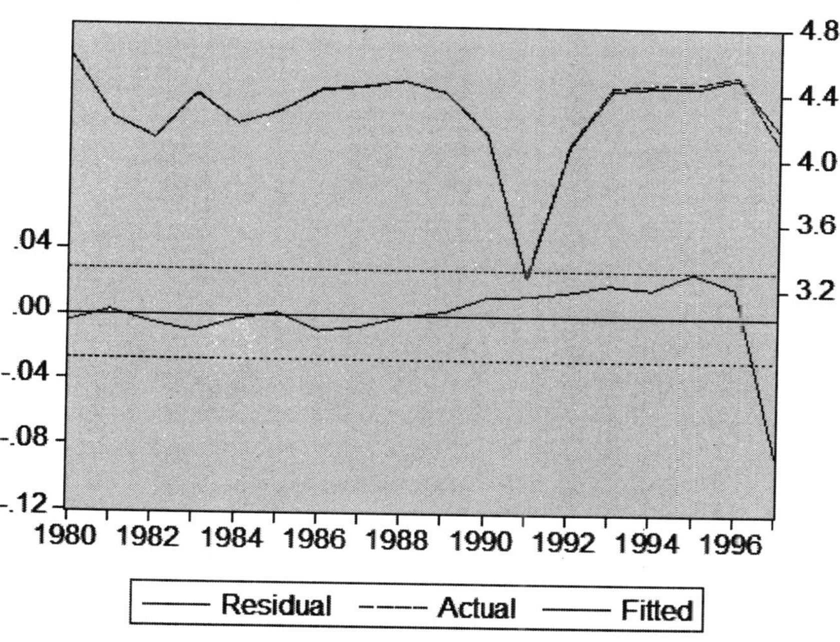

Fig. 9.7: Line Chart Estimated Non Linear Models for Regional Iron and Steel Industry at Current Price- Bihar

Table 9.8: Estimated Non Linear Models for Regional Iron and Steel Industry at Constant Price- Bihar

Variable	Coefficient	Std. Error	t-Statistic	Prob.
C	4.822918	0.283366	17.02008	0.0000
LOG(X1)	0.995934	0.031366	31.75235	0.0000
LOG(X2)	-0.011100	0.037019	-0.299850	0.7690
LOG(X3)	-1.030412	0.050971	-20.21560	0.0000
LOG(X4)	-0.001962	0.037627	-0.052138	0.9592
R-squared	0.993173	Mean dependent var		4.257563
Adjusted R-squared	0.991072	S.D. dependent var		0.294813
S.E. of regression	0.027856	Akaike info criterion		-4.093390
Sum squared resid	0.010088	Schwarz criterion		-3.846065

Prob (F-statistic) 0.000000

Estimation Equation:

LOG(Y) = C(1) + C(2)*LOG(X1) + C(3)*LOG(X2) + C(4)*LOG(X3) + C(5)*LOG(X4)

Substituted Coefficients:

LOG(Y) = 4.82291793 + 0.9959344661*LOG(X1) - 0.01110003362*LOG(X2) - 1.030412282*LOG(X3) - 0.001961791815*LOG(X4)

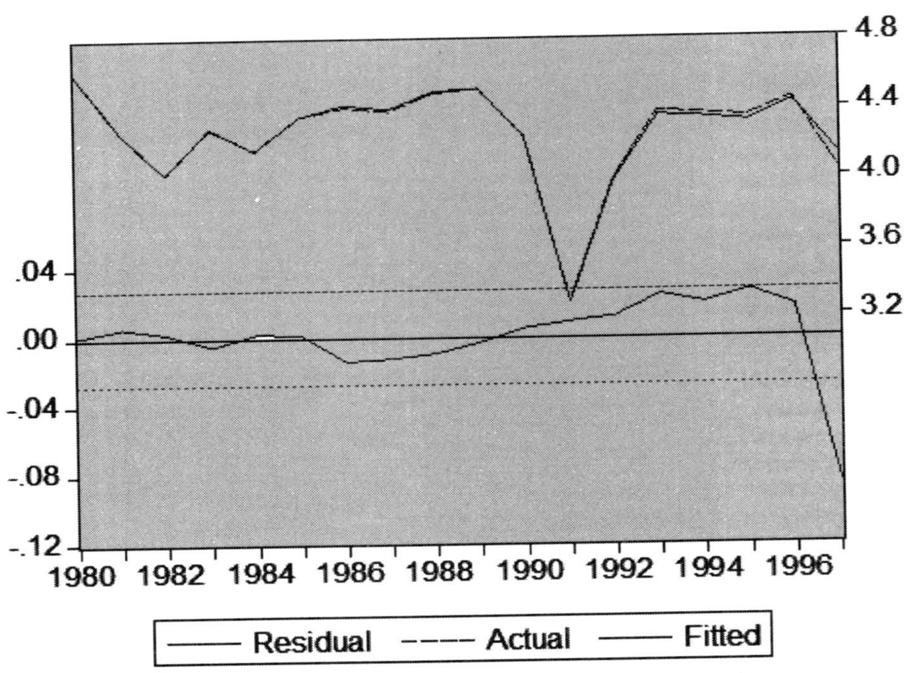

Fig. 9.8: Line Chart Estimated Non Linear Models for Regional Iron and Steel Industry at Constant Price- Bihar

The iron and steel industry is highly concentrated in Bihar due to availability of raw material. The non linear models at constant price and current price have higher R^2 values and hence provide a better fit. Variable x1(average wage rate) and x3 (productivity) are significant in explaining the variance in unit labour cost function. Average wage rate is having incremental impact and productivity has declining impact on unit labour cost. The non significant impact of unit material cost can be understood from the fact that raw materials required for the industry are available in abundance in Bihar. Iron ore and lime stones, the most important raw material of the industry are in abundance. And industries in Bihar also save much in transportation cost of these material. The non impactful nature of the variable x2 (unit material cost) indicate the relative change in unit material cost is much slower than average wage rate and productivity.

Table 9.9: Estimated Linear Models for Regional Iron and Steel Industry at Current Price-Delhi

Variable	Coefficient	Std. Error	t-Statistic	Prob.
C	100.6613	48.28321	2.084809	0.0574
X1	0.140133	0.026522	5.283711	0.0001
X2	-0.053230	0.488393	-0.108990	0.9149
X3	-0.142103	0.024756	-5.740085	0.0001
X4	0.003454	0.001518	2.274863	0.0405
R-squared	0.832303	Mean dependent var		96.93903
Adjusted R-squared	0.780704	S.D. dependent var		20.51096
S.E. of regression	9.605092	Akaike info criterion		7.592597
Sum squared resid	1199.351	Schwarz criterion		7.839923

Prob(F-statistic) 0.000058

Estimation Equation:

Y = C(1) + C(2)*X1 + C(3)*X2 + C(4)*X3 + C(5)*X4

Substituted Coefficients:

Y = 100.6612851 + 0.1401332543*X1 - 0.0532299369*X2 - 0.1421032421*X3 + 0.003453588907*X4

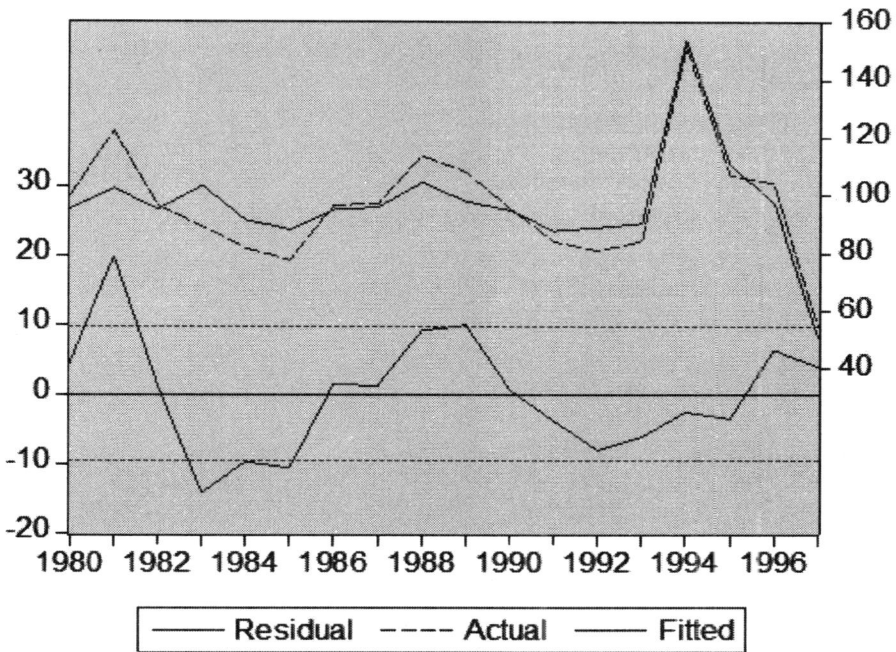

Fig. 9.9: Line Chart Estimated Linear Models for Regional Iron and Steel Industry at Current Price-Delhi

Table 9.10: Estimated Linear Models for Regional Iron and Steel Industry at Constant Price-Delhi

Variable	Coefficient	Std. Error	t-Statistic	Prob.
C	138.0455	30.49399	4.526972	0.0006
X1	0.725500	0.074033	9.799708	0.0000
X2	-0.425833	0.310483	-1.371516	0.1934
X3	-0.675328	0.064062	-10.54175	0.0000
X4	0.000714	0.001635	0.436702	0.6695
R-squared	0.930708	Mean dependent var		132.7701
Adjusted R-squared	0.909387	S.D. dependent var		38.28418
S.E. of regression	11.52430	Akaike info criterion		7.956925
Sum squared resid	1726.522	Schwarz criterion		8.204251

Prob(F-statistic) 0.000000

Estimation Equation:

Y = C(1) + C(2)*X1 + C(3)*X2 + C(4)*X3 + C(5)*X4

Substituted Coefficients:

Y = 138.0454593 + 0.7255001625*X1 - 0.4258329408*X2 - 0.6753284015*X3 + 0.0007137973156*X4

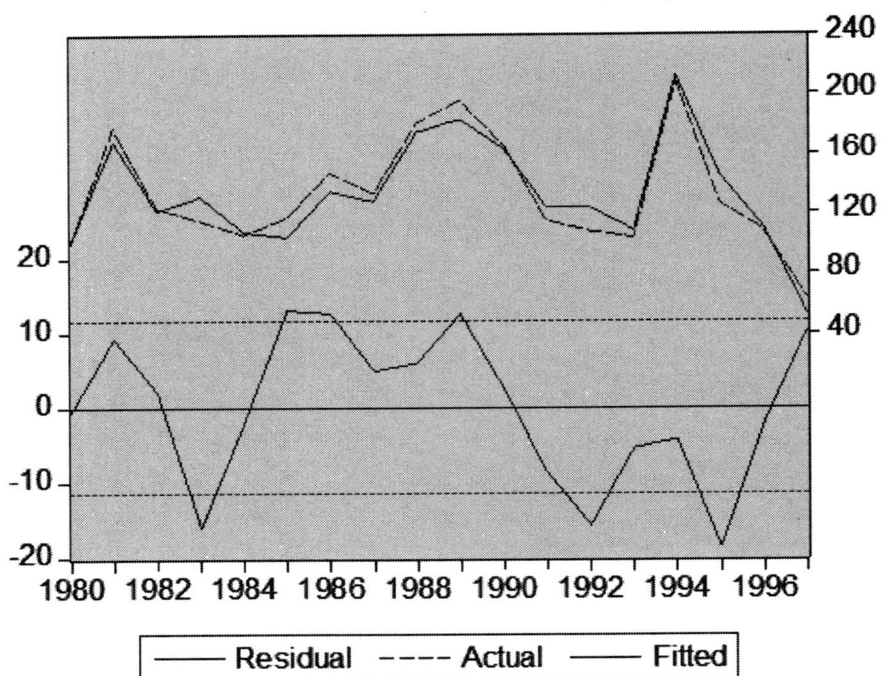

Fig. 9.10: Line Chart Estimated Linear Models for Regional Iron and Steel Industry at Constant Price-Delhi

Table 9.11: Estimated Non Linear Models for Regional Iron and Steel Industry at Current Price-Delhi

Variable	Coefficient	Std. Error	t-Statistic	Prob.
C	-2.924703	1.986026	-1.472641	0.1646
LOG(X1)	0.038614	0.140071	0.275676	0.7871
LOG(X2)	1.567631	0.407916	3.843028	0.0020
LOG(X3)	-0.158646	0.068562	-2.313908	0.0377
LOG(X4)	0.163996	0.085038	1.928502	0.0759
R-squared	0.555080	Mean dependent var		4.552948
Adjusted R-squared	0.418181	S.D. dependent var		0.213550
S.E. of regression	0.162890	Akaike info criterion		-0.561355
Sum squared resid	0.344929	Schwarz criterion		-0.314029
Prob(F-statistic)	0.023842			

Estimation Equation:

LOG(Y) = C(1) + C(2)*LOG(X1) + C(3)*LOG(X2) + C(4)*LOG(X3) + C(5)*LOG(X4)

Substituted Coefficients:

LOG(Y) = -2.924703379 + 0.03861419555*LOG(X1) + 1.567631173*LOG(X2) - 0.1586456079*LOG(X3) + 0.1639963729*LOG(X4)

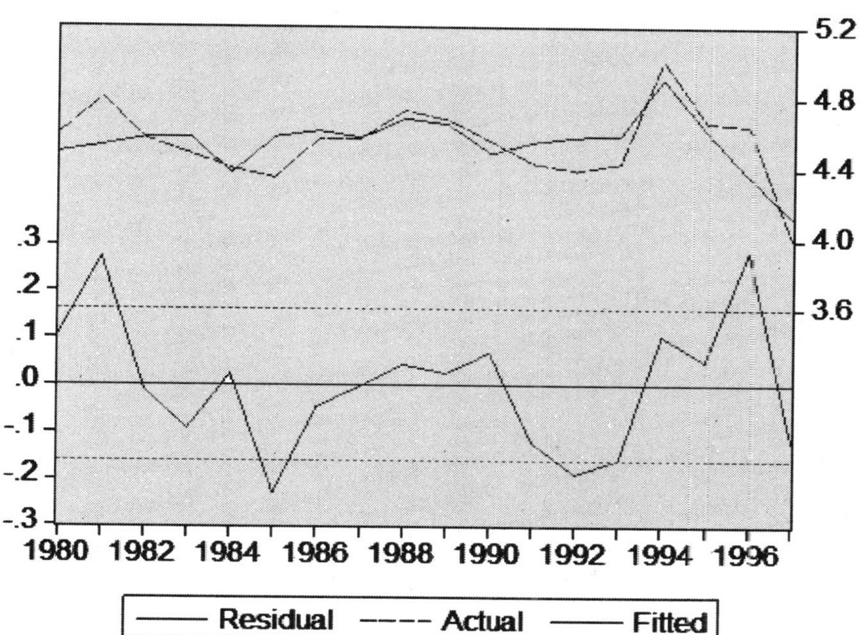

Fig. 9.11: Line Chart Estimated Non Linear Models for Regional Iron and Steel Industry at Current Price-Delhi

Table 9.12: Estimated Non Linear Models for Regional Iron and Steel Industry at Constant Price-Delhi

Variable	Coefficient	Std. Error	t-Statistic	Prob.
C	0.738469	1.846522	0.399924	0.6957
LOG(X1)	1.209307	0.315676	3.830851	0.0021
LOG(X2)	-0.082976	0.518414	-0.160057	0.8753
LOG(X3)	-0.164987	0.072272	-2.282858	0.0399
LOG(X4)	-0.155410	0.074383	-2.089317	0.0569
R-squared	0.675985	Mean dependent var		4.848921
Adjusted R-squared	0.576288	S.D. dependent var		0.293278
S.E. of regression	0.190904	Akaike info criterion		-0.243959
Sum squared resid	0.473776	Schwarz criterion		0.003366

Prob(F-statistic) 0.003553

Estimation Equation:

LOG(Y) = C(1) + C(2)*LOG(X1) + C(3)*LOG(X2) + C(4)*LOG(X3) + C(5)*LOG(X4)

Substituted Coefficients:

LOG(Y) = 0.7384686319 + 1.209306644*LOG(X1) - 0.08297561069*LOG(X2) - 0.1649869776*LOG(X3) - 0.1554101498*LOG(X4)

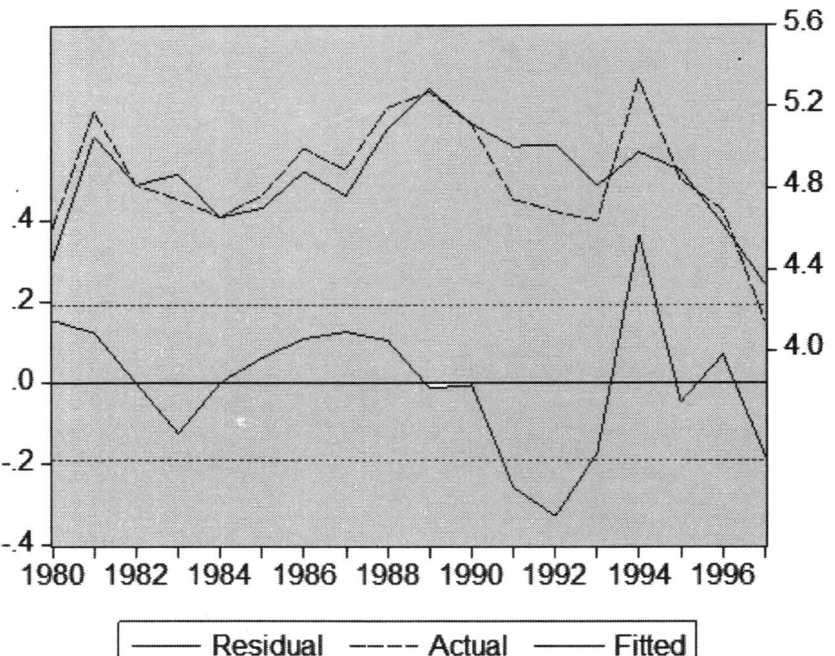

Fig. 9.12: Line Chart Estimated Non Linear Models for Regional Iron and Steel Industry at Constant Price-Delhi

Iron and steel is not a popular industry of Delhi, generally re-rolling mills are established here. The current price models provide better fit models. The non linear model has higher R^2 (.93) than linear model (0.83). Variable x1 (average wage rate) and x3 (productivity) provide explanation for variance in unit labour cost.

Table 9.13: Estimated Linear Models for Regional Iron and Steel Industry at Current Price-Karnataka

Variable	Coefficient	Std. Error	t-Statistic	Prob.
C	100.3379	23.88404	4.201044	0.0010
X1	0.101074	0.034183	2.956839	0.0111
X2	0.028804	0.201549	0.142915	0.8885
X3	-0.113423	0.020666	-5.488329	0.0001
X4	-0.003643	0.006720	-0.542024	0.5970
R-squared	0.845058	Mean dependent var		90.24530
Adjusted R-squared	0.797383	S.D. dependent var		16.98129
S.E. of regression	7.643784	Akaike info criterion		7.135796
Sum squared resid	759.5566	Schwarz criterion		7.383121
Prob(F-statistic)	0.000035			

Estimation Equation:

Y = C(1) + C(2)*X1 + C(3)*X2 + C(4)*X3 + C(5)*X4

Substituted Coefficients:

Y = 100.337907 + 0.1010740309*X1 + 0.02880428944*X2 - 0.1134232043*X3 - 0.003642640855*X4

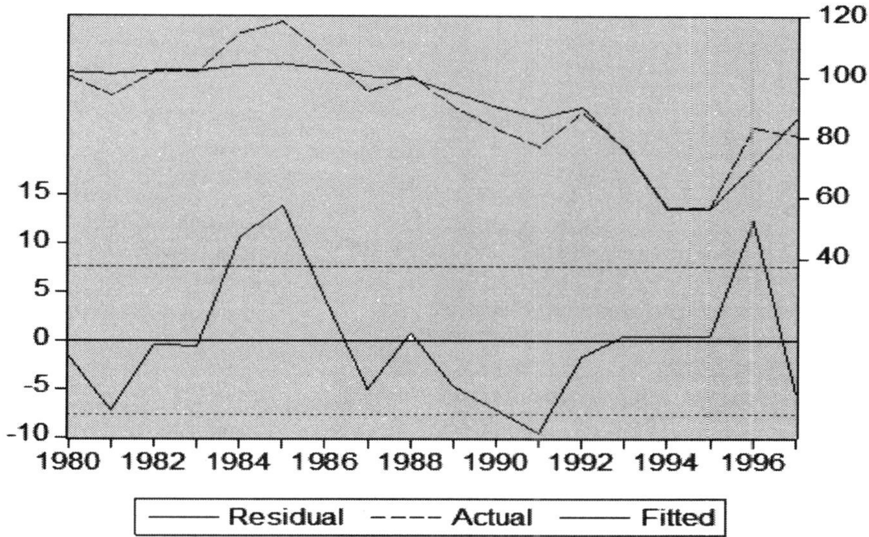

Fig. 9.13: Line Chart Estimated Linear Models for Regional Iron and Steel Industry at Current Price-Karnataka

Table 9.14: Estimated Linear Models for Regional Iron and Steel Industry at Constant Price-Karnataka

Variable	Coefficient	Std. Error	t-Statistic	Prob.
C	90.56423	14.63029	6.190188	0.0000
X1	0.416670	0.085843	4.853888	0.0003
X2	0.056023	0.107730	0.520028	0.6118
X3	-0.385530	0.048549	-7.941009	0.0000
X4	-0.007607	0.003804	-1.999881	0.0669
R-squared	0.904462	Mean dependent var		88.09341
Adjusted R-squared	0.875066	S.D. dependent var		19.27313
S.E. of regression	6.812283	Akaike info criterion		6.905465
Sum squared resid	603.2936	Schwarz criterion		7.152790

Prob(F-statistic) 0.000002

Estimation Equation:

Y = C(1) + C(2)*X1 + C(3)*X2 + C(4)*X3 + C(5)*X4

Substituted Coefficients:

Y = 90.56422805 + 0.4166703517*X1 + 0.0560226554*X2 - 0.3855302179*X3 - 0.007606958132*X4

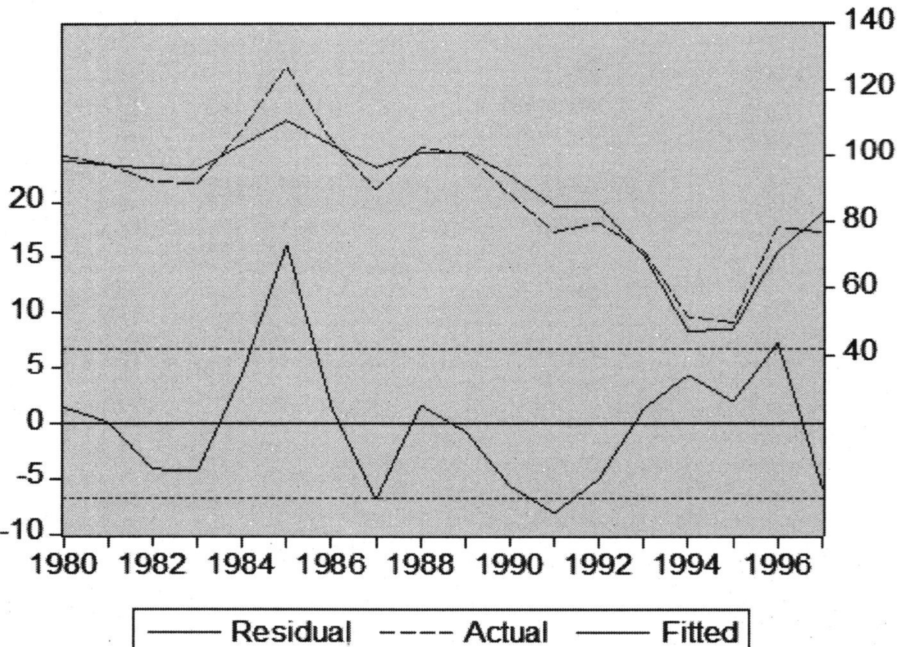

Fig. 9.14: Line Chart Estimated Linear Models for Regional Iron and Steel Industry at Constant Price-Karnataka

Table 9.15: Estimated Non Linear Models for Regional Iron and Steel Industry at Current Price- Karnataka

Variable	Coefficient	Std. Error	t-Statistic	Prob.
C	6.031323	0.472662	12.76033	0.0000
LOG(X1)	0.855052	0.063408	13.48488	0.0000
LOG(X2)	-0.278962	0.100803	-2.767405	0.0160
LOG(X3)	-0.830062	0.056344	-14.73207	0.0000
LOG(X4)	-0.046724	0.021179	-2.206151	0.0460
R-squared	0.975652	Mean dependent var		4.484014
Adjusted R-squared	0.968160	S.D. dependent var		0.203842
S.E. of regression	0.036373	Akaike info criterion		-3.559849
Sum squared resid	0.017199	Schwarz criterion		-3.312524
Prob(F-statistic)	0.000000			

Estimation Equation:

LOG(Y) = C(1) + C(2)*LOG(X1) + C(3)*LOG(X2) + C(4)*LOG(X3) + C(5)*LOG(X4)

Substituted Coefficients:

LOG(Y) = 6.031323475 + 0.8550523809*LOG(X1) - 0.2789618173*LOG(X2) - 0.8300619173*LOG(X3) - 0.04672357141*LOG(X4)

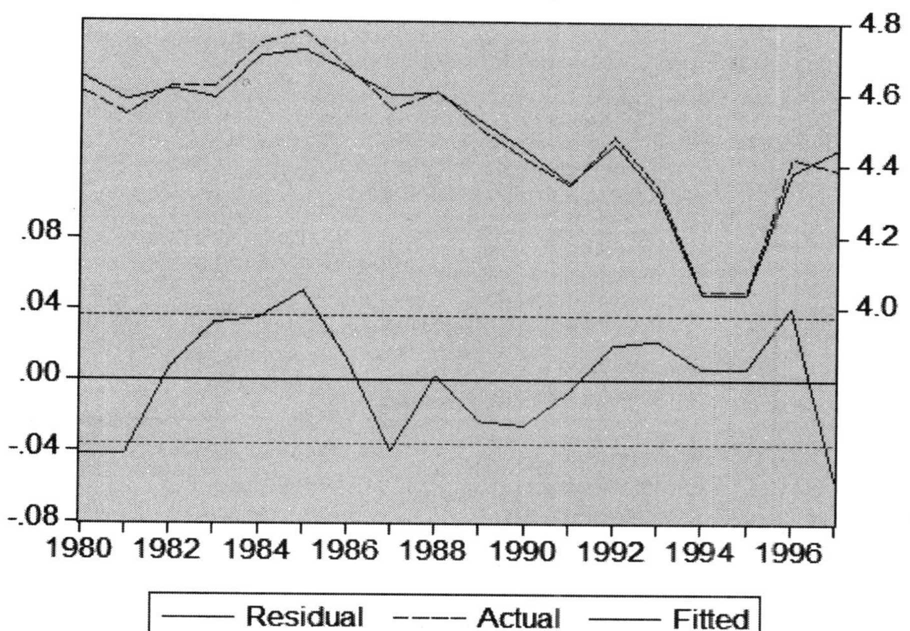

Fig. 9.15: Line Chart Estimated Non Linear Models for Regional Iron and Steel Industry at Current Price- Karnataka

Table 9.16: Estimated Non Linear Models for Regional Iron and Steel Industry at Constant Price- Karnataka

Variable	Coefficient	Std. Error	t-Statistic	Prob.
C	4.987780	0.447986	11.13378	0.0000
LOG(X1)	0.880927	0.065500	13.44933	0.0000
LOG(X2)	-0.094204	0.087909	-1.071615	0.3034
LOG(X3)	-0.807684	0.062886	-12.84364	0.0000
LOG(X4)	-0.053028	0.019501	-2.719217	0.0175
R-squared	0.975608	Mean dependent var		4.452938
Adjusted R-squared	0.968103	S.D. dependent var		0.240612
S.E. of regression	0.042973	Akaike info criterion		-3.226370
Sum squared resid	0.024006	Schwarz criterion		-2.979044

Prob(F-statistic) 0.000000

Estimation Equation:

LOG(Y) = C(1) + C(2)*LOG(X1) + C(3)*LOG(X2) + C(4)*LOG(X3) + C(5)*LOG(X4)

Substituted Coefficients:

LOG(Y) = 4.987780168 + 0.8809270344*LOG(X1) - 0.09420426399*LOG(X2) - 0.8076842663*LOG(X3) - 0.05302774537*LOG(X4)

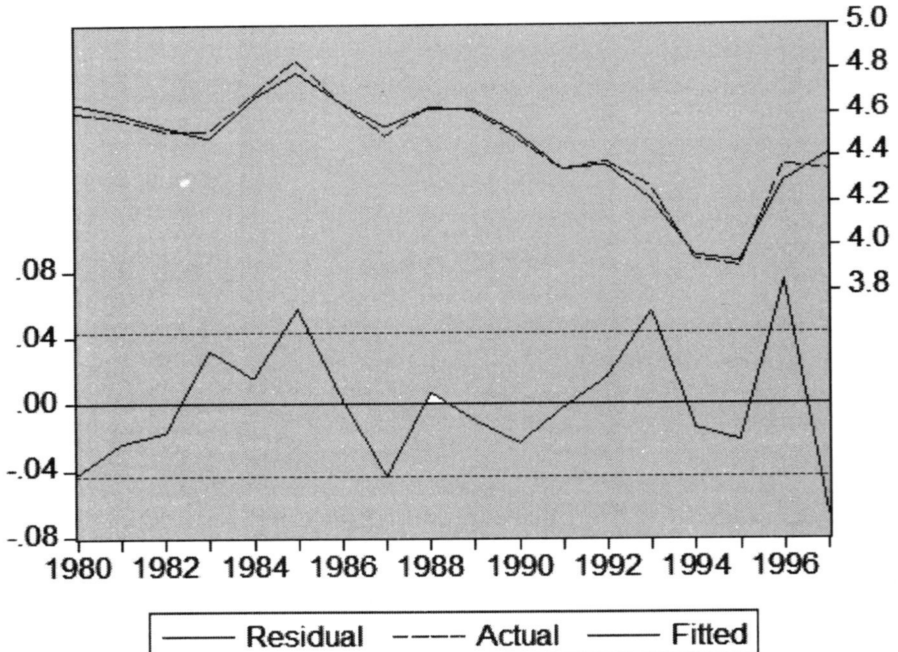

Fig. 9.16: Line Chart Estimated Non Linear Models for Regional Iron and Steel Industry at Constant Price- Karnataka

The non linear model provides better fit. Variable x1 (average wage rate) and x3 (productivity) have significant coefficient in the model and explain the variance in unit labour cost.

Table 9.17: Estimated Linear Models for Regional Iron and Steel Industry at Current Price- Maharashtra

Variable	Coefficient	Std. Error	t-Statistic	Prob.
C	152.0654	42.49732	3.578236	0.0034
X1	0.080207	0.037264	2.152387	0.0507
X2	-0.358351	0.387632	-0.924461	0.3721
X3	-0.173433	0.031632	-5.482785	0.0001
REPX4	0.010964	0.004548	2.410781	0.0314
R-squared	0.893461	Mean dependent var		85.87582
Adjusted R-squared	0.860680	S.D. dependent var		19.35949
S.E. of regression	7.226040	Akaike info criterion		7.023392
Sum squared resid	678.8034	Schwarz criterion		7.270718

Prob(F-statistic) 0.000003

Estimation Equation:

Y = C(1) + C(2)*X1 + C(3)*X2 + C(4)*X3 + C(5)*REPX4

Substituted Coefficients:

Y = 152.065423 + 0.08020664155*X1 - 0.3583507787*X2 - 0.1734325998*X3 + 0.01096400427*REPX4

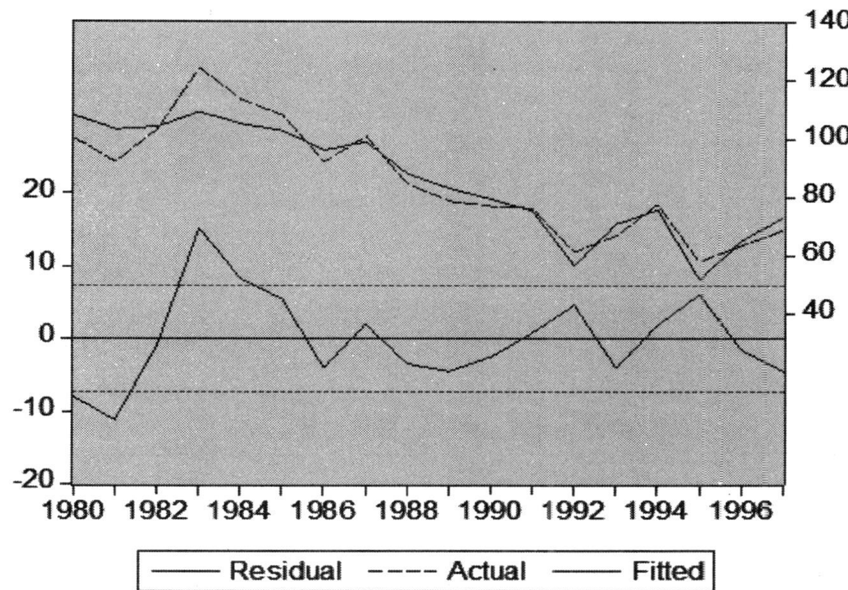

Fig. 9.17: Line Chart Estimated Linear Models for Regional Iron and Steel Industry at Current Price- Maharashtra

Table 9.18: Estimated Linear Models for Regional Iron and Steel Industry at Constant Price- Maharashtra

Variable	Coefficient	Std. Error	t-Statistic	Prob.
C	98.53066	17.06279	5.774592	0.0001
X1	0.065997	0.102265	0.645350	0.5299
X2	0.331833	0.180418	1.839245	0.0888
X3	-0.384638	0.045753	-8.406745	0.0000
REPX4	0.001555	0.002309	0.673307	0.5125
R-squared	0.957398	Mean dependent var		85.19768
Adjusted R-squared	0.944290	S.D. dependent var		20.01171
S.E. of regression	4.723364	Akaike info criterion		6.173053
Sum squared resid	290.0322	Schwarz criterion		6.420378

Prob(F-statistic) 0.000000

Estimation Equation:

Y = C(1) + C(2)*X1 + C(3)*X2 + C(4)*X3 + C(5)*REPX4

Substituted Coefficients:

Y = 98.53066266 + 0.06599684766*X1 + 0.3318332005*X2 - 0.3846379108*X3 + 0.001554679229*REPX4

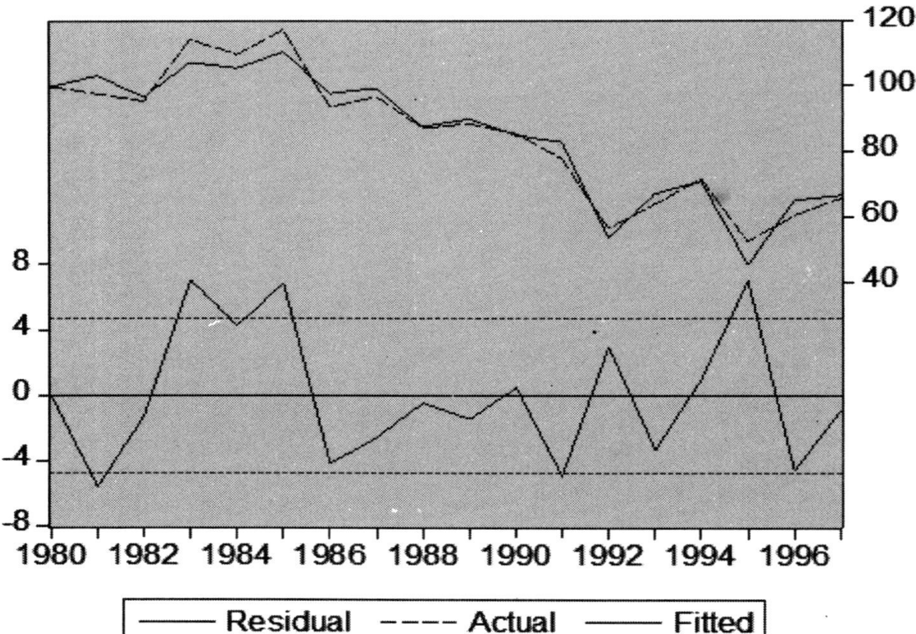

Fig. 9.18: Line Chart Estimated Linear Models for Regional Iron and Steel Industry at Constant Price- Maharashtra

Table 9.19: Estimated Non Linear Models for Regional Iron and Steel Industry at Current Price- Maharashtra

Variable	Coefficient	Std. Error	t-Statistic	Prob.
C	4.289005	0.592533	7.238427	0.0000
LOG(X1)	0.711290	0.056873	12.50673	0.0000
LOG(X2)	0.186279	0.119168	1.563169	0.1420
LOG(X3)	-0.828601	0.059034	-14.03593	0.0000
LOG(REPX4)	0.004706	0.027896	0.168692	0.8686
R-squared	0.988677	Mean dependent var		4.428907
Adjusted R-squared	0.985193	S.D. dependent var		0.225783
S.E. of regression	0.027475	Akaike info criterion		-4.120982
Sum squared resid	0.009813	Schwarz criterion		-3.873657

Prob(F-statistic) 0.000000

Estimation Equation:

LOG(Y) = C(1) + C(2)*LOG(X1) + C(3)*LOG(X2) + C(4)*LOG(X3) + C(5)*LOG(REPX4)

Substituted Coefficients:

LOG(Y) = 4.289004723 + 0.7112895417*LOG(X1) + 0.1862793546*LOG(X2) - 0.8286005568*LOG(X3) + 0.004705857687*LOG(REPX4)

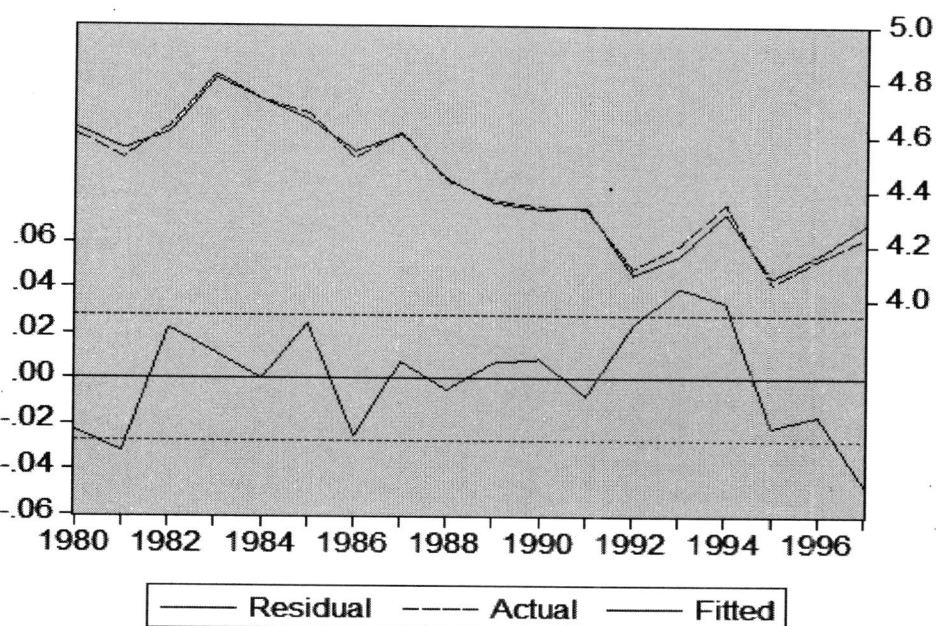

Fig. 9.19: Line Chart Estimated Non Linear Models for Regional Iron and Steel Industry at Current Price- Maharashtra

Table 9.20: Estimated Non Linear Models for Regional Iron and Steel Industry at Constant Price- Maharashtra

Variable	Coefficient	Std. Error	t-Statistic	Prob.
C	4.211954	0.442086	9.527458	0.0000
LOG(X1)	0.562049	0.106405	5.282179	0.0001
LOG(X2)	0.363408	0.090603	4.011004	0.0015
LOG(X3)	-0.826668	0.053717	-15.38922	0.0000
LOG(X4)	-0.019741	0.019797	-0.997183	0.3369
R-squared	0.992671	Mean dependent var		4.417096
Adjusted R-squared	0.990416	S.D. dependent var		0.247562
S.E. of regression	0.024235	Akaike info criterion		-4.371883
Sum squared resid	0.007636	Schwarz criterion		-4.124558

Prob(F-statistic) 0.000000

Estimation Equation:

LOG(Y) = C(1) + C(2)*LOG(X1) + C(3)*LOG(X2) + C(4)*LOG(X3) + C(5)*LOG(X4)

Substituted Coefficients:

LOG(Y) = 4.211953644 + 0.5620493763*LOG(X1) + 0.3634075516*LOG(X2) - 0.8266684188*LOG(X3) - 0.01974076849*LOG(X4)

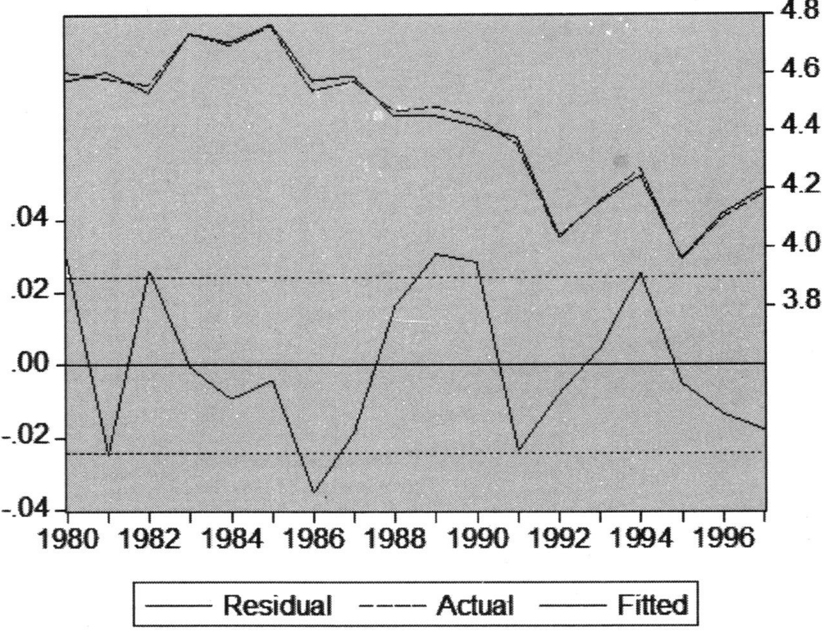

Fig. 9.20: Line Chart Estimated Non Linear Models for Regional Iron and Steel Industry at Constant Price- Maharashtra

The non linear model provides better fit. In current price models x3 (productivity) has significant coefficient. In the constant price model variable x1 (average wage rate) and x3 have significant coefficient and explain the variance in unit labour cost. The constant price non linear model provides best fit.

Table 9.21: Estimated Linear Models for Regional Iron and Steel Industry at Current Price-Punjab

Variable	Coefficient	Std. Error	t-Statistic	Prob.
C	147.1420	29.91830	4.918128	0.0003
X1	0.148773	0.063641	2.337671	0.0360
X2	-0.380339	0.305937	-1.243195	0.2358
X3	-0.215754	0.046048	-4.685448	0.0004
X4	0.007957	0.011610	0.685390	0.5051
R-squared	0.880396	Mean dependent var		92 09971
Adjusted R-squared	0.843595	S.D. dependent var		14.42088
S.E. of regression	5.703177	Akaike info criterion		6.550057
Sum squared resid	422.8410	Schwarz criterion		6.797383

Prob(F-statistic) 0.000007

Estimation Equation:

Y = C(1) + C(2)*X1 + C(3)*X2 + C(4)*X3 + C(5)*X4

Substituted Coefficients:

Y = 147.1420308 + 0.148772607*X1 - 0.3803388147*X2 - 0.2157535222*X3 + 0.00795709977*X4

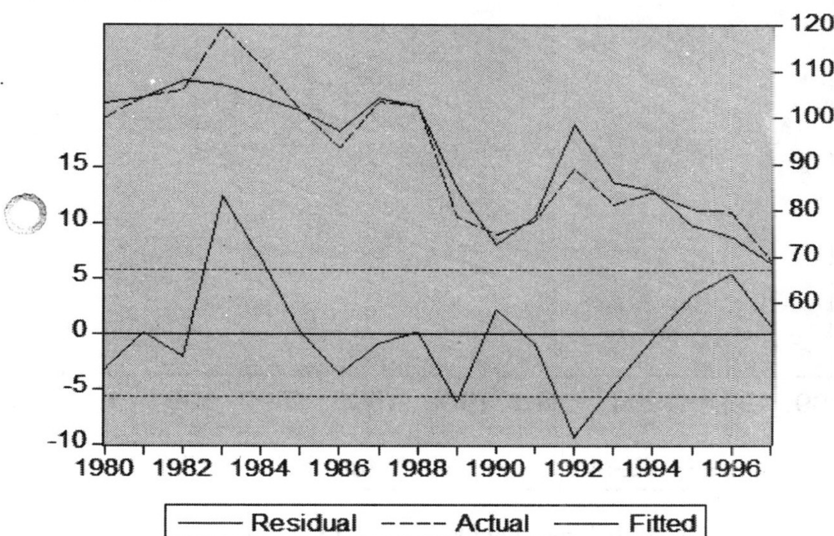

Fig. 9.21: Line Chart Estimated Linear Models for Regional Iron and Steel Industry at Current Price-Punjab

Table 9.22: Estimated Linear Models for Regional Iron and Steel Industry at Constant Price-Punjab

Variable	Coefficient	Std. Error	t-Statistic	Prob.
C	135.3944	10.30826	13.13455	0.0000
X1	0.302532	0.205937	1.469051	0.1656
X2	-0.191227	0.116889	-1.635966	0.1258
X3	-0.457642	0.118830	-3.851243	0.0020
X4	-0.005854	0.003725	-1.571338	0.1401
R-squared	0.937944	Mean dependent var		88.37920
Adjusted R-squared	0.918850	S.D. dependent var		14.68543
S.E. of regression	4.183415	Akaike info criterion		5.930266
Sum squared resid	227.5125	Schwarz criterion		6.177591

Prob(F-statistic) 0.000000

Estimation Equation:

Y = C(1) + C(2)*X1 + C(3)*X2 + C(4)*X3 + C(5)*X4

Substituted Coefficients:

Y = 135.3944482 + 0.3025319161*X1 - 0.1912265598*X2 - 0.4576415975*X3 - 0.005853734229*X4

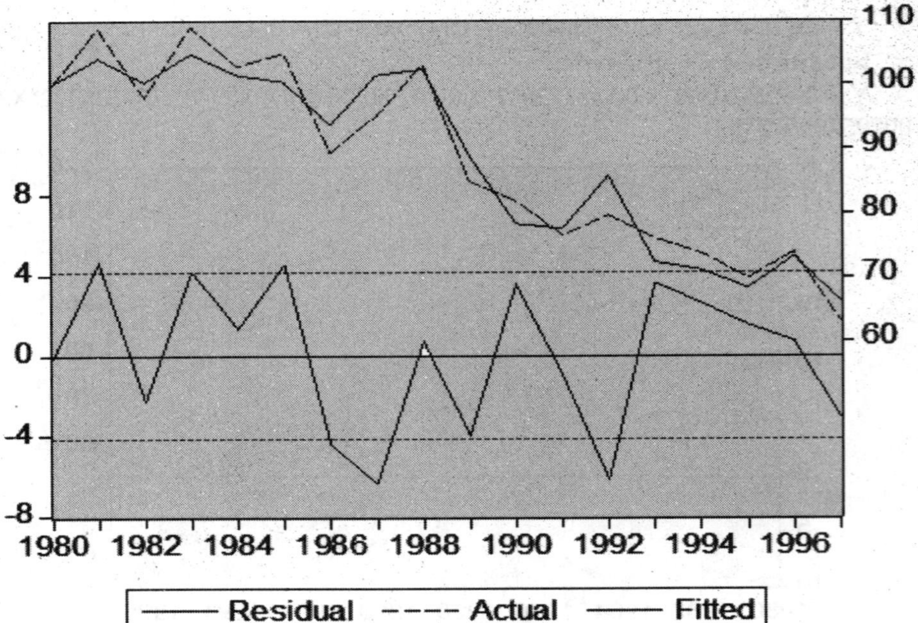

Fig. 9.22: Line Chart Estimated Linear Models for Regional Iron and Steel Industry at Constant Price-Punjab

Table 9.23: Estimated Non Linear Models for Regional Iron and Steel Industry at Current Price- Punjab

Variable	Coefficient	Std. Error	t-Statistic	Prob.
C	6.156027	0.718695	8.565566	0.0000
LOG(X1)	0.508630	0.131926	3.855426	0.0020
LOG(X2)	-0.179346	0.178245	-1.006179	0.3327
LOG(X3)	-0.715113	0.068861	-10.38486	0.0000
LOG(X4)	0.049285	0.057614	0.855438	0.4078
R-squared	0.969027	Mean dependent var		4.511263
Adjusted R-squared	0.959497	S.D. dependent var		0.156983
S.E. of regression	0.031593	Akaike info criterion		-3.841617
Sum squared resid	0.012976	Schwarz criterion		-3.594292

Prob(F-statistic) 0.000000

Estimation Equation:

LOG(Y) = C(1) + C(2)*LOG(X1) + C(3)*LOG(X2) + C(4)*LOG(X3) + C(5)*LOG(X4)

Substituted Coefficients:

LOG(Y) = 6.156027473 + 0.5086297342*LOG(X1) - 0.1793461944*LOG(X2) - 0.7151125334*LOG(X3) + 0.04928522205*LOG(X4)

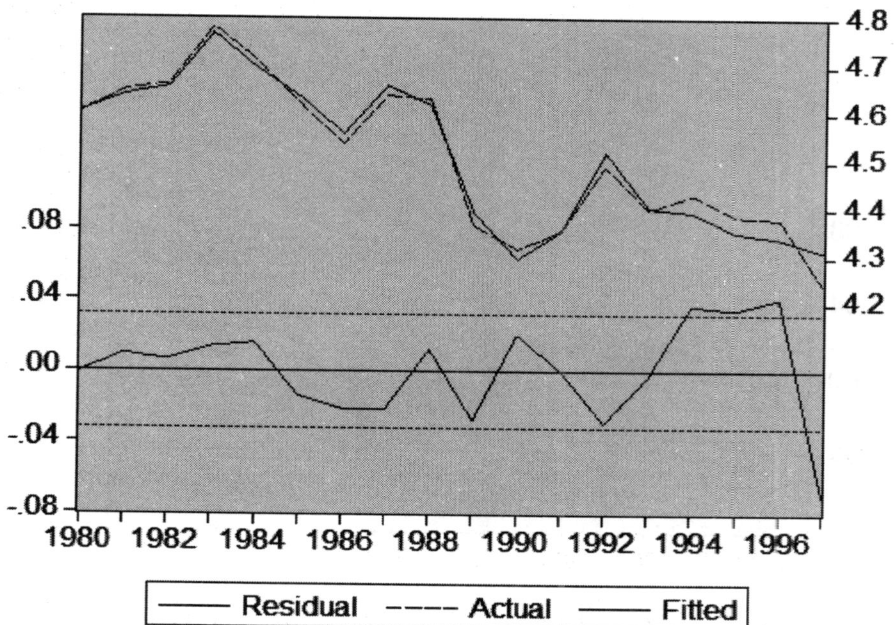

Fig. 9.23: Line Chart Estimated Non Linear Models for Regional Iron and Steel Industry at Current Price- Punjab

Table 9.24: Estimated Non Linear Models for Regional Iron and Steel Industry at Constant Price- Punjab

Variable	Coefficient	Std. Error	t-Statistic	Prob.
C	5.750179	0.577860	9.950808	0.0000
LOG(X1)	0.552519	0.243604	2.268106	0.0410
LOG(X2)	-0.095770	0.121004	-0.791463	0.4429
LOG(X3)	-0.618189	0.118591	-5.212787	0.0002
LOG(X4)	-0.087473	0.026732	-3.272270	0.0061
R-squared	0.962962	Mean dependent var		4.468249
Adjusted R-squared	0.951566	S.D. dependent var		0.169574
S.E. of regression	0.037320	Akaike info criterion		-3.508462
Sum squared resid	0.018106	Schwarz criterion		-3.261137

Prob(F-statistic) 0.000000

Estimation Equation:

LOG(Y) = C(1) + C(2)*LOG(X1) + C(3)*LOG(X2) + C(4)*LOG(X3) + C(5)*LOG(X4)

Substituted Coefficients:

LOG(Y) = 5.750179074 + 0.5525190066*LOG(X1) - 0.09577004294*LOG(X2) - 0.618189044*LOG(X3) - 0.08747340372*LOG(X4)

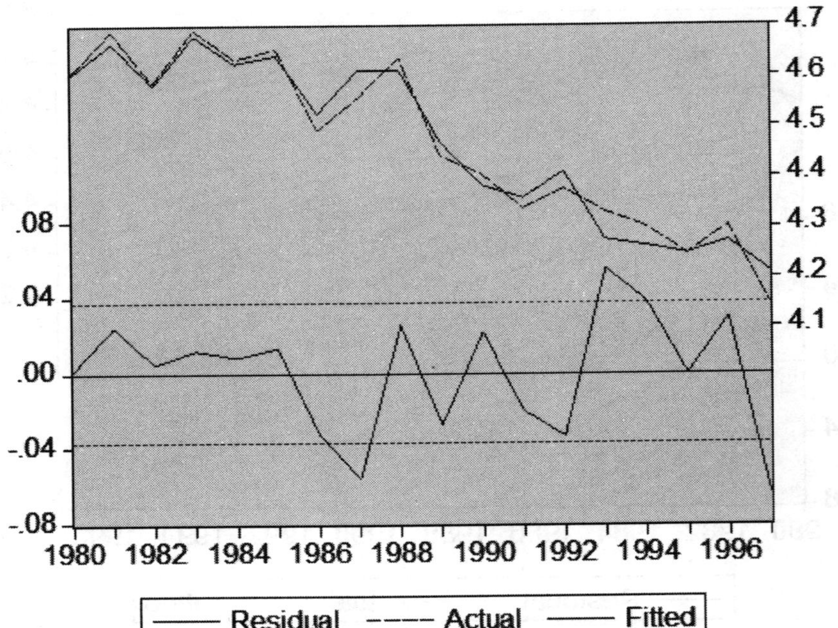

Fig. 9.24: Line Chart Estimated Non Linear Models for Regional Iron and Steel Industry at Constant Price- Punjab

Like other regions the non-linear models offer higher R^2 values, hence the better fit. Explanatory variables x1 and x3 have significant coefficients thus they explain the variance in independent variable unit labour cost.

Table 9.25: Estimated Linear Models for Regional Iron and Steel Industry at Current Price-Uttar Pradesh

Variable	Coefficient	Std. Error	t-Statistic	Prob.
C	59.06248	58.69821	1.006206	0.3327
X1	-0.048691	0.049758	-0.978573	0.3457
X2	0.494082	0.582324	0.848466	0.4115
X3	-0.100844	0.027608	-3.652658	0.0029
REPX4	0.037586	0.015193	2.473825	0.0279
R-squared	0.928562	Mean dependent var		71.62573
Adjusted R-squared	0.906581	S.D. dependent var		24.05939
S.E. of regression	7.353657	Akaike info criterion		7.058406
Sum squared resid	702.9916	Schwarz criterion		7.305731

Prob(F-statistic) 0.000000

Estimation Equation:

Y = C(1) + C(2)*X1 + C(3)*X2 + C(4)*X3 + C(5)*REPX4

Substituted Coefficients:

Y = 59.06247713 - 0.0486913981*X1 + 0.4940821372*X2 - 0.100844293*X3 + 0.03758599727*REPX4

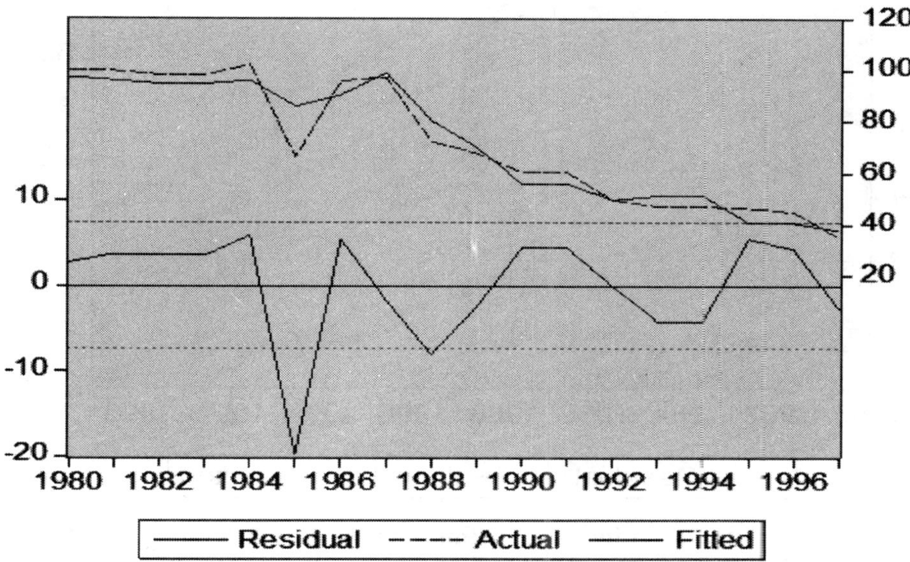

Fig. 9.25: Line Chart Estimated Linear Models for Regional Iron and Steel Industry at Current Price-Uttar Pradesh

Table 9.26: Estimated Linear Models for Regional Iron and Steel Industry at Constant Price-Uttar Pradesh

Variable	Coefficient	Std. Error	t-Statistic	Prob.
C	159.8727	18.28265	8.744502	0.0000
X1	0.189121	0.096347	1.962925	0.0714
X2	-0.523634	0.195041	-2.684738	0.0187
X3	-0.216241	0.047002	-4.600673	0.0005
X4	-0.012896	0.004210	-3.063371	0.0091
R-squared	0.959150	Mean dependent var		73.30648
Adjusted R-squared	0.946581	S.D. dependent var		24.97205
S.E. of regression	5.771704	Akaike info criterion		6.573945
Sum squared resid	433.0634	Schwarz criterion		6.821270

Prob(F-statistic) 0.000000

Estimation Equation:

Y = C(1) + C(2)*X1 + C(3)*X2 + C(4)*X3 + C(5)*X4

Substituted Coefficients:

Y = 159.8726884 + 0.1891214881*X1 - 0.5236336922*X2 - 0.2162413115*X3 - 0.01289562238*X4

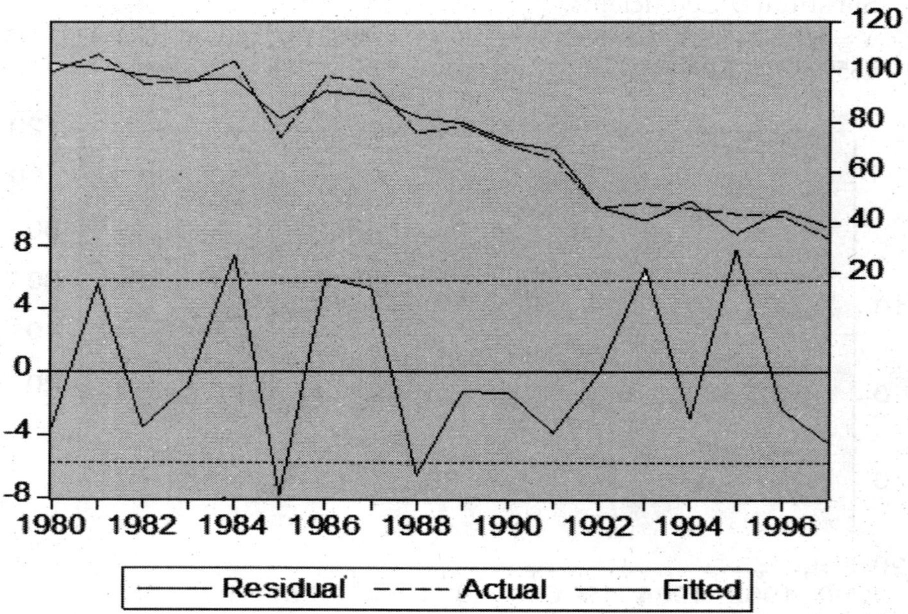

Fig. 9.26: Line Chart Estimated Linear Models for Regional Iron and Steel Industry at Constant Price-Uttar Pradesh

Table 9.27: Estimated Non Linear Models for Regional Iron and Steel Industry at Current Price- Uttar Pradesh

Variable	Coefficient	Std. Error	t-Statistic	Prob.
C	0.939498	3.374158	0.278439	0.7851
LOG(X1)	0.328606	0.188480	1.743458	0.1048
LOG(X2)	1.102313	0.777046	1.418595	0.1795
LOG(X3)	-0.684508	0.114336	-5.986817	0.0000
LOG(REPX4)	0.051066	0.076715	0.665656	0.5173
R-squared	0.954675	Mean dependent var		4.214357
Adjusted R-squared	0.940729	S.D. dependent var		0.354081
S.E. of regression	0.086204	Akaike info criterion		-1.834077
Sum squared resid	0.096604	Schwarz criterion		-1.586752

Prob (F-statistic) 0.000000

Estimation Equation:

LOG(Y) = C(1) + C(2)*LOG(X1) + C(3)*LOG(X2) + C(4)*LOG(X3) + C(5)*LOG(REPX4)

Substituted Coefficients:

LOG(Y) = 0.9394977173 + 0.3286061219*LOG(X1) + 1.102313005*LOG(X2) - 0.6845076686*LOG(X3) + 0.05106576556*LOG (REPX4)

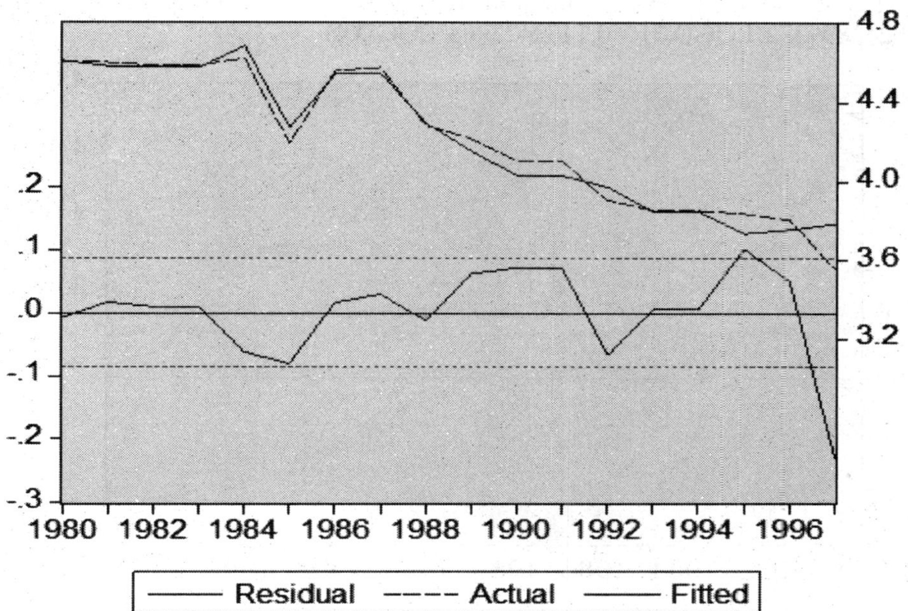

Fig. 9.27: Line Chart Estimated Non Linear Models for Regional Iron and Steel Industry at Current Price- Uttar Pradesh

Table 9.28: Estimated Non Linear Models for Regional Iron and Steel Industry at Constant Price - Uttar Pradesh

Variable	Coefficient	Std. Error	t-Statistic	Prob.
C	6.768976	1.215017	5.571094	0.0001
LOG(X1)	0.787423	0.175763	4.480016	0.0006
LOG(X2)	-0.580694	0.344137	-1.687390	0.1154
LOG(X3)	-0.524090	0.137624	-3.808128	0.0022
LOG(X4)	-0.145243	0.048222	-3.011975	0.0100
R-squared	0.961935	Mean dependent var		4.232264
Adjusted R-squared	0.950223	S.D. dependent var		0.375793
S.E. of regression	0.083843	Akaike info criterion		-1.889619
Sum squared resid	0.091384	Schwarz criterion		-1.642294
Log likelihood	22.00657	F-statistic		82.13011
Durbin-Watson stat	1.536283	Prob(F-statistic)		0.000000

Prob(F-statistic) 0.000000

Estimation Equation:

LOG(Y) = C(1) + C(2)*LOG(X1) + C(3)*LOG(X2) + C(4)*LOG(X3) + C(5)*LOG(X4)

Substituted Coefficients:

LOG(Y) = 6.768975736 + 0.7874231088*LOG(X1) - 0.5806938157*LOG(X2) - 0.5240899372*LOG(X3) - 0.1452425968*LOG(X4)

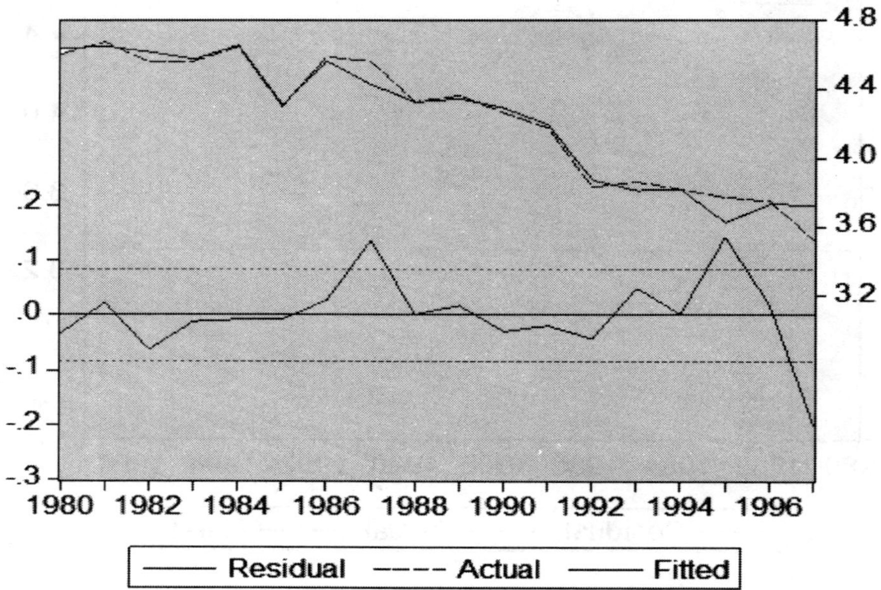

Fig. 9.28: Line Chart Estimated Non Linear Models for Regional Iron and Steel Industry at Constant Price- Uttar Pradesh

The iron and steel industry is not very developed in the state of Uttar Pradesh because the basic metal is not produced here. Most of the firms are engaged in re-rolling of the scrape and billets.

Like other regions the non-linear models offer higher R^2 values, hence the better fit. Explanatory variables x3 has significant coefficient thus Productivity only explains the variance in independent variable unit labour cost.

Table 9.29: Estimated Linear Models for Regional Iron and Steel Industry at Current Price - West Bengal

Variable	Coefficient	Std. Error	t-Statistic	Prob.
C	92.74735	17.46225	5.311305	0.0001
X1	0.318663	0.086940	3.665321	0.0029
X2	0.061853	0.163913	0.377355	0.7120
X3	-0.283456	0.081006	-3.499178	0.0039
X4	-0.010014	0.009914	-1.010093	0.3309
R-squared	0.629052	Mean dependent var		106.8177
Adjusted R-squared	0.514914	S.D. dependent var		11.53175
S.E. of regression	8.031646	Akaike info criterion		7.234789
Sum squared resid	838.5953	Schwarz criterion		7.482115

Prob(F-statistic) 0.008075

Estimation Equation:

Y = C(1) + C(2)*X1 + C(3)*X2 + C(4)*X3 + C(5)*X4

Substituted Coefficients:

Y = 92.74735453 + 0.3186630098*X1 + 0.06185331024*X2 - 0.2834555258*X3 - 0.01001374992*X4

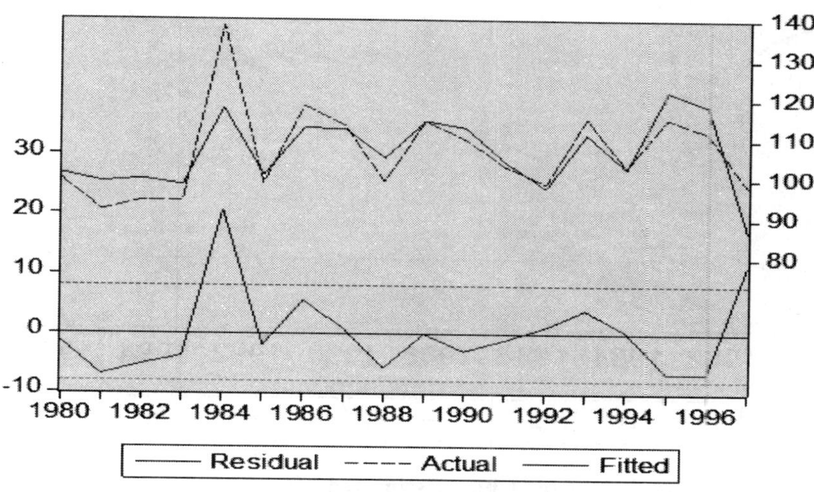

Fig. 9.29: Line Chart Estimated Linear Models for Regional Iron and Steel Industry at Current Price- West Bengal

Table 9.30: Estimated Linear Models for Regional Iron and Steel Industry at Constant Price- West Bengal

Variable	Coefficient	Std. Error	t-Statistic	Prob.
C	97.36694	9.529429	10.21750	0.0000
X1	0.962418	0.080915	11.89414	0.0000
X2	0.001374	0.053812	0.025530	0.9800
X3	-0.931246	0.094491	-9.855349	0.0000
X4	-0.001676	0.001740	-0.963166	0.3530
R-squared	0.947280	Mean dependent var		104.6903
Adjusted R-squared	0.931058	S.D. dependent var		13.28670
S.E. of regression	3.488660	Akaike info criterion		5.567046
Sum squared resid	158.2197	Schwarz criterion		5.814371

Prob(F-statistic) 0.000000

Estimation Equation:

Y = C(1) + C(2)*X1 + C(3)*X2 + C(4)*X3 + C(5)*X4

Substituted Coefficients:

Y = 97.36693848 + 0.9624179052*X1 + 0.001373811246*X2 - 0.9312457374*X3 - 0.001675566862*X4

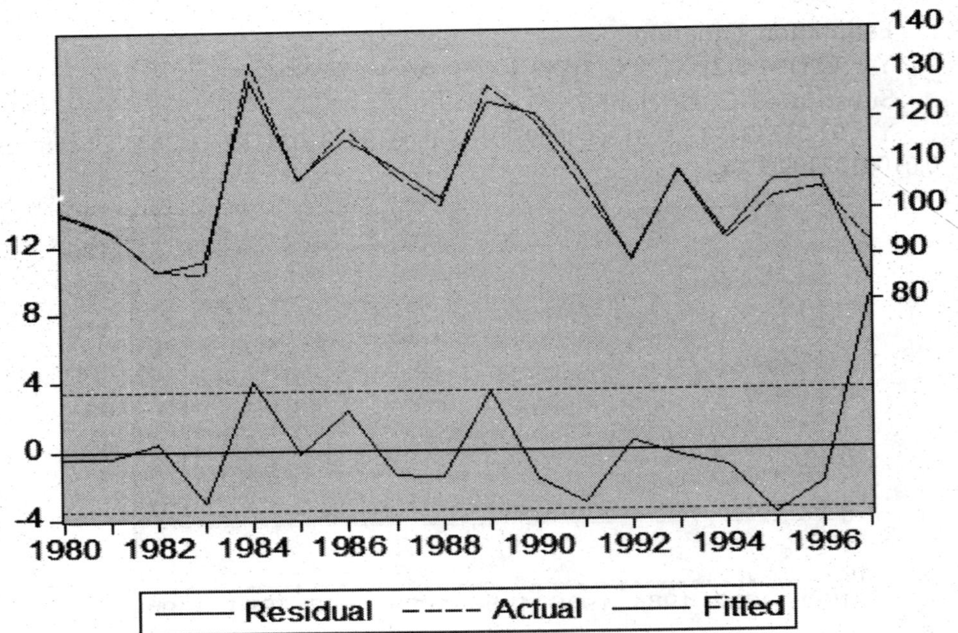

Fig. 9.30: Line Chart Estimated Linear Models for Regional Iron and Steel Industry at Constant Price- West Bengal

Table 9.31: Estimated Non Linear Models for Regional Iron and Steel Industry at Current Price - West Bengal

Variable	Coefficient	Std. Error	t-Statistic	Prob.
C	4.623813	0.227074	20.36258	0.0000
LOG(X1)	0.876523	0.053912	16.25852	0.0000
LOG(X2)	-0.000448	0.050585	-0.008865	0.9931
LOG(X3)	-0.873680	0.057627	-15.16087	0.0000
LOG(X4)	-0.005614	0.019781	-0.283822	0.7810
R-squared	0.966941	Mean dependent var		4.665926
Adjusted R-squared	0.956769	S.D. dependent var		0.103529
S.E. of regression	0.021526	Akaike info criterion		-4.608990
Sum squared resid	0.006024	Schwarz criterion		-4.361664

Prob(F-statistic) 0.000000

Estimation Equation:

LOG(Y) = C(1) + C(2)*LOG(X1) + C(3)*LOG(X2) + C(4)*LOG(X3) + C(5)*LOG(X4)

Substituted Coefficients:

LOG(Y) = 4.623812936 + 0.8765233994* LOG(X1) - 0.0004484600285* LOG(X2) - 0.87368046*LOG(X3) - 0.005614311717*LOG(X4)

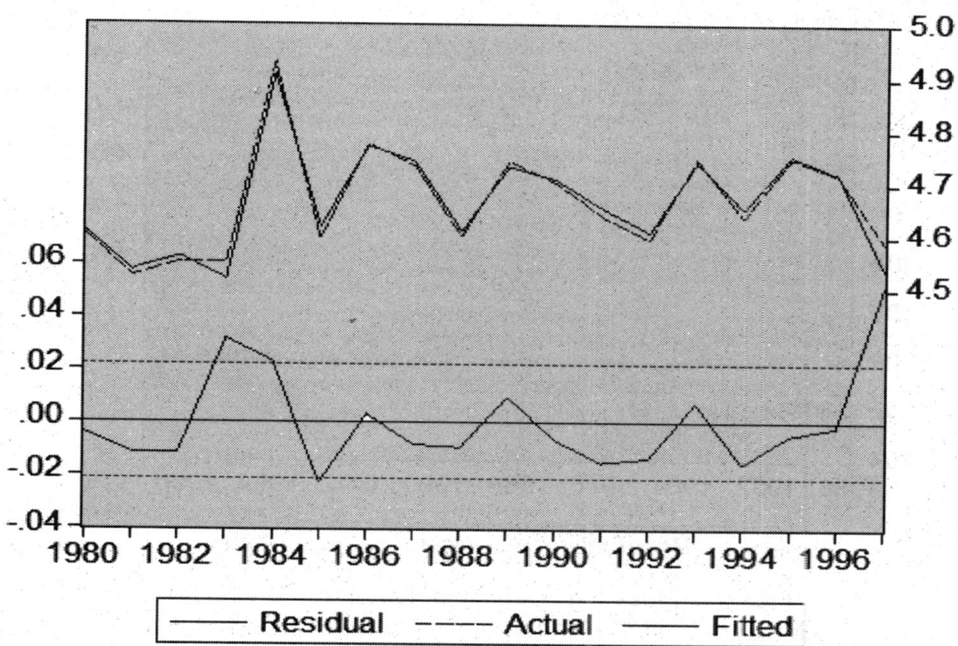

Fig. 9.31: Line Chart Estimated Non Linear Models for Regional Iron and Steel Industry at Current Price- West Bengal

Table 9.32: Estimated Non Linear Models for Regional Iron and Steel Industry at Constant Price - West Bengal

Variable	Coefficient	Std. Error	t-Statistic	Prob.
C	4.933100	0.278120	17.73728	0.0000
LOG(X1)	0.890948	0.041642	21.39539	0.0000
LOG(X2)	-0.019101	0.045056	-0.423945	0.6785
LOG(X3)	-0.945119	0.053880	-17.54110	0.0000
LOG(X4)	0.001486	0.007412	0.200493	0.8442
R-squared	0.980859	Mean dependent var		4.643639
Adjusted R-squared	0.974969	S.D. dependent var		0.124020
S.E. of regression	0.019621	Akaike info criterion		-4.794260
Sum squared resid	0.005005	Schwarz criterion		-4.546935

Prob(F-statistic) 0.000000

Estimation Equation:

LOG(Y) = C(1) + C(2)*LOG(X1) + C(3)*LOG(X2) + C(4)*LOG(X3) + C(5)*LOG(X4)

Substituted Coefficients:

LOG(Y) = 4.933100071 + 0.8909475104*LOG(X1) - 0.01910122529*LOG(X2) - 0.945118778*LOG(X3) + 0.001486112335*LOG(X4)

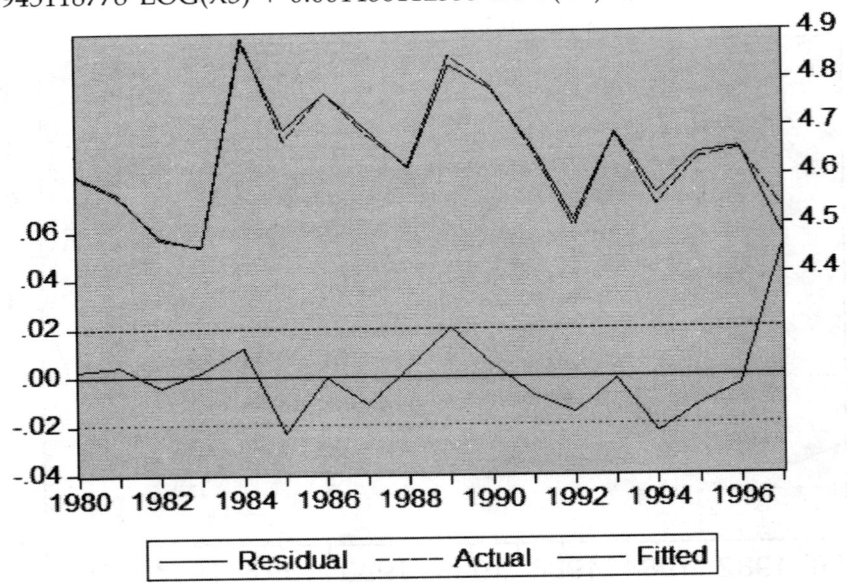

Fig. 9.32: Line Chart Estimated Non Linear Models for Regional Iron and Steel Industry at Constant Price - West Bengal

West Bengal is second important region of iron and steel industry. Availability of raw materials from nearby states (Bihar) and power has given great impetus to development in this state. On account of huge supply of coal and water, state has high capacity of power generation. Improving transportation facilities, investment by both private and public enterprises, availability of skilled workers has brought changes in productivity of firms in West Bengal.

Like other regions the non-linear models offer higher R^2 values, hence the better fit. Explanatory variables x1 and x3 have significant coefficients thus they explain the variance in independent variable unit labour cost.

Conclusion: In the estimated models for regional iron and steel industries, non-linear functional form of relationships provides the better fit to the data. The significant values of R^2 in all the cases, suggest that relevant variables were chosen for the model which explained, in most of the cases around 90% of the variance in unit labour cost. The declining trend of labour cost has been fully explained through the models. While raise in average wage rate has increased the unit labour cost in all regions, the improvement in productivity has reduced it. The technological investments were mostly done in decade of 1980-1990 the variable technological change although increased the R^2 value but did not appear as significant in relationships estimated. The magnitude of impacts of factors influencing unit labour cost, differ from region to region but general behavior of these factors is more or less similar.

ESTIMATION OF UNIT COST LABOUR FUNCTION IN REGIONAL COTTON TEXTILE INDUSTRY

Cotton textile industry of India is widely scattered all over India. So as to estimate the unit labour cost the important regions were considered and there models were estimated. The relationship of unit labour cost with Average wage rate, unit material cost, productivity and technological change were studied through linear and non linear models. This approach will enable us to compare the behavior and impacts of the factors in different regions of the country. These regions are: Andhra Pradesh, Delhi, Maharashtra, Madhya Pradesh, Rajasthan, Tamilnadu, Uttar Pradesh and West Bengal. The results are given below.

Table 9.33: Estimated Linear Models for Regional Cotton Textile Industry at Current Price-Andhra Pradesh

Variable	Coefficient	Std. Error	t-Statistic	Prob.
C	113.4830	15.98941	7.097383	0.0000
X1	-0.116492	0.059691	-1.951585	0.0729
X2	0.024116	0.167815	0.143704	0.8879
X3	-0.107552	0.023703	-4.537541	0.0006
X4	0.067842	0.017744	3.823355	0.0021
R-squared	0.904814	Mean dependent var		78.51227
Adjusted R-squared	0.875525	S.D. dependent var		23.26866
S.E. of regression	8.209405	Akaike info criterion		7.278571
Sum squared resid	876.1264	Schwarz criterion		7.525897

Prob(F-statistic) 0.000002

Estimation Equation:

Y = C(1) + C(2)*X1 + C(3)*X2 + C(4)*X3 + C(5)*X4

Substituted Coefficients:

Y = 113.4829833 - 0.1164916665*X1 + 0.02411575161*X2 - 0.1075523164*X3 + 0.06784244304*X4

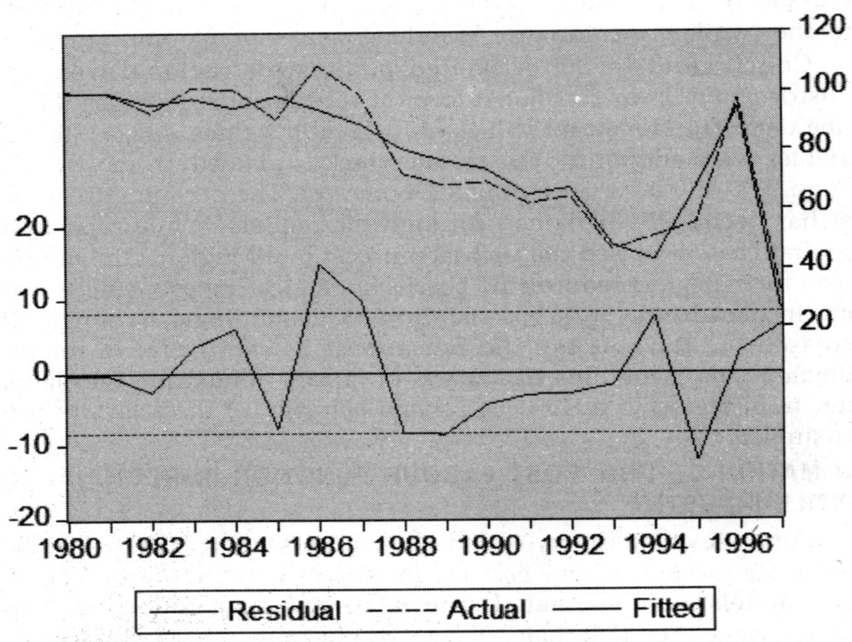

Fig. 9.33: Line Chart Estimated Linear Models for Regional Cotton Textile Industry at Current Price-Andhra Pradesh

Table 9.34: Estimated Linear Models for Regional Cotton Textile Industry at Constant Price-Andhra Pradesh

Variable	Coefficient	Std. Error	t-Statistic	Prob.
C	165.5801	24.46506	6.768021	0.0000
X1	-0.407410	0.189367	-2.151431	0.0508
X2	-0.079176	0.104250	-0.759485	0.4611
X3	-0.279988	0.040063	-6.988688	0.0000
X4	0.015288	0.008048	1.899629	0.0799
R-squared	0.928840	Mean dependent var		61.28375
Adjusted R-squared	0.906945	S.D. dependent var		21.84996
S.E. of regression	6.665309	Akaike info criterion		6.861843
Sum squared resid	577.5424	Schwarz criterion		7.109168

Prob(F-statistic) 0.000000

Estimation Equation:

Y = C(1) + C(2)*X1 + C(3)*X2 + C(4)*X3 + C(5)*X4

Substituted Coefficients:

Y = 165.5800536 - 0.4074104038*X1 - 0.07917604376*X2 - 0.2799878116*X3 + 0.01528787306*X4

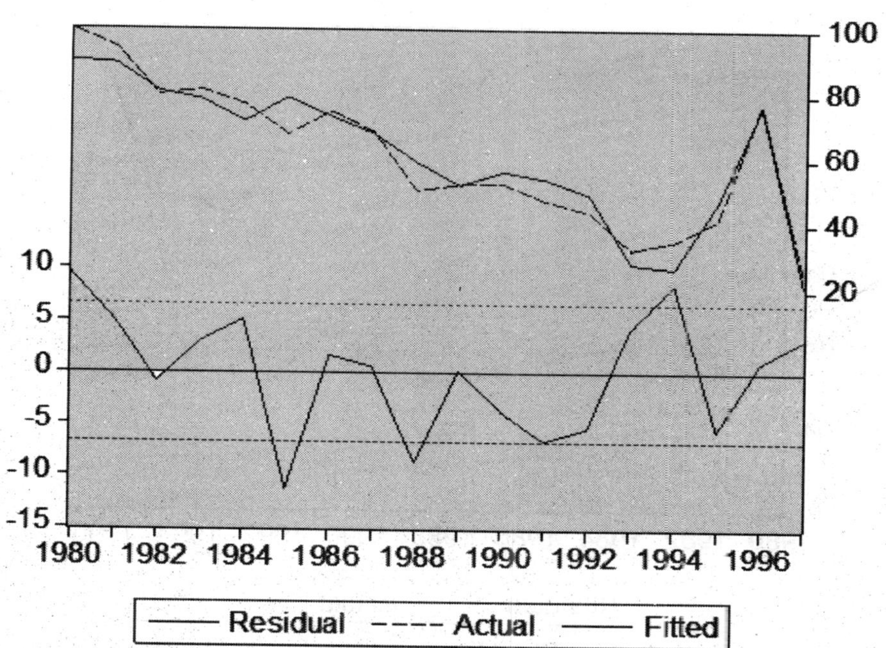

Fig. 9.34: Line Chart Estimated Linear Models for Regional Cotton Textile Industry at Constant Price-Andhra Pradesh

Table 9.35: Estimated Non Linear Models for Regional Cotton Textile Industry at Current Price-Andhra Pradesh

Variable	Coefficient	Std. Error	t-Statistic	Prob.
C	4.326710	0.271747	15.92186	0.0000
LOG(X1)	0.772688	0.095889	8.058190	0.0000
LOG(X2)	0.200195	0.067955	2.946011	0.0114
LOG(X3)	-0.845248	0.035471	-23.82930	0.0000
LOG(X4)	-0.071899	0.054659	-1.315405	0.2111
R-squared	0.994108	Mean dependent var		4.313700
Adjusted R-squared	0.992295	S.D. dependent var		0.340516
S.E. of regression	0.029889	Akaike info criterion		-3.952523
Sum squared resid	0.011614	Schwarz criterion		-3.705197
Prob(F-statistic)	0.000000			

Estimation Equation:

LOG(Y) = C(1) + C(2)*LOG(X1) + C(3)*LOG(X2) + C(4)*LOG(X3) + C(5)*LOG(X4)

Substituted Coefficients:

LOG(Y) = 4.326710254 + 0.772688078*LOG(X1) + 0.2001949193*LOG(X2) - 0.8452479194*LOG(X3) - 0.07189854361*LOG(X4)

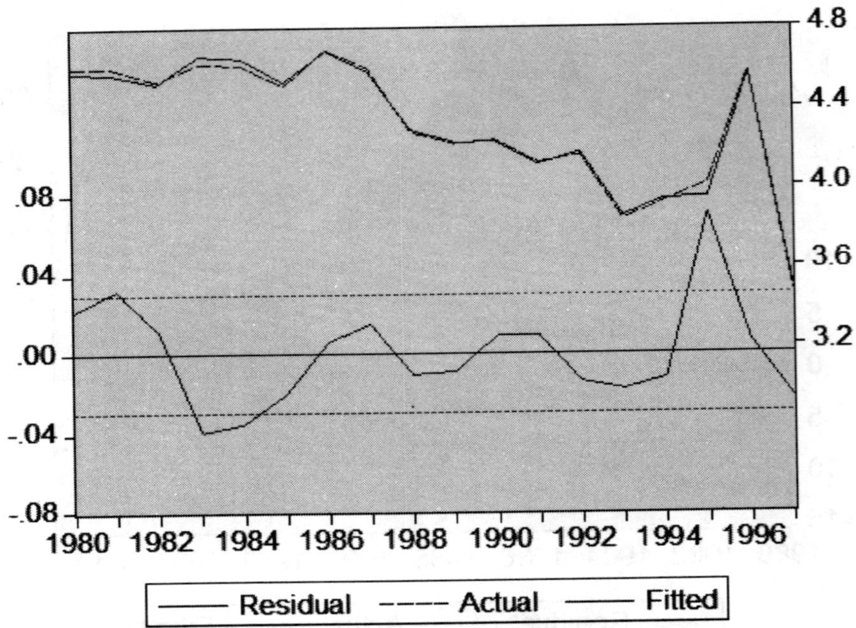

Fig. 9.35: Line Chart Estimated Non Linear Models for Regional Cotton Textile Industry at Current Price-Andhra Pradesh

Table 9.36: Estimated Non Linear Models for Regional Cotton Textile Industry at Constant Price-Andhra Pradesh

Variable	Coefficient	Std. Error	t-Statistic	Prob.
C	5.866808	0.865998	6.774620	0.0000
LOG(X1)	0.604164	0.141178	4.279453	0.0009
LOG(X2)	0.102752	0.078105	1.315567	0.2110
LOG(X3)	-0.925913	0.049653	-18.64749	0.0000
LOG(X4)	-0.061543	0.032168	-1.913159	0.0780
R-squared	0.994811	Mean dependent var		4.048134
Adjusted R-squared	0.993214	S.D. dependent var		0.391476
S.E. of regression	0.032248	Akaike info criterion		-3.800584
Sum squared resid	0.013519	Schwarz criterion		-3.553258

Prob(F-statistic) 0.000000

Estimation Equation:

LOG(Y) = C(1) + C(2)*LOG(X1) + C(3)*LOG(X2) + C(4)*LOG(X3) + C(5)*LOG(X4)

Substituted Coefficients:

LOG(Y) = 5.866807864 + 0.6041639339*LOG(X1) + 0.102752219*LOG(X2) - 0.9259126593*LOG(X3) - 0.06154298949*LOG(X4)

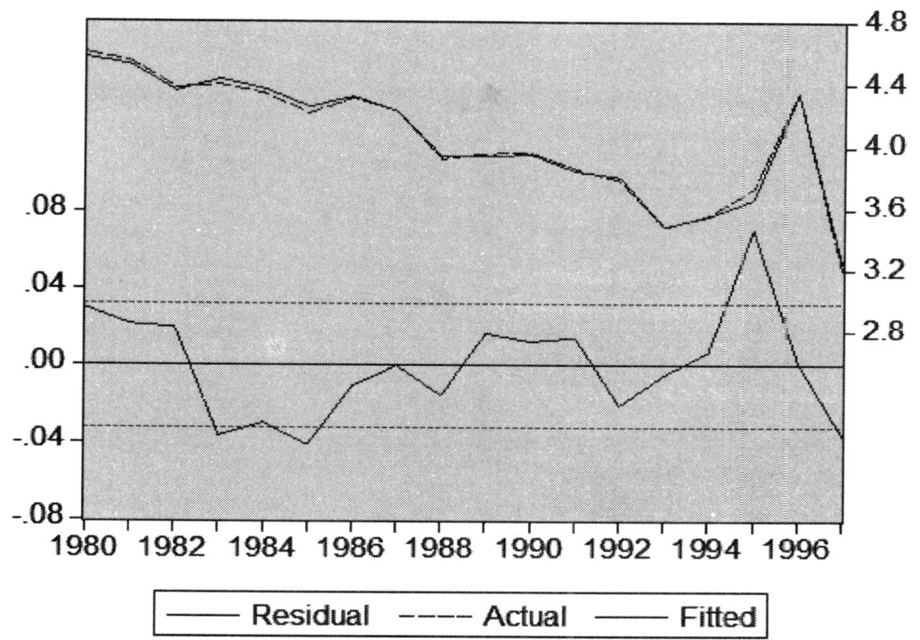

Fig. 9.36: Line Chart Estimated Non Linear Models for Regional Cotton Textile Industry at Constant Price-Andhra Pradesh

The estimates of the models above have high R^2 value. The R^2 value for non linear models is higher than linear models, x3 (productivity) is the factor having significant coefficient in all estimated models. The models at constant price, indicate x1 and x3 as factors with significant coefficient and thus are helpful in explaining the variance in data of unit labour cost.

Table 9.37: Estimated Linear Models for Regional Cotton Textile Industry at Current Price-Delhi

Variable	Coefficient	Std. Error	t-Statistic	Prob.
C	87.32057	27.72971	3.148990	0.0077
X1	-0.083640	0.060927	-1.372794	0.1930
X2	0.177093	0.241424	0.733535	0.4763
X3	0.035932	0.018013	1.994834	0.0675
X4	-0.045554	0.014936	-3.049923	0.0093
R-squared	0.732524	Mean dependent var		75.06394
Adjusted R-squared	0.650224	S.D. dependent var		22.04644
S.E. of regression	13.03868	Akaike info criterion		8.203851
Sum squared resid	2210.093	Schwarz criterion		8.451176

Prob(F-statistic) 0.001091

Estimation Equation:

Y = C(1) + C(2)*X1 + C(3)*X2 + C(4)*X3 + C(5)*X4

Substituted Coefficients:

Y = 87.32057042 - 0.08364021639*X1 + 0.177093165*X2 + 0.03593226023*X3 - 0.04555366743*X4

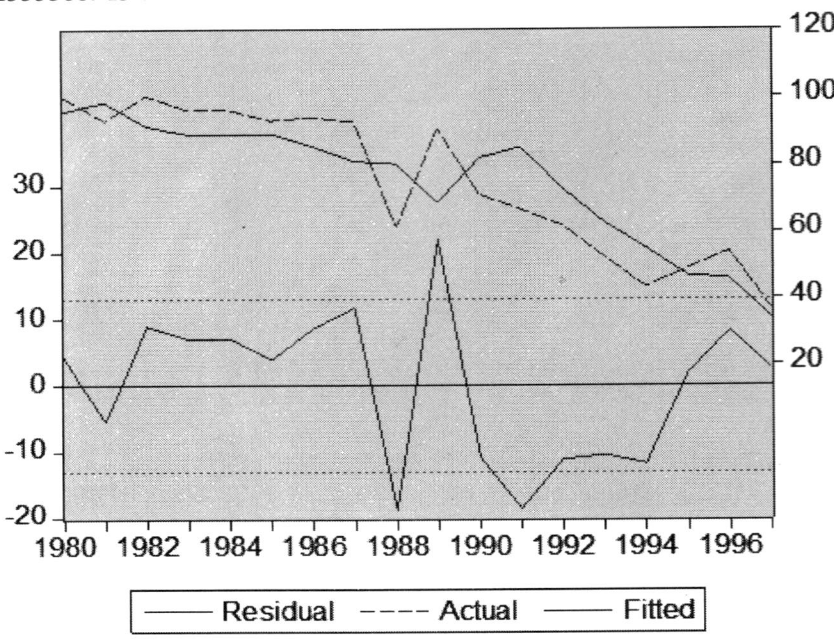

Fig. 9.37: Line Chart Estimated Linear Models for Regional Cotton Textile Industry at Current Price-Delhi

Table 9.38: Estimated Linear Models for Regional Cotton Textile Industry at Constant Price-Delhi

Variable	Coefficient	Std. Error	t-Statistic	Prob.
C	-4.245056	31.04897	-0.136721	0.8935
X1	0.154117	0.142594	1.080810	0.3010
X2	0.581127	0.201719	2.880877	0.0138
D(X3)	0.018058	0.030018	0.601554	0.5587
X4	-0.039559	0.007452	-5.308401	0.0002
R-squared	0.750223	Mean dependent var		56.25600
Adjusted R-squared	0.666964	S.D. dependent var		19.24072
S.E. of regression	11.10367	Akaike info criterion		7.892358
Sum squared resid	1479.499	Schwarz criterion		8.137421

Prob(F-statistic) 0.001336

Estimation Equation:

Y = C(1) + C(2)*X1 + C(3)*X2 + C(4)*D(X3) + C(5)*X4

Substituted Coefficients:

Y = -4.245056363 + 0.1541173876*X1 + 0.5811267692*X2 + 0.01805752711*D(X3) - 0.03955906712*X4

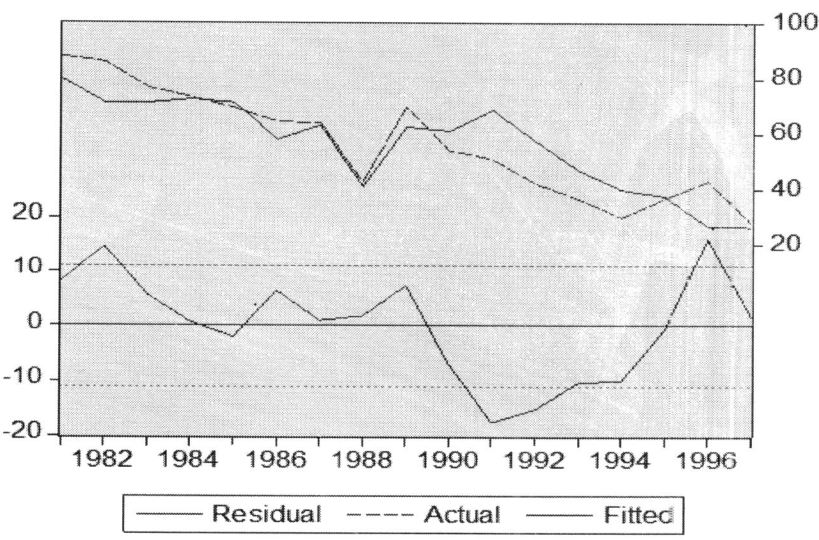

Fig. 9.38: Line Chart Estimated Linear Models for Regional Cotton Textile Industry at Constant Price-Delhi

Table 9.39: Estimated Non Linear Models for Regional Cotton Textile Industry at Current Price-Delhi

Variable	Coefficient	Std. Error	t-Statistic	Prob.
C	5.333446	0.863563	6.176095	0.0000
LOG(X1)	0.592225	0.159374	3.715938	0.0026
LOG(X2)	-0.073585	0.175145	-0.420135	0.6812
LOG(X3)	-0.703528	0.141970	-4.955452	0.0003
LOG(X4)	0.009177	0.096935	0.094669	0.9260
R-squared	0.934534	Mean dependent var		4.271724
Adjusted R-squared	0.914390	S.D. dependent var		0.325345
S.E. of regression	0.095193	Akaike info criterion		-1.635680
Sum squared resid	0.117803	Schwarz criterion		-1.388354

Prob(F-statistic) 0.000000

Estimation Equation:

LOG(Y) = C(1) + C(2)*LOG(X1) + C(3)*LOG(X2) + C(4)*LOG(X3) + C(5)*LOG(X4)

Substituted Coefficients:

LOG(Y) = 5.333446229 + 0.5922253853*LOG(X1) - 0.07358451972*LOG(X2) - 0.7035279584*LOG(X3) + 0.009176753481*LOG(X4)

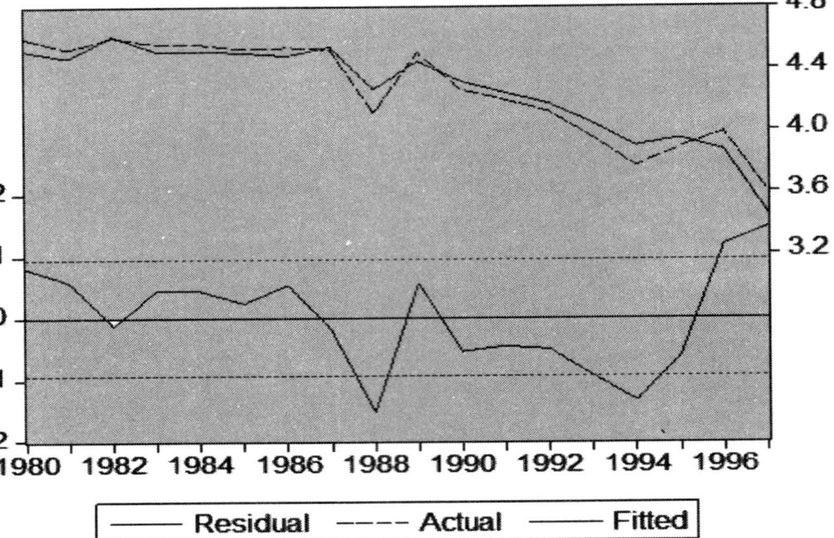

Fig. 9.39: Line Chart Estimated Non Linear Models for Regional Cotton Textile Industry at Current Price-Delhi

Table 9.40: Estimated Non Linear Models for Regional Cotton Textile Industry at Constant Price-Delhi

Variable	Coefficient	Std. Error	t-Statistic	Prob.
C	3.283479	1.197874	2.741089	0.0168
LOG(X1)	0.886437	0.195803	4.527190	0.0006
LOG(X2)	0.218694	0.216290	1.011116	0.3304
LOG(X3)	-0.793221	0.203677	-3.894512	0.0018
LOG(X4)	-0.062095	0.101669	-0.610753	0.5519
R-squared	0.934186	Mean dependent var		4.006029
Adjusted R-squared	0.913935	S.D. dependent var		0.381604
S.E. of regression	0.111950	Akaike info criterion		-1.311389
Sum squared resid	0.162927	Schwarz criterion		-1.064064

Prob(F-statistic) 0.000000

Estimation Equation:

LOG(Y) = C(1) + C(2)*LOG(X1) + C(3)*LOG(X2) + C(4)*LOG(X3) + C(5)*LOG(X4)

Substituted Coefficients:

LOG(Y) = 3.283478997 + 0.8864370798*LOG(X1) + 0.2186941469*LOG(X2) - 0.7932212571*LOG(X3) - 0.0620947082*LOG(X4)

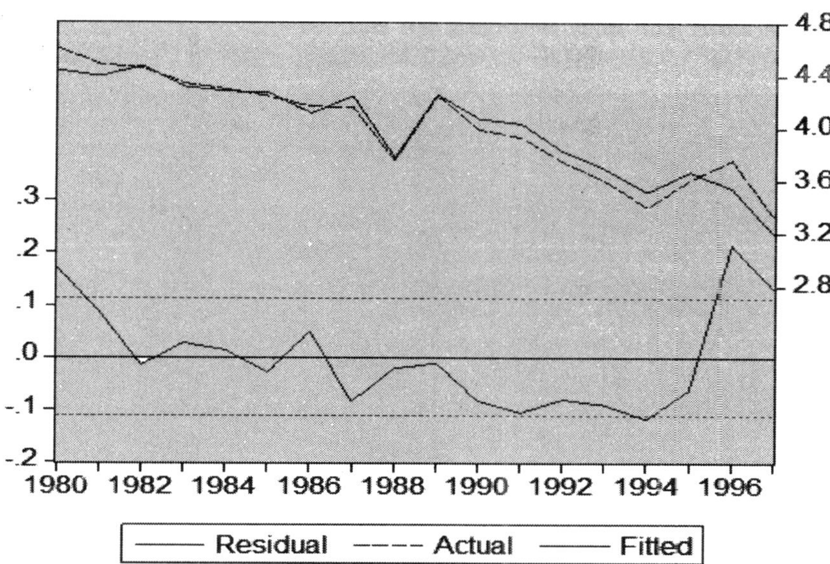

Fig. 9.40: Line Chart Estimated Non Linear Models for Regional Cotton Textile Industry at Constant Price-Delhi

The analysis of the above tables suggest that linear models with current price and constant price have much lower R2 values, 73% and 75% respectively. These models indicate that variable x2 unit material cost and x4 technological changes are the main factors impacting the unit labour cost of the industry, technological changes being present in all. In the non linear model with current price and constant price variables x1 (average wage rate) and x3 (productivity) are emerged as the factors explaining the variability of unit labour cost in the industry. Since the non linear models have much higher R^2 value without the need of correction of serial autocorrelation, the non linear models are used for interpretation.

Table 9.41: Estimated Linear Models for Regional Cotton Textile Industry at Current Price-Maharashtra

Variable	Coefficient	Std. Error	t-Statistic	Prob.
C	108.1821	20.68895	5.228983	0.0002
X1	0.185524	0.050803	3.651836	0.0029
X2	-0.019356	0.209983	-0.092180	0.9280
X3	-0.249117	0.063276	-3.937008	0.0017
REPX4	0.031412	0.024729	1.270244	0.2263
R-squared	0.889552	Mean dependent var		98.30943
Adjusted R-squared	0.855568	S.D. dependent var		13.18608
S.E. of regression	5.011268	Akaike info criterion		6.291388
Sum squared resid	326.4665	Schwarz criterion		6.538714
Prob(F-statistic)	0.000004			

Estimation Equation:

Y = C(1) + C(2)*X1 + C(3)*X2 + C(4)*X3 + C(5)*REPX4

Substituted Coefficients:

Y = 108.1821422 + 0.1855244235*X1 - 0.01935616065*X2 - 0.2491173928*X3 + 0.03141209144*REPX4

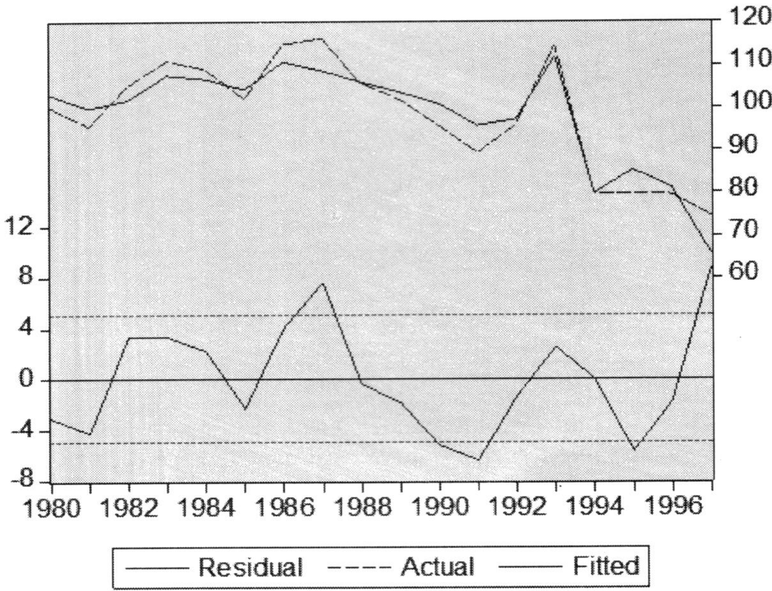

Fig. 9.41: Line Chart Estimated Linear Models for Regional Cotton Textile Industry at Current Price-Maharashtra

Table 9.42: Estimated Linear Models for Regional Cotton Textile Industry at Constant Price-Maharashtra

Variable	Coefficient	Std. Error	t-Statistic	Prob.
C	100.3437	22.11102	4.538174	0.0006
X1	-0.025446	0.150809	-0.168727	0.8686
X2	0.165743	0.167909	0.987100	0.3416
X3	-0.231215	0.089176	-2.592806	0.0223
REPX4	-0.009998	0.008346	-1.197911	0.2523
R-squared	0.920342	Mean dependent var		75.68562
Adjusted R-squared	0.895831	S.D. dependent var		12.46015
S.E. of regression	4.021533	Akaike info criterion		5.851336
Sum squared resid	210.2454	Schwarz criterion		6.098662

Prob(F-statistic) 0.000001

Estimation Equation:

Y = C(1) + C(2)*X1 + C(3)*X2 + C(4)*X3 + C(5)*REPX4

Substituted Coefficients:

Y = 100.3436809 - 0.0254456426*X1 + 0.1657430459*X2 - 0.2312152686*X3 - 0.009998004986*REPX4

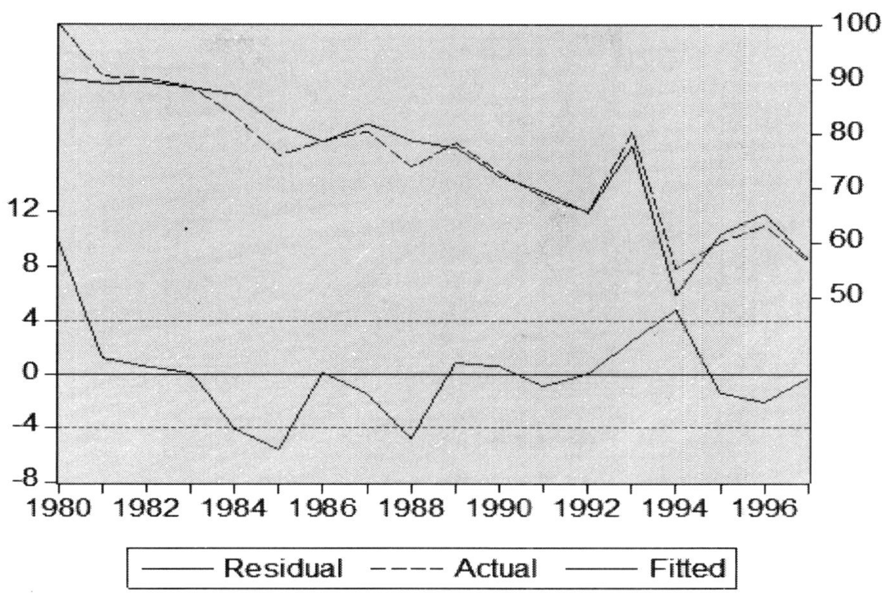

Fig. 9.42: Line Chart Estimated Linear Models for Regional Cotton Textile Industry at Constant Price-Maharashtra

Table 9.43: Estimated Non Linear Models for Regional Cotton Textile Industry at Current Price- Maharashtra

Variable	Coefficient	Std. Error	t-Statistic	Prob.
C	4.227260	0.727745	5.808708	0.0001
LOG(X1)	0.613297	0.075172	8.158636	0.0000
LOG(X2)	0.198431	0.159949	1.240584	0.2367
LOG(X3)	-0.752767	0.115166	-6.536371	0.0000
LOG(REPX4)	0.029068	0.075531	0.384846	0.7066
R-squared	0.946807	Mean dependent var		4.579166
Adjusted R-squared	0.930440	S.D. dependent var		0.139593
S.E. of regression	0.036817	Akaike info criterion		-3.535599
Sum squared resid	0.017621	Schwarz criterion		-3.288274

Prob(F-statistic) 0.000000

Estimation Equation:

LOG(Y) = LOG(C(1)) + C(2)*LOG(X1) + C(3)*LOG(X2) + C(4)*LOG(X3) + C(5)*LOG(REPX4)

Substituted Coefficients:

LOG(Y) = LOG(68.5291871295284) + 0.6132971077*LOG(X1) + 0.1984305387*LOG(X2) - 0.752766605*LOG(X3) + 0.02906768847*LOG(REPX4)

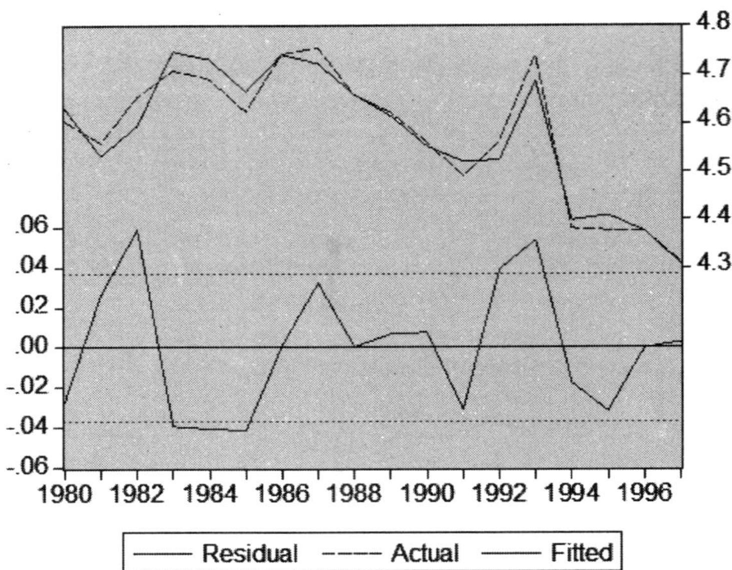

Fig. 9.43: Line Chart Estimated Non Linear Models for Regional Cotton Textile Industry at Current Price- Maharashtra

Table 9.44: Estimated Non Linear Models for Regional Cotton Textile Industry at Constant Price- Maharashtra

Variable	Coefficient	Std. Error	t-Statistic	Prob.
C	5.856014	1.043975	5.609343	0.0001
LOG(X1)	0.340761	0.142280	2.395002	0.0324
LOG(X2)	0.135053	0.151484	0.891538	0.3888
LOG(X3)	-0.732986	0.130703	-5.608025	0.0001
LOG(X4)	-0.022745	0.032235	-0.705620	0.4929
R-squared	0.967606	Mean dependent var		4.313464
Adjusted R-squared	0.957639	S.D. dependent var		0.168009
S.E. of regression	0.034579	Akaike info criterion		-3.660996
Sum squared resid	0.015544	Schwarz criterion		-3.413670

Prob(F-statistic) 0.000000

Estimation Equation:

LOG(Y) = C(1) + C(2)*LOG(X1) + C(3)*LOG(X2) + C(4)*LOG(X3) + C(5)*LOG(X4)

Substituted Coefficients:

LOG(Y) = 5.856014077 + 0.3407608256*LOG(X1) + 0.1350534381*LOG(X2) - 0.7329855931*LOG(X3) - 0.02274531492*LOG(X4)

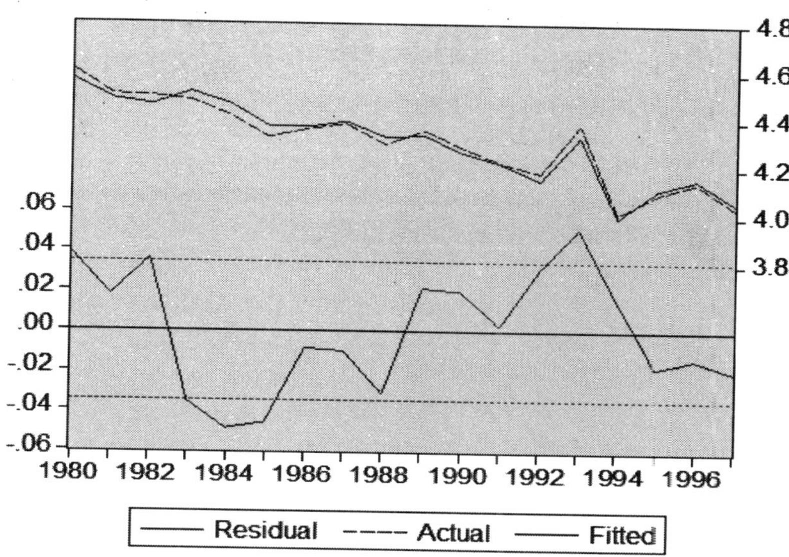

Fig. 9.44: Line Chart Estimated Non Linear Models for Regional Cotton Textile Industry at Constant Price- Maharashtra

Maharashtra has highly concentrated cotton textile industry. The above results indicate all the models are capable of explaining significant variation in unit labour cost. The linear model at current price indicate x1 (average wage rate) and x3 (productivity) are factors which are explaining around 89% variance in unit labour cost. The linear model at constant price indicates that only x3 is the factor with significant coefficient which explains around 92% variation in unit labour cost. The non linear models provide better fit. The non linear model with current price has x1 and x3 as significant factors explaining around 94% of variation in unit labour cost. The non linear model with constant price has x1 and x3 as significant factors explaining around 96% of variation in unit labour cost.

Table 9.45: Estimated Linear Models for Regional Cotton Textile Industry at Current Price-Madhya Pradesh

Variable	Coefficient	Std. Error	t-Statistic	Prob.
C	104.5369	28.01399	3.731596	0.0025
X1	-0.151657	0.061692	-2.458288	0.0288
X2	0.225788	0.282432	0.799444	0.4384
X3	0.009489	0.012264	0.773739	0.4529
X4	-0.023654	0.006549	-3.611826	0.0032
R-squared	0.930952	Mean dependent var		79.25248
Adjusted R-squared	0.909706	S.D. dependent var		34.02214
S.E. of regression	10.22328	Akaike info criterion		7.717344
Sum squared resid	1358.700	Schwarz criterion		7.964670

Prob(F-statistic) 0.000000

Estimation Equation:

Y = C(1) + C(2)*X1 + C(3)*X2 + C(4)*X3 + C(5)*X4

Substituted Coefficients:

Y = 104.5368947 - 0.1516570607*X1 + 0.2257883038*X2 + 0.009489063715*X3 - 0.02365406394*X4

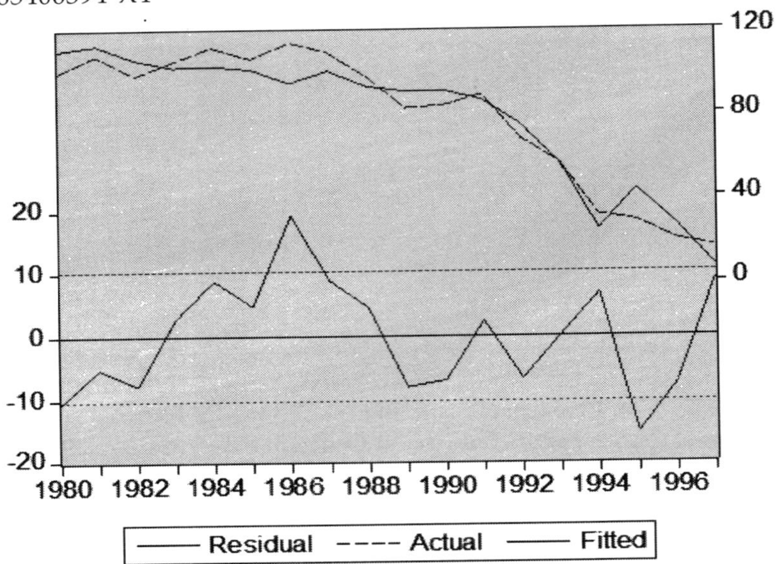

Fig. 9.45: Line Chart Estimated Linear Models for Regional Cotton Textile Industry at Current Price-Madhya Pradesh

Table 9.46: Estimated Linear Models for Regional Cotton Textile Industry at Constant Price-Madhya Pradesh

Variable	Coefficient	Std. Error	t-Statistic	Prob.
C	124.7424	62.76434	1.987472	0.0684
X1	-0.505253	0.477028	-1.059169	0.3088
X2	0.068559	0.322279	0.212733	0.8348
X3	0.037802	0.073821	0.512078	0.6172
X4	-0.029320	0.011396	-2.572746	0.0232
R-squared	0.850159	Mean dependent var		61.70697
Adjusted R-squared	0.804054	S.D. dependent var		28.73472
S.E. of regression	12.71964	Akaike info criterion		8.154305
Sum squared resid	2103.261	Schwarz criterion		8.401631

Prob(F-statistic) 0.000029

Estimation Equation:

Y = C(1) + C(2)*X1 + C(3)*X2 + C(4)*X3 + C(5)*X4

Substituted Coefficients:

Y = 124.74237 - 0.5052531391*X1 + 0.06855918793*X2 + 0.03780222313*X3 - 0.02931972839*X4

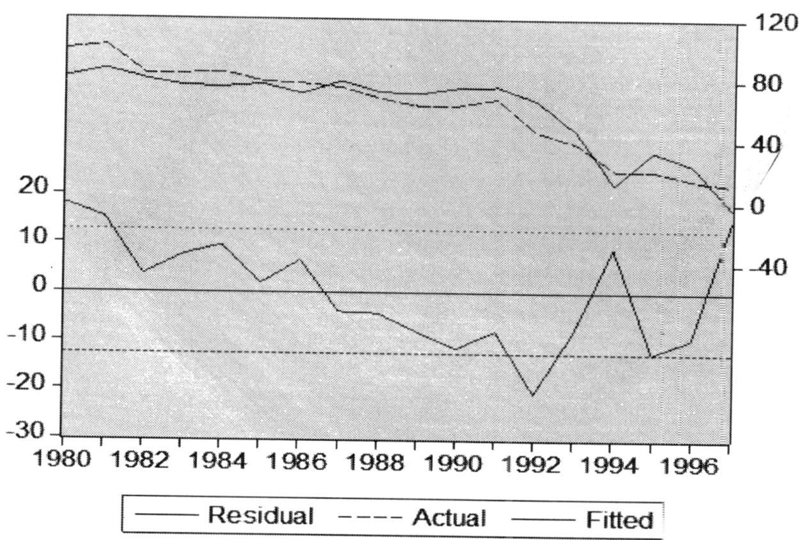

Fig. 9.46: Line Chart Estimated Linear Models for Regional Cotton Textile Industry at Constant Price-Madhya Pradesh

Table 9.47: Estimated Non Linear Models for Regional Cotton Textile Industry at Current Price-Madhya Pradesh

Variable	Coefficient	Std. Error	t-Statistic	Prob.
C	4.499108	0.655190	6.866878	0.0000
LOG(X1)	0.830143	0.071405	11.62580	0.0000
LOG(X2)	0.088825	0.161775	0.549063	0.5923
LOG(X3)	-0.858168	0.053385	-16.07523	0.0000
LOG(X4)	-0.037204	0.043436	-0.856530	0.4072
R-squared	0.995331	Mean dependent var		4.226854
Adjusted R-squared	0.993894	S.D. dependent var		0.635684
S.E. of regression	0.049673	Akaike info criterion		-2.936576
Sum squared resid	0.032076	Schwarz criterion		-2.689250

Prob(F-statistic) 0.000000

Estimation Equation:

LOG(Y) = LOG(C(1)) + C(2)*LOG(X1) + C(3)*LOG(X2) + C(4)*LOG(X3) + C(5)*LOG(X4)

Substituted Coefficients:

LOG(Y) = LOG(89.93684636832) + 0.8301428742*LOG(X1) + 0.08882469011*LOG(X2) - 0.8581682844*LOG(X3) - 0.03720447398*LOG(X4)

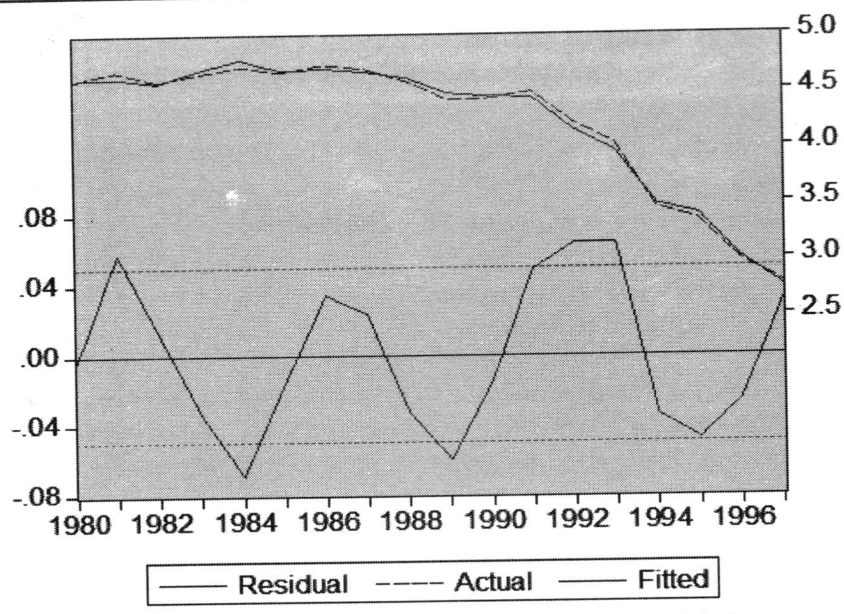

Fig. 9.47: Line Chart Estimated Non Linear Models for Regional Cotton Textile Industry at Current Price-Madhya Pradesh

Table 9.48: Estimated Non Linear Models for Regional Cotton Textile Industry at Constant Price-Madhya Pradesh

Variable	Coefficient	Std. Error	t-Statistic	Prob.
C	5.902608	1.038593	5.683273	0.0001
LOG(X1)	0.618500	0.142203	4.349412	0.0008
LOG(X2)	0.034107	0.132121	0.258151	0.8003
LOG(X3)	-0.881182	0.078306	-11.25312	0.0000
LOG(X4)	-0.054854	0.035790	-1.532637	0.1493
R-squared	0.996086	Mean dependent var		3.961116
Adjusted R-squared	0.994882	S.D. dependent var		0.660886
S.E. of regression	0.047282	Akaike info criterion		-3.035250
Sum squared resid	0.029062	Schwarz criterion		-2.787925

Prob(F-statistic) 0.000000

Estimation Equation:

LOG(Y) = C(1) + C(2)*LOG(X1) + C(3)*LOG(X2) + C(4)*LOG(X3) + C(5)*LOG(X4)

Substituted Coefficients:

LOG(Y) = 5.902607671 + 0.6184997994*LOG(X1) + 0.03410712799*LOG(X2) - 0.8811820518*LOG(X3) - 0.05485362828*LOG(X4)

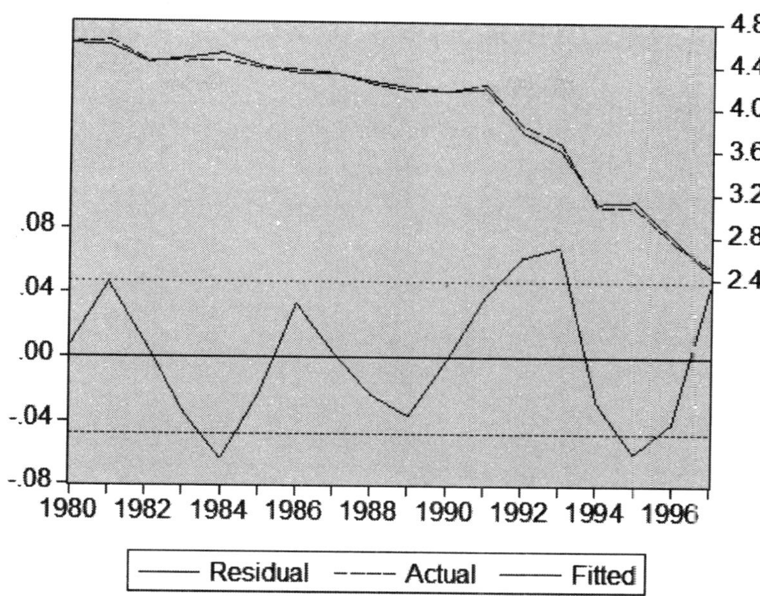

Fig. 9.48: Line Chart Estimated Non Linear Models for Regional Cotton Textile Industry at Constant Price-Madhya Pradesh

The non linear models provide a very good fir (R^2 = 99%) over linear model. The current price linear model indicates x1(average wage rate) and x4 (technological changes) as impactful factors explaining around 93% of variance in unit labour cost. In early 1990s Madhya Pradesh witnessed investment in technology and the impact on unit labour cost was also seen in later years. The linear model at constant price has R2 value of 85% with only x4 as significant. The non linear models identify the variables x1 and x3 as factors explaining the variation in unit labour cost.

Table 9.49: Estimated Linear Models for Regional Cotton Textile Industry at Current Price-Punjab

Variable	Coefficient	Std. Error	t-Statistic	Prob.
C	79.52097	25.01625	3.178773	0.0073
X1	0.091968	0.024266	3.789928	0.0022
X2	0.242477	0.232018	1.045076	0.3150
X3	-0.133352	0.016115	-8.275056	0.0000
REPX4	0.007591	0.005621	1.350348	0.1999
R-squared	0.914980	Mean dependent var		93.51806
Adjusted R-squared	0.888820	S.D. dependent var		11.97602
S.E. of regression	3.993247	Akaike info criterion		5.837219
Sum squared resid	207.2982	Schwarz criterion		6.084545

Prob(F-statistic) 0.000001

Estimation Equation:

Y = C(1) + C(2)*X1 + C(3)*X2 + C(4)*X3 + C(5)*REPX4

Substituted Coefficients:

Y = 79.52096791 + 0.09196787775*X1 + 0.2424768559*X2 - 0.1333523553*X3 + 0.007590665493*REPX4

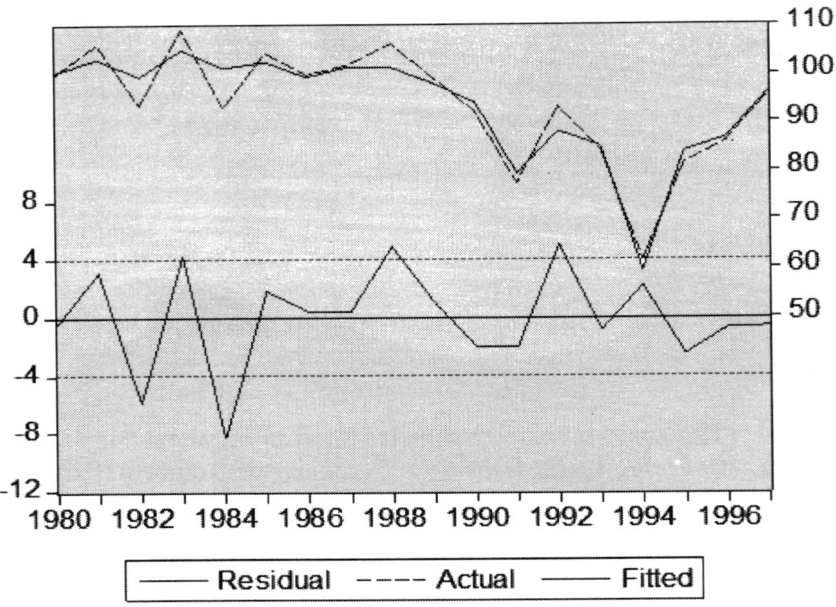

Fig. 9.49: Line Chart Estimated Linear Models for Regional Cotton Textile Industry at Current Price-Punjab

Table 9.50: Estimated Linear Models for Regional Cotton Textile Industry at Constant Price-Punjab

Variable	Coefficient	Std. Error	t-Statistic	Prob.
C	62.98316	39.49489	1.594717	0.1348
X1	0.242727	0.128408	1.890278	0.0812
X2	0.251092	0.321803	0.780268	0.4492
X3	-0.253300	0.041376	-6.121963	0.0000
X4	-0.001658	0.005641	-0.293985	0.7734
R-squared	0.855899	Mean dependent var		72.38463
Adjusted R-squared	0.811560	S.D. dependent var		14.06113
S.E. of regression	6.103889	Akaike info criterion		6.685862
Sum squared resid	484.3470	Schwarz criterion		6.933188

Prob(F-statistic) 0.000022

Estimation Equation:

Y = C(1) + C(2)*X1 + C(3)*X2 + C(4)*X3 + C(5)*X4

Substituted Coefficients:

Y = 62.98315533 + 0.2427269477*X1 + 0.2510924218*X2 - 0.2532997982*X3 - 0.001658328811*X4

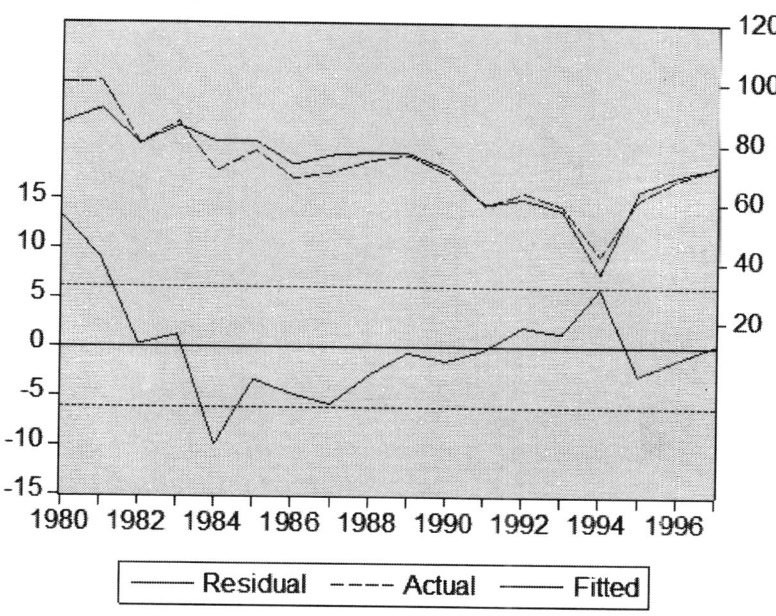

Fig. 9.50: Line Chart Estimated Linear Models for Regional Cotton Textile Industry at Constant Price-Punjab

Table 9.51: Estimated Non Linear Models for Regional Cotton Textile Industry at Current Price-Punjab

Variable	Coefficient	Std. Error	t-Statistic	Prob.
C	4.556085	0.955447	4.768538	0.0004
LOG(X1)	0.819681	0.108645	7.544591	0.0000
LOG(X2)	0.042261	0.196118	0.215488	0.8327
LOG(X3)	-0.805897	0.074999	-10.74544	0.0000
LOG(REPX4)	-0.045116	0.042321	-1.066028	0.3058
R-squared	0.942129	Mean dependent var		4.529430
Adjusted R-squared	0.924323	S.D. dependent var		0.140357
S.E. of regression	0.038611	Akaike info criterion		-3.440406
Sum squared resid	0.019381	Schwarz criterion		-3.193080

Prob(F-statistic) 0.000000

Estimation Equation:

LOG(Y) = LOG(C(1)) + C(2)*LOG(X1) + C(3)*LOG(X2) + C(4)*LOG(X3) + C(5)*LOG(REPX4)

Substituted Coefficients:

LOG(Y) =LOG(95.2099592217942) + 0.8196808008*LOG(X1) + 0.04226089581*LOG(X2) - 0.8058967372*LOG(X3) - 0.04511560312* LOG(REPX4)

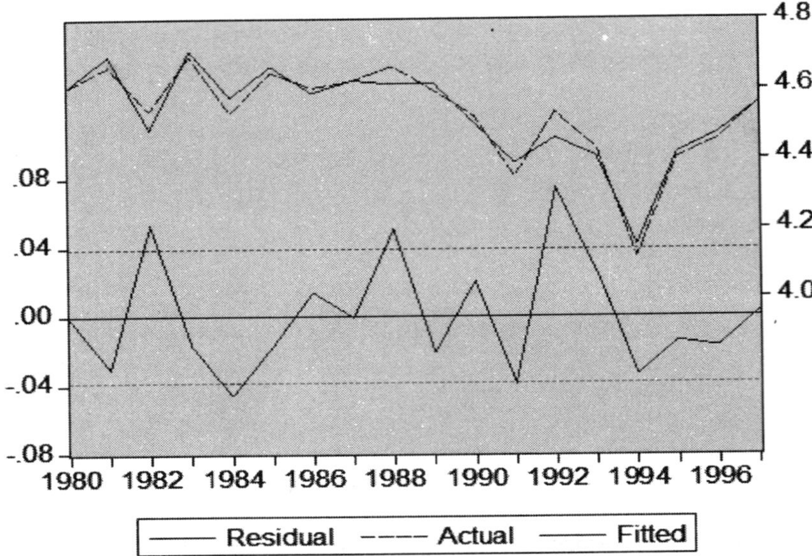

Fig. 9.51: Line Chart Estimated Non Linear Models for Regional Cotton Textile Industry at Current Price-Punjab

Table 9.52: Estimated Non Linear Models for Regional Cotton Textile Industry at Constant Price-Punjab

Variable	Coefficient	Std. Error	t-Statistic	Prob.
C	5.655675	0.986763	5.731545	0.0001
LOG(X1)	0.807277	0.097659	8.266251	0.0000
LOG(X2)	-0.165892	0.172229	-0.963204	0.3530
LOG(X3)	-0.807275	0.049234	-16.39667	0.0000
LOG(X4)	-0.065987	0.022995	-2.869635	0.0132
R-squared	0.979303	Mean dependent var		4.263723
Adjusted R-squared	0.972934	S.D. dependent var		0.199289
S.E. of regression	0.032786	Akaike info criterion		-3.767479
Sum squared resid	0.013974	Schwarz criterion		-3.520153

Prob(F-statistic) 0.000000

Estimation Equation:

LOG(Y) = C(1) + C(2)*LOG(X1) + C(3)*LOG(X2) + C(4)*LOG(X3) + C(5)*LOG(X4)

Substituted Coefficients:

LOG(Y) = 5.655675369 + 0.807276553*LOG(X1) - 0.1658918504*LOG(X2) - 0.8072747265*LOG(X3) - 0.06598669165*LOG(X4)

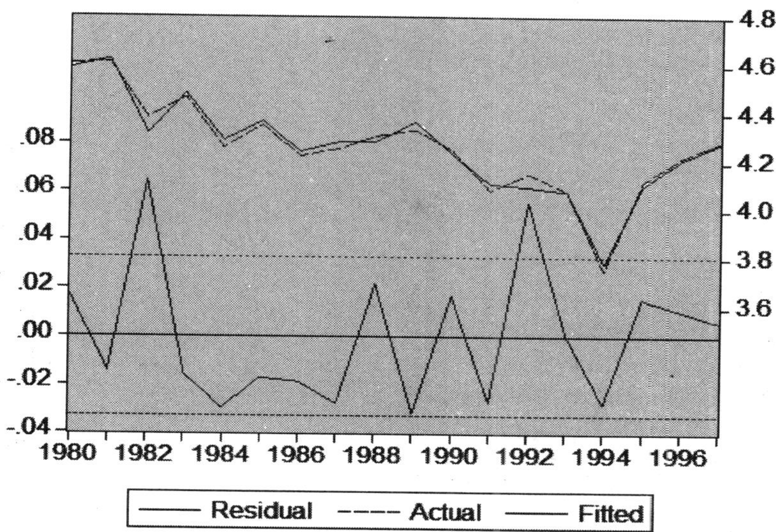

Fig. 9.52: Line Chart Estimated Non Linear Models for Regional Cotton Textile Industry at Constant Price-Punjab

The current price linear model indicates x1(average wage rate) and x3 (productivity) as impactful factors explaining around 91% of variance in unit labour cost.. The linear model at constant price has R^2 value of 85% with only x3 as significant. The non linear models provide better fit than linear models identify the variables x1 and x3 as factors explaining the variation in unit labour cost.

Table 9.53: Estimated Linear Models for Regional Cotton Textile Industry at Current Price-Rajasthan

Variable	Coefficient	Std. Error	t-Statistic	Prob.
C	53.15201	28.47926	1.866341	0.0847
X1	0.176798	0.084406	2.094616	0.0564
X2	0.401973	0.273645	1.468958	0.1656
X3	-0.201511	0.049012	-4.111468	0.0012
REPX4	0.031612	0.012247	2.581186	0.0228
R-squared	0.879872	Mean dependent var		79.96331
Adjusted R-squared	0.842910	S.D. dependent var		20.33125
S.E. of regression	8.058215	Akaike info criterion		7.241394
Sum squared resid	844.1527	Schwarz criterion		7.488720

Prob(F-statistic) 0.000007

Estimation Equation:

Y = C(1) + C(2)*X1 + C(3)*X2 + C(4)*X3 + C(5)*REPX4

Substituted Coefficients:

Y = 53.152009 + 0.1767977511*X1 + 0.401973397*X2 - 0.2015109678*X3 + 0.03161174485*REPX4

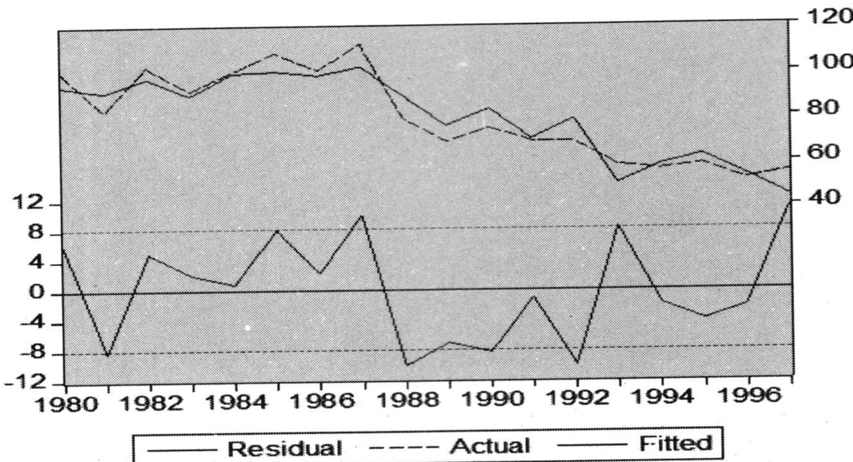

Fig. 9.53: Line Chart Estimated Linear Models for Regional Cotton Textile Industry at Current Price-Rajasthan

Table 9.54: Estimated Linear Models for Regional Cotton Textile Industry at Constant Price-Rajasthan

Variable	Coefficient	Std. Error	t-Statistic	Prob.
C	40.92926	26.27697	1.557610	0.1433
X1	0.531346	0.204924	2.592890	0.0223
X2	0.290530	0.153731	1.889867	0.0813
X3	-0.353575	0.043352	-8.155896	0.0000
X4	0.000518	0.005290	0.097982	0.9234
R-squared	0.929342	Mean dependent var		62.01792
Adjusted R-squared	0.907601	S.D. dependent var		18.70675
S.E. of regression	5.686314	Akaike info criterion		6.544135
Sum squared resid	420.3442	Schwarz criterion		6.791460

Prob(F-statistic) 0.000000

Estimation Equation:

Y = C(1) + C(2)*X1 + C(3)*X2 + C(4)*X3 + C(5)*X4

Substituted Coefficients:

Y = 40.92926222 + 0.5313455164*X1 + 0.2905301541*X2 - 0.3535748217*X3 + 0.0005183227602*X4

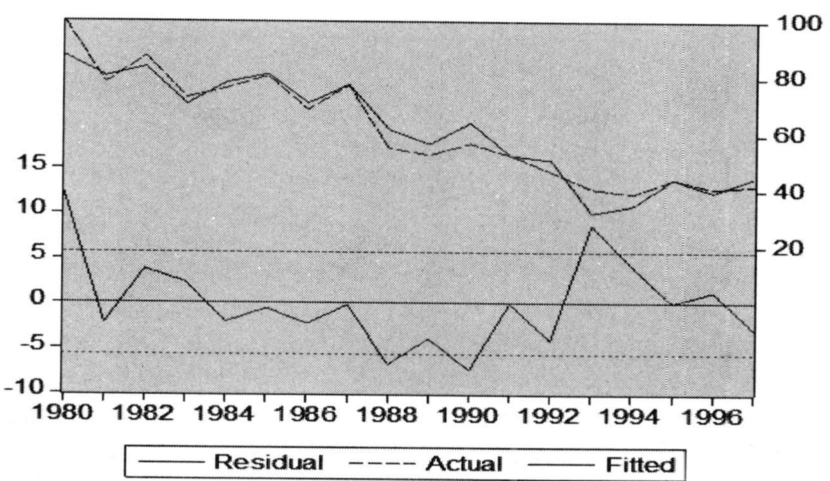

Fig. 9.54: Line Chart Estimated Linear Models for Regional Cotton Textile Industry at Constant Price-Rajasthan

Table 9.55: Estimated Non Linear Models for Regional Cotton Textile Industry at Current Price-Rajasthan

Variable	Coefficient	Std. Error	t-Statistic	Prob.
C	4.207880	0.282533	14.89341	0.0000
LOG(X1)	0.868645	0.052279	16.61540	0.0000
LOG(X2)	0.149705	0.059124	2.532038	0.0250
LOG(X3)	-0.949479	0.033513	-28.33192	0.0000
LOG(REPX4)	0.013425	0.015362	0.873878	0.3980
R-squared	0.995557	Mean dependent var		4.350269
Adjusted R-squared	0.994190	S.D. dependent var		0.259175
S.E. of regression	0.019755	Akaike info criterion		-4.780655
Sum squared resid	0.005074	Schwarz criterion		-4.533329

Prob(F-statistic) 0.000000

Estimation Equation:

LOG(Y) = LOG(C(1)) + C(2)*LOG(X1) + C(3)*LOG(X2) + C(4)*LOG(X3) + C(5)*LOG(REPX4)

Substituted Coefficients:

LOG(Y) = LOG(67.2138701316502)+ 0.8686446722*LOG(X1) + 0.1497054363*LOG(X2) - 0.9494785352*LOG(X3) + 0.01342494193*LOG(REPX4)

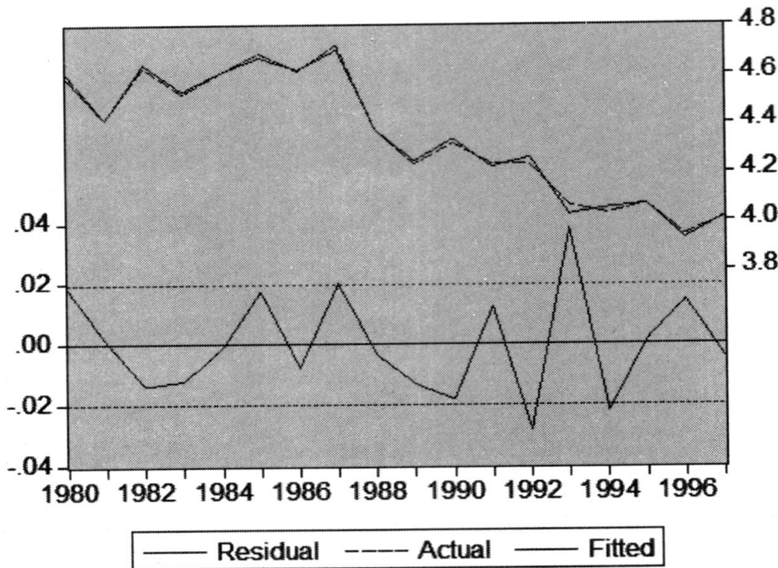

Fig. 9.55: Line Chart Estimated Non Linear Models for Regional Cotton Textile Industry at Current Price-Rajasthan

Table 9.56: Estimated Non Linear Models for Regional Cotton Textile Industry at Constant Price-Rajasthan

Variable	Coefficient	Std. Error	t-Statistic	Prob.
C	4.381058	0.447178	9.797122	0.0000
LOG(X1)	0.947054	0.084552	11.20079	0.0000
LOG(X2)	0.129480	0.051606	2.509012	0.0261
LOG(X3)	-1.025646	0.033367	-30.73818	0.0000
LOG(X4)	-0.007616	0.013302	-0.572563	0.5767
R-squared	0.995836	Mean dependent var		4.084567
Adjusted R-squared	0.994554	S.D. dependent var		0.301428
S.E. of regression	0.022244	Akaike info criterion		-4.543397
Sum squared resid	0.006432	Schwarz criterion		-4.296072

Prob(F-statistic) 0.000000

Estimation Equation:

LOG(Y) = C(1) + C(2)*LOG(X1) + C(3)*LOG(X2) + C(4)*LOG(X3) + C(5)*LOG(X4)

Substituted Coefficients:

LOG(Y) = 4.381057884 + 0.9470544173*LOG(X1) + 0.129480346*LOG(X2) - 1.025645977*LOG(X3) - 0.007615966581*LOG(X4)

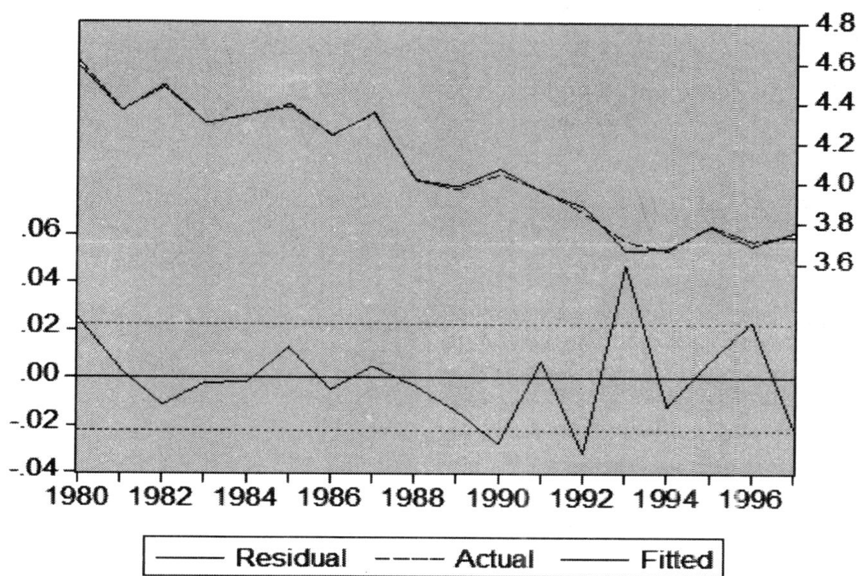

Fig. 9.56: Line Chart Estimated Non Linear Models for Regional Cotton Textile Industry at Constant Price-Rajasthan

The current price linear model indicates x3 (productivity) as impactful factors explaining around 87% of variance in unit labour cost. The linear model at constant price has R^2 value of 92% with x1 (average wage rate) and x3 as significant. The non linear models provide better fit than linear models. Non linear model at current price as well as the non linear model at constant price has R^2 of 99.5% explaining the variability of unit labour cost. The model identifies the variables x1 and x3 as factors explaining the variation in unit labour cost.

Table 9.57: Estimated Linear Models for Regional Cotton Textile Industry at Current Price-Tamilnadu

Variable	Coefficient	Std. Error	t-Statistic	Prob.
C	134.2833	22.13703	6.066006	0.0000
X1	-0.111673	0.046596	-2.396615	0.0323
X2	-0.174880	0.212349	-0.823550	0.4250
X3	-0.059953	0.025900	-2.314814	0.0376
REPX4	0.016451	0.005095	3.228964	0.0066
R-squared	0.956264	Mean dependent var		78.16133
Adjusted R-squared	0.942807	S.D. dependent var		19.41182
S.E. of regression	4.642335	Akaike info criterion		6.138445
Sum squared resid	280.1666	Schwarz criterion		6.385771

Prob(F-statistic) 0.000000

Estimation Equation:

Y = C(1) + C(2)*X1 + C(3)*X2 + C(4)*X3 + C(5)*REPX4

Substituted Coefficients:

Y = 134.2833494 - 0.1116725285*X1 - 0.1748803375*X2 - 0.05995254616*X3 + 0.01645135906*REPX4

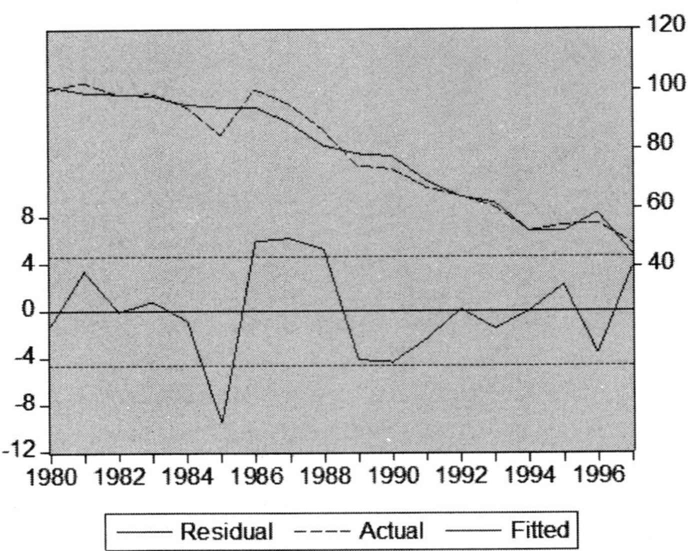

Fig. 9.57: Line Chart Estimated Linear Models for Regional Cotton Textile Industry at Current Price-Tamilnadu

Table 9.58: Estimated Linear Models for Regional Cotton Textile Industry at Constant Price-Tamilnadu

Variable	Coefficient	Std. Error	t-Statistic	Prob.
C	55.25872	38.76737	1.425393	0.1776
X1	0.208736	0.287801	0.725278	0.4811
X2	0.383387	0.243797	1.572567	0.1398
X3	-0.302489	0.062871	-4.811279	0.0003
X4	-0.000536	0.007302	-0.073465	0.9426
R-squared	0.909583	Mean dependent var		60.94429
Adjusted R-squared	0.881763	S.D. dependent var		19.69258
S.E. of regression	6.771413	Akaike info criterion		6.893430
Sum squared resid	596.0764	Schwarz criterion		7.140755

Prob(F-statistic) 0.000001

Estimation Equation:

Y = C(1) + C(2)*X1 + C(3)*X2 + C(4)*X3 + C(5)*X4

Substituted Coefficients:

Y = 55.25871859 + 0.2087355488*X1 + 0.3833874844*X2 - 0.3024889793*X3 - 0.0005364357576*X4

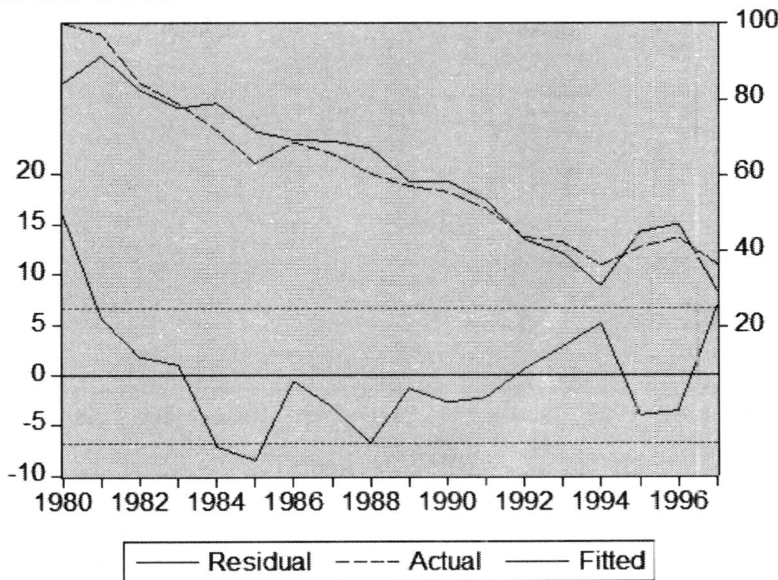

Fig. 9.58: Line Chart Estimated Linear Models for Regional Cotton Textile Industry at Constant Price-Tamilnadu

Table 9.59: Estimated Non Linear Models for Regional Cotton Textile Industry at Current Price-Tamilnadu

Variable	Coefficient	Std. Error	t-Statistic	Prob.
C	5.714697	0.544805	10.48943	0.0000
LOG(X1)	0.648560	0.079640	8.143610	0.0000
LOG(X2)	-0.106114	0.109863	-0.965874	0.3517
LOG(X3)	-0.767066	0.060922	-12.59087	0.0000
LOG(REPX4)	-0.013220	0.031824	-0.415421	0.6846
R-squared	0.994837	Mean dependent var		4.327410
Adjusted R-squared	0.993249	S.D. dependent var		0.262567
S.E. of regression	0.021574	Akaike info criterion		-4.604484
Sum squared resid	0.006051	Schwarz criterion		-4.357158

Prob(F-statistic) 0.000000

Estimation Equation:

LOG(Y) = LOG(C(1)) + C(2)*LOG(X1) + C(3)*LOG(X2) + C(4)*LOG(X3) + C(5)*LOG(REPX4)

Substituted Coefficients:

LOG(Y) = LOG(303.292192037951) + 0.6485598777*LOG(X1) - 0.1061141597*LOG(X2) - 0.7670656792*LOG(X3) - 0.01322017262*LOG(REPX4)

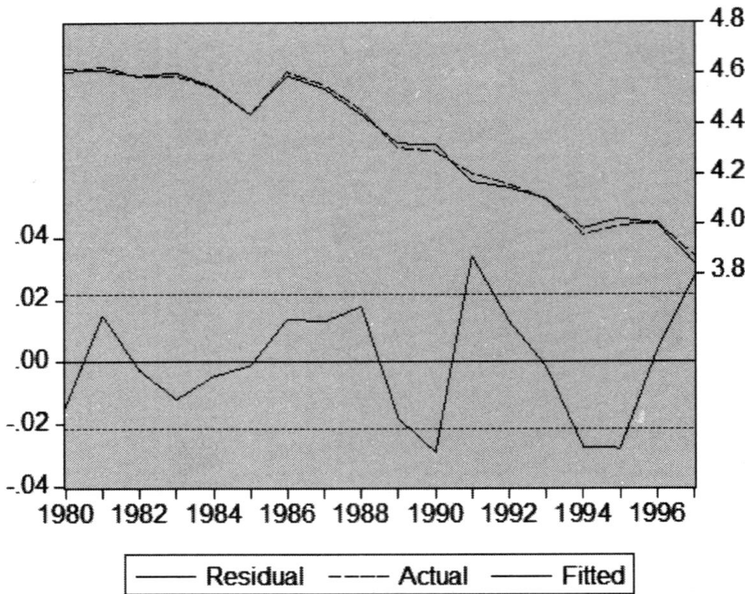

Fig. 9.59: Line Chart Estimated Non Linear Models for Regional Cotton Textile Industry at Current Price-Tamilnadu

Table 9.60: Estimated Non Linear Models for Regional Cotton Textile Industry at Constant Price-Tamilnadu

Variable	Coefficient	Std. Error	t-Statistic	Prob.
C	5.207462	0.707089	7.364644	0.0000
LOG(X1)	0.693703	0.121511	5.708968	0.0001
LOG(X2)	0.105122	0.098085	1.071742	0.3033
LOG(X3)	-0.890522	0.070362	-12.65625	0.0000
LOG(X4)	-0.047575	0.027010	-1.761381	0.1017
R-squared	0.994577	Mean dependent var		4.061699
Adjusted R-squared	0.992909	S.D. dependent var		0.319105
S.E. of regression	0.026871	Akaike info criterion		-4.165379
Sum squared resid	0.009387	Schwarz criterion		-3.918054

Prob(F-statistic) 0.000000

Estimation Equation:

LOG(Y) = C(1) + C(2)*LOG(X1) + C(3)*LOG(X2) + C(4)*LOG(X3) + C(5)*LOG(X4)

Substituted Coefficients:

LOG(Y) = 5.207461869 + 0.6937026912*LOG(X1) + 0.1051219188*LOG(X2) - 0.8905216768*LOG(X3) - 0.04757482845*LOG(X4)

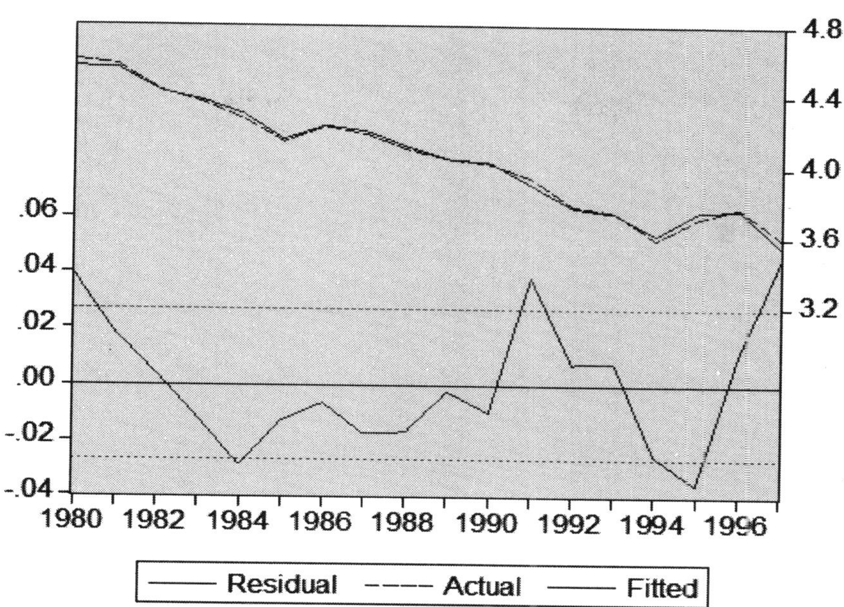

Fig. 9.60: Line Chart Estimated Non Linear Models for Regional Cotton Textile Industry at Constant Price-Tamilnadu

The current price linear model indicates x1(average wage rate), x3(productivity) x4 (technological change) as impactful factors explaining around 95% of variance in unit labour cost. The linear model at constant price has R^2 value of 90% with x3 as significant. The non linear models provide better fit than linear models. Non linear model at current price as well as the non linear model at constant price has R^2 of 99% explaining the variability of unit labour cost. The model identifies the variables x1 and x3 as factors explaining the variation in unit labour cost.

Table 9.61: Estimated Linear Models for Regional Cotton Textile Industry at Current Price-Uttar Pradesh

Variable	Coefficient	Std. Error	t-Statistic	Prob.
C	140.3774	38.77871	3.619959	0.0031
X1	0.217051	0.070150	3.094075	0.0085
X2	-0.313279	0.384405	-0.814971	0.4298
X3	-0.264652	0.054200	-4.882910	0.0003
REPX4	0.036836	0.006427	5.731036	0.0001
R-squared	0.861425	Mean dependent var		100.9694
Adjusted R-squared	0.818786	S.D. dependent var		17.84982
S.E. of regression	7.598530	Akaike info criterion		7.123920
Sum squared resid	750.5895	Schwarz criterion		7.371245
Prob(F-statistic)	0.000017			

Estimation Equation:

Y = C(1) + C(2)*X1 + C(3)*X2 + C(4)*X3 + C(5)*REPX4

Substituted Coefficients:

Y = 140.3773721 + 0.2170506374*X1 - 0.3132790116*X2 - 0.264651855*X3 + 0.03683613458*REPX4

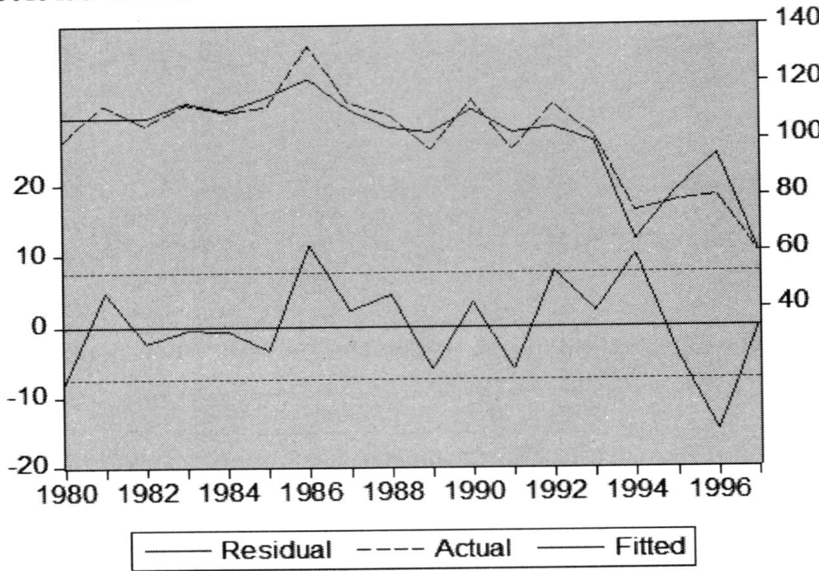

Fig. 9.61: Line Chart Estimated Linear Models for Regional Cotton Textile Industry at Current Price-Uttar Pradesh

Table 9.62: Estimated Linear Models for Regional Cotton Textile Industry at Constant Price-Uttar Pradesh

Variable	Coefficient	Std. Error	t-Statistic	Prob.
C	9.979999	33.37600	0.299017	0.7697
X1	1.143410	0.195353	5.853031	0.0001
X2	0.165267	0.222853	0.741594	0.4715
X3	-0.486947	0.072192	-6.745176	0.0000
X4	0.000983	0.005203	0.189025	0.8530
R-squared	0.880327	Mean dependent var		77.80081
Adjusted R-squared	0.843505	S.D. dependent var		15.95040
S.E. of regression	6.309897	Akaike info criterion		6.752249
Sum squared resid	517.5924	Schwarz criterion		6.999574

Prob(F-statistic) 0.000007

Estimation Equation:

Y = C(1) + C(2)*X1 + C(3)*X2 + C(4)*X3 + C(5)*X4

Substituted Coefficients:

Y = 9.979998586 + 1.143410058*X1 + 0.1652665872*X2 - 0.4869473882*X3 + 0.0009834756998*X4

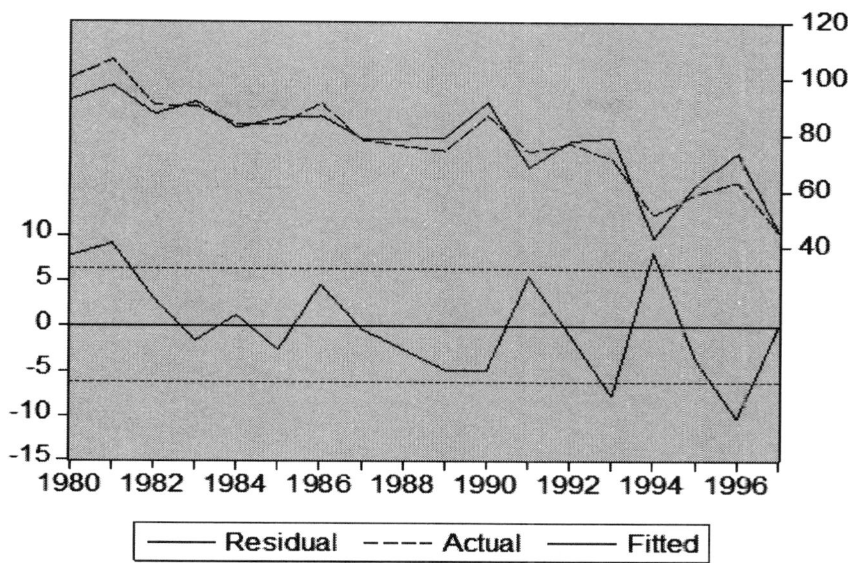

Fig. 9.62: Line Chart Estimated Linear Models for Regional Cotton Textile Industry at Constant Price-Uttar Pradesh

Table 9.63: Estimated Non Linear Models for Regional Cotton Textile Industry at Current Price-Uttar Pradesh

Variable	Coefficient	Std. Error	t-Statistic	Prob.
C	4.887828	0.555621	8.797047	0.0000
LOG(X1)	1.024499	0.056596	18.10191	0.0000
LOG(X2)	-0.089648	0.118726	-0.755086	0.4637
LOG(X3)	-0.950772	0.051054	-18.62294	0.0000
LOG(REPX4)	-0.046906	0.023727	-1.976882	0.0697
R-squared	0.988954	Mean dependent var		4.597975
Adjusted R-squared	0.985555	S.D. dependent var		0.195787
S.E. of regression	0.023531	Akaike info criterion		-4.430867
Sum squared resid	0.007198	Schwarz criterion		-4.183541

Prob(F-statistic) 0.000000

Estimation Equation:

LOG(Y) = C(1) + C(2)*LOG(X1) + C(3)*LOG(X2) + C(4)*LOG(X3) + C(5)*LOG(REPX4)

Substituted Coefficients:

LOG(Y) = 4.887827572 + 1.024499281*LOG(X1) - 0.08964799083*LOG(X2) - 0.9507718278*LOG(X3) - 0.046905933*LOG (REPX4)

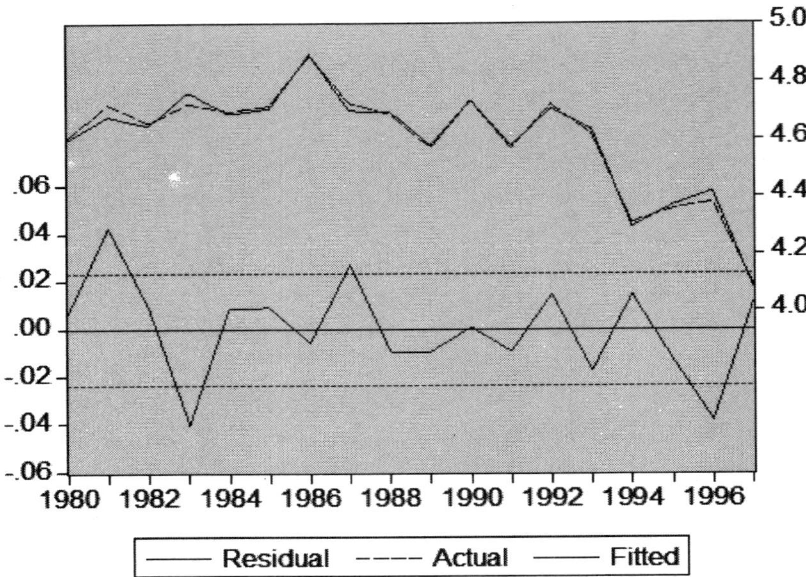

Fig. 9.63: Line Chart Estimated Non Linear Models for Regional Cotton Textile Industry at Current Price-Uttar Pradesh

Table 9.64: Estimated Non Linear Models for Regional Cotton Textile Industry at Constant Price -Uttar Pradesh

Variable	Coefficient	Std. Error	t-Statistic	Prob.
C	4.079110	0.325393	12.53595	0.0000
LOG(X1)	0.921449	0.039069	23.58513	0.0000
LOG(X2)	0.089400	0.070024	1.276708	0.2240
LOG(X3)	-0.864750	0.047322	-18.27363	0.0000
LOG(X4)	-0.033018	0.012524	-2.636454	0.0205
R-squared	0.993675	Mean dependent var		4.332236
Adjusted R-squared	0.991729	S.D. dependent var		0.221717
S.E. of regression	0.020164	Akaike info criterion		-4.739692
Sum squared resid	0.005286	Schwarz criterion		-4.492366

Prob(F-statistic) 0.000000

Estimation Equation:

LOG(Y) = C(1) + C(2)*LOG(X1) + C(3)*LOG(X2) + C(4)*LOG(X3) + C(5)*LOG(X4)

Substituted Coefficients:

LOG(Y) = 4.079110402 + 0.9214490712*LOG(X1) + 0.08940029612*LOG(X2) - 0.8647499842*LOG(X3) - 0.03301792608*LOG(X4)

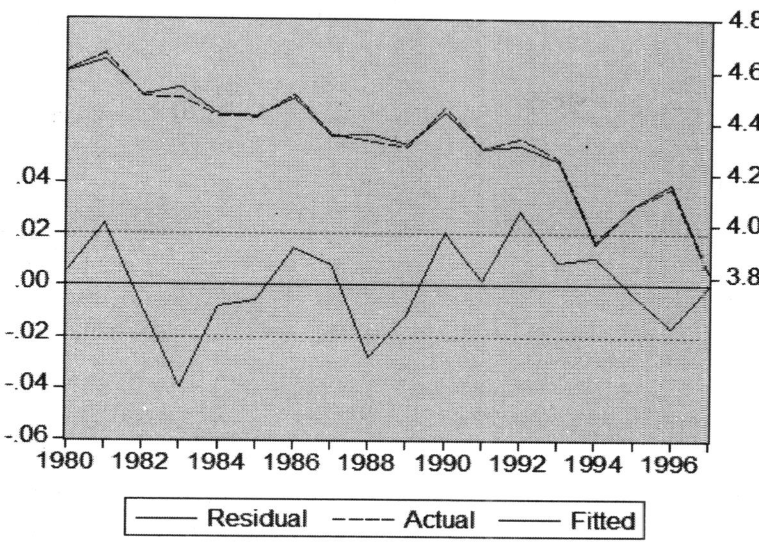

Fig. 9.64: Line Chart Estimated Non Linear Models for Regional Cotton Textile Industry at Constant Price -Uttar Pradesh

The current price linear model indicates x1(average wage rate), x3(productivity) repx4 (capital intensity) as impactful factors explaining around 86% of variance in unit labour cost. The linear model at constant price has R^2 value of 88% with x1 and x3 as significant. The non linear models provide better fit than linear models. Non linear model at current price has R^2 of 98.8% explaining the variability of unit labour cost. The model identifies the variables x1 and x3 as factors explaining the variation in unit labour cost. Non linear model at constant price has R^2 of 99.3% explaining the variability of unit labour cost. The model identifies the variables x1 and x3 and x4 (technological changes) as factors explaining the variation in unit labour cost.

Table 9.65: Estimated Linear Models for Regional Cotton Textile Industry at Current Price - West Bengal

Variable	Coefficient	Std. Error	t-Statistic	Prob.
C	114.6587	21.53617	5.324005	0.0001
X1	0.209760	0.038165	5.496138	0.0001
X2	-0.094002	0.202993	-0.463081	0.6510
X3	-0.238041	0.032839	-7.248827	0.0000
X4	0.010004	0.003550	2.818138	0.0145
R-squared	0.950597	Mean dependent var		94.03363
Adjusted R-squared	0.935397	S.D. dependent var		18.96443
S.E. of regression	4.820232	Akaike info criterion		6.213654
Sum squared resid	302.0502	Schwarz criterion		6.460980

Prob(F-statistic) 0.000000

Estimation Equation:

Y = C(1) + C(2)*X1 + C(3)*X2 + C(4)*X3 + C(5)*X4

Substituted Coefficients:

Y = 114.6586582 + 0.209759894*X1 - 0.09400222491*X2 - 0.2380411048*X3 + 0.01000369355*X4

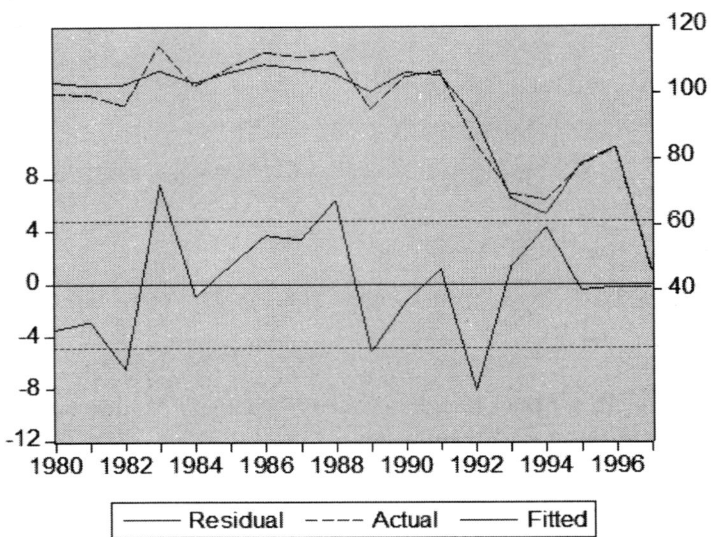

Fig. 9.65: Line Chart Estimated Linear Models for Regional Cotton Textile Industry at Current Price - West Bengal

Table 9.66: Estimated Linear Models for Regional Cotton Textile Industry at Constant Price- West Bengal

Variable	Coefficient	Std. Error	t-Statistic	Prob.
C	113.8551	21.65875	5.256773	0.0002
X1	0.082406	0.130463	0.631641	0.5386
X2	0.040380	0.148137	0.272586	0.7895
X3	-0.345114	0.037352	-9.239425	0.0000
X4	0.000520	0.001378	0.377558	0.7119
R-squared	0.971084	Mean dependent var		72.68657
Adjusted R-squared	0.962187	S.D. dependent var		17.33619
S.E. of regression	3.371125	Akaike info criterion		5.498503
Sum squared resid	147.7383	Schwarz criterion		5.745829

Prob(F-statistic) 0.000000

Estimation Equation:

Y = C(1) + C(2)*X1 + C(3)*X2 + C(4)*X3 + C(5)*X4

Substituted Coefficients:

Y = 113.8551415 + 0.08240582616*X1 + 0.04038007542*X2 - 0.3451136351*X3 + 0.0005203669363*X4

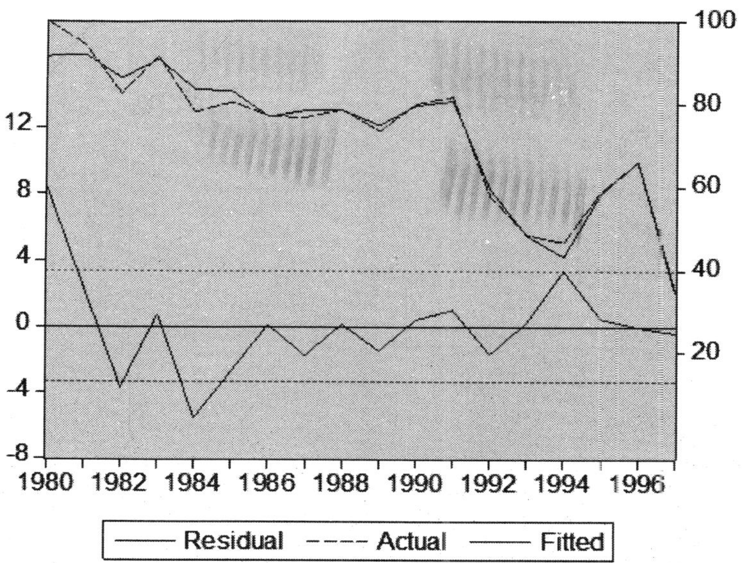

Fig. 9.66: Line Chart Estimated Linear Models for Regional Cotton Textile Industry at Constant Price- West Bengal

Table 9.67: Estimated Non Linear Models for Regional Cotton Textile Industry at Constant Price – West Bengal

Variable	Coefficient	Std. Error	t-Statistic	Prob.
C	4.624971	0.755716	6.119989	0.0000
LOG(X1)	1.035021	0.087498	11.82914	0.0000
LOG(X2)	0.023861	0.167332	0.142595	0.8888
LOG(X3)	-0.971145	0.098485	-9.860815	0.0000
LOG(X4)	-0.092497	0.040670	-2.274337	0.0405
R-squared	0.979227	Mean dependent var		4.519822
Adjusted R-squared	0.972835	S.D. dependent var		0.238230
S.E. of regression	0.039265	Akaike info criterion		-3.406851
Sum squared resid	0.020042	Schwarz criterion		-3.159526

Prob(F-statistic) 0.000000

Estimation Equation:

LOG(Y) = C(1) + C(2)*LOG(X1) + C(3)*LOG(X2) + C(4)*LOG(X3) + C(5)*LOG(X4)

Substituted Coefficients:

LOG(Y) = 4.624971293 + 1.035020545*LOG(X1) + 0.02386066715*LOG(X2) - 0.9711452448*LOG(X3) - 0.09249672033*LOG(X4)

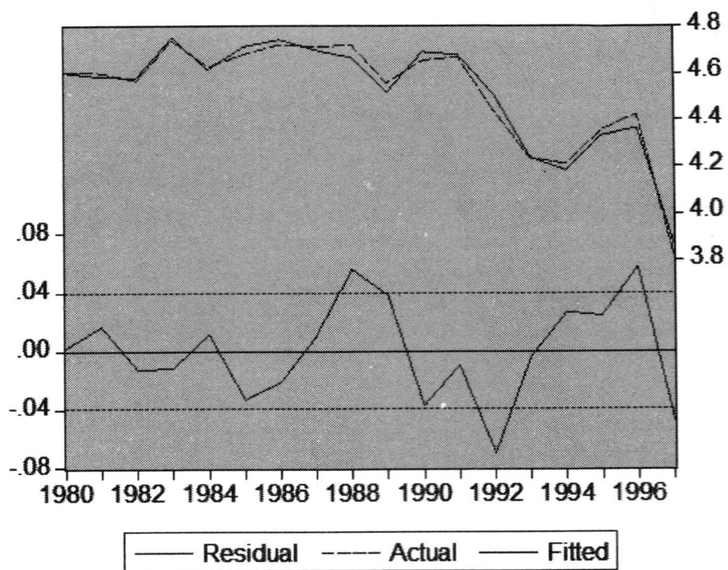

Fig. 9.67: Line Chart Estimated Non Linear Models for Regional Cotton Textile Industry at Constant Price – West Bengal

Table 9.68: Estimated Non Linear Models for Regional Cotton Textile Industry at Constant Price – West Bengal

Variable	Coefficient	Std. Error	t-Statistic	Prob.
C	4.098634	1.247001	3.286793	0.0059
LOG(X1)	1.099962	0.194689	5.649833	0.0001
LOG(X2)	0.081706	0.183332	0.445674	0.6632
LOG(X3)	-1.013705	0.098944	-10.24529	0.0000
LOG(X4)	-0.056684	0.026691	-2.123709	0.0535
R-squared	0.982140	Mean dependent var		4.254083
Adjusted R-squared	0.976645	S.D. dependent var		0.273846
S.E. of regression	0.041850	Akaike info criterion		-3.279311
Sum squared resid	0.022769	Schwarz criterion		-3.031985

Prob(F-statistic) 0.000000

Estimation Equation:

LOG(Y) = C(1) + C(2)*LOG(X1) + C(3)*LOG(X2) + C(4)*LOG(X3) + C(5)*LOG(X4)

Substituted Coefficients:

LOG(Y) = 4.098634198 + 1.099961766*LOG(X1) + 0.08170630956*LOG(X2) - 1.01370507*LOG(X3) - 0.05668384741*LOG(X4)

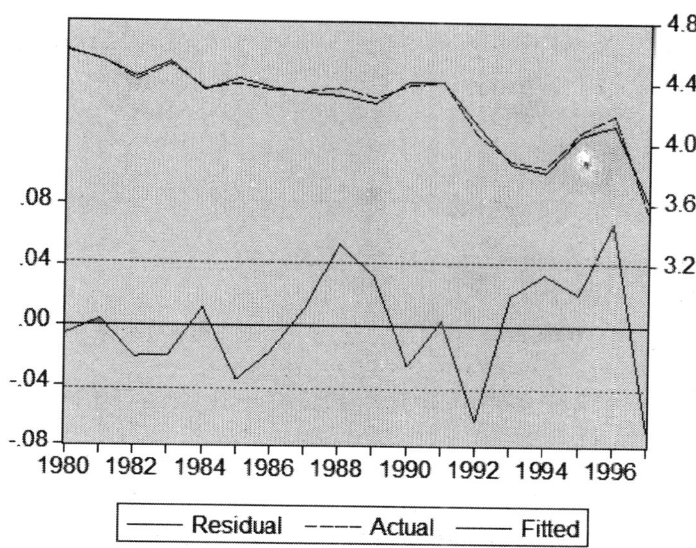

Fig. 9.68: Line Chart Estimated Non Linear Models for Regional Cotton Textile Industry at Constant Price – West Bengal

The current price linear model indicates x1(average wage rate), x3(productivity) and x4 (technological changes) as impactful factors explaining around 95% of variance in unit labour cost. The linear model at constant price has R^2 value of 97% with x3 as significant. The non linear models provide better fit than linear models. Non linear model at current price has R^2 of 97.9% explaining the variability of unit labour cost. The model identifies the variables x1 and x3 and x4 (technological changes) as factors explaining the variation in unit labour cost. Non linear model at constant price has R^2 of 98.2% explaining the variability of unit labour cost. The model identifies the variables x1 and x3 as factors explaining the variation in unit labour cost.

ESTIMATION OF UNIT COST LABOUR FUNCTION IN REGIONAL SUGAR INDUSTRY

Table 9.69: Estimated Linear Models for Regional Sugar Industry at Current Price - Bihar

Variable	Coefficient	Std. Error	t-Statistic	Prob.
C	72.70601	31.48062	2.309548	0.0380
X1	0.005857	0.019819	0.295507	0.7723
X2	0.273542	0.291495	0.938411	0.3651
X3	-0.086268	0.035361	-2.439623	0.0298
X4	0.001278	0.004023	0.317686	0.7558
R-squared	0.567423	Mean dependent var		84.58038
Adjusted R-squared	0.434322	S.D. dependent var		19.52735
S.E. of regression	14.68683	Akaike info criterion		8.441912
Sum squared resid	2804.138	Schwarz criterion		8.689238

Prob(F-statistic) 0.020203

Estimation Equation:

Y = C(1) + C(2)*X1 + C(3)*X2 + C(4)*X3 + C(5)*X4

Substituted Coefficients:

Y = 72.70601246 + 0.005856765529*X1 + 0.2735418345*X2 - 0.08626798725*X3 + 0.001278066311*X4

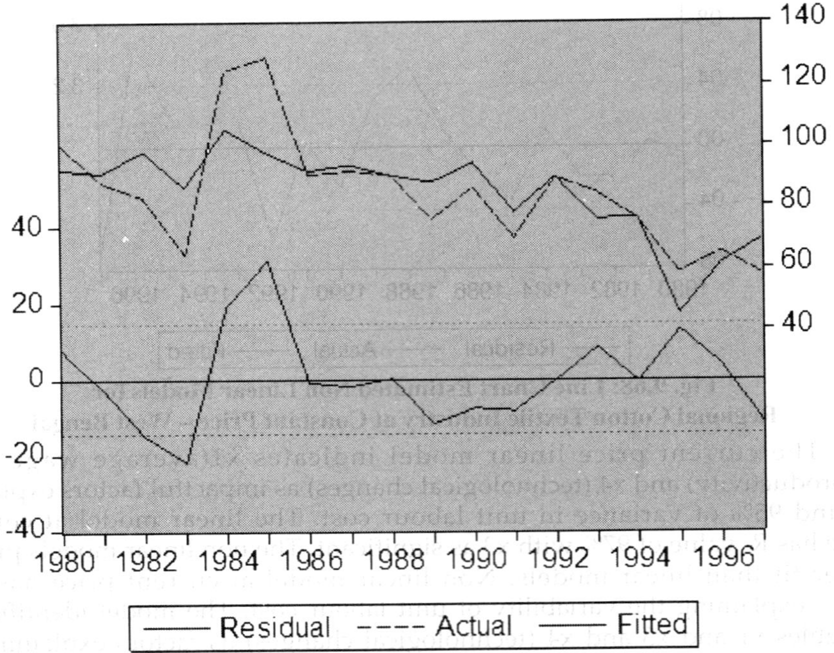

Fig. 9.69: Line Chart Estimated Linear Models for Regional Sugar Industry at Current Price- Bihar

Table 9.70: Estimated Linear Models for Regional Sugar Industry at Constant Price- Bihar

Variable	Coefficient	Std. Error	t-Statistic	Prob.
C	84.91955	15.95325	5.323027	0.0001
X1	-0.006615	0.020230	-0.326982	0.7489
X2	0.261753	0.147624	1.773105	0.0996
X3	-0.244965	0.047513	-5.155743	0.0002
X4	0.001167	0.000882	1.323888	0.2083
R-squared	0.826981	Mean dependent var		58.20729
Adjusted R-squared	0.773744	S.D. dependent var		17.76786
S.E. of regression	8.451526	Akaike info criterion		7.336704
Sum squared resid	928.5679	Schwarz criterion		7.584030

Prob(F-statistic) 0.000071

Estimation Equation:

Y = C(1) + C(2)*X1 + C(3)*X2 + C(4)*X3 + C(5)*X4

Substituted Coefficients:

Y = 84.91955378 - 0.006614712515*X1 + 0.2617532061*X2 - 0.2449653874*X3 + 0.001167157654*X4

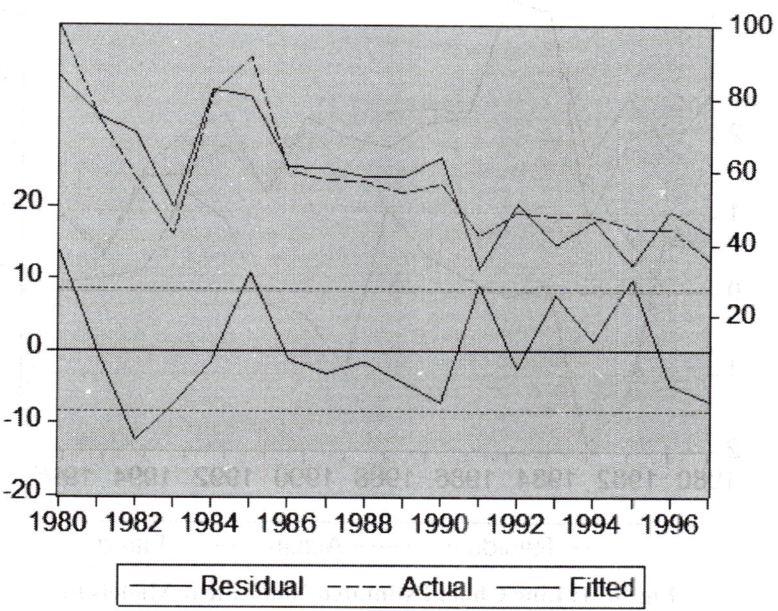

Fig. 9.70: Line Chart Estimated Linear Models for Regional Sugar Industry at Constant Price- Bihar

Table 9.71: Estimated Non Linear Models for Regional Sugar Industry at Current Price- Bihar

Variable	Coefficient	Std. Error	t-Statistic	Prob.
C	5.022793	1.038769	4.835330	0.0003
LOG(X1)	-0.127787	0.139755	-0.914361	0.3772
LOG(X2)	0.350229	0.237025	1.477604	0.1633
LOG(X3)	-0.573216	0.084144	-6.812338	0.0000
LOG(X4)	0.250310	0.108537	2.306226	0.0382
R-squared	0.839448	Mean dependent var		4.413729
Adjusted R-squared	0.790048	S.D. dependent var		0.223575
S.E. of regression	0.102443	Akaike info criterion		-1.488886
Sum squared resid	0.136430	Schwarz criterion		-1.241560

Prob(F-statistic) 0.000044

Estimation Equation:

LOG(Y) = C(1) + C(2)*LOG(X1) + C(3)*LOG(X2) + C(4)*LOG(X3) + C(5)*LOG(X4)

Substituted Coefficients:

LOG(Y) = 5.022792911 - 0.1277868288*LOG(X1) + 0.3502285811*LOG(X2) - 0.5732161473*LOG(X3) + 0.2503101658*LOG(X4)

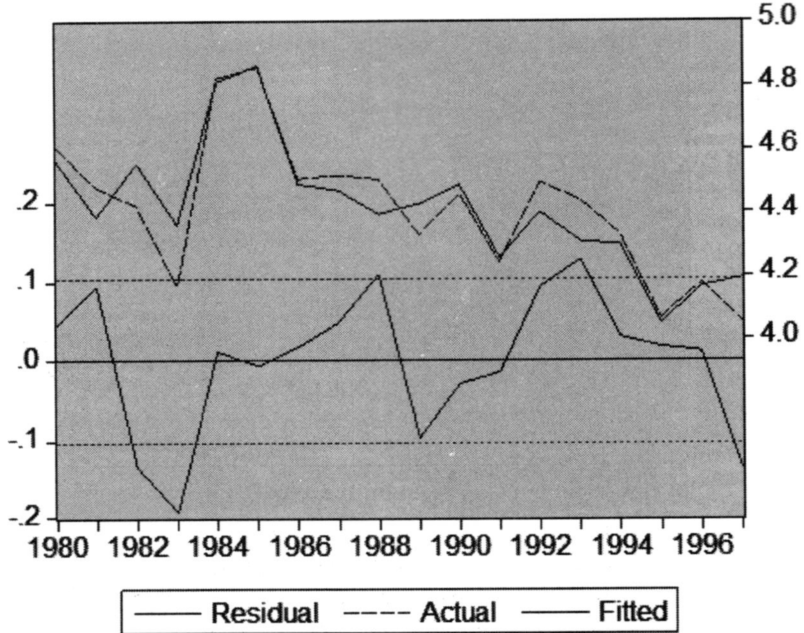

Fig. 9.71: Line Chart Estimated Non Linear Models for Regional Sugar Industry at Current Price-Bihar

Table 9.72: Estimated Non Linear Models for Regional Sugar Industry at Constant Price - Bihar

Variable	Coefficient	Std. Error	t-Statistic	Prob.
C	6.865803	0.838827	8.185003	0.0000
LOG(X1)	-0.070185	0.078390	-0.895340	0.3869
LOG(X2)	0.367723	0.150854	2.437605	0.0299
LOG(X3)	-0.850125	0.089994	-9.446419	0.0000
LOG(X4)	0.058004	0.039482	1.469147	0.1656
R-squared	0.941277	Mean dependent var		4.024980
Adjusted R-squared	0.923208	S.D. dependent var		0.279963
S.E. of regression	0.077581	Akaike info criterion		-2.044845
Sum squared resid	0.078245	Schwarz criterion		-1.797520

Prob(F-statistic) 0.000000

Estimation Equation:

LOG(Y) = C(1) + C(2)*LOG(X1) + C(3)*LOG(X2) + C(4)*LOG(X3) + C(5)*LOG(X4)

Substituted Coefficients:

LOG(Y) = 6.865802599 - 0.07018535262*LOG(X1) + 0.3677225744*LOG(X2) - 0.8501253709*LOG(X3) + 0.05800424154*LOG(X4)

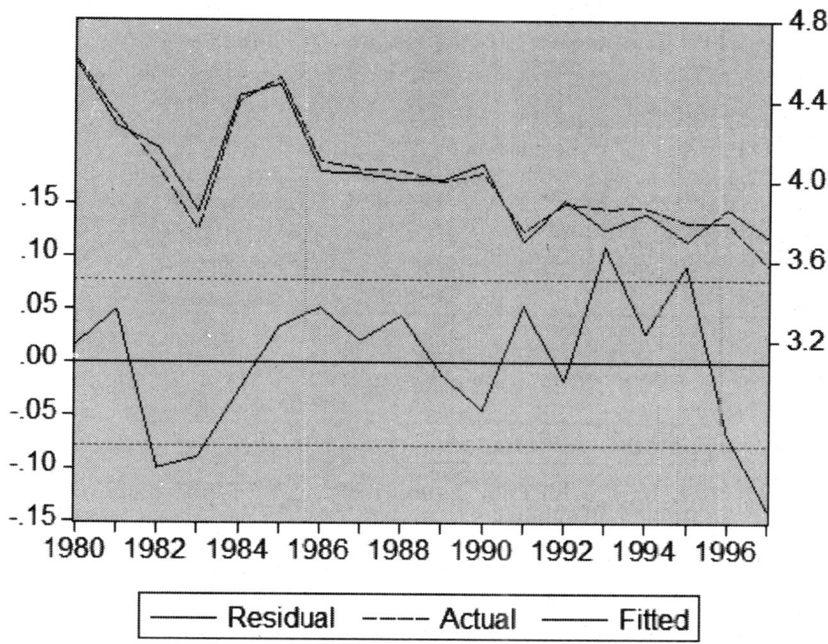

Fig. 9.72: Line Chart Estimated Non Linear Models for Regional Sugar Industry at Constant Price- Bihar

The current price linear model indicates x3(productivity) as impactful factors explaining around 56.7% of variance in unit labour cost. The explained variance in in this model in comparison to all other models of industries considered has explained much lesser variance with considered independent variables. The lesser R^2 indicate there are other lurking variables responsible for the variance in unit labour cost in sugar industry in Bihar. On removing the inflationary effect, the linear model at constant price has R^2 value of 82.6% with x3 as significant. The non linear models provide better fit than linear models. Non linear model at current price has R^2 of 83.9% explaining the variability of unit labour cost. The model identifies the variables x3 and x4 (technological changes) as factors explaining the variation in unit labour cost. Non linear model at constant price has R^2 of 94.12% explaining the variability of unit labour cost. The model identifies the variables x2 (unit material cost) and x3 as factors explaining the variation in unit labour cost.

Table 9.73: Estimated Linear Models for Regional Sugar Industry at Current Price- Maharashtra

Variable	Coefficient	Std. Error	t-Statistic	Prob.
C	166.9560	68.05653	2.453196	0.0290
X1	0.032456	0.028770	1.128111	0.2797
X2	-0.710040	0.707735	-1.003256	0.3340
X3	-0.231766	0.061965	-3.740278	0.0025
REPX4	0.111523	0.076692	1.454159	0.1696
R-squared	0.579426	Mean dependent var		90.04317
Adjusted R-squared	0.450018	S.D. dependent var		14.56909
S.E. of regression	10.80454	Akaike info criterion		7.827944
Sum squared resid	1517.596	Schwarz criterion		8.075269

Prob(F-statistic) 0.017106

Estimation Equation:

Y = C(1) + C(2)*X1 + C(3)*X2 + C(4)*X3 + C(5)*REPX4

Substituted Coefficients:

Y = 166.9560335 + 0.0324559376*X1 - 0.7100397059*X2 - 0.2317662636*X3 + 0.1115225056*REPX4

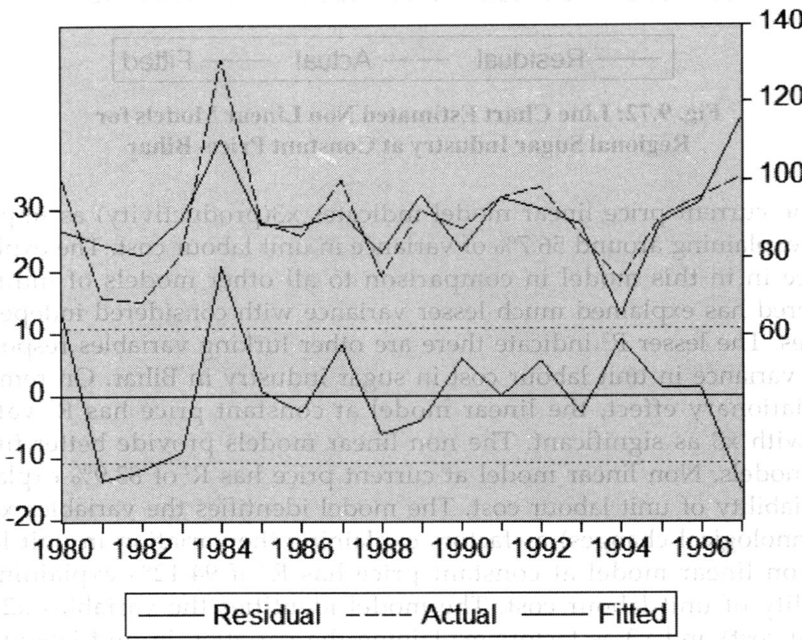

Fig. 9.73: Line Chart Estimated Linear Models for Regional Sugar Industry at Current Price- Maharashtra

Table 9.74: Estimated Linear Models for Regional Sugar Industry at Constant Price - Maharashtra

Variable	Coefficient	Std. Error	t-Statistic	Prob.
C	31.73727	35.92907	0.883331	0.3931
X1	0.054695	0.042914	1.274520	0.2248
X2	0.678992	0.350806	1.935522	0.0750
X3	-0.209515	0.054881	-3.817636	0.0021
X4	0.009759	0.009898	0.985946	0.3422
R-squared	0.709560	Mean dependent var		61.54895
Adjusted R-squared	0.620193	S.D. dependent var		13.46987
S.E. of regression	8.301275	Akaike info criterion		7.300828
Sum squared resid	895.8451	Schwarz criterion		7.548154

Prob(F-statistic) 0.001816

Estimation Equation:

Y = C(1) + C(2)*X1 + C(3)*X2 + C(4)*X3 + C(5)*X4

Substituted Coefficients:

Y = 31.73727182 + 0.0546945337*X1 + 0.6789921593*X2 - 0.2095153565*X3 + 0.009759168222*X4

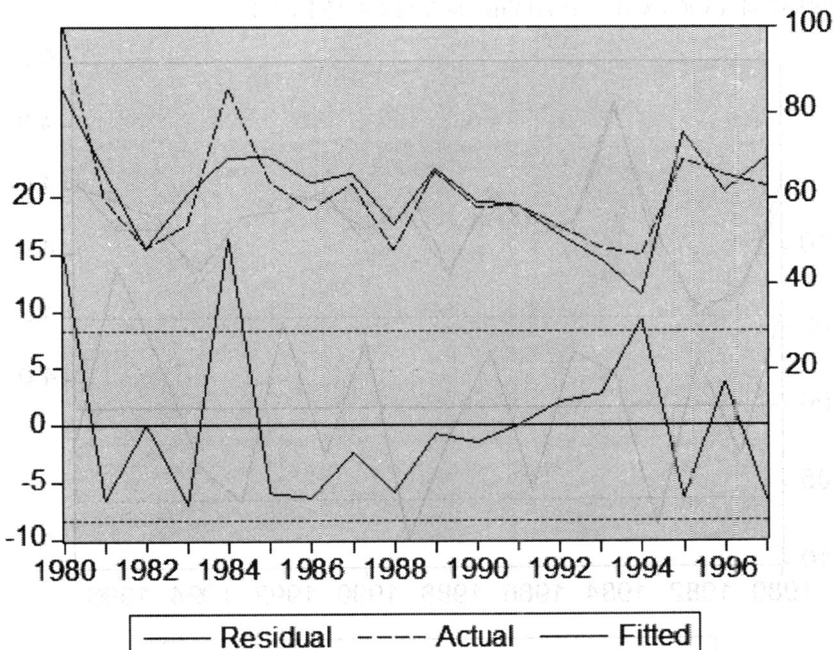

Fig. 9.74: Line Chart Estimated Linear Models for Regional Sugar Industry at Constant Price- Maharashtra

Table 9.75: Estimated Non Linear Models for Regional Sugar Industry at Current Price- Maharashtra

Variable	Coefficient	Std. Error	t-Statistic	Prob.
C	6.937410	1.534081	4.522193	0.0006
LOG(X1)	0.106972	0.068343	1.565239	0.1415
LOG(X2)	-0.341933	0.321146	-1.064725	0.3064
LOG(X3)	-0.988082	0.099139	-9.966677	0.0000
LOG(REPX4)	0.703567	0.112263	6.267149	0.0000
R-squared	0.893991	Mean dependent var		4.488552
Adjusted R-squared	0.861373	S.D. dependent var		0.156223
S.E. of regression	0.058166	Akaike info criterion		-2.620899
Sum squared resid	0.043983	Schwarz criterion		-2.373574
Prob(F-statistic)	0.000003			

Estimation Equation:

LOG(Y) = C(1) + C(2)*LOG(X1) + C(3)*LOG(X2) + C(4)*LOG(X3) + C(5)*LOG(REPX4)

Substituted Coefficients:

LOG(Y) = 6.937409536 + 0.1069724568*LOG(X1) - 0.3419326809*LOG(X2) - 0.9880815754*LOG(X3) + 0.7035670438*LOG(REPX4)

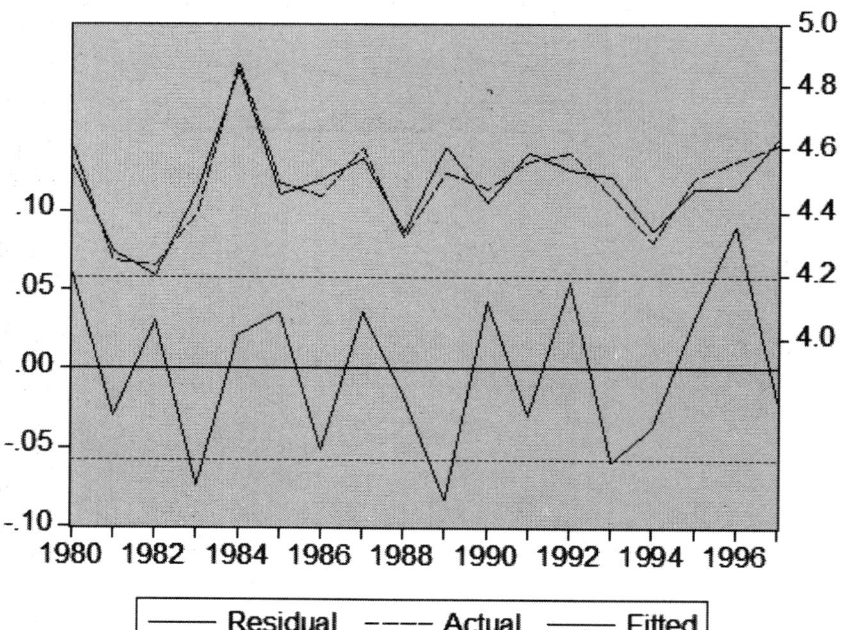

Fig. 9.75: Line Chart Estimated Non Linear Models for Regional Sugar Industry at Current Price- Maharashtra

Table 9.76: Estimated Non Linear Models for Regional Sugar Industry at Constant Price - Maharashtra

Variable	Coefficient	Std. Error	t-Statistic	Prob.
C	4.536191	2.042165	2.221266	0.0447
LOG(X1)	0.148922	0.172452	0.863556	0.4035
LOG(X2)	0.553374	0.347576	1.592093	0.1354
LOG(X3)	-0.845581	0.140250	-6.029109	0.0000
LOG(X4)	0.137555	0.086777	1.585161	0.1369
R-squared	0.828359	Mean dependent var		4.100140
Adjusted R-squared	0.775546	S.D. dependent var		0.198060
S.E. of regression	0.093834	Akaike info criterion		-1.664446
Sum squared resid	0.114463	Schwarz criterion		-1.417121
Prob(F-statistic)	0.000068			

Estimation Equation:

LOG(Y) = C(1) + C(2)*LOG(X1) + C(3)*LOG(X2) + C(4)*LOG(X3) + C(5)*LOG(X4)

Substituted Coefficients:

LOG(Y) = 4.536191118 + 0.1489216731*LOG(X1) + 0.5533740345*LOG(X2) - 0.8455807189*LOG(X3) + 0.1375553149*LOG(X4)

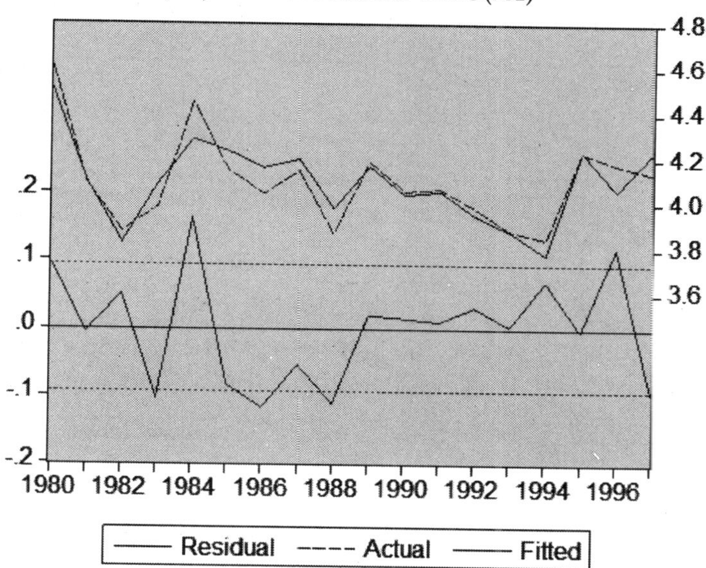

Fig. 9.76: Line Chart Estimated Non Linear Models for Regional Sugar Industry at Constant Price - Maharashtra

The current price linear model indicates x3(productivity) as impactful factors explaining around 57.9% of variance in unit labour cost. The explained variance in this model in comparison to all other models of industries considered has explained much lesser variance with considered independent variables. The lesser R^2 indicate there are other lurking variables responsible for the variance in unit labour cost in sugar industry in Bihar. On removing the inflationary effect, the linear model at constant price has R^2 value of 70.9% with x3 as significant. The non linear models provide better fit than linear models. Non linear model at current price has R^2 of 89.3% explaining the variability of unit labour cost. The model identifies the variables x3 and repx4 (capital intensity) as factors explaining the variation in unit labour cost. Non linear model at constant price has R^2 of 82.8% explaining the variability of unit labour cost. The model identifies the variables x3 as factors explaining the variation in unit labour cost.

Table 9.77: Estimated Linear Models for Regional Sugar Industry at Current Price - Tamilnadu

Variable	Coefficient	Std. Error	t-Statistic	Prob.
C	125.5785	46.05898	2.726471	0.0173
X1	0.027154	0.021871	1.241530	0.2363
X2	-0.339440	0.446660	-0.759953	0.4608
X3	-0.066738	0.043906	-1.520033	0.1524
X4	-0.000408	0.007384	-0.055230	0.9568
R-squared	0.492514	Mean dependent var		82.36426
Adjusted R-squared	0.336365	S.D. dependent var		11.66983
S.E. of regression	9.506689	Akaike info criterion		7.572001
Sum squared resid	1174.903	Schwarz criterion		7.819327

Prob (F-statistic) 0.051126

Estimation Equation:

Y = C(1) + C(2)*X1 + C(3)*X2 + C(4)*X3 + C(5)*X4

Substituted Coefficients:

Y = 125.5784911 + 0.02715378681*X1 - 0.3394403973*X2 - 0.06673789947*X3 - 0.000407833851*X4

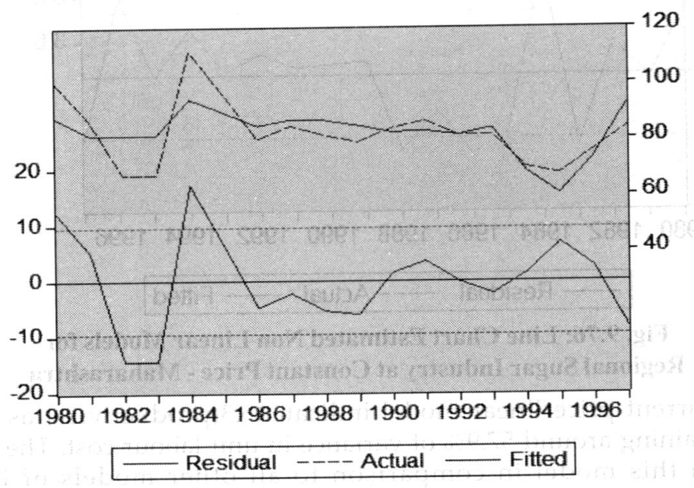

Fig. 9.77: Line Chart Estimated Linear Models for Regional Sugar Industry at Current Price - Tamilnadu

Table 9.78: Estimated Linear Models for Regional Sugar Industry at Constant Price- Tamilnadu

Variable	Coefficient	Std. Error	t-Statistic	Prob.
C	66.90171	21.67491	3.086597	0.0087
X1	0.024174	0.039946	0.605164	0.5555
X2	0.253840	0.207461	1.223553	0.2428
X3	-0.174382	0.050850	-3.429354	0.0045
X4	0.003570	0.004836	0.738080	0.4736
R-squared	0.665024	Mean dependent var		56.69582
Adjusted R-squared	0.561955	S.D. dependent var		14.10454
S.E. of regression	9.335087	Akaike info criterion		7.535570
Sum squared resid	1132.870	Schwarz criterion		7.782896
Prob(F-statistic)	0.004352			

Estimation Equation:

Y = C(1) + C(2)*X1 + C(3)*X2 + C(4)*X3 + C(5)*X4

Substituted Coefficients:

Y = 66.90170737 + 0.02417401739*X1 + 0.2538395588*X2 - 0.1743817931*X3 + 0.003569573646*X4

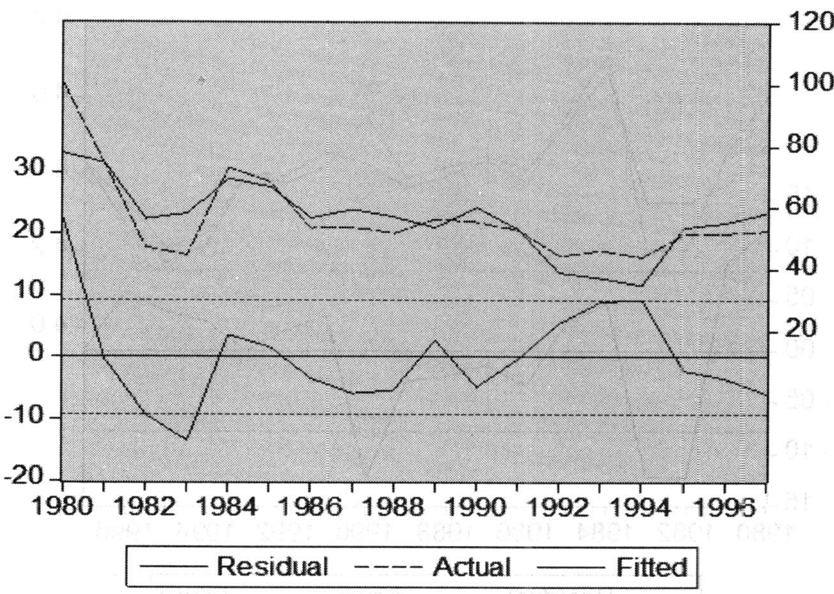

Fig. 9.78: Line Chart Estimated Linear Models for Regional Sugar Industry at Constant Price- Tamilnadu

Table 9.79: Estimated Non Linear Models for Regional Sugar Industry at Current Price -Tamilnadu

Variable	Coefficient	Std. Error	t-Statistic	Prob.
C	6.399786	1.532523	4.175981	0.0011
LOG(X1)	0.166991	0.084931	1.966208	0.0710
LOG(X2)	-0.234822	0.359457	-0.653268	0.5250
LOG(X3)	-0.491298	0.119139	-4.123739	0.0012
LOG(X4)	0.143502	0.060365	2.377236	0.0335
R-squared	0.750097	Mean dependent var		4.402069
Adjusted R-squared	0.673203	S.D. dependent var		0.137476
S.E. of regression	0.078590	Akaike info criterion		-2.019016
Sum squared resid	0.080293	Schwarz criterion		-1.771691

Prob(F-statistic) 0.000715

Estimation Equation:

LOG(Y) = C(1) + C(2)*LOG(X1) + C(3)*LOG(X2) + C(4)*LOG(X3) + C(5)*LOG(X4)

Substituted Coefficients:

LOG(Y) = 6.399786016 + 0.1669914072*LOG(X1) - 0.2348218544*LOG(X2) - 0.4912981965*LOG(X3) + 0.1435017738*LOG(X4)

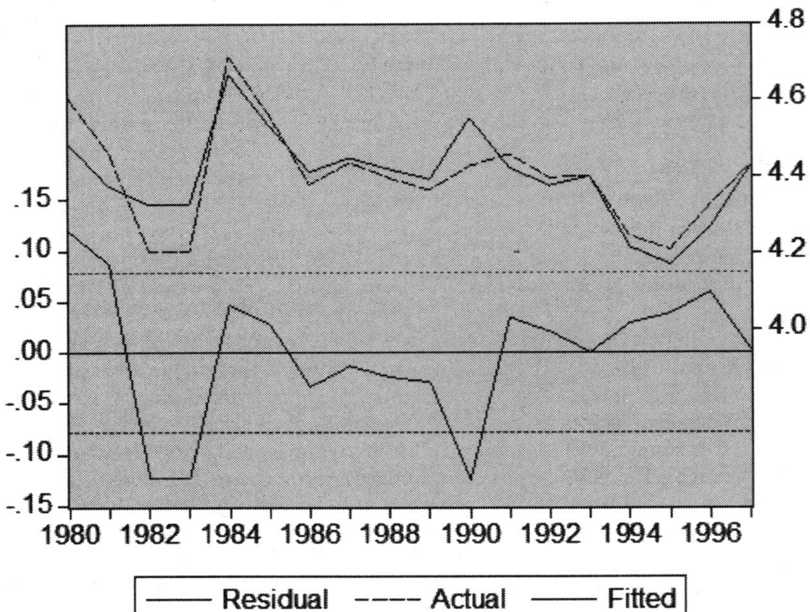

Fig. 9.79: Line Chart Estimated Non Linear Models for Regional Sugar Industry at Current Price-Tamilnadu

Table 9.80: Estimated Non Linear Models for Regional Sugar Industry at Constant Price -Tamilnadu

Variable	Coefficient	Std. Error	t-Statistic	Prob.
C	5.743472	0.892960	6.431945	0.0000
LOG(X1)	0.159796	0.089718	1.781089	0.0983
LOG(X2)	0.364251	0.171037	2.129662	0.0529
LOG(X3)	-0.886469	0.099814	-8.881239	0.0000
LOG(X4)	0.091923	0.037547	2.448205	0.0293
R-squared	0.909483	Mean dependent var		4.013733
Adjusted R-squared	0.881631	S.D. dependent var		0.215125
S.E. of regression	0.074013	Akaike info criterion		-2.139014
Sum squared resid	0.071213	Schwarz criterion		-1.891689

Prob(F-statistic) 0.000001

Estimation Equation:

LOG(Y) = C(1) + C(2)*LOG(X1) + C(3)*LOG(X2) + C(4)*LOG(X3) + C(5)*LOG(X4)

Substituted Coefficients:

LOG(Y) = 5.743471645 + 0.1597955472*LOG(X1) + 0.3642513024*LOG(X2) - 0.8864685448*LOG(X3) + 0.0919230692*LOG(X4)

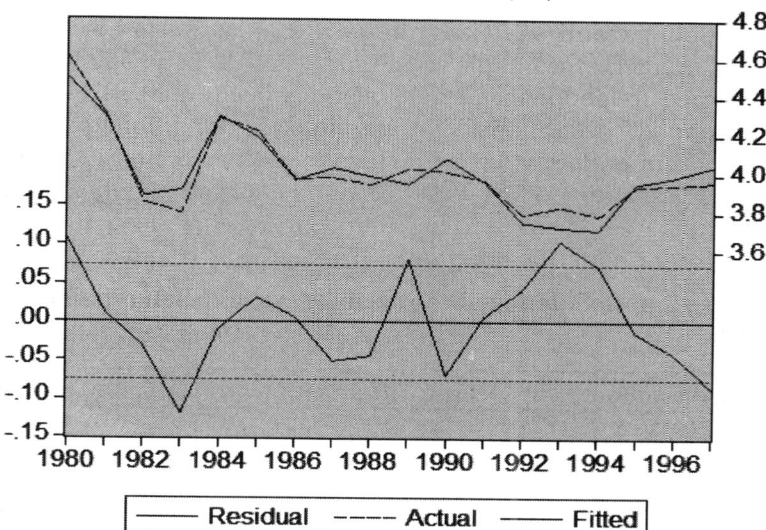

Fig. 9.80: Line Chart Estimated Non Linear Models for Regional Sugar Industry at Constant Price-Tamilnadu

The current price linear model indicates data inconsistencies as none of the coefficients of independent variable were found significant and R^2 value was also very low. On removing the inflationary effect, the linear model at constant price has R^2 value of 66.5% with x3 (productivity) as significant.

The non linear models provide better fit than linear models. Non linear model at current price has R^2 of 75% explaining the variability of unit labour cost. The model identifies the variables x3 and x4 (technological changes) as factors explaining the variation in unit labour cost. Non linear model at constant price has R^2 of 90.9% explaining the variability of unit labour cost. The model identifies the variables x3 and x4 as factors explaining the variation in unit labour cost.

Table 9.81: Estimated Linear Models for Regional Sugar Industry at Current Price-Uttar Pradesh

Variable	Coefficient	Std. Error	t-Statistic	Prob.
C	118.9269	21.57028	5.513464	0.0001
X1	0.039873	0.016990	2.346915	0.0354
X2	-0.202740	0.214506	-0.945146	0.3618
X3	-0.082966	0.026242	-3.161583	0.0075
X4	-0.004192	0.007625	-0.549737	0.5918
R-squared	0.775575	Mean dependent var		87.98180
Adjusted R-squared	0.706522	S.D. dependent var		9.991683
S.E. of regression	5.412860	Akaike info criterion		6.445565
Sum squared resid	380.8876	Schwarz criterion		6.692891

Prob(F-statistic) 0.000366

Estimation Equation:

Y = C(1) + C(2)*X1 + C(3)*X2 + C(4)*X3 + C(5)*X4

Substituted Coefficients:

Y = 118.9269474 + 0.03987314808*X1 - 0.2027396903*X2 - 0.08296586617*X3 - 0.004191719789*X4

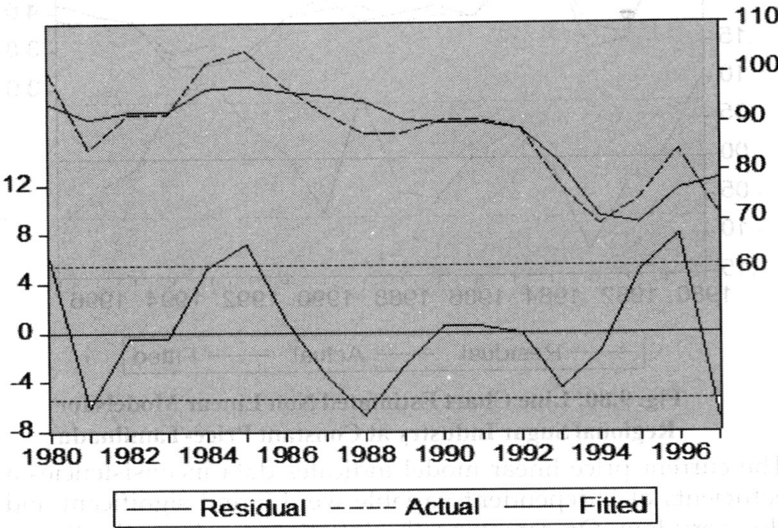

Fig. 9.81: Line Chart Estimated Linear Models for Regional Sugar Industry at Current Price-Uttar Pradesh

Table 9.82: Estimated Linear Models for Regional Sugar Industry at Constant Price-Uttar Pradesh

Variable	Coefficient	Std. Error	t-Statistic	Prob.
C	69.08563	22.11229	3.124309	0.0081
X1	-0.041802	0.053443	-0.782180	0.4481
X2	0.303505	0.208907	1.452825	0.1700
X3	-0.136983	0.057562	-2.379731	0.0333
X4	0.004476	0.004179	1.070897	0.3037
R-squared	0.771744	Mean dependent var		60.52596
Adjusted R-squared	0.701512	S.D. dependent var		13.32878
S.E. of regression	7.282057	Akaike info criterion		7.038837
Sum squared resid	689.3686	Schwarz criterion		7.286162

Prob(F-statistic) 0.000407

Estimation Equation:

Y = C(1) + C(2)*X1 + C(3)*X2 + C(4)*X3 + C(5)*X4

Substituted Coefficients:

Y = 69.08562664 - 0.04180226165*X1 + 0.3035054803*X2 - 0.1369826327*X3 + 0.004475667663*X4

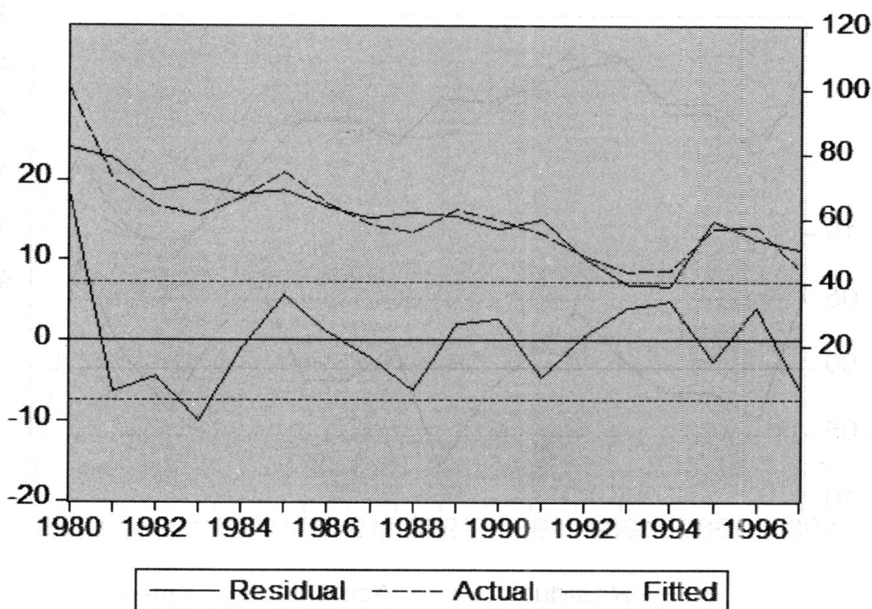

Fig. 9.82: Line Chart Estimated Linear Models for Regional Sugar Industry at Constant Price-Uttar Pradesh

Table 9.83: Estimated Non Linear Models for Regional Sugar Industry at Current Price-Uttar Pradesh

Variable	Coefficient	Std. Error	t-Statistic	Prob.
C	4.354828	0.903766	4.818533	0.0003
LOG(X1)	0.182887	0.076527	2.389845	0.0327
LOG(X2)	0.272357	0.220497	1.235194	0.2386
LOG(X3)	-0.543989	0.133225	-4.083248	0.0013
LOG(X4)	0.131164	0.111267	1.178824	0.2596
R-squared	0.853653	Mean dependent var		4.470805
Adjusted R-squared	0.808623	S.D. dependent var		0.116930
S.E. of regression	0.051153	Akaike info criterion		-2.877867
Sum squared resid	0.034016	Schwarz criterion		-2.630541

Prob(F-statistic) 0.000025

Estimation Equation:

LOG(Y) = C(1) + C(2)*LOG(X1) + C(3)*LOG(X2) + C(4)*LOG(X3) + C(5)*LOG(X4)

Substituted Coefficients:

LOG(Y) = 4.354828052 + 0.18288717*LOG(X1) + 0.2723571055*LOG(X2) - 0.5439886489*LOG(X3) + 0.1311639817*LOG(X4)

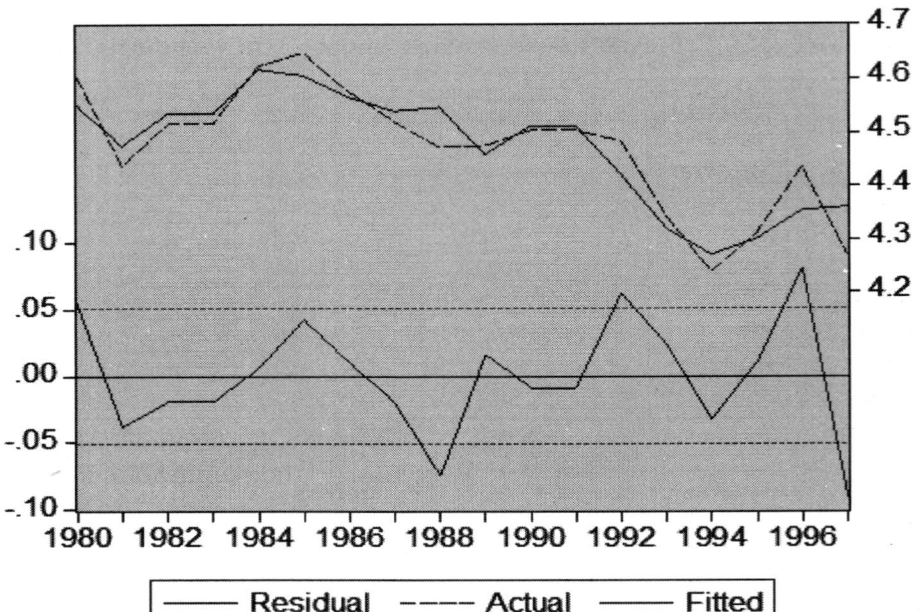

Fig. 9.83: Line Chart Estimated Non Linear Models for Regional Sugar Industry at Current Price-Uttar Pradesh

Table 9.84: Estimated Non Linear Models for Regional Sugar Industry at Constant Price-Uttar Pradesh

Variable	Coefficient	Std. Error	t-Statistic	Prob.
C	5.280358	1.094552	4.824219	0.0003
LOG(X1)	0.049337	0.120775	0.408504	0.6896
LOG(X2)	0.473173	0.179988	2.628910	0.0208
LOG(X3)	-0.760881	0.130157	-5.845874	0.0001
LOG(X4)	0.072774	0.051739	1.406567	0.1830
R-squared	0.923697	Mean dependent var		4.082336
Adjusted R-squared	0.900219	S.D. dependent var		0.205748
S.E. of regression	0.064992	Akaike info criterion		-2.398978
Sum squared resid	0.054911	Schwarz criterion		-2.151652

Prob(F-statistic) 0.000000

Estimation Equation:

LOG(Y) = C(1) + C(2)*LOG(X1) + C(3)*LOG(X2) + C(4)*LOG(X3) + C(5)*LOG(X4)

Substituted Coefficients:

LOG(Y) = 5.280357692 + 0.04933709534*LOG(X1) + 0.4731732034* LOG(X2) - 0.7608812042*LOG(X3) + 0.0727741708*LOG(X4)

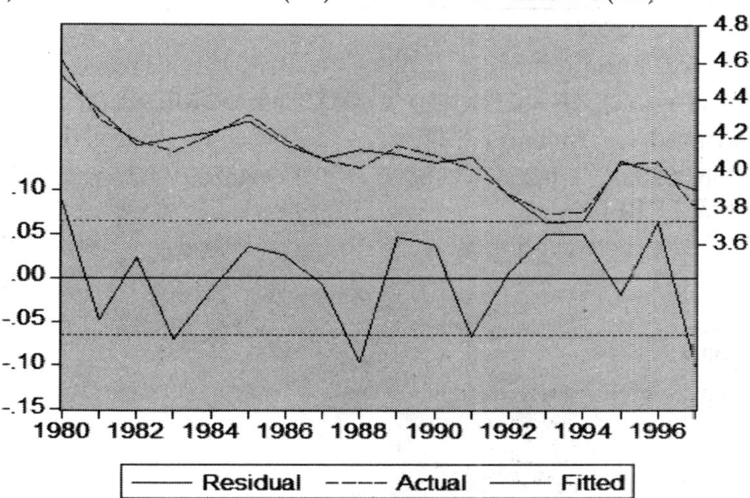

Fig. 9.84: Line Chart Estimated Non Linear Models for Regional Sugar Industry at Constant Price-Uttar Pradesh

Uttar Pradesh is key producer of sugar in India, primarily because of large cultivation of sugarcane. The current price linear model R^2 value is 77.5% with variable x1(average wage rate) and x3(productivity) having significant coefficients. On removing the inflationary effect, the linear model at constant price has R^2 value of 77.17% with x3 (productivity) as significant.

The non linear models provide better fit than linear models. Non linear model at current price has R^2 of 85.36% explaining the variability of unit labour cost. The model identifies the variables x1 and x3 as factors explaining the variation in unit labour cost. Non linear model at constant price has R^2 of 92.36% explaining the variability of unit labour cost. The model identifies the variables x2 (unit material cost) and x3 as factors explaining the variation in unit labour cost.

ESTIMATION OF UNIT COST LABOUR FUNCTION IN REGIONAL JUTE INDUSTRY

Table 9.85: Estimated Linear Models for Regional Jute Industry at Current Price- Andhra Pradesh

Variable	Coefficient	Std. Error	t-Statistic	Prob.
C	158.0578	36.76384	4.299274	0.0009
X1	0.256304	0.092280	2.777444	0.0157
X2	-0.459649	0.314648	-1.460837	0.1678
X3	-0.290815	0.105118	-2.766565	0.0160
REPX4	0.085765	0.045780	1.873398	0.0837
R-squared	0.703044	Mean dependent var		129.5830
Adjusted R-squared	0.611673	S.D. dependent var		20.16448
S.E. of regression	12.56567	Akaike info criterion		8.129947
Sum squared resid	2052.648	Schwarz criterion		8.377272

Prob(F-statistic) 0.002081

Estimation Equation:

Y = C(1) + C(2)*X1 + C(3)*X2 + C(4)*X3 + C(5)*REPX4

Substituted Coefficients:

Y = 158.0578272 + 0.2563035337*X1 - 0.4596487091*X2 - 0.2908145124*X3 + 0.08576493514*REPX4

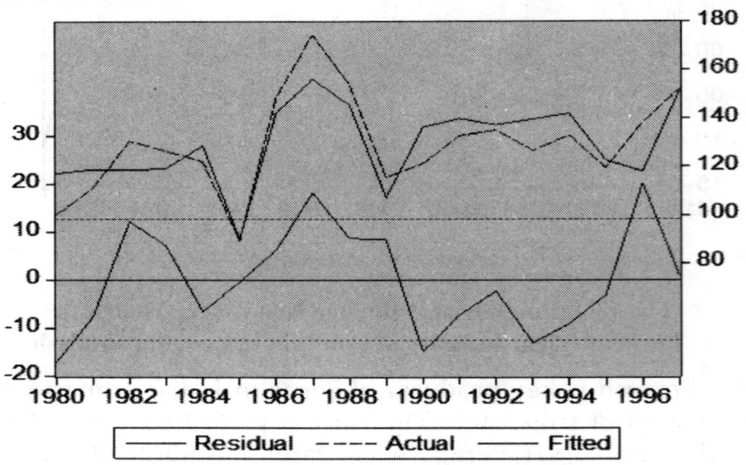

Fig. 9.85: Line Chart Estimated Linear Models for Regional Jute Industry at Current Price- Andhra Pradesh

Table 9.86: Estimated Linear Models for Regional Jute Industry at Constant Price - Andhra Pradesh

Variable	Coefficient	Std. Error	t-Statistic	Prob.
C	181.0296	28.54195	6.342580	0.0000
X1	0.457949	0.243076	1.883971	0.0821
X2	0.039255	0.158494	0.247676	0.8083
X3	-1.411850	0.195208	-7.232539	0.0000
X4	0.084508	0.024931	3.389678	0.0048
R-squared	0.829075	Mean dependent var		136.1569
Adjusted R-squared	0.776483	S.D. dependent var		23.84579
S.E. of regression	11.27371	Akaike info criterion		7.912957
Sum squared resid	1652.255	Schwarz criterion		8.160283

Prob (F-statistic) 0.000066

Estimation Equation:

Y = C(1) + C(2)*X1 + C(3)*X2 + C(4)*X3 + C(5)*X4

Substituted Coefficients:

Y = 181.0296094 + 0.4579485311*X1 + 0.03925528981*X2 - 1.411850357*X3 + 0.08450845112*X4

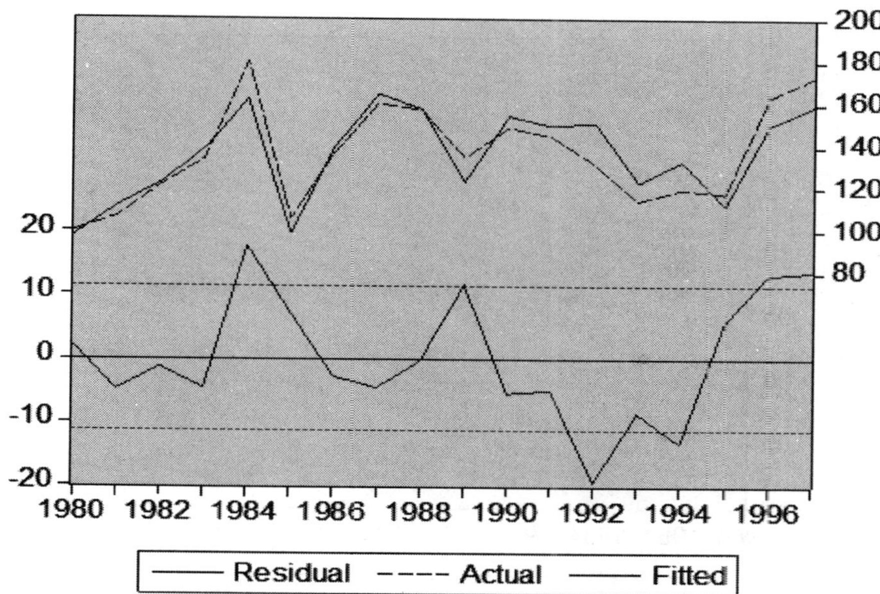

Fig. 9.86: Line Chart Estimated Linear Models for Regional Jute Industry at Constant Price- Andhra Pradesh

Table 9.87: Estimated Non Linear Models for Regional Jute Industry at Current Price-Andhra Pradesh

Variable	Coefficient	Std. Error	t-Statistic	Prob.
C	5.983345	0.976896	6.124854	0.0000
LOG(X1)	0.521943	0.118367	4.409516	0.0007
LOG(X2)	-0.421513	0.207482	-2.031560	0.0632
LOG(X3)	-0.493800	0.110616	-4.464113	0.0006
LOG(REPX4)	0.114537	0.060673	1.887781	0.0816
R-squared	0.839076	Mean dependent var		4.852671
Adjusted R-squared	0.789561	S.D. dependent var		0.158326
S.E. of regression	0.072630	Akaike info criterion		-2.176747
Sum squared resid	0.068576	Schwarz criterion		-1.929422

Prob (F-statistic) 0.000045

Estimation Equation:

LOG(Y) = C(1) + C(2)*LOG(X1) + C(3)*LOG(X2) + C(4)*LOG(X3) + C(5)*LOG(REPX4)

Substituted Coefficients:

LOG(Y) = 5.983344938 + 0.5219426215*LOG(X1) - 0.4215127321*LOG(X2) - 0.4938004901*LOG(X3) + 0.1145367733*LOG(REPX4)

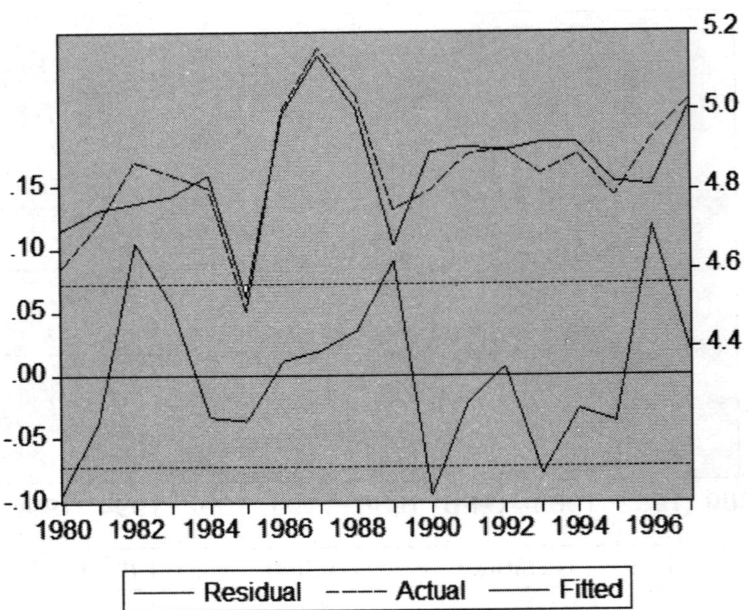

Fig. 9.87: Line Chart Estimated Non Linear Models for Regional Jute Industry at Current Price-Andhra Pradesh

Table 9.88: Estimated Non Linear Models for Regional Jute Industry at Constant Price-Andhra Pradesh

Variable	Coefficient	Std. Error	t-Statistic	Prob.
C	6.721999	1.037743	6.477521	0.0000
LOG(X1)	0.245610	0.204073	1.203542	0.2502
LOG(X2)	-0.059079	0.155342	-0.380315	0.7099
LOG(X3)	-0.834409	0.116550	-7.159237	0.0000
LOG(X4)	0.188542	0.052090	3.619532	0.0031
R-squared	0.843861	Mean dependent var		4.899318
Adjusted R-squared	0.795818	S.D. dependent var		0.175369
S.E. of regression	0.079243	Akaike info criterion		-2.002454
Sum squared resid	0.081634	Schwarz criterion		-1.755128

Prob(F-statistic) 0.000037

Estimation Equation:

LOG(Y) = C(1) + C(2)*LOG(X1) + C(3)*LOG(X2) + C(4)*LOG(X3) + C(5)*LOG(X4)

Substituted Coefficients:

LOG(Y) = 6.721999459 + 0.245610033*LOG(X1) - 0.05907910124*LOG(X2) - 0.8344091648*LOG(X3) + 0.1885423718*LOG(X4)

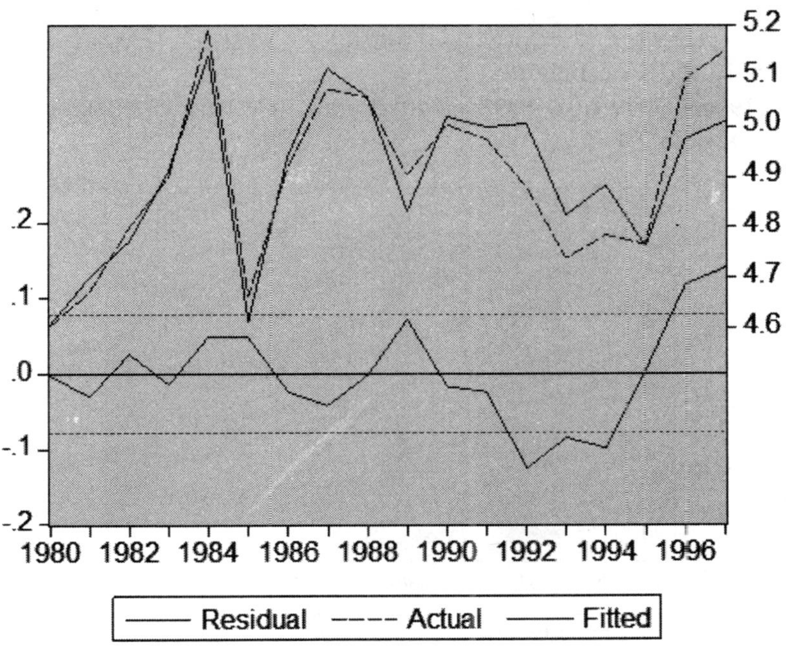

Fig. 9.88: Line Chart Estimated Non Linear Models for Regional Jute Industry at Constant Price-Andhra Pradesh

Like in all previous models the non linear models have better fit. The linear model with current price has R^2 value of 70.3% and identifies the explanatory variables as x1 (average wage rate) and x3 (productivity). The linear model with constant price has R^2 value of 82.9% and identifies the explanatory variables as x1 and x3 and x4 (technological changes). The non linear model with current price has R^2 value of 83.9% and identifies the explanatory variables as x1 and x3. The non linear model with constant price has R^2 value of 84.3% and identifies the explanatory variables as x3 and x4.

Table 9.89: Estimated Linear Models for Regional Jute Industry at Current Price-Uttar Pradesh

Variable	Coefficient	Std. Error	t-Statistic	Prob.
C	193.8940	34.07873	5.689590	0.0001
X1	0.098394	0.019611	5.017389	0.0002
X2	-0.743433	0.274928	-2.704097	0.0181
X3	-0.077155	0.029347	-2.629053	0.0208
X4	-0.001573	0.003251	-0.484048	0.6364
R-squared	0.871284	Mean dependent var		98.14804
Adjusted R-squared	0.831678	S.D. dependent var		30.48961
S.E. of regression	12.50898	Akaike info criterion		8.120903
Sum squared resid	2034.168	Schwarz criterion		8.368229

Prob(F-statistic) 0.000011

Estimation Equation:

Y = C(1) + C(2)*X1 + C(3)*X2 + C(4)*X3 + C(5)*X4

Substituted Coefficients:

Y = 193.8939849 + 0.09839396348*X1 - 0.7434330154*X2 - 0.07715477565*X3 - 0.001573404226*X4

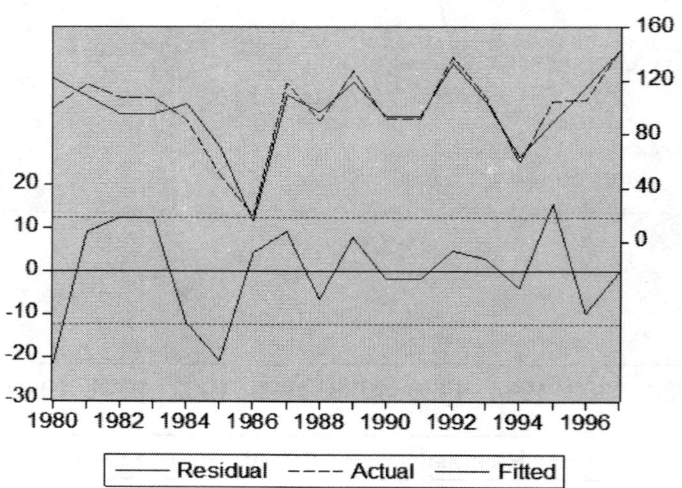

Fig. 9.89: Line Chart Estimated Linear Models for Regional Jute Industry at Current Price-Uttar Pradesh

Table 9.90: Estimated Linear Models for Regional Jute Industry at Constant Price-Uttar Pradesh

Variable	Coefficient	Std. Error	t-Statistic	Prob.
C	107.7663	30.54924	3.527626	0.0037
X1	0.655209	0.197635	3.315253	0.0056
X2	-0.390917	0.213300	-1.832714	0.0898
X3	-0.217552	0.040728	-5.341621	0.0001
X4	-0.004914	0.003082	-1.594399	0.1349
R-squared	0.805881	Mean dependent var		101.2781
Adjusted R-squared	0.746152	S.D. dependent var		31.88062
S.E. of regression	16.06251	Akaike info criterion		8.620986
Sum squared resid	3354.055	Schwarz criterion		8.868312

Prob(F-statistic) 0.000147

Estimation Equation:

Y = C(1) + C(2)*X1 + C(3)*X2 + C(4)*X3 + C(5)*X4

Substituted Coefficients:

Y = 107.7662983 + 0.6552093984*X1 - 0.3909174963*X2 - 0.2175521562*X3 - 0.00491397113*X4

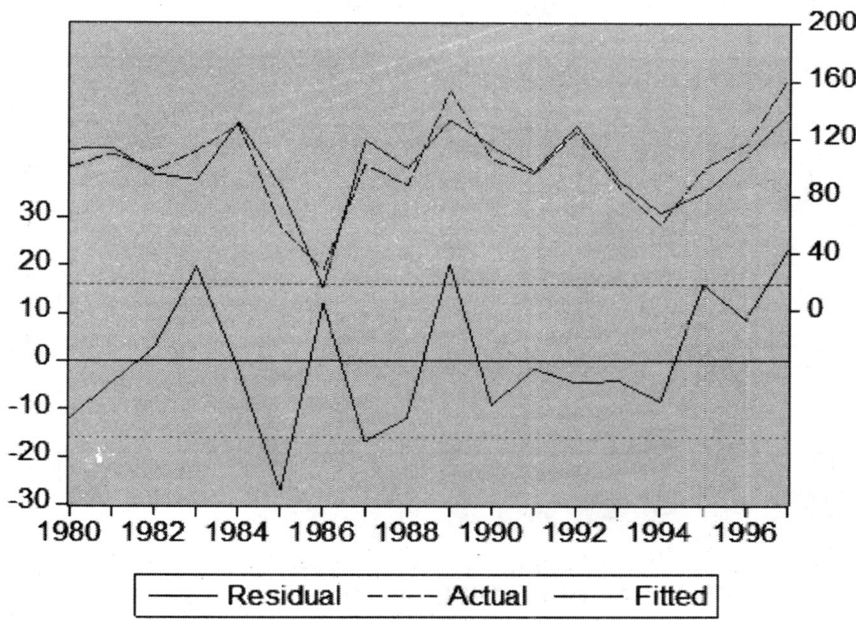

Fig. 9.90: Line Chart Estimated Linear Models for Regional Jute Industry at Constant Price-Uttar Pradesh

Table 9.91: Estimated Non Linear Models for Regional Jute Industry at Current Price - Uttar Pradesh

Variable	Coefficient	Std. Error	t-Statistic	Prob.
C	7.704534	2.061254	3.737790	0.0025
LOG(X1)	0.755376	0.121027	6.241398	0.0000
LOG(X2)	-0.623283	0.434778	-1.433565	0.1753
LOG(X3)	-0.806637	0.161878	-4.982992	0.0003
LOG(X4)	0.018332	0.113177	0.161974	0.8738
R-squared	0.923266	Mean dependent var		4.511089
Adjusted R-squared	0.899655	S.D. dependent var		0.464903
S.E. of regression	0.147269	Akaike info criterion		-0.762983
Sum squared resid	0.281945	Schwarz criterion		-0.515657

Prob(F-statistic) 0.000000

Estimation Equation:

LOG(Y) = C(1) + C(2)*LOG(X1) + C(3)*LOG(X2) + C(4)*LOG(X3) + C(5)*LOG(X4)

Substituted Coefficients:

LOG(Y) = 7.704534016 + 0.7553755064*LOG(X1) - 0.6232831021*LOG(X2) - 0.8066370389*LOG(X3) + 0.01833177454*LOG(X4)

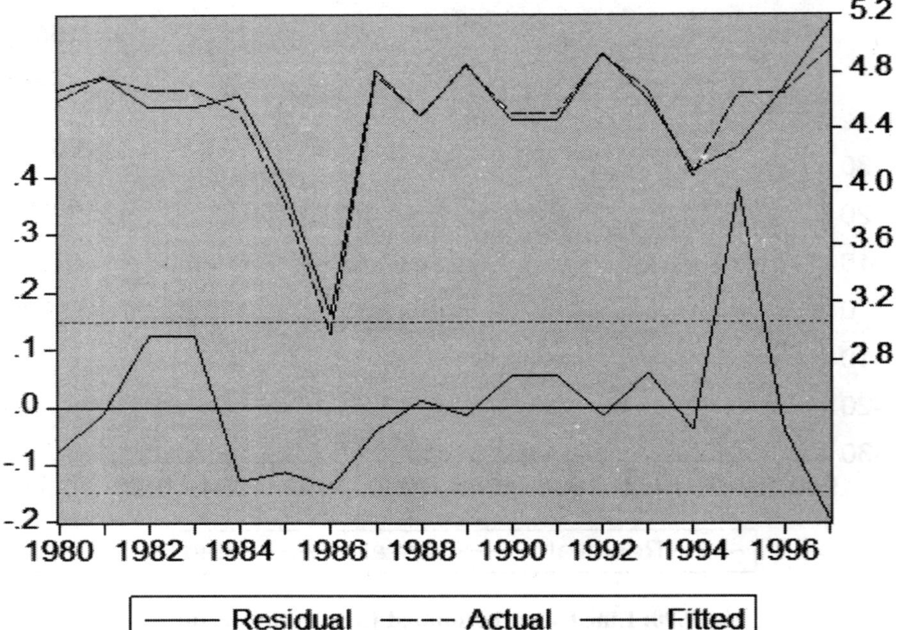

Fig. 9.91: Line Chart Estimated Non Linear Models for Regional Jute Industry at Current Price- Uttar Pradesh

Table 9.92: Estimated Non Linear Models for Regional Jute Industry at Constant Price - Uttar Pradesh

Variable	Coefficient	Std. Error	t-Statistic	Prob.
C	9.088415	1.356011	6.702317	0.0000
LOG(X1)	0.150324	0.203995	0.736899	0.4743
LOG(X2)	-0.386578	0.238192	-1.622966	0.1286
LOG(X3)	-0.834104	0.059984	-13.90533	0.0000
LOG(X4)	0.106387	0.048078	2.212783	0.0454
R-squared	0.950245	Mean dependent var		4.555691
Adjusted R-squared	0.934936	S.D. dependent var		0.398853
S.E. of regression	0.101738	Akaike info criterion		-1.502694
Sum squared resid	0.134559	Schwarz criterion		-1.255369

Estimation Equation:

LOG(Y) = C(1) + C(2)*LOG(X1) + C(3)*LOG(X2) + C(4)*LOG(X3) + C(5)*LOG(X4)

Substituted Coefficients:

LOG(Y) = 9.088415256 + 0.1503237621*LOG(X1) - 0.3865781797*LOG(X2) - 0.8341041552*LOG(X3) + 0.1063872622*LOG(X4)

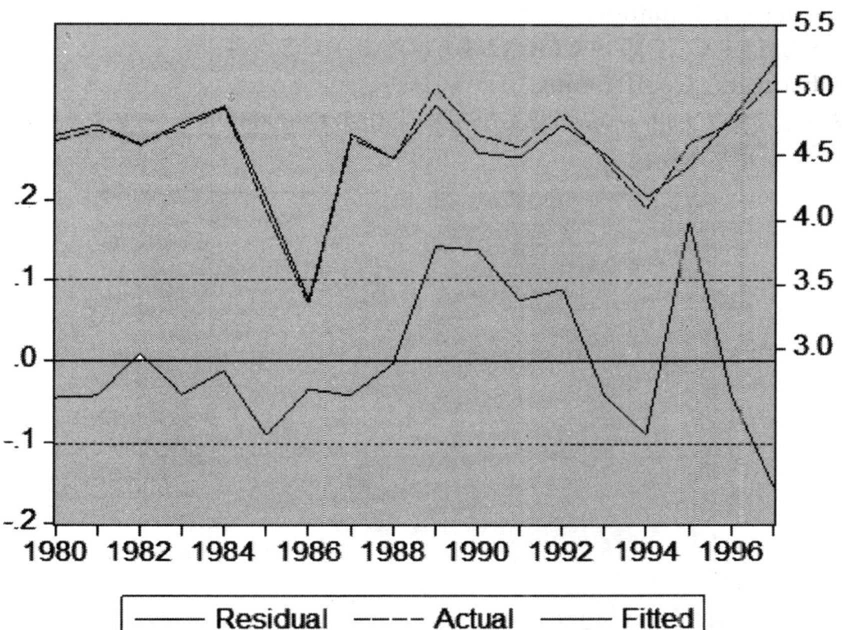

Fig. 9.92: Line Chart Estimated Non Linear Models for Regional Jute Industry at Constant Price- Uttar Pradesh

The linear model with current price has R^2 value of 87.12% and identifies the explanatory variables as x1 (average wage rate), x2 (unit material cost) and x3 (productivity). The linear model with constant price has R^2 value of 80.5% and identifies the explanatory variables as x1 and x3. The non linear model with current price has R^2 value of 92.32% and identifies the explanatory variables as x1 and x3. The non linear model with constant price has R^2 value of 95.02% and identifies the explanatory variables as x3 and x4.

Table 9.93: Estimated Linear Models for Regional Jute Industry at Current Price-West Bengal

Variable	Coefficient	Std. Error	t-Statistic	Prob.
C	137.9572	13.83463	9.971872	0.0000
X1	0.399454	0.034264	11.65815	0.0000
X2	-0.180907	0.120037	-1.507088	0.1557
X3	-0.497990	0.057796	-8.616314	0.0000
X4	0.012842	0.011518	1.114975	0.2850
R-squared	0.924619	Mean dependent var		112.6399
Adjusted R-squared	0.901425	S.D. dependent var		18.80747
S.E. of regression	5.904925	Akaike info criterion		6.619584
Sum squared resid	453.2858	Schwarz criterion		6.866909

Prob(F-statistic) 0.000000

Estimation Equation:

Y = C(1) + C(2)*X1 + C(3)*X2 + C(4)*X3 + C(5)*X4

Substituted Coefficients:

Y = 137.9571843 + 0.3994537065*X1 - 0.1809069085*X2 - 0.4979903641*X3 + 0.01284227265*X4

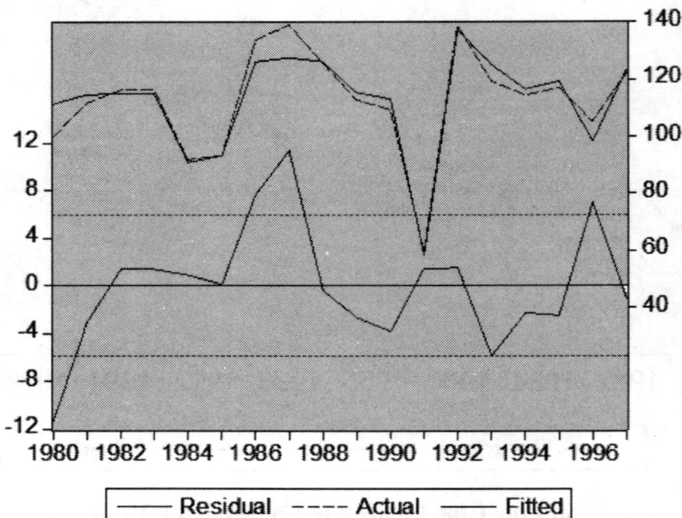

Fig. 9.93: Line Chart Estimated Linear Models for Regional Jute Industry at Current Price-West Bengal

Table 9.94: Estimated Linear Models for Regional Jute Industry at Constant Price-West Bengal

Variable	Coefficient	Std. Error	t-Statistic	Prob.
C	137.9442	8.014315	17.21223	0.0000
X1	1.012124	0.043728	23.14607	0.0000
X2	-0.062655	0.046187	-1.356547	0.1980
X3	-1.310669	0.076549	-17.12186	0.0000
X4	0.001132	0.002695	0.420116	0.6813
R-squared	0.978748	Mean dependent var		115.4497
Adjusted R-squared	0.972209	S.D. dependent var		17.51797
S.E. of regression	2.920342	Akaike info criterion		5.211412
Sum squared resid	110.8692	Schwarz criterion		5.458737

Prob(F-statistic) 0.000000

Estimation Equation:

Y = C(1) + C(2)*X1 + C(3)*X2 + C(4)*X3 + C(5)*X4

Substituted Coefficients:

Y = 137.9441975 + 1.012123996*X1 - 0.0626553572*X2 - 1.310668654*X3 + 0.0011324221*X4

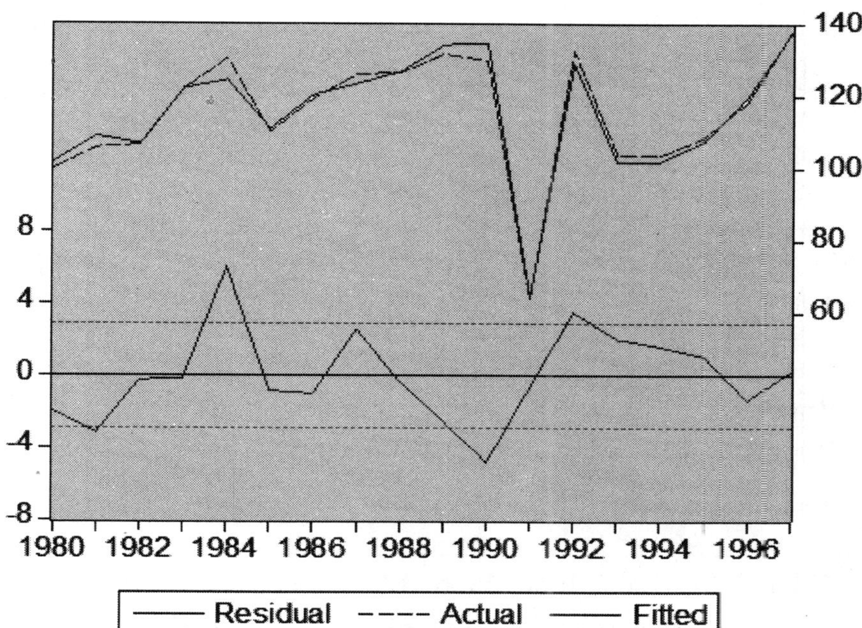

Fig. 9.94: Line Chart Estimated Linear Models for Regional Jute Industry at Constant Price-West Bengal

Table 9.95: Estimated Non Linear Models for Regional Jute Industry at Current Price - West Bengal

Variable	Coefficient	Std. Error	t-Statistic	Prob.
C	5.198717	0.315809	16.46156	0.0000
LOG(X1)	0.950649	0.034715	27.38415	0.0000
LOG(X2)	-0.104486	0.067455	-1.548981	0.1454
LOG(X3)	-0.957927	0.051741	-18.51404	0.0000
LOG(X4)	-0.007735	0.023854	-0.324275	0.7509
R-squared	0.984157	Mean dependent var		4.708322
Adjusted R-squared	0.979283	S.D. dependent var		0.193374
S.E. of regression	0.027833	Akaike info criterion		-4.095036
Sum squared resid	0.010071	Schwarz criterion		-3.847711

Prob(F-statistic) 0.000000

Estimation Equation:

LOG(Y) = C(1) + C(2)*LOG(X1) + C(3)*LOG(X2) + C(4)*LOG(X3) + C(5)*LOG(X4)

Substituted Coefficients:

LOG(Y) = 5.198716993 + 0.9506491816*LOG(X1) - 0.1044861233*LOG(X2) - 0.9579274753*LOG(X3) - 0.007735303339*LOG(X4)

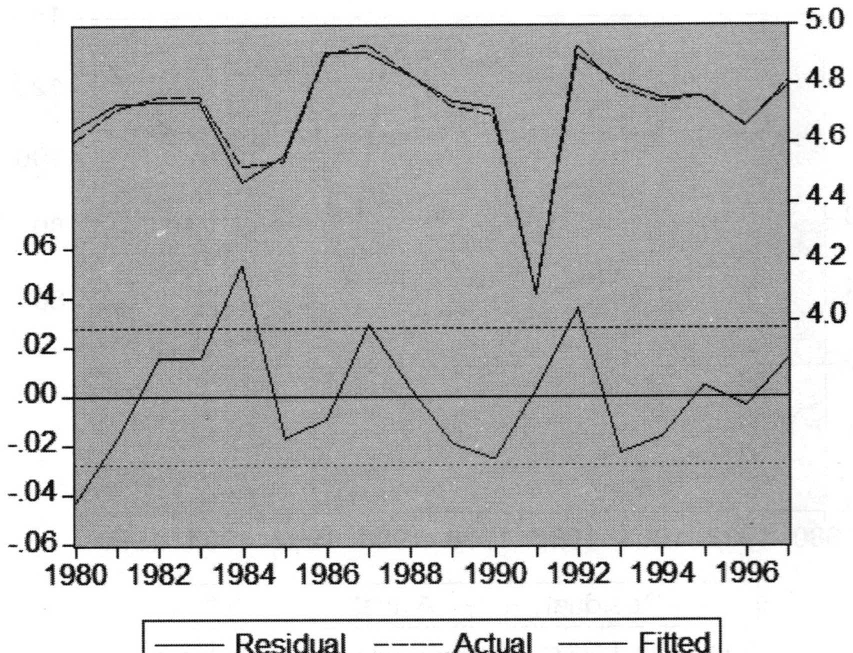

Fig. 9.95: Line Chart Estimated Linear Models for Regional Jute Industry at Current Price - West Bengal

Table 9.96: Estimated Non Linear Models for Regional Jute Industry at Constant Price - West Bengal

Variable	Coefficient	Std. Error	t-Statistic	Prob.
C	5.782167	0.273944	21.10709	0.0000
LOG(X1)	0.954803	0.027764	34.39008	0.0000
LOG(X2)	-0.100024	0.045171	-2.214327	0.0453
LOG(X3)	-1.121428	0.048389	-23.17513	0.0000
LOG(X4)	0.013867	0.008707	1.592630	0.1352
R-squared	0.989920	Mean dependent var		4.735659
Adjusted R-squared	0.986819	S.D. dependent var		0.176185
S.E. of regression	0.020228	Akaike info criterion		-4.733394
Sum squared resid	0.005319	Schwarz criterion		-4.486068

Prob(F-statistic) 0.000000

Estimation Equation:

LOG(Y) = C(1) + C(2)*LOG(X1) + C(3)*LOG(X2) + C(4)*LOG(X3) + C(5)*LOG(X4)

Substituted Coefficients:

LOG(Y) = 5.78216726 + 0.9548025157*LOG(X1) - 0.1000235316*LOG(X2) - 1.12142755*LOG(X3) + 0.01386696499*LOG(X4)

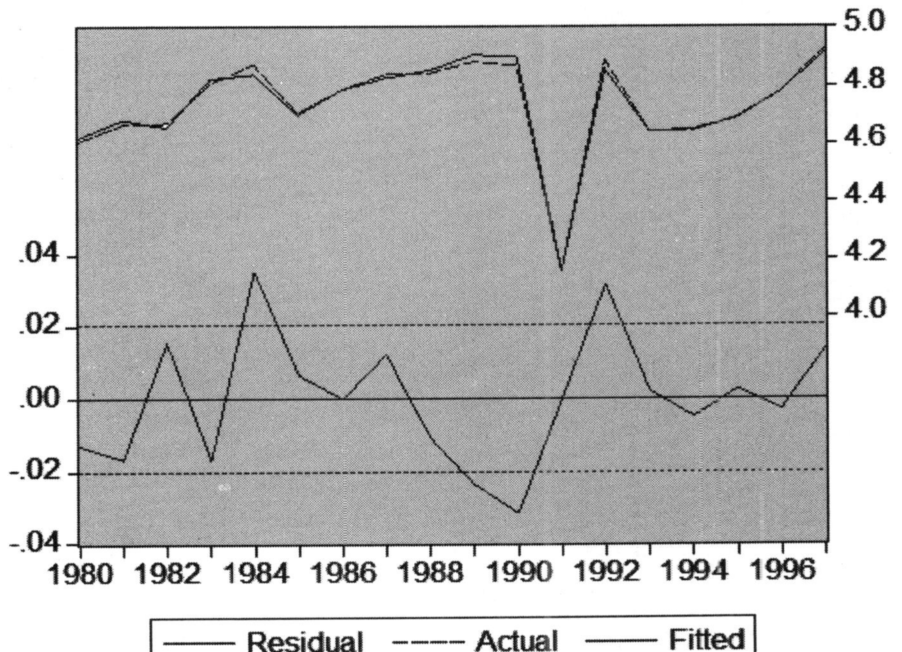

Fig. 9.96: Line Chart Estimated Non Linear Models for Regional Jute Industry at Constant Price- West Bengal

West Bengal is the leading state in jute. The linear model with current price has R^2 value of 92.46% and identifies the explanatory variables as x1 (average wage rate) and x3 (productivity). The linear model with constant price has R^2 value of 97.87% and identifies the explanatory variables as x1 and x3 and x4 (technological changes). The non linear model with current price has R^2 value of 98.41% and identifies the explanatory variables as x1 and x3. The non linear model with constant price has R^2 value of 84.3% and identifies the explanatory variables as x1 x2 (unit material cost) and x3.

10

Summary and Conclusion

Theoretically as well as empirically the present study provides a scientific analysis labour cost administration in selected Indian industries. It brings to fore the important changes that are taking place, and estimates the impact of factors influencing the unit labour cost in the selected industries of India.

In spite of raising wages, the unit labour cost in the selected industries has gone down. This decline has been caused mainly due to positive impact of increasing productivity; very few models indicate the positive impact of technological changes or capital intensity. A critical analysis further suggests that the unit labour cost varies for region to region and industry to industry. The proportion of labour cost is highest in cotton textile industries, lower in iron & steel and jute industries and lowest in sugar industries.

The study of regional patterns suggest that in all the selected industries, excepting jute labour cost is higher in regions where there is more concentration of the industries. This implies that location of industries has not been influenced by economical labour resources, but other factors like economies in utilizing other resources like raw material. The marginal change these variables bring in unit labour cost has been estimated in the models and is provided by coefficient of the variables in the model. If the coefficient is significant the absolute value of the coefficient is considered as the amount of change contributed to unit labour cost by one unit of that variable in the direction according to the sign of the coefficient. The conclusions on the basis of current price based estimates that intensive use of capital is not the factor that reduces unit labour cost in certain industries must be deduced with caution. This relationship should be accounted to price mechanism. Anyhow, the insignificant value of regression coefficient of x2 indicates the possibility of under-utilization of installed capacities, use of old plants and recruitment of workers in higher grades to handle new technology at work. When installed capacities at work are not fully utilized, the fixed overhead charges of the labour can not be spread over wide range of output and hence the investment in capital remains ineffective to certain extent in reducing the unit labour cost per unit of the product. Similarly the employment of skilled workers, which is desired as a process of mechanization and technological changes, prevents labour cost from being reduced in spite of substitution of capital for worker.

In the cotton textile industry, the degree of impact of the factors that affect unit labour cost also varies from region to region, but every unit of change in productivity has positive impact on unit labour cost and every unit of change in average wage rate has negative impact. The impact of productivity being larger has contributed to the decline in unit labour cost. Findings indicate that there is a decline in employment levels in composite mills in the cotton textile industry in India. This shift can be attributed towards more capital-intensive technologies. The increased capital-intensity generally contributes in an improvement in health and safety conditions within the mills which in turn help in raised levels of productivity. Statistically it was found that in the causal relationship, wages and labour costs are directly correlated also productivity and total cost of production are directly correlated. Technological changes or capital intensity contributes to unit labour cost by reducing it. The regions in which technological change was significant in econometric models were: Andhra Pradesh, Madhya Pradesh, Punjab, Uttar Pradesh and West Bengal. The unit material cost was found significant for the region Andhra Pradesh and Uttar Pradesh only.

Similarly the impact is also been measured in other industries. In the sugar industry every one percent rises in the wages or in capital intensity there is an impact of increment in unit labour cost. Average wage rate was found significant. Although, capital intensity was not found significant in all the regions, the regions where technological changes or capital intensity contributed were Maharashtra, Tamilnadu, Andhra Pradesh and Uttar Pradesh. This implies the industries in these regions have invested in improving their technology of production or up gradation of capacities. The other regions where capital intensity and technological changes were not found significant were: all India, Bihar and West Bengal. On the contrary, every one percent rise in productivity growth or in material cost reduces unit labour cost. The unit material cost contributed significantly in Maharashtra, Andhra Pradesh and Uttar Pradesh. Relative to supplies of capital and energy, in iron and steel industries the workers have gained but not in cotton textiles industry.

The behavior of the factors affecting the unit labour cost is the same in the jute industry, average wage rate and growth of productivity being the chief factor that reduces unit labour cost. Estimates of impact shat that every one percent rise in capital intensity or technological change was also observed in the regions of Andhra Pradesh and Uttar Pradesh, which is understandable as the industries in these regions are relatively new in comparison of jute industries in West Bengal. One the other hand every one percent rise in productivity reduces the unit labour cost and every one percent rise in average wage rate increases the unit labour cost. The impact of productivity being stronger than the average wage rate, the decline in unit labour cost was witnessed.

There are various factors that tend to lift or lower the cost of labour, wages and productivity. But the combined as well as individual effect of these factors, vary on different conditions. Generally the increasing return to scale during the period of the study and productivity of labour vis-à-vis its cost reduces unit labour cost in the selected industries of India. The rate of growth of wage earnings has been falling along with employment, the capital deepening has been accompanied by gains in labour productivity and gains in productivity is associated with falling unit labour cost.

The hypothesis is not supported that, labour is a variable factor rather than a fixed factor; therefore for industries operating under increasing return, any increase in the number of workers will improve the marginal productivity of the labour. For industries operating under diminishing return, any increase in the number of workers will decrease the marginal productivity of the labour.

Productivity is affected by multiple factors. Behind productivity lie all the dynamic forces of economic life. Improved techniques, technically trained workers and efficiency in use of labour may be the important factors influencing productivity growth in India. Generally speaking the capital intensive techniques of production and efficiency of labour have helped in the growth of productivity in major industries of India.

The present analysis thus focuses on an encouraging feature of the industrial development of India, namely, improvement in rate of productivity growth and corresponding decline in unit labour cost. The real pace of advancement is slow in some of the major industries, but it is bound to be rapid, as the techniques of production continue to improve. If industrial units make an effect to utilize fully installed capacities of the industries. The raise of technical education in India is expected to contribute to further advancement in productivity. The economic conditions of late 1990 and early 2000 are further support the production activities at higher efficiency. The expansion of economy would lead to the increase in demand and improvement in all the economic variables including the average wage rate.

Bibliography

Ahluwalia, I. (1985). *Industrial Growth in India: Stagnation Since the Mid-Sixties.* Delhi: Oxford University Press.

Ahluwalia, I. (1992). *Productivity and Growth in Indian Manufacturing.* Delhi: Oxford University Press.

Ambekar Institute for Labour Studies. (2009). *Living Wage Survey For India's Garment And Textile Workers In Selected Regions.* Indonesia.

Balakrishnan, P., & Pushpangandan, K. (1998, Aug). What Do we Know About Productivity Growth in Indian Industries? *Economic and Political Weekly,* 2241-46.

Beri, G.C. (1962). *Measurement of Production and Productivity in Indian Industry.* Bombay: Asia Publishing House.

Bhattacharya, B. B., & Mitra, A. (1994). Employment, Labour Productivity and Wage Rate in Public and Organised Private Sectors in Context of Structural Reforms. *The Indian Journal of Labour Economics, 37* (2), 163-73.

Brenner, M. (2002). Defining and Measuring a Global Living Wage: Theoretical and Conceptual Issues. *PEERI:Global Labor Standards and Living Wages.* University of Massachusetts, Amherst.

Burange, L. G., & Yamini, S. (2010). *Competitiveness of the Firms in Indian Iron and Steel Industry.* Retrieved from Working Paper UDE33/2/2010.

Cambridge capital controversy. (2009, Sep). Retrieved Jan. 21, 2010.

Carneiro, A. (2007). What is Required for Growth? *Business Strategy Series, 8* (1), 51-57.

celex-text-52002DC0332. (2009, 8 13). Retrieved April 26, 2010, from Eur-Lex Access to European Union Law.

Chand, S., & Sen, K. (2002). Trade Liberalization and Productivity Growth: Evidence from Indian Manufacturing. *Review of Development Economics, 6* (1), 120-132.

Commision, P. (2001a). *Approach to the Tenth Five Year Plan (2002-07).* New Delhi: Planning Commission.

Commission, P. (1981, Jan 18). *Planning Commission, Government of India: Five Year Plans*. Retrieved December 24, 2009.

Denison. (1967). *Why Growth Rates Differ.* Washington: The Brookings Institution Press.

Denison, E. (1969, May). Some Major Issues in Productivity Analysis. *Survey of Current Business, 49* (5), pp. 1-28.

Duque, J. C., Ramos, R., & Suriñach, J. (2006). Wages and Productivity: The Role of Labour Market Institutions in OECD Countries. *Empirica, 33* (4), 231-243.

Flatau, P. (2002, Summer). *Hicks's The Theory of Wages: its Place in the History of Neoclassical Distribution Theory*. Retrieved May 15, 2010.

Fonesca, A. J. (1964). *Wage Determination and Organised Labour inIndia.* Bombay: Oxford University Press.

Gangopadhyay, S., & Wadhwa, W. (1998, May). Economics Reforms and Labour. *Economic and Political Weekly*, 42-48.

Goldar, B. N. (1987). Employment Growth in Indian Industry. *Indian Journal ofIndustrial Relation, 22* (3), 271-85.

Goldar, B. N. (1986). *Productivity Growth in Indian Industry.* New Delhi: Allied Publisher Pvt. Ltd.

Griliches. (1960). Measuring Inputs in Agriculture: A Critical Survey. *Jounal of Farm Economics,* 1398-427.

Griliches, Z., & Jorgenson, D. W. (1976). The Explanation of Productivity Change: Capital Input. *Review of Economic Studies,* 34, 256.

Gujrati, D. N., & Sangeetha. (2007). *Basic Econometrics.* New Delhi: Tata McGrawhill Education Pvt. Ltd.

ILO. (1959). *Labour Costs in European Industries.*

India, G. o. (2003). *Statistical Data for Labour*. Retrieved.

Industrial Policy. (1991, July 24). Retrieved Aug 25, 2008.

Jha, R., Murty, M., Paul, S., & Rao, B.B. (1993, Oct). An Analysis of Technological Change, Factor Substitution and Economies of Scale in Manufacturing Industries in India. *Applied Economics,* 1137.

Johri, C.K., & Agarwal, N.C. (1966). Inter Industry Wage Structure in India, 1951-1961: An Analysis. *Indian Journal of Industrial Relations,* 379-413.

Jorgenson. (1966). The Embodiment Hypothesis. *Journal of Political Economy,* 1-17.

Jorgenson, & Griliches. (1967). The Explanation of Productivity Change. *Review of Economics,* 249-80.

Jorgenson, D.W. (n.d.). The Economics of Productivity. *The International Library of Critical Writings in Economics,* 236.

Jose, A.V. (1994). Earnings, Employment and Productivity Trends in Organised Industries in India. In L.K. Despande, & G. Rodgers, *Indian Labour Market and Economic Structural Change.* Delhi: B R Publishing Corporation.

Joshi, V., & Little, I. (1994). *India: Macroeconomics and Political Economy 1964-1991.* Delhi: Oxford University Press.

Kabiria, M., & Tisdell, C. (1985). International Comparisons of Learning Curves and Productivity. *Management International Review (MIR), 25* (4), 66-72.

Kambhampati, U.S. (2003, June). Trade Reforms and the Efficiency of Firms in India. *Oxford Development Studies, 31* (2), pp. 219-233.

Kambhampati, U., & Howell, J. (1998). *Journal of International Development, 10* (4), 439-452.

Kendrick, J.W. (1973). *Post War Productivity Trends in U.S. 1948-69.* New York: National Bureau of Economic Resaerch.

Kumar, U., & Mishra, P. (2008). Trade Liberalization and Wage Inequality: Evidence from India. *Review of Development Economics, 12* (8), 291-311.

Kuznet, S. (1978). Technological Innovations and Economics Growth. In M. Kranzberg, *Technological Innovation: A Critical Review of Current Knowlegdge* (pp. 335-56). San Francisco: San Francisco Press.

Kuznets, S. (1971). *Economic Growth of Nations.* Cambridge: Harvard University Press.

Labour Bureau, M. o. (2012, April 12). *Statistical Data for Labour.* Retrieved April 15, 2012, from Labour Bureau, Govt. of India.

Maheshwari, P. C. (1968). Trends of Labour Costs in Major Industries of India since 1947 to 1962. AU. Agra University.

Marjit, S., & Singh, N. (1995). Technology and Indian Industry. In D. Mukherjee, *Indian Industry, Policies and Performance.* Delhi: Oxford University Press.

Mehta, S.S. (1980). *Productivity, Production Function and Techniocal Change: A Survey of Some Indian Industries.* New Delhi: Concept Publishing Co.

Mitra, D., & Ural, B.P. (2008). Indian Manufacturing: A Slow Sector in a Rapidly Growing Economy. *Journal of International Trade & Economic Development, 17* (4), 525-559.

MoF. (2002). *Economic Survey 2001/02.* New Delhi: Economic Division, Ministry of Finance.

Nagaraj, R. (1990, Oct 13). Industrial Growth: Future Evidence and Towards an Explanation and Issues. *Economics and Political Weekly, 15* (41).

Narayan, L. (2003). *Productivity and Wages in Indian Industries.* Delhi: Discovery Publishing House.

nic code 87. (1987). Retrieved Dec 20, 2009.

Panagariya, A. (2003, Nov 6). *pana*. Retrieved Aug 25, 2008.

Papola, T. S. (1972). Inter Industry Wage Structure: Technology Hypothesis. *Anveshak*, 50-74.

Papola, T.S. (1970). *Principles of Wage Determination: An Empirical Study.* Bombay: Somaiya Publications Pvt. Ltd.

Pradhan, G., & Barik, K. (1998). Fluctuating Total Factor Productivity in India: Evidence form Selceted Polluting Industries. *Economica nd Political Weekly*, M25-30.

Rajan, R. (2005, Dec 26). *From Bharat To India, A Commentary*. Retrieved August 28, 2008, from International Monetary Fund.

Rao, J.M. (1996a). Manufacturing Productivity Growth: Method and Measurement. *Economic and Political Weekly*, 2927-36.

Razack, A., Devadoss, S., & Holland, D. (2009). A General Equilibrium Analysis of Production Subsidy in a Harris-Todaro Developing Economy: An Application to India. *Applied Economics, 41* (21), 2767-2777.

Rosen, G. (1959). Industrial Change in India. Delhi: Asian Publising House.

Salter, W. (1969). *Productivity and Tecnical Change.* Cambridge: Cambridge University Press.

Sanga, K. (1964). *Productivity and Economic Growth*. Bombay: Asia Publishing House.

Sen, K. (2008). Trade Policy and Wage Inequality: Evidence from Indian Manufacturing. *Indian Growth and Development Review, 1* (2), 147-171.

Shivamaggi, B.H., Rajgopalan, N., & Venkatachalam, T.R. (1968). Wages, Labour Productivity and Cost of Production. *Economic and Political Weekly*, 710-16.

Singh, N.P., Singh, P., & Singh, R. P. (2007). Sugar Industry in Uttar Pradesh: Efficiency Still Holds the Key. *Agricultural Economics Research Review*, 157-170.

Sinha, J.N., & Sawhney, P. K. (1970). *Wages and Productivity in Selected Indian Industries*. New Delhi : Vikas Publishing House.

Solow, R.M. (1970). *Growth Theory: An Exposition*. New York: Oxford University Press.

Solow, R.M. (1970). *Growth Theory: An Exposition*. New York: Oxford University Press.

Solow, R.M. (1957). Technical Change and the Aggregate Production Function. *Review of Economics and Statistics, 39* (3), 312-20.

Stigler, G. (1947). *Trends in Output and Employment*. New York: National Bureau of Economic Research.

Subrahmanyam, G. (1984). Some Conceptual Issues in Productivity Measurement. *Pranjan, 13* (2), 182.

Subrahmanyam, G. (1984). Some Conceptual Issues in Productivity Measurement. *Prajnan*, 182.

Suri, G.K., & Sastry, C.M. (1974). Deerminants of Workers Money Earnings and Income Policy. *Productivity*, 97-112.

Tulpule, B., & Datta, R. C. (1988, October). Real Wages in Indian Industries. *Economic and Political Weekly*, 2275-78.

Verma, P. (1973). Regional Wages and Economic Development: A Case Study of Manufacturing Wages in India, 1950-1960. *Journal of Development Studies, 10* (1), 16-33.

Verma, P. (1992). Trends and Structures of Wagesin Indian Industries. *Productivity, 33* (2), 270-75.

Index

❖ ❖ ❖ ❖